A Window to Hotel Management

A Window to Hotel Management

Ashim Gupta

RANDOM PUBLICATIONS
NEW DELHI (INDIA)

A Window to Hotel Management

ISBN 978-93-5111-332-4

Published in 2014 in India by

RANDOM PUBLICATIONS

4376-A/4B, Gali Murari Lal, Ansari Road
New Delhi-110 002
Phone : +91-11-43580356, +91-11-23289044
e-mail: randomexports@gmail.com, sales@randompublications.com, info@randompublications.com

Reprinted 2026

Type Setting by : Keystoneprintads, Delhi-110051

Preface

There are many different industries all over the world. Different industry works in different sectors. But there are few industries which are called successful business. And also there are many industries which are called business. There is a long way between business and successful business. Business becomes successful by a proper management system. So the management system is very important in the sector of development.

Hotel management is the executive level of a hotel. This management position will oversee all aspects of running a hotel. This will be in the form of the hotel, housekeeping, restaurant, meetings, etc.

A cardinal part of hospitality industry, hotel management has wide employment opportunities. Moreover, with globalisation gaining acceptance with more and more countries, the hotel management industry is truly becoming global.

As hotel chain owners are opening new hotels in various big and small cities, requirement for trained hotel management professionals is huge. Although considered one of the most glamorous careers, hotel management requires professionals who can keep their cool even in the most challenging situations.

The management system that manages all things about hotel business is called hotel management. Another way, the hotel management is the perfect management techniques including hotel administration, accounts, marketing, maintenance, housekeeping, food and beverage management and catering. This management system runs the hotel properly and manages every single thing according to the way it should be.

Mistakes are banned in this type of management system. Because proper management depends on how perfectly it managed. So each and every person related to this hotel management system should be careful and should be aware of responsibility.

The book is organized around the hotel management system model which serves as a guide to understand management functions and related techniques.

I would like to thank my team for standing beside me throughout my career and writing this book. My special thanks go to "Random Publications" who have published the book.

— Ashim Gupta

Contents

1

Introduction to Hotel

A hotel is an establishment that provides paid lodging, usually on a short-term basis. Hotels often provide a number of additional guest services such as a restaurant, a swimming pool or childcare. Some hotels have conference services and meeting rooms and encourage groups to hold conventions and meetings at their location.

Hotels differ from motels in that most motels have drive-up, exterior entrances to the rooms, while hotels tend to have interior entrances to the rooms, which may increase guests' safety and present a more upmarket image.

In Australia, a hotel may also be an establishment that serves alcoholic drinks, and usually meals in a casual setting but which does not necessarily provide accommodation. This type of establishment would more usually be called a pub or bar in other countries. In general use in Australia the terms '"hotel" and pub are usually taken to be synonymous.

In India, the word may also refer to a restaurant since the best restaurants were always situated next to a good hotel.

The word hotel derives from the French hotel, which referred to a French version of a townhouse, not a place offering accommodation (in contemporary usage, hôtel has the meaning of "hotel", and hotel particular is used for the old meaning). The French spelling (with the circumflex) was once also used in English, but is now rare. The circumflex replaces the 's' once preceding the 't' in the earlier hostel spelling, which over time received a new, but closely related meaning.

SERVICES AND FACILITIES

Basic accommodation of a room with only a bed, a cupboard, a small table and a washstand has largely been replaced by rooms with en-suite bathrooms and climate control. Other features found may be a telephone, an alarm clock, a TV, and broadband Internet connectivity. Food and drink may be supplied by a mini-bar (which often includes a small refrigerator) containing snacks and drinks (to be paid for on departure), and tea and coffee making facilities (cups, spoons, an electric kettle and sachets containing instant coffee, tea bags, sugar, and creamer or milk).

In the United Kingdom a hotel is required by law to serve food and drinks to all comers within certain stated hours; to avoid this requirement it is not uncommon to come across "private hotels" which are not subject to this requirement. However, in Japan the capsule hotel supplies minimal facilities and room space.

The cost and quality of hotels are usually indicative of the range and type of services available. Due to the enormous increase in tourism worldwide during the last decades of the 20th century, standards, especially those of smaller establishments, have improved considerably. For the sake of greater comparability, rating systems have been introduced, with the one to five stars classification being most common.

TYPES OF HOTELS

Boutique Hotels

Boutique hotel is a term originating in North America to describe intimate, usually luxurious or quirky hotel environments. Boutique hotels differentiate themselves from larger chain/branded hotels and motels by providing personalized level accommodation and services / facilities.

Sometimes known as "design hotels" or "lifestyle hotels," boutique hotels began in the 1980s in major cities like New York, London, and San Francisco. Very often it is the Morgans Hotel in Murray Hill of New York, that is awarded with the title of first boutique hotel in the world. It was opened by Ian Schrager in 1984 according to a design by Andrée Putman.

Typically boutique hotels are furnished in a themed, stylish and/or aspirational manner. Although usually considerably smaller than a mainstream hotel (often ranging from 3 to 100 guest rooms), boutique hotels can often have hundreds of rooms in major cities. Guest rooms and suites are fitted with telephony and Wi-Fi Internet, air-conditioning, honesty bars and often cable/pay TV. Guest services are attended to by 24 hour hotel staff. Many boutique hotels have on-site dining facilities, and the majority offer bars and lounges which may also be open to the general public.

Despite this definition, the popularity of the boutique term and concept has lead to some confusion about the term. Boutique hotels have typically been unique properties operated by individuals or companies with a small collection. However, their successes have prompted established multi-national hotel companies to establish their own brands. The most notable is Starwood Hotels and Resorts' W Hotels.

Currently, there is one publication dedicated to the boutique hotel, boutique DESIGN magazine, which is published quarterly. Boutique hotel resources are more commonly available online. One such site dedicated to boutique hotels is Tablet Hotels. There are also a number of sytlized design and coffee table books highlighting various properties throughout the world.

Apartment Hotel

An Apartment Hotel is a type of accommodation, described as "a serviced apartment complex that uses a hotel style booking system". It is similar to renting an apartment, but with no fixed contracts and occupants can 'check-out' whenever they wish.

Apartment hotels are flexible types of accommodation; instead of the rigid format of a hotel room an apartment hotel complex usually offers a complete fully fitted apartment. These complexes are usually custom built, and similar to a hotel complex contain a varied amount of apartments. The length of stay in these apartment hotels are very varied with anywhere from a few days to months or even years. Prices tend to be cheaper than hotels. The people that stay in apartment hotels use them as a home from home therefore they are usually fitted with everything the average home would require.

Apartment hotels were first created in holiday destinations as accommodation for families that needed to 'live' in an apartment rather than 'stay' as they would in a hotel. The apartments would provide a 'holiday home' but generally be serviced. Later on these apartments evolved to be complete homes, allowing occupants to do everything they would at home, such as cleaning, washing and cooking.

Essentially the apartment hotel combines the flexibility of apartment living with the service of a hotel. Many of the apartments take advantage of prime locations with panoramic views of cities seen through wall to ceiling windows. Suites usually include high quality finishes, broadband connection & interactive TV, servicing and integrated kitchen and bathroom. High quality leather sofas in the living area and king size beds bring the hotel experience to a whole new level. Those are the luxuries, they also come with the basics: satellite or cable TV, washer, dryer, dishwasher, cooker, oven, fridge, freezer, sink, shower, bath, wardrobes, all the furnishings to be expected in a luxury home.

Bed and Breakfast

A Bed and Breakfast often referred to as a B&B is a type of boarding house typically operating out of a large single family residence.

Guests are accommodated at night in private bedrooms and breakfast is served in the morning - either in the bedroom or, more commonly, in a dining room or the host's kitchen. Bathrooms can be private or shared (with other guests or with the family in smaller establishments) or en-suite (where the ablutions are directly accessed from the guest's bedroom).

B&Bs may be operated either as a primary occupation or as a secondary source of income. Staff often consists of the house's owners and members of their family who live there. Guests are usually expected to pay for their stay upon arrival and leave before noon (or earlier) on the day of departure. A big advantage of this type of hosted accommodation is the local knowledge of the host. When guests stay more than one night, in some smaller B&Bs they will be expected to be away from the B&B during the main part of the day. This arrangement, however, may not be inconvenient since many popular B&Bs are located in beach and mountain areas, such as Hawaii, New England, and Colorado where daytime recreation and tourism activities are popular. One advantage of staying at a B&B is readier access to popular locations "off the beaten path" which may not be convenient to the city center.

Because most B&Bs are small, rarely with room for more than about 2-12 guests, it is advisable for anyone wanting to stay at a bed and breakfast to make reservations well in advance of their travel date. Consultation with a qualified travel agent knowledgeable in this type of accommodation may be helpful; However, many B&Bs belong to associations and have a web presence. Be aware that prices and tariffs described in various books and travel guides are often obsolete by the time they are published.

The B&B arrangement is actually a very old one; before the 20th century, it was quite normal for country travellers to spend the night at a private house rather than an inn, and the custom persists in many parts of the world. However, prior to the 19th century, this was strictly an informal arrangement constrained by acquaintance and social rank; a doctor might stay with a doctor or pharmacist, while a nobleman would only stay with the local gentry. The abbreviation of 'B&B' on roadside signs first became popular in the British Isles.

In the British Isles, breakfast is usually cooked on demand for the guest and usually features bacon, eggs, sausages, tomatoes, mushrooms, baked beans, etc. but increasingly, because of either a desire of owners to economise or guests to minimise their calorie intake, a 'continental breakfast' is becoming more common.

In the British Isles where hotel prices are often outrageous, B&B's are a budget option and this tradition continues in many parts of the world.

However, many B&Bs in North America and New Zealand often consciously seek to recall earlier days; they are frequently established in attractive older houses that have been renovated and filled with antique furniture. In some cases in North America an existing inn will relabel itself as a "B&B" to improve business and move itself `up-market'.

In Ireland, most B&Bs serve a traditional Irish breakfast as a point of pride. In Cuba, which opened up to tourism in the 1990s after the financial support of the Soviet Union ended, a form of B&B called casa particular ("private home") became the main form of accommodation outside the tourist resorts.

The term "bed and breakfast" is also used to refer to a meal plan where breakfast is the only meal provided, commonly in package holidays, in a major hotel that may provide other meals to only some customers.

As they are often run by amateurs, with little lodge management experience, strict laws should govern the operation of B&Bs. However, regulations vary in each jurisdiction both in content and extent and in enforcement. The most common regulations B&Bs must follow pertain to safety. They are required to have fire resistance, a sufficient fire escape plan in place, and smoke detectors in each guest room.

Capsule Hotel

A capsule hotel, is a hotel system of extremely dense occupancy. Guest space is reduced in size to a modular plastic or fibreglass block roughly 2 m by 1 m by 1.25 m, providing room to sleep and little more, although facilities usually include a television and other electronic entertainment. These capsules are then grouped and stacked, two units high. Luggage is usually stored in a locker away from the capsule. Privacy is maintained by a curtain at the open end of the capsule but noise pollution can be high. Washing facilities are communal and there are often restaurants, or at least vending machines, and other entertainment facilities.

This style of hotel accommodation was developed in Japan and has not gained acceptance outside of the country. The Japanese capsule hotels vary widely in size, some having only fifty or so capsules and others over 700. They are often male-only. There are also capsule hotels with separate male and female sleeping quarters. Clothes and shoes are sometimes exchanged for a yukata and slippers on entry. A towel may also be provided. The benefit of these hotels is convenience and price, usually around ¥2000-4000 a night 21-29, $25–34, £15–20). Such hotels are not necessarily regarded as only an option for those with lower incomes—a typical customer would be the business salaryman after a night of drinking who has missed the last train home. Some capsule hotels offer low daytime discounts for those needing an afternoon nap.

The first capsule hotel was the Capsule Inn Osaka, designed by Kisho Kurokawa and located in the Umeda district of Osaka. It opened on February 1, 1979 and the initial room rate was ¥1,600.

These rooms can be seen in the movie The Fast and the Furious: Tokyo Drift. They were also used as a basis for sets in the film The Fifth Element. They also appear in the cyberpunk novel Neuromancer under the name of "coffin hotel."

Casa Particular

Casa particular is a phrase meaning private accommodation or private homestays in Cuba, very similar to bed and breakfast although it can also take the form of vacation rental. When the meaning is clear the term is often shortened to simply casa.

A casa particular is basically a private family establishment that provides paid lodging, usually on a short-term basis. In general under this term you can find full apartment and houses, rooms inside people homes, mini-apartments or rooms with separate entrance (studio or efficiency type rooms). It is also considered a type of boarding house typically operated out of a single family residence where guests can be accommodated at night in private bedrooms (which may or may not be equipped with private baths) and where breakfast, sometimes continental and sometimes the full English variety, is served in the morning. The business may be operated either as a primary occupation or as a secondary source of income, and the staff often consists of the house's owner(s) and members of their family who live there.

Because they are usually small, rarely with room for more than about 5-6 guests, it is advisable for anyone wanting to stay at a particular casa particular during high season to make advance reservations. However, outside the season there is no need because there are often many such casas, causing competition and opening opportunities to strike a deal. Prices can then drop to 15 euro or even less for longer stays. During high season they can rise to over 30 euro. Many belong to associations, have a web presence, and are described in various books and travel guides.

Casas particulares can be recognised by a small sign on the door, with two blue triangles ('roofs') against a white background, which the owners obtain after paying a fixed per-room annual tax.

In some Cuban cities and tourist resorts, like Varadero, Playa Santa Lucia and Guardalavaca, local authorities determined that casas particulares would represent a threat to the hotel industry, and passed some legislation placing regulations and limits on the industry forbidding the operation of these establishments.

"Casa particular" literally means "private house" but it started to be used to mean "private accommodation" in 1997, when the Cuban government finally allowed Cubans to rent out rooms in their houses or apartments to tourists, providing Cuban families with new sources of income. As any other type of accommodation in Cuba such as hotels, camping and motels were owned by the government, the term "casa particular" stated that this kind of paid lodging was privately operated.

Services and Facilities

All rooms are clean, safe and upgraded to tourist standards. It ranges from basic accommodation of a room with a bed, a closet, a small table to full furnished independent apartments upgraded to western standards. Other features found may be a telephone, an alarm clock, and a TV. Food and drink may be supplied by a mini-bar (which often includes a small refrigerator) containing snacks and drinks (to be paid for on departure).

It is possible to have breakfast/dinner in the casa for price. Often breakfasts/dinners sold will decide if case owner will break even or not. So if it becomes clear that one plans to generally eat out, the price may go up because this is an important source of income.

Casas particulares have several advantages over other types of lodgings:

- The guest can quickly develop genuine Cuban relationships and become deeply involved in the culture of the country. Before he/she knows it, the guest will be part of the family. In a big resort one may only meet hotel workers and other tourists.
- The guest will enjoy the free and easy atmosphere, feel completely at home in the casa particular and will be able to invite friends over. The current regulations for state-run hotels don't allow to have Cuban guests invited to hotel rooms.
- It is almost always cheaper to stay in a private room than in a hotel.
- "Guests" are not usually allowed into the hotels. Usually one can take one local "guest" into his rented casa-particular.
- By renting a casa particular, the guest will be directly contributing to a person or family's standard of living. This is often obvious through the fact that casas particulares are freshly painted.

The cost and quality of casas particulares are usually indicative of the accommodation type and type of services available. Most of the casas particulares are rented for short term to travellers. Long term accommodation is also provided by some casas, especially for foreign students. In Havana, the casas particulares are usually family apartments and a smaller number of them are houses. In other cities, private accommodation is provided mainly in family houses.

Types of Casas Particulares rentals:

- Private Room: a room is rented out most of the times with private bathroom and a key to the apartment/house is usually given to the guest.
- Private Room with independent entrance. Sometimes the house/ apartment is split in order to allow this.
- Apartment: the guest can enjoy the privacy and independency of a full furnished apartment for his/her vacations. Sometimes this apartment is part of house being split by a wall usually with a connecting door.
- Studio-type or mini-apartment: it is not an apartment with several rooms but just the bedroom, a kitchen-living-dining room and a bathroom.

Condo-hotel

A condo-hotel or a hotel-condo is a building used as both a condominium and a hotel. This type of residential building meets several needs that make it attractive. As development costs increase, the cost of hotel development can make developing new hotels difficult, especially in major cities. By selling the units as condos, the developer moves much of the development cost to the condo owners. By owning units that can be rented as hotel rooms, the owners are able to get a return on their investment allowing them the ability to own a residence in a resort or major city.

It should be noted that the U.S. Government is very strict about the type of advertising that can be done vis a vis Condo Hotel projects. Some condo projects have advertised themselves as "Real Estate Investments" - since the value of these condos as a real estate investment is not entirely clear - the U.S. Government currently disallows use of this reference when advertising condo hotels.

Condo hotels have been criticized in California for allowing developers to skirt laws designed to protect public access to beaches. Because such a facility has hotel rooms, it can be classified as a public accommodation, even though the majority of the units are privately held, and the facility does little to accommodate the public.

DEVELOPMENT PROCESS OF HOTEL INDUSTRY

The ability to add value and to create a sustainable hotel project ultimately starts from the first brush on paper and opportunities for this are all the way through to the final touch of paint on the finished product.

The crisis has had a huge impact on all real estate development, including hotels. But due to the gap between hotel supply and demand across the country there remains great opportunities for hotel projects.

Hotels are typically more complex to develop compared with other asset classes, as their design is tailored to the brand operating the business.

The design of these can also have an impact on the overall profitability of the hotel operation, as design deficiencies affect the operation of a hotel and ultimately have a negative impact on the bottom line — and hence asset value. In order to reduce the risk of developing a hotel, which may not be commercially successful, it is important to seek advice from a hospitality consultant, who will ultimately act as the commercial conscience of the developer.

At the start of the development, prior to building and design stage, the most important question to answer is "is the project viable?" Demand and supply factors for the hotel project need to be identified in order to understand the dynamics of the future operation — to basically understand who will be the target audience for the hotel and build for that. A developer needs to have an understanding of the estimated cash-flow income of the future operation from the opening day of the hotel. This will then provide any potential investor with a comfort level that debt can be serviced from the operation.

When hotels are part of a wider scheme, the design and development of the hotel needs to be in line with the overall development vision of the scheme.

In a resort environment, it is important to understand the relationship between hotel, golf, spa, residential and other facilities, and in an urban mixed-use scheme.

The hotel will, more often than not, be managed by a professional hotel operator. It is always of benefit to ask a consultant to run a competitive tender processes (be it tailored or to the wider market) when looking for a hotel company to manage your property, as this provides the opportunity to drive the process in order to achieve the best commercial deal terms available in the market. These contracts typically run for 15-25 years and key terms agreed at the beginning will have a major impact going forward.

Hotels are particularly sensitive to market changes, economic downturns and to alterations in supply and demand — for example when competitive hotels open up next to your own hotel this can severely impact performance. It is better to have all advice and information prior to decisions being taken on concept, design, architecture style, number of rooms, size of facilities, star classification and so on — to avoid the need to either redo all the aforesaid or to face the possibility of building a hotel which no operator wants to manage or which will not be commercially viable.

THE ART AND SCIENCE OF OPENING A HOTEL

PRE-OPENING STAFF PLAN

The pre-opening staffing begins with an organizational chart with all positions. Once the titles and staff counts by position are finalized, then spreadsheets are created to include the position titles, start dates, pay rates, bonus, transfer allowances, and number of full-time equivalents (FTEs) for all positions.

The pre-opening staff plan is a comprehensive document that states who is hired, when they start, how much they are paid, and whether or not they are allocated a relocation allowance and benefit costs. Each of these pieces is used to build the pre-opening staff plan budget. If hiring has already begun and the opening date changes, the budget must be amended. Hiring a position that does not conform to the plan, such as bringing on a renowned chef one month earlier than planned, also requires the budget be modified.

PRE-OPENING BUDGET

The OPM develops and manages the preopening budget. This budget typically consists of three major categories; labour cost (40 per cent), sales and marketing efforts (40 per cent), and miscellaneous (20 per cent).

The labour cost is taken directly from the pre-opening staff plan. Sales and marketing activities comprise advertising, collateral, public relations, and travel to see clients. Rounding out the budget are all of the miscellaneous items. These include office space rental before moving into the hotel, utilities (power, water, Internet, and telephone), human resources recruitment (ads, headhunters, drug testing, etc.), training materials, association dues, and licenses and permits (business, liquor, sales tax collection, etc.).

If the hotel opening date is delayed for any reason, the pre-opening budget is affected. Additional costs include labour, office rent, utilities, and marketing efforts. If the opening date changes within three weeks of the original plan, major costs are encountered, as most of the staff is already hired.

OPERATIONAL SUPPLIES AND EQUIPMENT (OS&E)

The largest and most complex aspect of the OPM's responsibility is specifying, quantifying, and budgeting for the operational supplies and equipment (OS&E) list. This budget typically pencils out to $8,000 to $10,000 per guest room for a typical four-star property. The list of goods typically exceeds 2,500 line items. Add a little more for a full-service resort; deduct a little for an in-city business hotel.

The OS&E comprises all of the items that are not nailed down, with the exception of the furniture, fixtures, and equipment (FF&E). The FF&E is typically specified and ordered by the interior designer. Typical guest room items include bedding (frames, box springs, mattresses, mattress pads, sheets, pillows, pillowcases, towels, etc.), clock radios, hangers, laundry bags, laundry tickets, iron, ironing board, ironing board organizer, luggage rack, guest amenities (soap, shampoo, lotion, etc.), hair dryer, shower curtains, and shower curtain hooks.

Housekeeping equipment includes vacuums (guest room and wide-area units), carpet shampooers, carpet extractors, housekeeper carts, laundry bins, garbage trucks, valet delivery carts, and shelving, to name a few of many items. Housekeeping must also keep an inventory of guest request items including humidifiers, dehumidifiers, cribs, high chairs, rollaway beds, bedboards, spare pillows, towels, amenities, refrigerators, laundry soap, and so on.

ON-LINE PRICING: AN ANALYSIS OF HOTEL COMPANY PRACTICES

Both industry cost structure and the perishable nature of the product make effective distribution particularly important in the hotel sector. A hotel room left unsold on any particular night cannot be stored and subsequently offered to the customer at a later date.

Thus, selling each room each night at an optimum price is critical to a hotel's long-term success. To achieve this, hotel companies use a variety of different distribution channels to help sell their product, and also manipulate price in response to demand using sophisticated yield management systems in an attempt to maximize revenues. While direct sales are most common, extensive use is normally made of a variety of intermediaries, including travel agents, tour operators, marketing consortia, and representative companies. However, the importance of electronic routes has grown significantly in recent years.

Statistics quoted in the Horwath Worldwide Hotel Industry Studies, direct reservations fell from approximately 39% in 1995 to just 33% in 1999, with the corresponding growth being focused exclusively in electronic channels. And while hotels continue to make extensive use of the travel agent-orientated Global Distribution Systems (GDS), end user consumer adoption of the Internet as a mainstream commerce medium has prompted a change in the way in which the hotel product is being distributed.

Table. Composition of Worldwide Hotel Advanced Reservations

Composition of Advanced Reservations	1995	1996	1997	1998	1999
Direct enquiry	38.3	36.9	35.1	34.0	33.5
Own reservations system	18.9	14.5	14.0	14.7	14.2
Independent reservations system	6.0	5.2	5.3	4.3	5.1
Travel agents	15.7	18.1	19.8	20.7	20.4
Tour operator	12.7	16.5	18.1	16.4	15.9
Hotel representatives	8.4 (Other)	5.7	4.3	6.5	5.9
Transportation company		2.3	2.0	1.6	2.2
Web site/Internet		0.8	1.4	1.8	2.8

The Web has dramatically changed the way people communicate, research information, make decisions, and particularly the way in which they buy goods and services. Travel products in particular have proven to be some of the most suitable for sale online.

The typical profile of an Internet user—affluent, frequent traveller who spends above average on leisure and entertainment—is an attractive market for travel suppliers. Furthermore, from a consumer perspective, in an increasingly wired world, purchasing travel online has become faster, easier, and more convenient than contacting a travel agent or telephoning a supplier directly. As a result, online travel revenues are forecast to grow sharply. For example, online travel sales will more than triple in the next 5 years from US$24 billion in 2001 to US$64 billion in 2007.

Booking volumes are also forecast to climb, with the Travel Industry Association of America estimating that by 2002 between 6% and 10% of all travel reservations will originate on the Web. This will make travel the highest grossing online product, nearly doubling that of PC hardware—the traditional top selling product. E-Commerce analysts Jupiter Media Metrix are even more enthusiastic, predicting that over 22% of all travel bookings will be made online by 2007—an 11% increase over the next 5 years. Key to successful selling online is the issue of price. Recent research has shown that consumers have become more value conscious. For example, a recent study by BIGResearch found that nearly three quarters of travel consumers were unwilling to buy online unless they felt they were getting a good deal. Furthermore, studies by Gomez, Hospitality Sales and Marketing Association International, the Travel Industry Association of America, Jeong and Lambert, and PhoCusWright have all identified price as being one of the key motivating factors that encourages consumers to purchase travel online.

For example, the PhoCusWright study found that competitive pricing is the best way to attract customers. When travellers who haven't bought online were asked what would encourage them to do so, 64% said that saving money would make them more interested. No other benefit—saving time, getting bonus loyalty club points, more control, or obtaining better information—came close to this level of response.

HOTEL PRICING ON THE WEB

Recent studies have shown that online travel purchasers tend to be price driven. For example, according to Yesawich, Pepperdine and Brown, almost 6 out of 10 leisure travellers now actively seek the "lowest possible price" for travel services. Similarly, a recent Forrester Research study found that 66% of all buyers used an online discount in the past 12 months to buy travel online, and a study by the Joint Hospitality Industry Congress found that there is a real expectation among consumers that Internet prices will be lower than those in the "bricks and mortar" world.

Such a perception has developed for several reasons. First, many of the most wellknown Internet retailers compete with traditional outlets based, to a large extent, on price. As a result, there is an assumption among Web users that the same is true for travel products. Secondly, many consumers are aware of the lower distribution costs associated with Web channels. As Jack Geddes, Managing Director Sales and Marketing Asia, Radisson Hotels Worldwide, has pointed out "Consumers now understand that suppliers are cutting costs through this channel and expect savings to be passed onto them, as well as being rewarded for making the booking themselves".

Such expectations are being reinforced by the budget airline sector, which offers significant discounts for online bookings. Companies such as EasyJet, RyanAir, and Buzz estimate that by avoiding telesales and travel agents, they can make savings of up to 30%—which they pass on to customers in the form of lower fares. Lastly, many hotels use the Web to sell last minute deals—packages at relatively low prices but with short lead times. While such promotions can help dispose of distressed inventory, they have also resulted in the public associating rooms sold over the Internet with cheaper prices.

These factors have combined to make consumers associate online booking with good value. However, in the case of hotel own branded Web sites, industry practice seems to be the opposite of theory. In their 1999 survey,

O'Connor and Horan found that, in the majority of cases, rates obtained over hotel Web sites were significantly higher than those obtained by contacting the hotel company's Central Reservations Office. Often the rate quoted by the company's Web site was substantially higher, despite the associated lower cost of distribution.

However, this study was limited in that it only focused on direct sales over hotel chains' own branded Web sites. Hotel electronic distribution is rapidly evolving and a large number of other online consumerfocused channels are now available, with most chains using multiple routes to get their product to the consumer.

The availability of so many alternative points-of-sale poses some interesting questions. Is there consistency between the rates and availability being offered over alternative channels? Research has shown that consumers shopping for travel online almost always check more than one site before purchasing.

Jupiter Media Metrix, for the hotel product 10% of bookers visit one site, another 43% visit two or three sites, and 22% visit four or more sites. Online purchasers have become increasingly intolerant of inconsistent information, and may react to disparate rates on different channels by purchasing from the company's competitor. Furthermore, if rates are not consistent across channels, is any particular route consistently cheaper? And lastly, if rates are different over alternative channels, is the pricing strategy logical from both the consumer's and the hotel's perspective?

METHODOLOGY AND LIMITATION OF THE STUDY

Hotel Internet use have been limited. Murphy focused on rating the content of hotel Web sites, while Van Hoof and Combrink attempted to measure managers' perceptions of, and attitudes towards, the Internet. Web reservations facilities were investigated in detail in a prior paper by the author. However, the issue of pricing over multiple simultaneous travel distribution channels does not appear to have been the subject of extensive systematic research to date. The objectives, therefore, of this study were to analyse the rates being offered to consumers over hotel electronic distribution channels and to subsequently identify the pricing strategies being used by the hotel companies.

Obviously, an exhaustive analysis of the rates being offered by all hotels would be impossible. However, as the use of both technology and electronic distribution has in the past been lead by the major international hotel chains, an analysis of their efforts was thought to be indicative of developments in the field. As a result, it was decided to focus the study on the Behaviour of the top 50 international hotel brands.

While this strategy means that the findings are not representative of the industry as a whole and thus the results not generally applicable, it does allow an accurate benchmark of trends as they currently stand to be established. The companies were chosen based on the ranking of the top 50 hotel brands published in *Hotels* magazine in July 2000. Two companies were removed from the listing as they are in effect resorts, only distribute their rooms as part of packages, and thus their products are not directly comparable. Furthermore, three companies neither offered online reservations facilities on their own Web site nor were they listed on any of the other channels studied. Thus, the results reflect the findings for 45 hotel brands for which consistent data could be found.

Five major types of electronic B2C distribution channels were identified from the literature and leading examples of each category selected for inclusion in the study. In addition to the chain's own Web site, these included channels that draw their data/ reservations engine from the Global Distribution Systems; those that are based upon the databases/reservation engine of the Switch companies; and pure Web-based channels that require their inventory/ reservations database to be maintained online.

While not collectively exhaustive, these represent the majority of the non-direct-to-hotel reservations. Omitted from the study were the "nameyour- price"/"auction" style Web sites, which, due to their bidding pricing structure, were not comparable and thus could not be included. Voice channels were also incorporated into the study for comparison purposes by analysing the rates offered by the toll-free number to the Central Reservations Office (CRO). Data were collected by iteratively reserving a double room for specified dates in a selected property from each of the brands using each of the distribution channels. Where the product requested was available on the system, both the number of rates displayed and the lowest rate available were recorded for analysis. The hotel company's Central Reservation Office was subsequently telephoned and the same product requested.

In the latter case, the first rate quoted by the telesales agent was recorded. This process was repeated for five sets of alternative dates to reduce the possibility of error due to systems malfunctions or other exceptional circumstances. The order in which the channels were polled was also varied to minimize the effect of yield management systems.

SUMMARY OF RESEARCH FINDINGS

Number of Channels Used

Each of the major hotel brands uses multiple simultaneous distribution channels, with the mean number of channels being 4.68. The most commonly used channels were over voice through the company's Central Reservation Office and through the company's corporate Web site. Those companies that did not use voice were in the economy sector, and, although outside the scope of the study, it could be speculated that their abstinence from using this channel could be a reaction to the high operating costs of this channel. The level of use of a company's own Web site was also found to be high, with nearly 97% of the brands surveyed offering the facility to make an online reservation in this manner. It is interesting to note that this represents a considerable advancement in comparison to prior surveys, which found that only approximately 50% of the major hotel companies provided such online facilities. Thus, there appears to have been major growth in the use of the Web as a direct selling medium by the hotel industry over the past 2 years.

Table. Channels Used by the Major Hotel Brands

Channel	Number	Percentage
Hotel company Web site	44	97%
Microsoft Expedia	38	84%
Travelocity.com	35	78%
TravelWeb	34	76%
WorldRes	14	31%
Voice (CRO)	44	97%

In contrast, usage of the other channels investigated was lower. Approximately four fifths of the major brands used the GDS-based intermediaries Microsoft Expedia and Travelocity, three quarters used TravelWeb, and only approximately one third used WorldRes at the time of the study. These findings are not in themselves surprising. Both Expedia and Travelocity draw their data from the major GDS, and as the majority of the hotel brands represented in the study are business focused, representation on the GDS and thus their subsequent listing on these channels was to be expected. Similarly, TravelWeb draws its data from THISCO (The Hotel Industry Switching Company), and thus any of the hotel brands that use this as their switch service could be expected to leverage their investment by make inventory available for sale over TravelWeb—the switch's consumer-focused Website. However, the low usage of WorldRes is surprising.

With the exception of through a company's own Web site, using WorldRes has the lowest potential transaction cost and thus would appear to be an attractive channel for use by hotel companies. However, in practice, it does not list the properties of many of the major hotel brands.

Examination of its property database reveals a large percentage of independent hotels, bed and breakfasts, and smaller hotel chains, yet the question has to be asked as to why the major brands do not exploit this distribution channel?

Rates Available

With the exception of the toll-free number (where the first rate offered was accepted), each of the channels analysed offered multiple rates to the customer.

Each channel presented an average of five rates in response to the request, with more being offered to the customer in the case of Travelocity than through the other channels surveyed.

Table. Number of Rates Offered to the Customer

Channel	Mean	SD	Maximum	Minimum
Hotel company Web site	4.27	3.6	19	1
Microsoft Expedia	3.66	1.4	5	1
Travelocity.com	6.07	3.3	16	2
TravelWeb	5.62	3.6	17	1
WorldRes	4.58	3.8	12	1
Voice (CRO)	1.00	—	—	—

Presenting a variety of rates to the customer has both positive and negative implications. From a positive perspective, it offers the potential customer a choice and allows them to match their needs with the products being sold. On the other hand, presenting multiple rates without adequate product differentiation can create confusion in the mind of the customer as to what they are getting for their money.

This is best demonstrated by an example encountered in the study, where a property had 17 different rates available for a particular date on TravelWeb, with few (if any) discernable differences identifiable in the rate descriptions. Clearly such a scenario would be confusing and frustrating for any customer wishing to book that property.

In terms of which channel is consistently cheapest, such a broad generalization is difficult to make. However, based on an analysis of the rates found in the study and making allowances for rounding and currency conversions, it can be seen that prices across each of the channels were comparable, with the average price for the requested room being in the range of US$163. There were two noticeable exceptions to this trend. Microsoft Expedia was consistently marginally cheaper than any of the other channels and the rates found on WorldRes were in general more expensive.

Table. Average Rates Offered to the Customer

Channel	Mean	SD
Hotel company Web site	159	112
Microsoft Expedia	152	116
Travelocity.com	166	134
TravelWeb	162	115
WorldRes	181	168
Voice (CRO)	163	117

Such findings are surprising in that, as was explained earlier, the transaction costs associated with each channel vary greatly. Expedia, as an online travel agency, has a higher cost of distribution from the hotel's perspective, and thus it would be logical to assume that rates offered over this channel would reflect these higher associated costs. Similarly, because WorldRes's transaction costs are relatively low in comparison with the other channels surveyed, it should in theory be offering the cheapest rates if hotel companies were matching their rates to the associated cost of using the channel. However, in practice, in general the rates quoted on WorldRes were the highest found on any the channels surveyed. Clearly, when selling the hotel product online, there does not appear to be a relationship between the cost of using the distribution channel and the rate offered.

However, simply examining broad averages often hides valuable information. If the brands studied are subdivided into classifications based on their targeted market segment, a different picture emerges.

Table. Market Sector Analysis

	Cheapest Channel			
Channel	**Economy**	**Mid-Priced**	**Luxury**	**Chi-Square**
All rates equal	46%	21%	28%	0.016*
Hotel company Web site	26%	47%	8%	0.036*
Online intermediary	26%	21%	31%	0.370
Voice (CRO)	9%	11%	2%	0.600
Microsoft Expedia	14%	11%	22%	0.030*
Travelocity.com	3%	5%	4%	0.750
TravelWeb	9%	5%	4%	0.900
WorldRes	0%	0%	0%	
	Most Expensive Channel			
Channel	**Economy**	**Mid-Priced**	**Luxury**	**Chi-Square**
Hotel company Web site	14%	16%	34%	0.011*
Online intermediary	9%	26%	17%	0.221
Voice (CRO)	31%	37%	21%	0.440
Microsoft Expedia	0%	21%	7%	0.017*
Travelocity.com	3%	5%	10%	0.450
TravelWeb	0%	0%	0%	
WorldRes	6%	0%	0%	0.240

Note:

Columns may not total 100% due to rounding.

*The association is significant at the 95% confidence level.

Hotels at the lower end of the market are far more likely to offer consistent rates across all channels used. While it could be speculated that the reason for this might be because economy properties are more likely to have a single fixed price for their product irrespective of demand, it could also be due to a more consistent pricing strategy on the part of the hotel companies involved when addressing a relatively price-sensitive market. Furthermore, it can be seen that consumers at the lower ends of the market are far more likely to obtain lower rates through direct channels. For economy brands, direct sales over the company's own Web site was cheapest nearly one quarter of the time, with a further 46% offering the same rate irrespective of the channel used. Thus, a consumer making a reservation for an economy room on a hotel company's Web site would find the cheapest rate on this channel three times out four.

With mid-priced products, the chain Web site is even more likely to give the best rate, offering the cheapest rate nearly half of the time.

However, at the upper end of the market the situation was very different. Hotel company Web sites gave the cheapest rate in less than 10% of cases, but quoted the highest rate in over one third of cases.

The evidence is clear. If you want to stay in upmarket hotels, avoid booking on their Web site if you are searching for good value! Instead, the online intermediaries (in particular Microsoft Expedia) offer the highest probability of finding the cheapest rate available for such upper-end properties.

It is also clear from the data that a hotel company's Central Reservation Office, accessed through a toll-free number, is not the place to obtain cheaper rates. Irrespective of the market segment, there is a higher probability of obtaining the most expensive rate through this channel, and bookings through this route were almost never the cheapest available. However, this finding is to a large extent a factor of the survey methodology used. With voice, the first rate quoted was the one recorded for analysis. In many cases, other (lower) rates were quoted when the researcher indicated that he did not want to make a booking, suggesting that some degree of haggling would have resulted in significant lower prices on this channel.

CONCLUSIONS

It can be seen that both the range of channels through which hotels can be booked and the complexity of these channels have grown. This study represents the first major attempt to understand hotel company's pricing strategies over electronic routes. Bookings made on five major consumer-focused online travel sites were analysed to determine if a logical pricing strategy could be established.

The study revealed that the majority of hotel brands now use multiple simultaneous electronic channels of distribution, making their product available to a relatively wide audience. While the use of voice through a Central Reservation Office has fallen slightly, there has been a growth in the availability of hotel company's own Web site, with 19 out of 20 of companies now making their product available for sale in this manner. The differences between this and earlier published research indicate a major expansion in the use of the Web as a direct selling medium on the part of the hotel industry, perhaps accompanied by a realization of its benefits in comparison with other, more traditional, electronic channels of distribution.

Most companies offer multiple rates to customers over each channel utilized. It is interesting to note the large number of companies that now have consistent pricing across all channels. Research found less than 10% of companies had consistent pricing and cited the lack of integration between the various inventory databases used to manage inventory as a possible cause. Yet over one third of brands now offer consistent pricing across multiple channels, indicating progression in the industry's management of electronic distribution in the interim.

Although no single distribution channel is consistently cheapest, in-depth analysis does reveal a link between the market being targeted and price. Firstly, cheaper prices can rarely be obtained over voice channels, irrespective of market segment. From the data it can be seen that consumers are more likely to find cheaper prices on hotel chains' own Web sites in the economy and mid-price segments. More upmarket hotel brands are, on the other hand, more likely to quote more expensive prices on their own Web site than on other channels. Perhaps this is a reaction by the brands at the lower end of the market to the price sensitivity of their customer, or alternatively a realization that at least some of the cost savings generated by direct selling should morally and ethically be passed onto the consumer. In any case, it represents a more progressive and realistic pricing strategy than that of the upper- end brands, who in many cases are charging their highest prices over the channel that represents their lowest cost of distribution.

And what are the implications of these findings for the consumer? First, it is clear that for those with a taste for more upscale products, the hotel brand's own Web site is not the place to shop, as better value can be obtained in most cases through other channels.

More interesting, however is the fact that, in general, prices have become more or less equal across many of the channels investigated, and thus by implication, across many other electronic distribution channels as well. It is well established that time is a valuable commodity in today's society.

Because the number and variety of ways that a consumer can book a hotel room have become undeniably complex, the cost associated with searching through even a small number of the many alternative consumer-focused channels currently available in the marketplace in an attempt to find a cheap price has also grown dramatically. Given that this study has found that many of the rates being offered over alternative channels are more or less the same for the majority of hotels, the question must be asked as to whether spending time and energy searching for the cheapest rate is worthwhile.

THE LODGING INDUSTRY

Lodging (or a holiday accommodation) is a type of residential accommodation. People who travel and stay away from home for more than a day need lodging for sleep, rest, safety, shelter from cold temperatures or rain, storage of luggage and access to common household functions.

Lodgings may be *self catering* in which case no food is laid on but cooking facilities are available.

Lodging is done in a hotel, hostel or hostal, a private home (commercial, *i.e.* a bed and breakfast, a guest house, a vacation rental, or non-commercially, with members of hospitality services or in the home of friends), in a tent, caravan/camper (often on a campsite). In addition there are make-shift solutions.

MARKETING BASICS FOR THE SMALL HOTEL BUSINESS

The essence of marketing is to understand your customers' needs and develop a plan that surrounds those needs. Let's face it anyone that has a business has a desire to grow their business. The most effective way to grow and expand your business is by focusing on organic growth.

You can increase organic growth in four different ways. They include:

- Acquiring more customers
- Persuading each customer to buy more products
- Persuading each customer to buy more expensive products or up selling each customer
- Persuading each customer to buy more profitable products

All four of these increase your revenue and profit. Let me encourage you to focus on the first which is to acquire more customers. Why? Because by acquiring more customers you increase your customer base and your revenues then come from a larger base.

How can you use marketing to acquire more customers?

- Spend time researching and create a strategic marketing plan.
- Guide your product development to reach out to customers you aren't currently attracting.
- Price your products and services competitively.
- Develop your message and materials based on solution marketing.

The Importance of a Target Market

When it comes to your customers keep in mind the importance of target marketing. The reason this is important is that only a proportion of the population is likely to purchase any products or service. By taking time pitch your sales and marketing efforts to the correct niche market you will be more productive and not waste your efforts or time.

It's important to consider your virtual segmentation by selecting particular verticals to present your offerings to. Those verticals will have the particular likelihood of purchasing your products and services. Again, this saves you from wasting valuable time and money.

Marketing Differs between Small hotels and larger hotels

If you are like the majority of small hotel business owners your marketing budget is limited. The most effective way to market a small hotel business is to create a well rounded programme that combines sales activities with your marketing tactics. Your sales activities will not only decrease your out-of-pocket marketing expense but it also adds the value of interacting with your prospective customers and clients. This interaction will provide you with research that is priceless.

Small hotel businesses typically have a limited marketing budget if any at all. Does that mean you can't run with the big dogs? Absolutely not. It just means you have to think a little more creatively. How about launching your marketing campaign by doing one of the following:

- Call your vendors or associates and ask them to participate with you in co-op advertising.
- Take some time to send your existing customers' referrals and buying incentives.
- Have you thought about introducing yourself to the media? Free publicity has the potential to boost your business. By doing this you position yourself as an expert in your field.
- Invite people into your place of business by piggybacking onto an event. Is there a concert coming to town, are you willing to sell those tickets? It could mean free radio publicity. If that is not your cup of tea, how about a walkathon that is taking place in your area, why not be a public outreach and distribute their material?

When you do spend money on marketing, do not forget to create a way to track those marketing efforts. You can do this by coding your ads, using multiple toll-free telephone numbers, and asking prospects where they heard about you. This enables you to notice when a marketing tactic stops working. You can then quickly replace it with a better choice or method. By being diligent in your marketing and creating an easy strategy such as holding yourself accountable to contact ten customers or potential customers daily five days a week you will see your business grow at an exceptional rate. The great thing is it will not take a large marketing budget to make it happen.

PROSPECT

For people who think this is the industry for them, they really think about their personality and be sure they can thrive (and survive) in the atmosphere. It truly is different from anything else. It is critical that they work for a hotel while they are still in school, preferably in a few different hotels, and departments, so they can get a feel for it and know where they would be the happiest and most successful. The growth in the services sector of the worldwide economy has been phenomenal in the last 25 years.

In the United States, services currently account for more than 75 percent of the gross domestic product (GDP), which is a popular measure of an economy's productivity. Similarly, on an international scale, services continue to account for an ever-increasing percentage of economic activity. Most new jobs are created in the service sector, and the growth in the hospitality and tourism industry is a major contributor.

Until the mid-1980s, the emphasis within the marketing community was on products. Now services have surpassed products and have taken on a more important role in marketing. Services, such as those offered by providers in the hospitality and tourism industry, have developed marketing strategies and practices that are unique. It has been established that the strategies, tactics, and practices that have been used successfully for product marketers do not always work successfully for those who market services. With the distinct differences between products and services in mind, the field of services marketing has evolved.

Services Defined

Unlike products, which are tangible, services are usually intangible. A service is not a physical good; rather, it is the performance of an act or a deed. This performance often requires consumers to be present during the production or delivery of the service. Service industries, including hospitality and tourism, are actually selling consumers an experience.

Services have been defined to "include all economic activities whose output is not a physical product or construction, is generally consumed at the time it is produced, and provides added value in forms (such as convenience, amusement, timeliness, comfort or health) that are essentially intangible concerns of its first purchaser." Service employees such as front desk agents, housekeepers, hostesses, wait staff, car rental agents, flight attendants, and travel agents are responsible for creating positive experiences for customers.

These frontline employees are critical to the success of service firms and play boundary-spanning roles because of their direct contact with customers. These roles are important because customers' perceptions of service firms are formed as a result of their dealings with the boundary-spanning employees. Several reasons underlie the remarkable growth in services.

The numerous reasons for this growth:

- *Changing patterns of government regulation:* The reduction in government regulation has spurred the growth of services. In recent years, there has been a very noticeable shift toward the government taking a much less active role in the regulation of business activities.

The most noteworthy of these shifts have been in the airline, trucking, telecommunication, and electrical generation and distribution industries. All of these industries have seen significant changes, as the barriers to entry have been removed and regulations governing such marketing elements as price have also been relaxed or entirely removed.

- *Relaxation of professional association restrictions on marketing:* A new element of competition has been introduced into professions such as law and medicine as more of the practitioners in these areas advertise their services. Bans or restrictions on promotion have been largely removed. Within the hospitality and tourism industry, standards have also changed. We have seen an increase in advertising focusing on direct comparisons, or attacks, on competitors' products and services. This type of advertising strategy creates, or sustains, the perception of superiority in the mind of the consumer in favor of the brand being advertised.
- *Privatization of some public and nonprofit services:* The term privatization was first used in Great Britain when the government adopted the policy of returning national industries from government to private ownership. This transformation has resulted in a greater emphasis on cost containment and a clearer focus on customers' needs. Later, in Central and Eastern Europe, following the fall of communism, we witnessed a continuing transformation from planned or government-run economies to market-driven economies fueled by private companies. Many of these countries' governments have released the control of airlines and travel agencies to private firms.
- *Technological innovation:* Technology continues to alter the way firms do business and interact with consumers. In all types of businesses, consumers take a more active role in the service delivery process. For example, airlines, in an effort to reduce labour costs and increase speed of service to customers, have aggressively promoted self-check-in, both at the ticket counter and through their Web sites prior to arrival at the airport. Customers print boarding passes, receipts, and other documents without intervention by an airline employee. Express checkout for hotel guests has been in place for many years, but hotel chains continue to experiment with ways to enhance the service, thereby reducing labour costs and/or increasing the customers' perceived value.

In other settings, touch-screen computers collect feedback from guests, in much the same manner that comment cards have been used previously. The ease with which a company can maintain and access a database has permitted the development of sophisticated reservation systems and has led to more sophisticated frequent traveler Programmes. The use of more sophisticated reservations and property management systems has allowed hospitality and tourism firms to improve the level of service provided to guests. Guest history data serve as another example of how a hospitality organization can use technology to gain a competitive advantage. If a hotel guest requests a specific type of pillow, staff can record this preference within the individual's guest history file. When this guest checks into another hotel operated by the chain, the items that were previously requested can be waiting, without the guest even having to request them.

- *Growth in service chains and franchise networks:* Much of the growth in service firms, including the hospitality industry, has been the direct result of franchising efforts by some of the major companies. Franchising represents a contractual arrangement whereby one firm (the franchisor) licenses a number of other firms (the franchisees) to use the franchisor's name and business practices. Notable lodging organizations such as Choice Hotels International and Marriott International, as well as food service firms such as McDonald's, Burger King, Taco Bell, and Wendy's, have all used franchising as a major vehicle for growth. The continued growth of the hospitality industry by means of franchising has put additional stress on independent owners and operators. In fact, each year the percentage of hospitality and tourism operations that are independently operated decreases.
- *Internationalization and globalization:* Increasing shareholder value often remains directly associated with increasing company sales and profits, and globalization is one means of achieving this. As more and more of the prime locations are developed domestically, companies look internationally for expansion opportunities. This has been particularly true for fast-food franchisors: a significant proportion of their expansion during the last few years has occurred outside of their traditional domestic markets.
- *Pressures to improve productivity:* In many industries within the service economy, competition stays very intense. This factor, when combined with the pressure from investors for higher returns on capital, has resulted in pressure to increase productivity and reduce costs. In many cases, managers seek to reduce labour costs by running leaner operations or using technology to replace humans for some tasks An example of this was when Delta Airlines encouraged passengers to check in via the Internet, thereby reducing the number of passengers who wanted to check in at the airport. They offered an incentive of 1,000 extra frequent-flyer miles to any passenger who used this service. While increasing productivity and profits remains

a highly desirable goal, it must not be done at the expense of longterm customer satisfaction. Without long-term satisfaction, future profitability may exist in jeopardy.

- *The service quality movement:* With the advent of consumerism, the public's perception is that service quality has declined. In response, successful firms are using the customer's perception of quality to set performance standards, rather than relying solely on operationally defined standards for service quality. They often conduct extensive research to determine the key elements that impact the customer's perception of service quality. When Ritz-Carlton won the Malcolm Baldrige National Quality Award, this was tangible evidence that paying careful attention to customers' service expectations can have a dramatic impact on the firm.
- *Expansion of leasing and rental businesses:* The expansion of businesses that lease equipment and personnel to firms has been a contributing factor in the growth of the service sector. More and more firms are looking to outsource some elements of their operation, and they often start with elements that are not part of the firm's core product or business. For example, most hotels that host meetings and conventions have outsourced the servicing of the audiovisual needs of groups to a company that specializes in that type of business. The company in turn leases the audiovisual equipment to groups that are holding meetings in the hotel. The company is able to provide more up-to-date and specialized equipment to groups than the hotel might if it provided the service itself. The hotel does not have to maintain an inventory of equipment, and therefore capital costs are reduced.
- *Manufacturers as service providers:* Some of the firms that traditionally manufactured and distributed tangible products have found it profitable to provide services as well. For example, most automobile manufacturers have consumer credit agencies to facilitate the leasing and purchasing of automobiles. In the hospitality industry, PepsiCo decided to enter the restaurant industry and distribute its products through acquisitions such as Taco Bell and KFC, but the company later reconsidered this strategy and sold these brands to Yum! Brands, Inc. In the computer industry, firms such as IBM and Hewlett-Packard provide services in addition to hardware and software. In most cases, the profit margins on services are higher than on products, contributing significantly to the bottom line of the firm.
- *Pressures on public and nonprofit organizations to find new income sources:* All organizations are under pressure to increase sales, which often

becomes difficult within the traditional products that a firm sells. There are many reasons for this, but increasing competition and mature industries are often contributing factors. In an effort to find new sources of income, firms often seek new services that will generate new net sales, without cannibalizing sales of existing products. For example, a limousine company might expand its city tour business in addition to the other services offered.

- *Hiring and promotion of innovative managers:* In the past, managers in the service industries often spent their entire careers within a single industry, or perhaps even with the same firm. This situation no longer reintroduction to services marketing mains the same, especially at the corporate level of management. Firms often hire individuals from other industries to provide a fresh perspective and fresh ideas. The results can become dramatic. One such individual is Steven Bollenback, president and CEO of Hilton Hotels. Prior to his very positive impact on Hilton Hotels, he had engineered innovative financing at both Marriott International and Trump Hotels and Resorts.

SEGMENTATION IN A HOTEL CHAIN

Consider, for example, the needs of business customers and vacation customers at "Wolverine Inns" a fictitious name for a major mid-priced hotel chain we worked with recently. The chain recently segmented its franchisees according to which segment of customers they are most likely to serve, based on the idea that downtown properties cater more to the business customer segment and leisure-area properties cater more to the vacation customer segment.

The matrices are used to set priorities for quality improvement. The company's satisfaction and loyalty survey covers eight general quality areas or customer benefits (reservation process, staff, facilities, grounds, bathroom, room, breakfast, and perceived value) and each area is rated on a variety of attributes. For the moment, just look at the impact and performance aspects of the eight types of benefit. Later we will take up the issue of setting priorities among the attributes that provide each benefit, such as the friendliness, helpfulness, efficiency, and grooming and appearance of the hotel staff.

The vertical axes show how each type of property performs on each of the eight benefits using a weighted average of customers' attribute ratings (on a scale where 1 is poor and 5 is excellent). Both downtown and leisure-area properties, for example, perform very well on the quality of the reservations process. The horizontal axes show the relative importance of each benefit as revealed by its statistical impact on overall satisfaction.

For example, the impact score of.75 for quality of the room for the downtown properties shows that as room quality increases by 10 percent, satisfaction increases by 7.5 percent (10 percent ×.75). (This example is based on standardized scale values.)

The results reveal vast differences in the drivers of satisfaction across the two property types. Business customers who frequent downtown Wolverine Inn locations look for the hotel to simply provide a clean and comfortable room. They use the hotel for a place to get a good night's sleep and have little interest in its other services. In contrast, a much wider variety of factors drive satisfaction for the vacation customers who frequent the chain's leisure-area properties. The quality of the room is secondary to the quality of service and advice that the staff provides. The quality of the grounds, bathroom, and breakfast are also more important for the vacation customer.

As hotel manager at any given property, you would certainly want to know impact and performance levels for your target customers. Assuming the described results for individual hotels, the downtown manager would see improving the quality of the rooms as the greatest priority, given its high impact and currently moderate performance. In contrast, the manager of the leisure-area property would see improving the quality of the staff as relatively more important. Neither manager would have much incentive to do anything about perceived value—the customers' view of the price they are paying for the experience—even though it is far and away the lowest performance area in both cases, because the survey results show that neither group of customers cares much about it. Lowering prices would be costly for the hotel and would make it more difficult to sustain improvements in areas that matter to the customers, so it's best to avoid this step unless the hotel has an incentive to change its customer base to one that regards the current price level as a barrier rather than a minor irritant.

After deciding which customer levels to include in the measurement system and what customers or market segments to include, the next step is to ask what level of generality or detail about the lens of the customer the system should contain. Customer satisfaction is a complex matter, made up of the way the customer perceives the concrete attributes of a product, the benefits the customer derives from those attributes, and the personal values that the product supports. All these elements reside with the customer and are beyond the company's direct control, so we refer to them as *external quality factors*. Measurement systems vary in the amount of detail they provide about external factors such as these.

For example, macro-level measurement systems such as the American Customer Satisfaction Index (ACSI) only include very general differences in external perceptions of overall quality and value as drivers of satisfaction and loyalty. Quality is itself measured using customer ratings of the levels of customization and reliability provided, while value is measured using customer perceptions of the price or prices paid for the quality received. The purpose of measurement systems such as the ACSI is, however, to provide quality, value, satisfaction, and loyalty benchmarks across a very wide range of firms, industry groupings (including products, services, retailers, and government and public agencies), and even countries. Such broad-based comparisons require a measurement system that emphasizes generality and comparability as opposed to depth and detail.

If your goal is to improve or radically reinvent goods and services, you'll need a more detailed and comprehensive information system. It should include information on the range of concrete attributes and abstract benefits that might drive satisfaction and require improvement.

In subsequent chapters we will discuss how to develop these more detailed or in-depth measurement systems for the purpose of measuring and managing customer data for a particular product or service and market segment. Remember that the information in the measurement system is designed to leverage either incremental (evolutionary) or innovative (revolutionary) activities, or both. For example, when Volvo discovered that its customers found its manual transmissions difficult to shift (an attribute-level problem), it translated the problem into one of changing certain parts that immediately reduced complaints.

In contrast, when product or service designers are pursuing major innovations, they shift upward from the attribute level to more abstract customer benefits and personal values as input to the design process. Developing a fuel cell or electric vehicle, for example, requires matching the benefits and consequences that the new technology provides (such as zero emissions and moderate performance) with the benefits and values that are important to target customers (such as a willingness to trade off vehicle performance for environmental impact). Product or service design is then a process of developing a whole new configuration of product and service attributes to better serve customer needs.

We are often asked when to engage in revolutionary innovation rather than more evolutionary continuous improvement. The key, of course, is to avoid focusing on one to the exclusion of the other, but rather to balance both activities. Masaaki Imai, who was instrumental in developing the *kaizen* or continuous improvement process, emphasizes the importance of maintaining a balance among three activities: maintaining the quality of existing products, services, or processes; achieving kaizen or continuous improvement; and achieving innovation. The temptation, Imai argues, is to focus only on innovation as a means of making rapid changes and leapfrogging the competition. This ignores the long-term benefits that continuous improvement brings to a company.

When all three activities are balanced, the result is a formidable competitive advantage. Disney is a great example of an organization that consistently manages to balance all three activities. The regular development of new characters for use in movies, television shows, and theme parks is a constant source of innovation. At the same time, Disney works to maintain or keep improving every stage of its customers' experience. The combination has created a legendary service organization that is built on a quality foundation *and* reinvents itself on a regular basis.

Measuring quality, customer satisfaction, and loyalty should be an ongoing, repetitive process. It is difficult, however, to make general recommendations about just how frequently to measure. The frequency varies from company to company and depends on the audience, the stability or volatility of the product or service, and the nature of the market. For instance, if you have relatively few customers it may not be desirable to survey them too often. Needless to say, your customers should never feel that the process is burdensome. And once you do a survey and set some priorities, be sure to implement the changes before you launch another survey. Otherwise, your customers will ask the obvious question: "Why should I bother filling out this survey when you didn't pay any attention to the last one?"

A product's life cycle also affects the frequency of measurement. You need frequent contact with customers early on, when the market is evolving and changes to the product or service can have a great impact on a company's success. Consider the battle between Ericsson and Nokia in the cellular phone market. The early adopters of cellular phones were businesspeople. They simply wanted a reliable phone, which gave Ericsson the edge. But Ericsson did not keep up with the evolution of customer needs in the market and emergence of new market segments that demanded more features and design improvements. This allowed Nokia to achieve a greater advantage as the market evolved.

Later in a product's life cycle, customers are much harder to attract, more valuable to keep, and more costly to lose, so again you want close and frequent customer contacts. And, of course, it is always important to listen carefully to customers when the threat of competition has increased. The general point is that contact with customers should become more frequent during certain critical stages of the product life cycle and market dynamics.

Keeping these contingencies in mind, we recommend a customer satisfaction survey at least yearly. More frequent surveys are likely to have little effect on your improvement efforts when the product and the market are stable. If competition is really active and is moving quickly in a market, it may be necessary to carry out more frequent studies—perhaps even on a quarterly basis. But make sure you have enough resources to process and implement the findings, or the efforts are wasted. It is often a good compromise to measure every six months in times of change.

Finally, remember that there's a difference between customer measures and surveys as the basis of a measurement and management system and more informal surveys or methods designed to take a quick pulse or to identify problems as they occur. The latter methods typically focus on the most recent episode or transaction with a customer (such as the latest stay at the hotel or visit to the bookstore), and are often loosely structured (an informal interview by the manager or an open-ended "opinion" card). Their value toward allocating resources and deciding strategy is limited. At the same time, they may be a valuable source of information for service managers or front-line service personnel to catch and resolve certain classes of problems as they occur.

Providing external quality and customer satisfaction depends directly on the quality of your company's internal processes, operating policies, strategies, and plans. Whether your company provides products or services (or both), quality management provides a solid foundation for developing and deploying strategy and measuring quality through the lens of the customer. As you move through subsequent chapters, you will see the three basic strategies of quality management.

We will describe the use of reference models or benchmarks to interpret and analyze customer data. We will show you how to optimize rather than maximize customer satisfaction and loyalty by setting priorities for quality improvement. Finally, we will describe ways to maximize use of available resources to implement the change. Policy deployment and its variants, including balanced performance measures, are important tools for creating a more universal and consistent focus. These approaches provide companies with a means of translating their customer strategies into action.

Just where to begin building the system requires decisions regarding which customers to include, or system breadth, and how much detail to provide, or system depth. You want to include the kinds of customers that drive business performance.

To do this, you will need to ask "which of our internal or external customers are both a source of future profits and have a choice about where they take their business?" To drive profitability, produce and deliver high-quality products and services to satisfy and retain these customers. When including customers in the measurement system, remember that customers do not all value the same things and behave in the same way. Build your customer measurement systems on an understanding of how your customer base at any given level (such as retail or end-user) is segmented.

Segmentation is a process of identifying individuals or populations of customers with unique needs and wants. By paying attention to segment differences you will avoid the pitfall of setting priorities based on "average" customers who don't exist. In your planning process, also consider just how much detail you will need to measure and how you will use your measurement system.

At a general level, macro-level customer measurement systems provide for broad-based comparisons and benchmarking but give only general guidance about what companies should improve (such as product or service quality or value). In this book, the focus is on measurement systems that are more specific to the company or segment; they provide detailed information regarding concrete product or service attributes as well as information about more abstract consequences and benefits. By continually improving the concrete attributes of existing offerings and finding completely new ways to provide customer benefits, you can leverage your customer data to create a truly exemplary level of performance and competitive advantage.

To link internal quality to profitability, you have to find out how customers see the products and services they purchase and consume. Your first step (and the subject of this chapter) will be to develop a model of how customers view your firm's products, services, and activities—the "lens of the customer" that will guide the rest of your efforts.

As discussed earlier, people inside an organization too often develop customer surveys from their own perspective, or how they believe customers view their products and services.

The result is a survey or measurement instrument that embodies the lens of the organization rather than the lens of the customer. You'll often see airline surveys organized in this fashion, for example, full of questions broken out by organizational activity (check-in, preflight service, food and beverage, flight crews, and cabin environment). A survey that aligns question areas with organizational responsibility in this fashion does have the advantage of producing recommendations that are fairly straightforward to implement. If the survey results and prioritysetting process indicate that flight crews are most in need of improvement, then the responsibility for making improvements within the organization is clear.

Unfortunately, this type of survey may warp or entirely miss issues that cross organizational boundaries, as when flight crews get blamed for being short-tempered about carry-on baggage that should never have been allowed into the cabin in the first place. Customers tend to form opinions regarding such benefits as service, convenience, and safety that cut across the functional areas of an organization. It is essential, therefore, that the measurement system be based squarely on the lens of the customer. In addition, having a survey instrument that better captures the customers' perception of the company makes the data easier to analyze. We are able to explain more variation in key customer evaluations and behaviours, such as satisfaction and loyalty, when the questionnaire is based on the customers' view. For an airline, such a questionnaire might address a whole range of activities from seat reservations through boarding to baggage claim under the heading of convenience, and everything from the gate lobby staff to the seat cushions under the heading of comfort.

The concrete attributes of a product or service and the abstract benefits it generates occupy different levels in the customers' lens. This distinction is very useful but may take some getting used to.

The rectangular objects at the left-hand side represent the concrete aspects or dimensions on which customers can readily report performance via survey measures (such as whether a sales staff keeps its appointments and returns telephone calls and e-mail messages). The circular objects to the right of the attributes represent the relatively abstract or *latent* variables that capture the benefits or consequences that the attributes provide or, at an even more abstract level, the personal values that they serve. For simplicity, we will refer to all the abstract drivers of satisfaction and loyalty as *benefits.*

As in a traditional marketing perspective, the customer satisfaction model embodies the view that products and services compete primarily on the benefits they provide or the needs they fulfill. The concrete attributes of the product or service are only the means to these more abstract ends. Letters, e-mail messages, and faxes all, for example, provide the benefit of communication. You can thus view benefits as the primary drivers of satisfaction in the lens. Notice, however, that benefits may be measured using different numbers of concrete attributes.

Satisfaction in the model is defined as a customer's overall evaluation of the purchase and consumption experience with a product, service, or provider. This definition is quite different from transaction-specific definitions of satisfaction that capture a customer's immediate reaction to a particular episode or experience.

Why discard the immediate response in favour of a more cumulative or overall definition of satisfaction? Although it seems more remote, the latter turns out to be more directly tied to customers' repurchase intentions and behaviour. Customers' repurchase decisions are affected by their entire purchase and consumption history with a company or brand, not just the last trip to the restaurant or last shipment from a supplier. Although we list loyalty, broadly defined, as the desired outcome of satisfaction, there are other constructs we could have shown there as well. Customer satisfaction may also lead to an enhanced reputation and greater brand equity for the company, which will in turn attract additional customers who are disposed to develop loyalty of their own.

The also see overall satisfaction and loyalty in circles, treating them as abstract constructs that can be measured in concrete terms. Overall satisfaction is reflected in different concrete satisfaction measures, which might include a satisfaction scale, how the product or service performs overall versus customer expectations, performance versus an ideal product or service in the category, and performance versus "best in class" competitors.

Similarly, loyalty may be measured using a variety of behavioural intentions (ratings of the likelihood that customers will return, will purchase other products and services from the company, or will speak positively of their experience to others) or actual behaviours (such as whether customers do return, how often they return and how much they purchase when they do, and whether they bring or refer additional customers). Note the dotted arrow that runs from an attribute-benefit cluster directly to customer loyalty.

This captures the possibility that customers' intentions or decisions to repurchase are affected directly by certain benefits. In a recent study of satisfaction with hair care providers, for example, we found that the quality of the haircut, the relationship with the stylist, and the atmosphere of the salon all affect loyalty via overall satisfaction. However, the timeliness and ease of scheduling an appointment have direct effects on loyalty in addition to their effects on satisfaction. Price can also affect loyalty directly— customers are likely to weigh price or value much more when evaluating loyalty than when evaluating satisfaction. "I love his work, but I can't afford to go back every month"

You can't develop the lens of the customer by sitting around and reflecting on how customers view the world. Instead, you need in-depth, qualitative research to show you the issues from the customers' own perspective. Keep in mind that the goal of conducting qualitative research (such as interviews and focus groups) is not to immediately set priorities for quality improvement— it is to identify a comprehensive range of issues (benefits and attributes) that potentially drive satisfaction, loyalty, and profitability.

The customer sample that you use at this stage of the research should represent a good cross-section or range of customers from the population or target market of interest, but it need not be truly random as you're not looking for statistical validity at this point. The lens or model that results from this qualitative research provides the foundation for more systematic survey research, which in turn becomes the primary basis for setting priorities when you get to that stage of the process.

Marketing books offer a wide choice of qualitative methods that you can use to identify product and service attributes and the customer benefits they provide—one-on-one interviews, group interviews or focus groups, protocol methods (having customers "think out loud" while using or evaluating a product or service), and a variety of observation techniques. Here, we focus on one qualitative technique that is particularly well suited to the development of a customer model or lens: the *critical incident technique* (CIT).

The CIT can be used to identify satisfaction drivers for a range of internal and external customers. It typically involves an interview in which individuals or groups of customers are asked to provide a list of the things that they like and dislike about the product, service, or company in question. According to Bob Hayes, an expert on the CIT approach, "A critical incident is a specific example of the service or product that describes either *positive* or *negative* performance. A positive example is a characteristic of the service or product that the customer would like to see every time he or she receives that service or product. A negative example is a characteristic of the service or product that would make the customer question the quality of the company."

The critical incidents themselves should be as specific as possible in describing a single feature of the customer's purchase and consumption experience. Hayes argues that a good critical incident should cover a single behaviour or characteristic, and should either describe the service provider in behavioural terms or describe the service or product using specific adjectives. One retailer noted positively that "the range (variety) of products is good"—pointing to a particular characteristic of the tires (the available range) using a specific adjective (good). Another retailer noted negatively that "regional representatives arrive too seldom"—pointing to a specific behaviour of the local salesperson (waiting too long between visits).

If the critical incidents are too general, the interviewer needs to ask additional questions to clarify what the customer really has in mind. For each specific incident, it is also useful to ask the customer for comments on the significance and consequences of the incident.

Such questions will elicit valuable information for the next stage of the process, categorizing the incidents into attributes and benefit groupings. When encouraged to elaborate, for example, the retailer who praised the product range pointed out that carrying a range of tire products allowed him to offer "a tire for almost every customer that walks into my store." The one who said the regional representative arrived too seldom said that "he should come every month ...just to see how things are going."

Overall, the CIT process involves a number of steps that are helpful to describe using an activity-based flowchart. Step 1 is to compile and assess whatever relevant secondary research or knowledge pertaining to the lens of the customer already exists within the company. (One should avoid, of course, any biases from the lens of the organization.) Perhaps similar studies have been conducted in slightly different research contexts that shed light on how customers view the product or service. Step 2 is to make initial visits to different customers early in the process. We have found this important for two reasons. First, the visits will provide firsthand observations of the

2

Hospitality Management

INTRODUCTION

It's important for people to know what you stand for. It's equally important that they know what you won't stand for. The twenty-first century began with a flurry of high-profile scandals involving managers in a wide variety of industries, ranging from high-tech firms to pharmaceutical manufacturers.

Many very successful business-people found themselves behind bars for their ethical transgressions. The topic of business ethics is receiving increasing coverage in all media, including newspapers, business periodicals, television, radio, and even the Internet, while the pressures on businesses to perform continue to increase.

With continued technological advancement, political upheaval, increased global competition, changing demographics, and pressure from stockholders, maintaining one's ethical integrity will become both more difficult and more important. In 1993 a large group of hospitality industry executives were asked, "What skills and abilities do students need to obtain to be successful in the hospitality industry?"

The number one answer was "business ethics." There is little evidence to suggest the answer would be any different today. One thing is clear: Ethical behaviour is important, and all of you will be facing situations in which you will need to make difficult decisions that you will base on your ethical beliefs and value systems.

Individual Ethics

Ethics is defined as "the system or code of morals of a particular person, religion, group, or profession." As such, ethical beliefs may vary from person to person. There are three basic individual approaches to ethics that are reflected in the behaviour of people. First is the moral rights approach, which judges the consistency of decisions and behaviors with the maintenance of certain fundamental personal and group liberties and privileges such as life, freedom, health, privacy, and property. Second is the justice approach, which judges the consistency of decisions and behaviors with the maintenance of equity, fairness, and impartiality in the distribution of costs and benefits among individuals. Third is the utilitarian approach, which judges the effects of decisions and behaviors on providing the greatest good for the greatest number of people.

Business Ethics

Business ethics in Western society emerged with the growth in capitalism in sixteenth-century Europe. Up to that time it was largely believed that it was immoral to produce goods for profit. With the Protestant Reformation came the belief that a diligent worker pleased God, and that the wealth that was acquired from business activities was a sign that God was pleased. Good businesspeople could be good human beings by satisfying the needs of customers and providing employment for workers.

Today there is a common belief among many organizations that good ethics is good business. This idea has evolved into the concept of social responsibility, and some companies, such as HVS and the Ecotel concept, have stressed the importance of energy conservation, recycling, and minimal disturbance of ecological systems in property development. It is too soon to tell if there is a positive relationship between social responsibility and profits, but there are clearly increasing numbers of companies who want to be known as being socially responsible. It is important to note that operating within the legal system may not be an adequate basis for evaluating the ethics of a business decision.

Overview of the Incidents

Among the following cases, "Sunspot Resorts" involves the construction of a new resort in a developing country. "The Hawaiian Village" deals with the issue of employee theft. "A Dog-Eat-Dog World" describes a subordinate whose boss "fudges" data to obtain a business account. "Seaside Plantations" presents a situation involving misleading advertising. "The Decision to serve" involves the issue of serving liquor to minors. In analyzing these incidents, you should think about the relationship between ethics and the law. It should also become apparent to you which individual approach to ethics you favour.

Case 1 -Sunspot Resorts

Sunspot Resorts, Incorporated, is a publicly held international hotel firm that specializes in luxury resorts in exotic locations. Sunspot has in the last 20 years focused on oceanfront development all over the world in locations such as Greece, Cyprus, Mexico, Indonesia, Australia, and South America. It has opened three resorts in the Caribbean region over the last several years and is hoping to begin construction of another property in Barbados in the near future. Real estate negotiations for the purchase of a seafront location have stalled, however, because of complaints from environmental groups and local citizens. These groups are protesting be- cause they feel that development will disrupt the fragile relationships of life on the reef that is immediately offshore. The environmentalists say they have seen many instances in which developers destroyed pristine land and exploited native populations. They are determined not to let this happen in Barbados, and they have assembled the people and financial support to put up a major battle if necessary. The local residents have seen many changes in their island in the last several years. They are not totally opposed to development because it provides employment opportunities and tax revenues, but in the past developers have made promises they have not kept and, as a result, many parts of the island have been ruined.

Sunspot has handled similar situations in the past by emphasizing the poor economic conditions in the host country and by promising jobs that will benefit the local community, even though it has often had difficulty in providing these jobs. Sunspot management has found that the skill level of the local labour pool has typically been low, and the firm has found it easier and less expensive to import most managerial and supervisory personnel from the United States or Europe rather than training the local people.

This time, however, the strategy does not seem to be working, and the local community is resisting Sunspot's advances in order to retain the pristine nature of the area. To date, several hundred thousand dollars have been invested in the planning and design of the resort at corporate headquarters in Seattle.

The Corporate President of Sunspot has made it clear that he wants a resort in this locale because of its unique environment and profit potential, and the annual bonus of the Regional Vice President (RVP) is based on progress on the proposed development. The RVP has been in contact with the government of Barbados to push the economic perspective, and he has hired an attorney to attempt to portray the environmentalists as radical obstructionists.

Several local businesspersons have approached him, suggesting that they might know a way to overcome the resistance to the project, but they have implied that some sort of bribe might be necessary to do so.

Sunspot stock has recently gone up several points on the New York Stock Exchange (NYSE), based on anticipated profits from this highly publicized development that was enthusiastically presented in Sunspot's annual report and meeting, where it was announced that the opening would take place in 18 months.

1. What are the important issues in this situation?
2. Who are the primary customers of Sunspot?
3. What recommendations would you make to Sunspot management?

Case 2 -The Hawaiian Village

Allison Webb was employed by the Hawaiian Village as the Supervisor for all Food and Beverage Cashiers. She thoroughly enjoyed her job and the working relationship she had with her employees. Ms. Webb directly supervised 45 cashiers and was expected to train these employees, as well as the 29 bartenders whom she indirectly supervised. She was also responsible for balancing all of the cash drawers, Programming the computers at all of the food and beverage outlets, and depositing all revenues collected from her cashiers.

Because of the largely financial nature of her job, Allison was supervised by the Accounting Department, not the Food and Beverage Department. Throughout the time she worked at the Hawaiian Village, she had been evaluated as a "good" to "excellent" employee. Allison had found her work environment to be excellent as well, except for two unfortunate incidents of sexual harassment, which she felt warranted the two separate grievances she had filed over the past 18 months.

In the summer approaching Allison's tenth year with the Village, it became necessary for her Accounts Clerk to question a cashier at the Seaside Hut, one of the hotel's beverage outlets, regarding a corporate ac-count. This particular corporation had been extended a line of credit at the hotel, with its food and beverage transactions being recorded on vouchers. After defaulting on several payments, however, the corporation's credit was revoked by the Accounting Office and the cashier at the Seaside Hut was notified that "cash only" would be accepted for this account. Nonetheless, the Accounts Clerk had a voucher from the Seaside Hut showing credit sales to this corporate customer.

The Accounts Clerk was trying to confirm that a mistake had been made in recording the sales on a credit voucher and that cash had actually been collected.

The cashier did, in fact, remember collecting cash payments for this particular customer and happened to mention to the Accounts Clerk that she had handed the money to the hostess for recording. The Accounts Clerk found this suspicious, and she notified Ms. Webb of the situation, drawing specific attention to the fact that the hostess had been in physical possession of the money.

Further investigation by Allison revealed that the hostess at the Seaside Hut used her seniority to convince the cashier that she was entitled to access the cash drawer, record payments, and make deposits. The hostess also frequently complained to the cashier about her job, lamenting her low position and its lack of recognition. Responding to the norms of the work area and the hostess's negative attitude about her job, the cashier deferred to the hostess without really thinking beyond the cashier's immediate responsibility of ringing up customer sales.

Another problem Allison found was that the Controller's Office had set up a system without cross-checks on the recording of payments and deposits. With no other employee required to verify these amounts, the hostess had complete autonomy to manipulate the Seaside Hut's ledger. The hostess had been recording cash payments of certain corporate customers as credit sales, using readily available vouchers, while pocketing the cash.

The Seaside Hut being a relatively small outlet, Allison surmised that the hostess had assumed that its operation was dismissed by the Accounting Office as trivial and that her embezzlement would go undetected—which it had, for two years. In fact, if she had not written a credit voucher on an account that, unbeknownst to her, had been converted to "cash only," her theft may have continued.

Following this discovery, Allison promptly spoke to her immediate supervisor, Bill Tompkins. She felt that not only should disciplinary action be initiated, but that the flaw in the system should be corrected as well. After obtaining all of the information from Allison, Bill assured her that he would address the situation. Committed to her role as a supervisor, Allison wrote up the Seaside Hut cashier, citing her negligence in adhering to proper procedure. From their training, all cashiers knew that at no time were they to transfer cash to any person other than the appropriate accounting personnel.

The next week Allison went on vacation, pleased that it was her investigation that had revealed an inherent problem in the system and confident that Bill, working with the Controller's Office, would be able to correct it. Upon returning after a week's absence, she learned that the hostess and the manager of the outlet had been fired. Although feeling somewhat sorry for the Seaside Hut manager, Allison resumed her nor-mal work with enthusiasm. At the end of her shift she was called to the office of the Assistant Controller, Harry Brunson, her supervisor's boss. Without any forewarning, Mr. Brunson terminated her, claiming she was negligent in not having performed an audit of the outlet. Mr. Brunson claimed that the Controller's Office expected her to have done an audit as part of her routine job responsibilities. Allison left Mr. Brunson's office in a state of shock and anger.

Later, at home that evening, she attempted to assess the whole situation. Sitting at her desk, she began to outline the events and the reasons for her termination. She did not believe the argument that she was actually expected to conduct an audit, as she was not a trained accountant. As Supervisor of Food and Beverage Cashiers, she doubted she would have had the authority to audit the Seaside Hut, which operated under the jurisdiction of the Controller's Office. Allison had not forgotten that it was procedures designed by the Controller's Office that had enabled the hostess to embezzle sales money, and later in the week she was to learn that except for the firing of the Seaside Hut manager and hostess, no action had been taken to correct the problem.

Regarding audits, however, she decided that if, in fact, they were one of her responsibilities, it had not been made clear to her either by her supervisor, Bill, or in the job description of Supervisor of Food and Beverage Cashiers, which was vague and outdated. Allison concluded that there were two probable reasons why she was fired.

One was that she was simply being used as a scapegoat to protect the accountants in the Controller's Office, who were more than likely the ones responsible for running audits. The other was that her three male superiors saw her as a troublemaker, in that she had revealed their inappropriately devised accounting procedure and had filed two sexual harassment grievances.

Allison toyed with her pencil and considered filing charges against the Hawaiian Village for sexual discrimination and wrongful discharge:

1. How did this situation come about?
2. Was Allison at fault for any of the problems?
3. Who could have prevented this situation from happening? How?

Case 3 - A Dog-Eat-Dog World

Jackie Luden had been working at the Kingswood Conference Center for almost two years. It was a wonderful place to work, as the facilities were state-of-the-art and her fellow employees were extremely competent. Because of the nature of the conference center business, she found that she worked primarily Monday through Friday and seldom at night.

She spent the first year of her employment in the front office training rotation and had become familiar with the operations of the front desk, reservations, and guest services. For the last nine months she had been working in the Sales Department and had reached a point where she was actively involved in developing and making presentations to potential clients. Her background in statistics and computers had prepared her particularly well for this new position.

Jackie had spent the last several weeks doing research and preparing a presentation to the executive board of a medium-sized manufacturing firm.

Kingswood was attempting to get this company to sign a multiyear contract to use the facility for its management development training Programmes.

If Kingswood was successful, the contract would be worth several hundred thousand dollars. The presentation, however, did not go as Jackie had expected, and she had two major complaints. She felt that her work had not been well represented, first, in that she had not received credit for what she had done and, second, that Ericka, the Sales Manager who had actually made the presentation, had altered a lot of her material and falsified some information.

Several days after the presentation Jackie approached Ericka to discuss the situation. When Jackie entered Ericka's office she found that Ericka was exuberant about getting the account, and Ericka initiated their conversation by congratulating Jackie for her hard work. Although Ericka was excited and was attempting to make Jackie feel good about the success, this only made Jackie feel more uncomfortable about what she had to say. Ericka was surprised to learn that Jackie had come to see her about a problem and was even more surprised that the problem was about the new account.

Jackie began by asking why some of the information she had worked so hard on researching had either been changed or left out of the presentation entirely. Ericka responded by asking, "We wanted to get the account, didn't we?" This made Jackie very uneasy, as in a discussion prior to the presentation Ericka had assured her that everything in Jackie's report was perfect and that no changes were necessary. Jackie said that she felt it was dishonest to the customer to falsify information, but Ericka reverted to her previous argument that her actions were in the best interest of the company. Ericka did not understand Jackie's disappointment, because they had gotten the account, and replied simply, "It's a dog-eat-dog world out there."

As Ericka continued to praise Jackie for all the hard work she had done, Jackie felt that this was an opportune time to question her about the lack of credit she received at the presentation. Ericka explained that she did not get the recognition because she was her subordinate, saying, "It simply doesn't work that way." She informed Jackie that the higher she gets in the company hierarchy, the more credit she will get, no matter who does the work.

Still annoyed by the situation, Jackie requested that any changes or "falsifications" in her work not be made in the future or, at least, if they were, that she would like to be informed. She told Ericka that she would feel better if she was able to expect any changes, rather than have them surprise her, and asked if they could meet prior to the next presentation to go over the material.

Although Ericka noted that the word "falsifications" was much too strong, she agreed to meet and notify Jackie of any changes the day before the next presentation:

1. Who was right in this situation?
2. How often do you think this type of incident occurs?
3. What would you do if you were Jackie?
4. What are some of the possible costs involved?

Case 4 – Seaside Plantations

Liza Slater was a Property Manager with more than 10 years of experience specializing in resorts and 20 years in the hospitality industry. She had previously been the Director of Property Management for Seaside Plantations, a beach resort located on Bayside Island that catered to both families and convention business. In this position, Liza was responsible for the communication between the resort operating company and the individual owners of the condominiums in Seaside Plantation's rental Programme. Liza had been in this position for five years and had developed a good working relationship of trust and mutual respect with the condominium owners. She left the position because of her family and their growing needs.

Two years later a powerful storm struck the island and nearly destroyed Seaside Plantations. Liza felt a responsibility to return to the re-sort to help the property owners, who had experienced great losses, both economical and emotional. Because most of the condominium owners lived in other, distant locations, they desperately needed an agent on the island to help them through the reconstruction period and to prepare their villas again for rental. Time was of the essence, as most property owners had suffered enormous loss of rental income as a result of the storm.

The original property management company for whom Liza had worked had offices and front desk check-in on the premises. This company closed, however, after the storm and was eventually sold to a new company, Condominiums, Inc., who then occupied the vacated space. In the meantime, Liza accepted a position with a competitor, Oaks Proper-ties, a prominent resort rental company.

Oaks Properties owned and operated two other villa resort rental Programmes in the area and had just purchased a villa rental company on Bayside Island that was located 3 miles from Seaside Plantations. Inasmuch as Oaks Properties did not have previous rental experience on this island, they were particularly interested in hiring Liza because she was so familiar with the Seaside Plantations property, the property owners, and their condominiums. Liza's responsibilities included the day-to-day supervision of the office, including reservations, front desk activities, and property management functions, as well as overseeing both the housekeeping and maintenance operations.

Although she lived at the resort, she had to travel the 3 miles to the office and was on call 7 days a week, 24 hours a day. Marketing was handled exclusively by the home office located on another island. The owners of Oaks Properties had decided to compete aggressively on Bayside Island in an effort to increase their market share in both reservations and number of villas in their Seaside Plantations rental Programme. They used the Seaside Plantations name throughout all of the advertising without specifically identifying themselves as Oaks Properties, a rental/property management agency for the resort.

This strategy was carried into their brochures, telephone advertising, and conference sales. Prospective guests assumed they were reaching the on-site reservations office for Seaside Plantations, rather than a separately located rental agency. Callers thought that they were making reservations directly with Seaside Plantations and that their stay would include certain amenities of the resort. Bookings made through the competing on-site property management company, Condominium, Inc., for instance, offered golf and tennis privileges at reduced rates, a free summer children's Programme, free transportation within Seaside Plantations, and convenient charging privileges at the front desk for all food and clothing outlets.

Although Oaks Properties offered slightly lower rental rates, its check-in desk was located 3 miles from the front gate of the resort, it did not offer special amenities, and it required full payment for the accommodations within two weeks of booking the reservation, which was nonrefundable 14 days prior to arrival. Although Liza did not approve of Oaks Properties's strategy, she initially had some ability to correct the misperceptions of potential guests by instructing her reservations staff to provide complete information to the guests when they were inquiring or booking reservations.

During the second year of operations, Oaks Properties's management decided that the three reservation offices located on separate islands should be consolidated, and the reservation function was moved to the main office. Because of this move, the satellite operating office that Liza managed no longer had control over the information that was given to the prospective guest prior to making the reservation.

Management also decided that the staff should be cut in half on Bayside Island because this office no longer handled reservations. This did not allow for sufficient staff to handle the problems of the property owners or guest services. Difficulties for Liza and her staff began soon after this consolidation. Oaks Properties invested heavily in marketing its properties. All types of advertising had the name "Seaside Plantations" prominently displayed, with only a small-lettered notation of "Oaks Properties" and the address. The reservations office, now under control of the home office, answered the telephone, "Seaside Plantations Reservations," not "Oaks Properties." The 800 directory listed "Seaside Plantations Accommodations," which in reality was the 800 number for Oaks Properties.

The change caused a great deal of confusion for guests, particularly in regard to check-in procedures. Because many of the guests did not realize they were renting through Oaks Properties, they would go to the main resort front desk, run by Condominiums, Inc., where they would be directed to the Oaks Properties office, 3 miles away, to check in. During the busy summer months it was not unusual for guests to slowly creep along in congested traffic to reach Seaside Plantations, where they would then wait at the front desk only to be sent back the 3 miles. Often the delay caused by the check-in confusion would be more than 45 minutes and was typically endured in subtropical heat. Many guests had small children in their cars and had been traveling for several hours. By the time they finally arrived at Oaks Properties to check in, they were hot, tired, and terribly irritated.

Oaks Properties policies gave Liza and her staff no way to appease these guests. They could merely point out that no misrepresentation had occurred, inasmuch as the name and address of Oaks Properties did appear on the brochure and reservation confirmation. The only positive information they could provide was that Oaks Property's rental rates were slightly lower than those of Condominiums, Inc. In addition, because the deposit was now nonrefundable, guests would forfeit their money if they did not keep their reservations.

Although this was an extremely upsetting situation for Liza and her staff, there were other equally distressing occurrences. Oaks Properties did not operate its Bayside Island office, including the front desk, on a 24-hour basis. When the office closed at 8:00 P.M., check-in information was left in a box for the guest to pick up.

Guests arriving late at night, most having gone directly to the resort first were greeted by a rental packet and key when they returned to Oaks Properties. Often the security office or the front desk of Seaside Plantations would call Liza at home to handle an irate guest. On these occasions, she was forced to leave her two children unattended, sometimes after midnight, to unlock the door of a condominium while trying to calm the guest. Even if the staff and Liza survived the check-in, there were other troubles. Included in the summer rates charged by Condominiums, Inc. at Seaside Plantations was a free all-day children's Programme. Many families visited the resort during the summer, and this was an important amenity.

A sign was prominently displayed on the main road by the resort that read "Registration for the Children's Programme." Although the programme was available only to guests who booked through Condominiums, Inc., all guests driving to their accommodations could not fail to see this sign. Guests who had made their reservations through Oaks Properties would often try to register their children in the Programme, only to be told that they could not. Once again Liza and her staff had very angry guests on their hands, and once again they could only point out that the guests paid a lower rate for the accommodations through Oaks Properties.

In addition to Liza's misgivings regarding the marketing and management practices of Oaks Properties, its compensation policy further complicated her predicament. Liza was paid a base salary that no longer met her financial needs.

The company had eliminated any base salary in-creases and had decided instead that any additional compensation would be received in the form of a bonus for performance. Part of the bonus it paid Liza was based on how much she "comped" guests to appease them. Although Liza often felt that a guest was entitled to some recompension, the less she "gave away" in the form of complimentary gifts or services, the more she received for her bonus. She was also paid a very large fee every time she obtained a new rental unit for Oaks

Properties. This put her in the position of having to be aggressive in securing villas for its rental programme when she did not personally feel that its operating methods were ethical.

Liza's integrity and values were very important to her, but as a single parent she felt she had no alternative except to do her best for Oaks Properties until another comparable position could be found. She was also bound to Oaks Properties by her sense of fairness. Although she had been approached by several direct competitors, she did not think that joining their organizations would be appropriate.

Once again, the end came when Liza put her family's needs first. She realized that not only was she suffering from the stress of her job, but that her children were as well. The ethical dilemmas she faced every day left her emotionally drained. The long hours she worked, with little or no opportunity to leave the island, as she was to be "on call" around the clock, left her physically exhausted.

She had for some time been unavailable to give her children the attention they needed:

1. Evaluate the strategy of Oaks Properties.
2. What impact did the strategy have on employees?
3. What could Liza have done in this situation?
4. Make a prediction about the future of Oaks Properties.

Case 5 - The Decision to Serve

David Anderson was the Assistant Manager of an upscale restaurant in Philadelphia. On a beautiful summer afternoon he noticed two attractive young ladies enter the restaurant and head for the lounge area, which contained a bar and also had small tables where light meals were served. He assumed that they were going to eat lunch in the lounge. Ten minutes later David was approached by Josh, one of his servers, who told him that he was in a situation that made him feel uncomfortable. Josh explained that the hostess had seated two young ladies in his section in the outside seating area that was adjacent to the sidewalk in front of the restaurant.

This area was under an awning and separated from the side-walk by a short decorative iron fence, but diners were clearly visible from the sidewalk and street. He said that both of the women had cocktails, and he felt that they were underage and he did not know what to do. David looked out and noted that the two ladies were the same ones he had seen enter the restaurant earlier. He went to the bar and asked Julie, the bartender, if she had served the two ladies drinks, to which she replied that she had. He asked her if she had asked for identification, and she told him that she had not.

David then approached the table where the two were sitting and asked them for identification. One had a driver's license that showed she had recently turned 21, and the other said she had forgotten her identification. David informed the one without identification that he would need to remove her drink, as the restaurant had liability issues related to serving underage people. He told her that she would be reimbursed for the drink and offered to provide her with a complimentary nonalcoholic beverage.

When David took the beverage, the woman immediately began to complain loudly, got up from the table, went into the restaurant, and began yelling at the server, saying that her father was joining them soon and would rectify the situation. The General Manager approached David about the ruckus, and David explained the circumstances. In the mean-time, the young lady returned to her table, and the two women were soon joined by an older man. At this point the General Manager approached the table and had a brief conversation with the man and the young ladies. He apologized for the incident and offered them a complimentary round of drinks and dinner as compensation for their inconvenience.

The General Manager (GM) then approached David and explained to him what he had done and said the older man had vouched for the age of the young lady lacking any identification. It was never made clear as to whether the man was actually the father of either of the ladies. The GM went on to explain that the policy of the restaurant was to not ask for identification, especially for attractive women, unless it was obvious that the person was underage—which David felt was indeed the case in this situation. He continued to explain to David that having attractive women in the restaurant was good for business, that it was like free advertising, and that this was something they did not teach you in school.

A few minutes later Josh approached David and apologized for creating the problem. David thanked him and made no comment about the General Manager's decision, even though he thought it was wrong. David then approached the table to make sure that the man and two young ladies were enjoying their dinner. He asked if there was anything else he could do, to which the man replied that everything was fine and apologized for the confusion.

The two young ladies said nothing:

1. How did this situation come about?
2. Was David's action appropriate? Why or why not?
3. What would Josh do in a similar situation in the future?
4. Evaluate the General Manager's performance.

HOSPITALITY DIRECTIONS

The hospitality sector has adopted numerous strategies, approaches and measures in response to the challenge of sustainable development. The sector has particularly used environmental management systems and tools to demonstrate commitment to an environmentally friendly work ethic. Many multinational and independent hotel companies have introduced environmental management practices at the property level.

These include:

- Environmental management systems and tools
- Education, awareness creation, training and information dissemination
- Voluntary initiatives
- Multi-stakeholder communication and consultation
- Environmental reporting
- Implementation of the Rio principles

Ideally, the framework for this involves defining an environmental policy and building a management system to measure environmental impacts and compliance with the policy and local regulations, as well as documenting the system's performance for inspection and auditing purposes. Such environmental management systems (EMS) help businesses to evaluate manages and reduces their negative environmental impacts by providing a methodology to integrate environment management into business operations in a systematic manner.

Connected Thinking

Businesses are increasingly being asked to shoulder responsibility for their social, ethical and environmental impacts, with this pressure particularly keenly felt in consumer-facing industries. While for many hospitality companies interest in the sector started with environmental management issues, the focus has now widened to include social and economic impacts, more broadly defined as Corporate Responsibility.

The travel industry of course drives demand for hotel accommodation and between 1950 and 2000 the number of journeys taken by international tourists, including business travellers, increased nearly 28 fold. This year alone 840million tourist arrivals are forecast globally, and by 2020 the figure could reach 1,580 million.

Fears that numbers of this size are unlikely to be sustainable have led to calls for less air travel and for more personal and Corporate Responsibility. However, despite some progress, Jonathon Porritt, Chair of the UK Sustainable Development Commission, recently commented on the travel industry:

> "The industry cannot begin to claim that it's even remotely responsible. Our collective efforts to date are hopelessly inadequate".

In January 2006, PricewaterhouseCoopers undertook new research into 14 of Europe's leading hotel groups, accounting for some 1.5 million rooms globally. We tested these hotel companies against 11 key components of Corporate Responsibility to assess the relevance of Corporate Responsibility to their businesses, the expectations of key stakeholders, and how well the sector is performing. This article presents the results of this research and also assesses some of the future challenges the sector must tackle.

Overall, our research shows that:

- Some progress has been made, but the sector lags behind other European industries in responding to Corporate Responsibility challenges;
- Because of the complexity of the sector it is not easy for hotel companies, and others in the industry value chain, to respond too many of the issues without engaging with their business partners;
- Long term, there is a clear business advantage for those who get their Corporate Responsibility response right but real risks for those who don't.
- "The industry creates buildings full of air conditioning and there's no comment on how waste is being disposed of. For an 'eco' agenda to be meaningful, hoteliers have to look at the repercussions of what they're doing from the beginning. Yes, a large number of hotels now have light-saving devices. They ask us to hang up our towels. But that's not enough. Let's be honest: these are often just mechanisms for the hotelier to manage costs".

Mark Banning-Taylor, owner of upscale hotel and lodge development, Moonlight Head, Australia.

While consumer awareness of Corporate Responsibility in the hospitality industry is still in its inception, consumers are becoming more active in directing their spending towards goods and services that meet their ethical expectations and boycotting companies and brands which they view as exploitative. This is particularly apparent in the clothing and grocery sectors.

Corporate Responsibility

Over the past few years, a wide range of stakeholders have become increasingly interested in the social, ethical and environmental performance of the hospitality industry, including the media, investors and rating agencies, consumers, employees, governments and non- governmental organisations (NGOs):

The media is paying ever-greater attention to sustainability issues. Much of this interest has previously focused on the retail sector, for example, with headline- grabbing statements on issues such as child labour. Such exposes have had a considerable impact and in some cases have led to boycotting of certain consumer brands with a consequent impact on shareholder value. The hospitality sector cannot shy away from these issues any more than the retail sector can. Current headlines are focusing on topics such as climate change, the impact of global travel, worker exploitation, binge drinking and obesity.

This media attention has amplified the need for companies in the sector to not only establish systems and controls to monitor supplier performance, but also to develop reporting mechanisms to demonstrate to external audiences what actions they are taking to ensure high standards of Corporate Responsibility.

Governments across Europe are also taking an increasing interest in Corporate Responsibility, although they are not currently a key driver for change in the sector. Initiatives in place include, for example, at the EU level, the European Commission's White Paper on Corporate Social Responsibility, which contains guidance on labour standards.

Many corporate investment companies are now screening their investments according to a range of social and environmental criteria. Additionally, rating indices such as FTSE4Good and the Dow Jones Sustainability Indices (DJSI) include ratings on hospitality companies on the basis of their performance in this area. For example, the DJSI has an assessment category covering "hotels, restaurants, bars and recreational services". As of September 2005, DJSI had identified Accor, Compass Group, McDonald's, Sodexho and Starbucks as sustainability leaders. The Socially Responsible Investment (SRI) market is expected to expand significantly in the next decade with a greater scrutiny of performance in this area.

A November 2005 report on Responsible Tourism from First Choice, based on more than 1,000 people questioned by market research firm Mintel, found that a quarter of respondents were concerned about the impact of tourism on the environment of the countries they visited and 28 per cent were prepared to pay a small supplement to offset the carbon emissions of their flights. One in five said that it was important that their visit benefited local communities. More than half said they would be happy to take more public transport to explore on holiday (54 per cent), half said they would recycle on holiday (50 per cent), and four out of 10 said they would accept local drinks if this meant fewer imports (44 per cent).

Other suggestions included:

- Reducing the changes of towels and bedlinen (34 per cent)
- Buying locally produced souvenirs (32 per cent)
- Borrowing brochures from travel agents to avoid wastage (30 per cent)
- Accepting a smaller range of food in hotel buffets to reduce wastage (20 per cent)
- Reducing the number of holidays taken (14 per cent)
- Spending a couple of hours to help with local projects such as beach cleaning (11 per cent)
- Paying more for a holiday so a higher proportion can benefit the local community (11 per cent).

First Choice Mainstream Sector managing director Dermot Blastland commented on the findings that:

- "We and other travel companies need to make it as easy as possible for people to do the right thing while they are away. It also means we need to show our customers how, with their help we can make a positive difference and preserve holiday destinations for future generations".

Increasing numbers of travel companies appear to be responding to consumer concerns. Several mainstream companies now include information or advice about ethical, social or environmental issues in their brochures, and niche companies specialising in 'eco-friendly' or 'responsible' travel have sprung up in recent years. For example, Earth, a London-based travel company focusing on luxury properties. The company has made a soft environmental impact, by being small and respectful of the landscape and local culture. Amanresorts follow ecologically sympathetic architectural principles and tend to be small and sensitive developments.

Additionally, the travel industry is starting to respond. British Airways has recently launched a scheme where its customers can choose to offset the carbon dioxide emissions created during their flights. Customers can pay via a link from the airline's website for the cost of the emissions created by their journey. For example, a return flight to Madrid will cost £5 and a return flight to Johannesburg will cost £13.30.

The money raised will be used by an organisation called Climate Care to invest in sustainable energy projects that tackle global warming by reducing carbon dioxide levels. Climate Care's projects include a scheme in South Africa that has distributed 50,000 energy efficient lamps this year via school groups as part of an environmental awareness campaign. In India, Climate Care's support means schools are able to use stoves that run on renewable energy briquettes made from crop waste rather than liquid petroleum gas. Customers can offset their carbon emissions via the booking confirmation form when they book British Airways flights.

Responsible Organisations

Employees are increasingly demanding assurances from their employers regarding the management of a broad range of Corporate Responsibility issues. Employee concern is the most commonly cited reason for companies producing Corporate Responsibility reports. This is supported by research by the Work Foundation and the Virtuous Circle Ltd, 'Achieving High Performance: CSR at the heart of business', which found a strong positive correlation between companies that are seen to take their responsibilities towards society seriously and those seen as a good employer to work for.

NGOs are increasingly looking at the practices of the hospitality industry. Although such organisations do not have any direct power to force change in the sector, the publicity that NGO campaigns can generate is an important driver of business behaviour. In the summer of 2004, Tourism Concern started a campaign looking at working conditions in the tourism sector. They conducted research in five popular holiday destinations – Bali, Mexico, the Dominican Republic, Egypt, and the Canary Islands. The research revealed examples of exploitative labour conditions.

These included over-dependence on tips, long working hours, unpaid overtime, stress, lack of secure contracts, poor training and almost no promotion opportunities for locally employed people. Their research also found that tour operators often use their considerable purchasing power to force down prices in much the same way as supermarkets do when imposing price cuts on farmers.

The result is invariably cost-cutting and longer hours for the lowest paid workers. Those who suffer most are the socially weaker and less skilled staff members, a high proportion of whom are women. In response to this research, Tourism Concern is now calling on all tour operators to 'audit' labour standards across the tourism supply chain. The industry is currently considering its Europe Edition response to this specific campaign. Additionally, Federation of Tour Operators (FTO) members last year signed a statement of commitment to sustainable development and management of tourism.

The statement commits members to making a positive contribution to the natural and cultural environment and to generate benefits for host communities. Members are committed in the future to following the FTO Integrated Responsible Tourism Programme, which is currently under development.

Challenges Facing the Hospitality Industry

Irrespective of wherever individual hospitality companies have got to in their thinking on Corporate Responsibility, the issue is clearly here to stay, indeed with issues such as climate change coming further to the forefront in 2006, many are likely to become more pressing. In the hospitality industry, it will affect daily activities including location and site decisions, employment issues, management of the supply chain, and customer treatment and management. Sustainable tourism is about preserving popular destinations, the environment and its resources. We have got to get it right for this generation and beyond.

Within the hotel and travel sector, various initiatives and standards have been established to try to better define what Corporate Responsibility means for the sector. Such initiatives include the International Tourism Partnership and the International Eco-tourism Society. In addition, various award programmes now exist to recognise good performance in Corporate Responsibility in the sector.

For example:

- International Hotel & Restaurant Association's Environmental Award: launched in 1990 and conducted with the UNEP, the United Nation's Environment Programme and sponsored by American Express. Judges include Conservation International, Green Globe 21 and ITP. The award recognises the efforts being made to 'green' the hotel industry from within.
- British Airways Tourism for Tomorrow awards launched in 1991 by British Airways and, since 2004, under the auspices of World Travel and Tourism Council (WTTC), Tourism for Tomorrow recognises and promotes best practice in travel and tourism development around the world.
- Conservation International & National Geographic Traveller: Traveller magazine and Conservation International together launched the 2004 World Legacy Awards, a global campaign to promote environmentally, culturally, and socially responsible tourism practices across a wider spectrum of the tourism industry, with the goal of "protecting the Earth's natural and cultural heritage".
- Conde Nast Traveller's Ecotourism Awards: These awards have been set up to recognise properties, tour operators, and destinations committed to preserving the local environment, assisting and employing the people who live there, and educating the guests who visit. Organisations can nominate themselves for entry to the awards, after which a panel of industry judges vote on the finalists.

What do stakeholders expect from companies who are serious about addressing Corporate Responsibility? Leading companies follow the same broad principles, although these may differ in their application and emphasis. First, stakeholders, be they staff, customers, shareholders or the community at large, expect to see commitment from the top of an organisation – this means leadership and advocacy. If employees, communities and customers do not actually see repeated evidence of this commitment, then the organisation will lack credibility.

"My priorities for 2005 are to continue our focus on generating shareholder value through further disposals of hotel assets, returning additional funds to shareholders, and retaining and enhancing our powerful brand positions and infrastructures. We will also maintain our focus on Corporate Social Responsibility, where we seek to be an industry leader." - Andrew Cosslett, CEO of IHG.

They view their contribution and buy-in as essential in assessing environmental, social and economic dimensions of hospitality management, and in balancing short-term priorities against long term needs.

The ITP is a programme of The Prince of Wales International Business Leaders Forum (IBLF) and exists to inspire and provide global leadership for responsible business in hotels, travel and tourism. The initiative builds on the success of the International Hotels Environment Initiative (IHEI) launched in 1992.

Organisations including airlines, car hire companies and tour operators through to existing hotel chain members and non government organisations (NGO) all work together within ITP to promote responsible practical actions that ensure sustainable solutions. Partners are drawn together to work on specific projects to drive actions and awareness in areas that affect responsible travel and tourism. The ITP also assists hotel, travel and tourism companies define and build a leadership role in responsible business by contributing to policy dialogues, pioneering new approaches to changing business and development agendas and by providing practical business solutions.

The ITP has developed "BenchmarkHotel" - an environmental benchmarking tool designed to help hotels around the world improve their environmental performance.

The International Eco-tourism Society (TIES)

TIES was founded in 1990 and is the largest and oldest ecotourism organisation in the world dedicated to generating and disseminating information about ecotourism. It currently has members in more than 70 countries.

The organisation membership includes academics, consultants, conservation professionals and organizations, governments, architects, tour operators, lodge owners and managers, general development experts, and ecotourists. TIES provides guidelines and standards, training, technical assistance, research and publications to foster sound ecotourism development.

This is a very tricky process for a company to get right. All too often, "engagement" is a one-way dialogue, with the company telling stakeholders the decisions that it has made. This risks engendering alienation and, potentially, opposition from stakeholders who feel insulted rather than consulted.

Effective engagement, by contrast, is invaluable in shaping corporate strategy, understanding upcoming risks and opportunities, and providing a suitable response and feedback. It is best practice, for example, to refer directly to stakeholder concerns and corresponding actions in corporate reports. Publishing your Corporate Responsibility strategy and defining priorities for action is also a key part of best practice.

Corporate commitments should then be enshrined in "policy" – which could be a formal sustainability policy, code of practice or some guiding principles. This policy should be effectively communicated and implemented, for example through objectives and performance targets/indicators. It should be monitored through appropriate control processes and management systems, such as the ISO 14001 environmental management standard.

Performance indicators should be determined, with regular reports disclosing performance. Best practice is to have these reports assured by an independent third party. Corporate Responsibility is still a relatively new concept for the hospitality industry.

However, by taking action now and reporting to stakeholders on progress made, forward- looking companies do have the opportunity to gain a leadership position in this respect. Adopting such a leadership position would have corresponding potential long term beneficial impacts on critical business areas such as customer and staff recruitment and retention, ultimately translating into shareholder value.

In order to look at how the industry is currently responding to the Corporate Responsibility agenda, PricewaterhouseCoopers conducted new research into the Corporate Responsibility activities of Europe's 14 largest publicly listed hotel companies in January 2004.

Together these hotels accounted for more than 1.5 million hotel rooms across the world in 2004. Our research examined how each company was responding on 11 key components of Corporate Responsibility, such as their overall level of disclosure, policies in place, management systems and stakeholder engagement. The research was based solely on publicly available information, for example, through company websites, investor briefings and annual reports. This research builds on previous work by PwC in 2001 to examine the implementation of environmental policies in European hotels.

PwC's research found that 10 out of 14 of Europe's leading hotel companies provided at least some information relating to Corporate Responsibility in their published information. For example, Accor's website contains an interactive web-based Corporate Responsibility report.

Research results: how well are Europe's leading 14 hotel groups responding to the Corporate Responsibility agenda? Accor's website contains interactive sections on its responsibilities towards shareholders, For example, while most companies did have Corporate Responsibility, environmental or social polices in place, only three of the 14 companies stated that they had conducted a Corporate Responsibility risk assessment. Additionally, only four of the companies had made a clear link between their Corporate Responsibility activities and business strategies. This lack of risk assessment and connection with broader business strategy could mean that many of these companies are not currently deriving real business benefits from their Corporate Responsibility activities.

Environmental Policy

In terms of policy disclosure, nine out of the 14 companies had environmental policies in place.

Accor, Hilton Group and Whitbread all disclosed a significant amount of information on their environmental performance:

- Hilton Group reported on the use of the Hilton Environmental Reporting tool (HER) and staff training (15,000 staff to date). Hilton group also publicly report their target of a 10 per cent reduction in utility consumption across the UK and Ireland by 2006
- Accor publicly disclosed that, in 2004, 26 properties were awarded ISO14001 certification. Significant disclosure was also provided in areas such as water and energy consumption, waste, biodiversity, and environmental building design
- Whitbread published a stand alone environment report, which received third party assurance. The report contained considerable disclosure on environmental performance, e.g. reductions in C02 emissions, water, energy consumption, and recycling was also provided.

Whitbread refer to their Environment Management System (EMS) in their report. Detailed information on how Accor sees its responsibilities towards customers, employees, suppliers, the environment, local communities and shareholders. Likewise, Hilton Group plc has published a detailed "Responsible Business" report for the last three years. This report contains information on Hilton's vision and core values, corporate governance and key Corporate Responsibility issues, defined as people, equal opportunities and diversity, human rights, health and safety, environment, business practice, customers, products and services, business partners and supply chain and communities/charities.

For companies that did not produce standalone Corporate Responsibility reports, disclosure was usually focused on case study examples of particular developments or initiatives that were initiated with Corporate Responsibility in mind. These ranged from employee volunteering schemes, to monitoring working conditions across the supply chain, to providing details of community impacts in terms of working with local people to provide employment opportunities. These examples demonstrate how, to some extent, all hotel companies are actively considering Corporate Responsibility in their operations, and in doing so, are focusing on the full range of issues – not simply environment, health and safety.

Once we dug below the surface, we found the organisations we benchmarked had markedly different levels of Corporate Responsibility activity. In terms of disclosure on 'social' areas of Corporate Responsibility, ten out of the 14 companies benchmarked publish information on policies in this regard.

Areas covered by many included:

- People issues

- Diversity
- Equal opportunities
- Community/charitable donations

However, fewer companies reported their activities in emerging issues such as:

- Human rights and
- Supplier management

One exception to this was Intercontinental Hotels Group (IHG), who have publicly stated their commitment to the Universal Declaration on Human Rights and the International Labour Organisation's (ILO's) core conventions. Another notable exception was Accor's significant disclosure on its programme in place to monitor the social and ethical performance of its key suppliers.

However, where applicable, none of the hotels covered within the survey disclosed any significant information on the environmental or social performance of their franchised hotels. Rather, the sector is currently focusing on the activities of directly owned and managed properties. Looking to the future, it is likely that stakeholders will expect the sector to also disclose the performance of franchised hotels. In addition, it would be prudent for companies to include coverage of these franchised properties in Corporate Responsibility programmes as franchised hotels do have the ability to cause significant reputation and brand damage if found lacking in sensitive Corporate Responsibility issues, such as child labour and minimum wage payments.

In terms of Corporate Responsibility board sponsorship, the research found that only 4 of the 14 companies publicly articulated a board level commitment to Corporate Responsibility. Such board level sponsorship is critical to Corporate Responsibility programmes being taken seriously by external audiences. IHG is a good example of a company that has made a clear, board-level, commitment to Corporate Responsibility:

"We need to build an IHG culture. A culture that's focussed on driving returns for our owners and on supporting each other in a more collaborative way. Part of the culture will be about raising our commitment still further to helping the communities in which we operate. As an organisation we will increase our commitment to Corporate Social Responsibility and ensure that we are industry leading in this area. Not just because it helps to drive the culture which it does, but because it increasingly helps attract talented people to the business." - Andrew Cosslett CEO IHG.

Looking at the implementation of management systems to actively monitor and control elements of Corporate Responsibility such as environment, health and safety, only five organisations claimed to have established management systems, and three more were in the process of developing them. One company that does disclose details of its Corporate Responsibility management systems are Rezidor SAS, which has an established Responsible Business (RB) programme. The programme focuses on three key areas: taking Responsibility for the health and safety of employees and guests, respecting social and ethical issues in the company, as well as in the community, and reducing negative impacts on the environment.

The operational responsibility for the RB programme lies with the Hotel Managers, who are supported by the RB co-coordinators at each hotel. In 2003, a regional structure was added, supporting the hotels at a regional level and providing a liaison between the hotels and the Corporate Director of Environmental and Social Affairs. The local RB action plans guide the hotels in what measures and actions they will implement during the year to improve performance.

Six companies within the benchmark provided details of their stakeholder engagement plans and a further two provided limited details with a commitment to future activity in this area. However, even for these six companies that did disclose information on engagement, the level of disclosure was limited. It is increasingly expected that companies will publicly disclose who they believe their key stakeholders are and what activities/processes they have in place to engage with these key stakeholder groups. The hotel industry is significantly behind other sectors in this area, for example, British Telecom has a highly established process of stakeholder engagement.

Looking at disclosure on actual performance, just four of the 14 organisations were able to publish meaningful data on Corporate Responsibility type parametres (e.g. health and safety, resource use, waste production, community consultation); while four more produced some limited data. For example, the Hilton Group plc reported in its most recent Corporate Responsibility report that 'team member satisfaction scores have increased across the world by up to 7 per cent from 2003, averaging at 75 per cent.' Hilton was also the only company in the survey to have third party assurance over their reported information on Corporate Responsibility, although three other companies did provide assurance in some limited areas.

What conclusion should we draw from this information? Perhaps the majority of hotel companies are focusing on Corporate Responsibility, but not publicly talking about it? Or, alternatively that they recognise that Corporate Responsibility is important but have not fully implemented the necessary processes or controls throughout their business. Alternatively, there could be a more complex explanation. Perhaps the industry's current response results from the complex value chain and business partner relationships in the hospitality sector generally.

Individual companies may not always be responsible for the direct buying relationship with the customer, often being dependent on other companies up and down the value chain in terms of Corporate Responsibility related impacts. Whatever the explanation, it is clear that progress has been made in terms of implementing environmental policies for many in the sector since PricewaterhouseCoopers examined this issue of Hospitality Directions.

However, the sector is behind other European industries, e.g. the retail sector, in terms of Corporate Responsibility reporting, and faces a challenging agenda to catch up and respond effectively to the concerns of stakeholders.

Indeed, in the 2004 Business in the Community Corporate Responsibilty Index, of the top 100 quoted companies from a Corporate Responsibilty perspective, only four came from the leisure and hotels sector. By comparison, a sector such as Banks and Utilities had 11 apiece. However, this could partly be explained by relatively few hotel companies being quoted on the FTSE 100 and FTSE 250.

Looking Towards the Future

Many companies in the hospitality industry are currently not making the most of the Corporate Responsibility agenda. While it can easily appear to business as a threat and a recipe for extra burdens, the reality is that Corporate Responsibility related issues present real business opportunities. In a recently published report by the leading global business organisation, the World Business Council for Sustainable Development, "From Challenge to Opportunity: the role of business in tomorrow's society", business leaders in a number of major companies have produced a model for tomorrow's global business. It is based on recognising and capturing the opportunities that are presented by societal and environmental concerns.

By focusing on the issue strategically, companies which address Corporate Responsibility are likely to achieve better community relationships, save money through operational efficiencies and differentiate themselves as responsible and accountable companies. Transparent and accountable behaviour helps to build stakeholder trust and enhance corporate reputation, both long-term drivers of value. Other sectors such as the European retail, telecommunications, pharmaceutical and extractive industries have already started to yield such benefits through established Corporate Responsibility programmes.

There are several steps that the hospitality industry will have to take to embed Corporate Responsibility into the way it does business day-to-day. The most immediate steps include instituting the right policies, processes, and systems for monitoring and reporting performance.

Additionally, for such Corporate Responsibility programmes to be credible, it is important to ensure the following:

- A serious commitment to Corporate Responsibility is shown from the top of the organisation;
- Stakeholders are actively involved in decision making;
- Corporate Responsibility strategy is published, with defined priorities for action;
- Corporate commitments are enshrined in policy; and

- Performance indicators are determined, with regular reports disclosing performance.

Overall, the biggest challenge for the sector will be to win over the 'hearts and minds' and thus the behaviour of the company. This is a longer term and more complex process, and will demand cross industry collaboration, but is essential for Corporate Responsibility to really 'stick'. Many leading hospitality companies have made a start, but achieving maximum value from Corporate Responsibility will be far from simple. It will require a clear sense of direction, a commitment from the organisation, robust planning and strong implementation to deliver.

HOSPITALITY SERVICE

The concept of Hospitality Services, also known as "accommodation sharing", "hospitality exchange", and "home stay networks", refers to centrally organized social networks of individuals who trade accommodation without monetary exchange.

While this concept could also include house swapping or even time share plans, it has come to be associated mostly with travellers and tourists staying with one another free of charge. Since the 1990s, these services have increasingly moved away from using printed catalogs and phone trees to connect users towards Internet websites. These have grown exponentially since 2000 and today it is estimated that well over 100,000 people are registered users of these networks. These vary in operational structure, place different emphasis on graphical vs. textual formatting, and cater disproportionately to specific geographic regions.

In 1949, Bob Luitweiler founded the first hospitality service called Servas Open Doors as a cross national, non-profit, volunteer run organization advocating interracial and international peace. The next earliest began in 1965 when John Wilcock set up the Traveller's Directory, originally as a listing of his mutual friends willing to host each other when traveling. This later became the Hospitality Exchange in 1988 when Joy Lily rescued the organization from imminent demise.

Hospitality Club is the direct successor Hospex, the first Internet-based service, operating out of Poland since 1992. It is currently the largest hospitality exchange network, growing rapidly.

CouchSurfing is a newer but also rapidly growing hospitality exchange organization founded in 2004. Just as all the individual services have their own individual creation stories and organizational histories (often including demise and resurrection), many also have specific niche markets that they cater to including students, activists, religious pilgrims, and even occupational groups like police officers. However, the trend in recent years points to a greater consolidation of users in networks without a specific group, value, or lifestyle affiliation.

In essence, these systems employ reciprocity – users gain access to other users' information only by posting their own. Required fields normally include name and contact information, though newer services encourage users to include more detailed personal material, including likes and dislikes, hopes and dreams, and even photographs. Of course, more information included tends to improve the chances that someone will find them trustworthy enough to host or stay with while traveling. It is very much akin to online dating services.

Staying in private homes means that travellers can save lots of money on accommodation that they would usually be spending on hotels or hostels. Used over a long period of time (2 to 4 weeks), this strategy can cut overall travel budgets in half, or even more combined with hitchhiking. These savings can then be passed on towards more generously patronizing local establishments or simply staying abroad for longer periods of time.

Many tourist vacations today are sold in package form, often including flights, hotels, rental cars, sightseeing tours, and coupons for chain restaurants and bars. While this makes purchasing more convenient, it also puts more money in the hands of large multinational corporations exploiting the synergy strategy of marketing their products in the context of their subsidiary companies operating in other markets. Many years ago, this might have been termed collusion; today, however, it is the norm. This comes at the expense of locally owned independent businesses. Accommodation sharing helps to break apart this monopoly and hopefully redirects some of the tourist revenue back to the local or national economy.

While this is especially important in more rural travel venues where hotels are often built in very picturesque, though fragile environments, every night stayed at a local's home means that much less demand for such hotel rooms. Also, if accommodation sharing does in fact increase the length of average stays, it may reduce the amount of trips to and from different locations and back home again, thus reducing the overall fuel expenditures in the process.

Ostensibly, one of the primary reasons we travel is to experience what life is like for people living in other countries. Making interpersonal connections and fostering understanding of different cultures may in the long run also be important to international relations. However, even in our increasingly globalized world supposedly rife with diversity, in many popular travel destinations we find tourists milling around "tourist enclaves" where the companies they patronize back home have set up shop to cater to their desires while they are abroad.

Sociologist George Ritzer has referred to this phenomenon as the "McDonaldisation of society" and the more recently, the "globalization of nothing". The location of hotels near these centres only fosters more convenient envelopment of the tourist dollar. During hospitality exchanges, hosts want to show off their local knowledge and exciting "off the map" venues. Not only may travellers get a distinctly different experience, but they will also get a feel for the everyday lives of local residents.

These systems foster richer and more convenient travel experiences not so much on the premise of altruism, but on the basis of social exchange theory. Implicit in the agreement to host travellers is the ability to ask to be hosted by them in the future. If one enjoys having interesting guests in their home, this works out well for both parties. It works comparatively better if you are visited by travellers from a locale you find particularly attractive. Thus, hosting someone from New York City in Gainesville, FL seems to be an unbelievable opportunity. Moreover, if you are a Westerner visiting someone in a developing nation, your stay might be the only way that this individual or family could afford a trip to a rich nation. This may mean more than just a relaxing vacation for such disadvantaged parties.

Tourism has always searched for these two qualities, but much like Midas and his golden touch, the reach of tourism has to a large extent destroyed the opportunity to encounter them in most places. Unluckily, the experience has been thoroughly commodified by everyone who wanted to secure their opportunity to make a buck in the process. Accommodation sharing offers a way out of this bind and a viable alternative to having one's desires manipulated by corporate conglomerates who never had the best interests of the place or the people foremost in their minds.

There is no contractual agreement between users in these systems. Reservations are made, but if they are for some reason broken, there is no higher authority to which one could plead for a refund or other compensation. The only repercussion will be the poor rating you give that user and your only consolation will be that your warning will deter others from visiting or hosting them. For those who feel insecure unless their travel arrangements are written in stone before departure, this system will not be comforting.

There is a chance that guest and host will not get along. Perhaps there will be scheduling or ideological conflicts. Maybe you will find that hosts or visitors have misrepresented themselves. Perhaps the experience will not live up to your expectations. Intense interpersonal communications in advance and a flexibility once you have arrived is your best bet. These experiences require additional planning and courtesy towards the demands of your host. Thus, your living conditions, length of stay, and overall experience will be circumscribed by the living conditions you enter into.

The average user is a young white person who speaks English and lives in a developed nation. While there are many users who do not fit this description, the more different they are, the less likely they will be involved. This is especially true for persons living in the developing world who likely do not have easy access to the fundamental prerequisite for using these services: computers and the Internet. Thus, the sample population found in searches of these databases are really much less diverse than a geographical representation of worldwide users might suggest. There is a distinct possibility that someone will abuse the system and that innocent users (especially women) will get hurt. All services include disclaimers that require users to waive their rights to hold anyone but themselves responsible for any harm that may come to them in using the system.

They advise that the best defence mechanism is to only involve oneself with users that have extensive personal information and interpersonal networks within the system that have been verified by others. It does seem entirely plausible that someone clever and patient enough might be able to invent an entire group of complex user identities and build histories convincing enough to fool even more cautious patrons. Still, the difference between these systems and the other social networking platforms popular nowadays on the web (such as MySpace, Tribe, Orkut, LiveJournal and Ebay) is that any agreement reached through the accommodation sharing medium is contingent on actually meeting other people face-to-face.

Other web scams are easier because interpersonal interactions rely so much on putative identities that are never actually verified in the real world. However, this does not diminish the greater risk to physical well being that this kind of traveling by definition must entertain. The best advice is to meet unknown persons in public spaces first, and try to meet some of their acquaintances in person before agreeing to a hospitality exchange.

INDIAN HOSPITALITY

In 2004-05, Visakhapatnam was the market leader in terms of occupancy, registering occupancy of 80.6 per cent. Bangalore achieved the second-highest occupancy at 79.8 per cent. It also had the highest (ARR), across all categories among the 30 cities, with an ARR of Rs 6,762. New Delhi was the second highest, registering an ARR of Rs 5,498. All India average occupancy was 63.6 per cent, an increase of 3.9 per cent occupancy points above the previous year's level, or 6.5 per cent in real terms. All India ARR increased by 26.9 per cent over the previous year.

Star category-wise occupancies ranged between 46.3 per cent to 72.1 per cent. Average rates showed a much greater spread, from Rs 5,499 for five-star deluxe hotels to Rs 643 for one-star hotels, an increase of Rs 1,052 and Rs 140, respectively, from the previous year. The All India average revenue per available room (RevPAR) increased substantially, from Rs 1,605 in 2003-04 to Rs 2,170 in 2004-05, reflecting an increase of 35.2 per cent. In the eight years of the survey, this has been the second-highest RevPAR growth (the highest was 46.2 per cent in 2003-04).

Rooms revenue, generally considered being the most important source of a hotel's overall profitability, was 57.7 per cent of total revenue for five-star deluxe hotels, 60.1 per cent of total revenue for five-star hotels and 56.6 per cent for four-star hotels. Overall (across all hotels) it represented 57.3 per cent of total revenue (an increase of 5.7 per cent from 2003-04). Food & Beverage revenue represented 28.3 per cent of total revenue across all hotels, a decrease of 4.6 per cent from last year. (This reflects the increased share of rooms revenue in the total of 100). The all India average of Rooms department expense as a percentage of Rooms revenue declined further from 17.8 per cent in 2003-04 to 14.7 per cent in 2004-05.

Similarly, the all India average Food & Beverage department expense as a percentage of Food & Beverage revenue declined from 55.9 per cent in 2003-04 to 53.9 per cent in 2004-05. Minor Operated department expense as a percentage of Minor Operated department revenue registered an increase from 53.7 per cent in 2003-04 to 58.8 per cent in 2004-05. Telephone and other department expense, at 64.3 per cent of total revenue, was the highest departmental expense. Total departmental expense as a percentage of total departmental revenue reflected a further decline, from 37.4 per cent in 2002-03 and 33.7 per cent in 2003-04 to 30.9 per cent in 2004-05. This is partly owing to higher ARRs.

Percentage of foreign guests increased to 28.3 per cent in 2004-05, compared to 25.0 per cent in 2003-04, primarily as the percentage of foreign business travellers grew. Of the foreign guests, the UK provided the largest demand, at 16.2 per cent, followed by USA, at 12.8 per cent, and France at 7.2 per cent. Domestic guests continue to be the most important segment for the Indian hotel industry, accounting for 71.7 per cent of all guests in 2004-05, though this has decreased marginally from 75 per cent in 2003-04 and 76.9 per cent in 2002-03.

All India average stay of a business traveller has increased from two days to 2.4 days.There is an increase in foreign business travellers utilising five-star deluxe, five-star, four-star hotels and heritage hotels from 27 per cent, 18.6 per cent, 11.4 per cent and 11.7 per cent, respectively, in 2003-04 to 28.1 per cent, 21.4 per cent,13.7 per cent and 14.1 per cent, respectively, in 2004-05. Owing to all India increased occupancy, property operations and maintenance expenses per available room (PAR) has increased from Rs 69,735 in 2003-04 to Rs 91,981 in 2004-05. Average monthly occupancy was highest in December (at 71.7 per cent), followed by November (at 67.8 per cent) and January, February (at 65.8 per cent).

Direct enquiry and advance reservations by travel agents and tour operators cumulatively comprise 75.9 per cent of reservation source for the Indian hotel industry. Five-star deluxe hotels are making the best use of GDS as 8.1 per cent of the total reservations for five-star deluxe hotels come from GDS, against the all India average of 1.7 per cent. GDS reservations generally provide higher room rates compared to the other channels.

Print advertising is the most popular medium used by the Indian hotel industry with the all India average at 92.2 per cent of hotels using it, followed by 82.5 per cent using direct mails. Radio advertising features as the least utilised marketing media at 8.4 per cent, followed by merchandising at 24.5 per cent, by the Indian hotel industry in 2004-05. All five-star deluxe hotels (sample size 32) used the hotel website at 100 per cent as a marketing medium in 2004-05.

Credit cards as a mode of transaction increased from 27.7 per cent and 30.4 per cent in 2002-03 and 2003-04, respectively to 32.5 per cent in 2004-05. Credit cards remained the most popular method of payment at five-star deluxe hotels at 47.4 per cent. Visa (41.8 per cent) was the most widely used credit card by hotel guests in 2004-05, followed by Mastercard (37 per cent). American Express charged the highest credit card commission at 2.9 per cent against 1.7 per cent by Visa and Mastercard.

Comparison with the results of the survey in 2004-05 with the previous year, shows that nearly all categories (except one-star hotels) saw an increase in occupancy and a significant increase in average rate (except heritage hotels). This resulted in a major increase in RevPAR across all categories with the highest RevPAR growth in four-star hotels at 41.9 per cent and an all India RevPAR growth at 35.2 per cent. The demand for rooms has been positive and owing to lack of adequate new supply, hotels in nearly all categories have managed to simultaneously increase the occupancy and average rates.

Among environmental issues, electricity consumption is the most monitored attribute, followed by water consumption. Five-star deluxe and five-star hotels continue to monitor environmental issues most closely. Energy expenses accounted for 8.9 per cent of total revenue in 2004-05 against 10.5 per cent of total revenue in 2003-04 and 12.3 per cent in 2002-03. This may be partly attributed to rising revenues and partly to the increase in efforts made to conserve energy by the industry in India.

Other Significant Trends

All India average revenue per hotel has grown significantly, from Rs 9.15 crore during 2003-04 to Rs 11.49 crore during 2004-05, and is expected to see further improvement in the next few years owing to an increase in occupancy and average rate. House Profit (Gross Operating Profit after deducting franchise and management fees) as a percentage of revenue increased from 34.8 per cent in 2003-04 to 40.7 per cent in 2004-05. The all India average net income (income before depreciation, interest payments and taxes) per hotel also increased, from Rs 2.80 crore (34.8 per cent) in 2003-04 to Rs 4.08 crore (40.7 per cent) in 2004-05, reflecting the overall health of the industry.

July has the lowest monthly occupancy in the year. However, occupancy for all months was higher in 2004-05 compared to the last five years. The year 2004-05 saw a continuation of the growth momentum experience by the hotel industry in 2003-04. Most cities saw occupancy levels improve over the previous year and, consecutively for two years, both occupancy and average room rates have improved.

City Trends

The following paragraphs detail the expectations of new supply and performance for 19 important hotel markets, based on research undertaken and forecasts made by HVS International.

New Delhi

Occupancy witnessed a growth of 10.82 per cent in 2004-05. Average rates registered an increase of 29.43 per cent. The National Capital Region is expected to see an estimated 27 new hotels, serviced apartments and mixed-use developments with approximately 4,900 rooms in various categories over the next three to four years, with nearly 20 new hotels to be in Gurgaon alone. The new supply will start entering the market in 2007-08. This growth will be supported by significantly improved road and transport infrastructure (a six-lane section of National Highway 8 connecting Delhi and Gurgaon will open in late 2006), privatisation of the Delhi airport and demand induced by the Commonwealth Games, to be held in Delhi in 2010. There will be further increase in hotel activity, especially in the mid-market and budget segment, after the much-awaited auction of sites by the Delhi Development Authority (DDA).

Mumbai

Citywide occupancy in Mumbai increased by 13.0 per cent and average rate witnessed an increase of 40.6 per cent in 2004-05. Mumbai (including Navi-Mumbai) is expected to see 19 new hotels, serviced apartments and mixed-use developments with approximately 4,950 rooms in various categories over the next three to four years.

The bulk of the new supply will enter the Mumbai market by 2008-09. Most companies setting up operations in Mumbai now prefer to locate to new commercial districts in the suburbs like Andheri, Bandra-Kurla and Malad, and other periphery areas like Navi-Mumbai and Mulund; and, hotel development has shifted to these areas. Now, with availability of commercial space in the mills area, places like Parel, Lower Parel, Worli and Mahalaxmi will see increased hotel development activity. This is more so with the proposed development of Bandra-Worli Sea Link, which will significantly reduce the travel time between Bandra and central Mumbai.

Kolkata

Kolkata is expected to see 12 new hotels, serviced apartments and mixed-use developments with approximately 2,000 rooms entering the market in various categories over the next few years. The city is becoming a preferred location for conferences and seminars due to the relatively easy availability of space and at a lower cost as compared to other metros. It is also the commercial capital of the northeast region, with most companies basing their headquarters in the city.

Pune

Pune is expected to see 11 new hotels, serviced apartments and mixed-use developments with approximately 1,600 rooms in various categories over the next three to four years. The addition to supply, although quite high, is likely to be successfully absorbed, taking into account Pune's low room base of approximately 800 rooms and a continuous growth in the city's IT, ITeS, BPO and manufacturing industries.

Chennai

Chennai witnessed an occupancy increase of 15.7 per cent, following a decline for two consecutive years. The city saw a simultaneous increase in average rate by approximately 15.6 per cent. Chennai is expected to see 14 new hotels, serviced apartments and mixed-use developments with approximately 2,900 rooms in various categories over the next few years. The Old Mahabalipuram Road (OMR) connecting Chennai with Mahabalipuram is being developed as an IT corridor to house various IT and ITeS companies. As existing tech parks are full to capacity, software companies are also looking at sick industrial unit areas such as Guindy, Taramani, Ambattur and Padi, which are being converted into software technology parks (STPs). We see Chennai as a stable market and expect it to continue to show improvements in occupancy and average rate in the next few years.

Bengaluru

Bangalore's hotel market grew marginally in terms of occupancy and by approximately 64.5 per cent in terms of the average room rate. This is on the back of very high demand and lack of new supply. Approximately 7.0 million square feet of commercial space is likely to be absorbed this fiscal year (2005-06). Bangalore is expected to see, at last count, 27 new hotels, serviced apartments and mixed-use developments with approximately 6,100 rooms in various categories over the next few years. With work on the international airport having commenced the northern areas of the city will see pronounced commercial and hotel development activity. The first phase of the airport is estimated to open by October 2008. Road infrastructure, however, remains the biggest challenge for the city.

Goa

Goa is expected to see development of eight new hotels with approximately 1,200 rooms in various categories over the next 2-3 years. Goa is an extremely promising market with the highest average length (amongst the key cities) of stay by both foreign and domestic guests. The proposed Mopa airport is anticipated to witness much higher traffic flow than the airport at Dabolim. Accompanying the airport project will be a new ground transportation system, which will benefit the whole of Goa.

Agra

Agra has seen an increase in occupancy of 22.9 per cent. Average rates have decreased marginally by 1.4 per cent. This may be partly attributed to a higher base surveyed in 2003-04 and an increase in smaller hotels participating in the survey. Tourists typically make a day trip to Agra from Delhi; the increase in occupancy is owing to the meetings & conference segment, which has seen a significant growth for two consecutive years.

Ahmedabad

The survey indicates an occupancy decline of 7.7 per cent and a decrease in average rate by 8.9 per cent. This may again be due to change in composition of hotels participating in the survey. However, HVS's independent research indicates an estimated 15.0 per cent increase in both occupancy and average rate. Hotel activity will increase in the city owing to expected commercial growth on CG Road, Ashram Road, Satellite Road and SG Highway-particularly from the pharma, financial sector, telecom, retail, textiles, BPO and IT services.

Kochi

The survey indicates a decrease in occupancy of 4.2 per cent and a decrease in average rate by 22.3 per cent. This may be partly attributed to a variation in the hotels participating in the survey and does not reflect the true market condition.

The city's hotel demand generators are mainly tourism related, with commercial demand borne out of shipping, Kochi Port, Cochin Shipyard, oil refineries and marine and agro export industries based in the city. Banking, financial services, insurance and the telecom sectors have seen growth over the past two years.

Hyderabad

In Hyderabad, overall occupancy increased by 3.3 per cent. Average rates registered an increase of 13.4 per cent over the previous year. HITEC City, HITEX, Genome Valley and ICICI Knowledge Park demonstrate the state's commitment to create world class infrastructure. The convention centre opening in 2006, with approximately 75,000 square feet of conferencing facility and 55 break-out rooms, is the first of its kind in South Asia. The convention centre will induce substantial demand for rooms in the city. The Hyderabad market will continue to witness a strong increase in occupancy and average rate in the next few years.

Jaipur

Occupancy levels increased by 14.2 per cent in 2004-05 and average rates increased by 10.0 per cent over the previous year. Besides being a preferred tourist and wedding destination, the city of Jaipur is gaining prominence as a commercial destination as well. This is owing to increased travel by buyers for gems, jewellery and textiles. With the proposal for a Jaipur special economic zone (SEZ), an international airport and an ethnic village, the city will see development of new hotel projects (approximately 1,200 rooms). There is a chance of Jaipur facing an oversupply of rooms in 3-4 years.

Lucknow

Occupancy levels increased marginally by 0.6 per cent in 2004-05 and average rates increased by 10.0 per cent over the previous year. Lucknow has been a very stable market and is witnessing a rise in average rate for the last two years. Lately, Lucknow has also seen increased retail activity.

Nagpur

Nagpur witnessed a decline in occupancy by 10.1 per cent and a decrease in average rates by 5.5 per cent from the previous year. The Nagpur market has now declined for two years consecutively.

Thiruvananthapuram

The city witnessed a decrease in occupancy of 7.0 per cent, and a growth in average room rate of 38.6 per cent. Being the state capital, the city is a hub of political activity.

Moreover, Thiruvananthapuram, with its famous beaches, is among the top tourist destinations in India. The city has grown as a tourist and commercial centre, with the international airport being one of the gateways into Kerala.

Udagamandalam (Ooty)

Ooty city has seen a decline in occupancy by 9.0 per cent and an increase in average rate by 15.6 per cent. Mainly a tourist destination, Ooty is known for its picturesque locales. The city is unlikely to see any major hotel activity in the next 2-3 years.

Udaipur

Citywide occupancy increased by 19.25 per cent in 2004-05. Average rate showed a steep increase of 53.65 per cent. The increase in the average rate may be partly attributed to the inclusion of luxury/heritage hotels in the survey. Udaipur has lately seen an increase in international events and is attracting many domestic off-site meetings, conferences and weddings as well.

Vadodara

Citywide occupancy increased marginally from 62.5 per cent in 2003-04 to 62.6 per cent in 2004-05. Similarly, the average rate increased from Rs 458 in 2003-04 to Rs467 in 2004-05. The Gujarat government has also been promoting the state as a commercial destination and is giving incentives to various companies.

Visakhapatnam

Visakhapatnam witnessed a steep increase in occupancy by 15.0 per cent in 2004-05 and an increase in average rates by 18.4 per cent. In the past, the city experienced rapid industrialization with the onset of major industries: an oil refinery, a large fertilizer factory, the Hindustan Zinc smelter and the Visakhapatnam steel plant.

PROFESSIONAL IN HOSPITALITY INDUSTRY

The hospitality industry can offer a promising future for IT professionals wanting to make an exciting career. In recent years, the scope of IT professionals in this industry has been on the upswing.

International brands are coming to India bringing along state-of-the-art technologies, which other local brands will need to match up to. This has begun to open up new avenues for the IT professional to implement, learn and to develop.

The accelerated infusion of computerised systems and sub-system transactions sweeping the hospitality industry has spurred IT professionals to look at the industry as a potential workplace.

The challenge to integrate computer interface and the need to accelerate upgradation of technology usage so as to lower costs has added allure to this industry. Just six years ago, all the IT professionals wanted to do was set base within the IT industry. But today the non-IT companies, including hotels, are proving to be equally lucrative. Jobs that are being targeted are in the areas of database management and administration, security and technical support. In fact, the hospitality industry holds sway over other industries as well. It is one sector which cannot choose to outsource simply because of the security aspect and a dedicated in-house team is considered to be better equipped to solve problems.

The worth of IT professionals is well recognised by the industry and an IT job is as important in hotels as in any other industry. No hotel can run without IT support these days. Moreover, the hotel industry offers unique challenges that make it more attractive to the IT professionals.

EDP Domain

The basic responsibility of the EDP or IT department in a hotel is to maintain all the computer systems, cater to troubleshooting of all hotel management software such as Fidelio, Point of Sale (POS) management system, Materials Management System (MMS), BOSS, etc, over and above managing the hotel's website. From the guests' point of view, IT should solve any frustrating computer-related problems.

Information management plays a very important role in hotels on a daily basis for successful management requirements of internal and external customers. With automation coming to the fore, there are packages used to support the needs of a unit or a group. This package may either be customised or taken off the shelf.

To oversee the smooth functioning of the software package being used, most hotels have an EDP department where the manager is required to enhance the usability of the package. But this can be a remote requirement since in most cases the package bought by the unit comes with an after-sales service option. Indeed, the management laps up any form of automation, which may support the hotel's cause to generate customer satisfaction and retention. IT requires constant upgradation and bringing in new advancements which involves the finance department at every step. Moreover, IT being in the know-how of valuable and confidential information related to finance, it is the finance department in many hotels that oversees the IT department.

The Right Man

The industry considers certain qualities as necessary for becoming a successful head of the hotel industry. These include job knowledge in becoming a successful IT head, knowledge in setting up networks, experience with various software packages (Micros, Fidelio), familiarity with different types of servers, switches, routers, etc.

One should be in a position to work under pressure and meet timelines. The IT professional must be up-to-date and aware of new technologies introduced in the market. Other than this, he must be an effective listener, a team player and a quick learner.

An IT professional can grow in the hotel industry starting as an executive and moving up to become head of the department. There are various growth positions, but it calls for total dedication and continual improvement. When selecting candidates, hotels generally look for persons with good personality traits - the ability to communicate, educational qualification to match the post and experience.

Other than the candidates' qualifications and personality traits, we also look for resourcefulness, his ability to keep abreast with new developments with in-depth knowledge of the technicalities and the ability to solve problems not just over the phone but attend to the needs personally. The aspirant should have good management skills and be a team player.

Growth Potential

This is one industry that makes an effort to constantly utilise its funds for upgradation and introduction of new technologies. Every IT professional wants to be associated with and learn about new technologies. The hotel industry gives such IT professionals a chance to broaden their horizons thus making it an attractive option.

One's growth is determined by one's capability and willingness to work. The pay is very rewarding. One's remuneration does not stop at the monthly pay package - there are hosts of incentives given while on the job. Over and above this, performance-based benefits and schemes provided make working for the hospitality industry that much more rewarding.

3

Housekeeping in a Hotel Industry

INTRODUCTION

Hotel housekeeping departments can be considered hotel ambassadors because of their dedication and responsibility in maintaining the hotel's image. Housekeeping performs detailed work in guest rooms and hotel areas to provide a clean, comfortable environment for hotel guests to enjoy.

Through cleaning and organizing public spaces, housekeeping departments ensure that what the guests see and experience result in a positive impression of the property:

- *Function*: The primary role of the hotel's housekeeping department is cleaning guest rooms. Housekeeping works closely with front desk operations to communicate when rooms are clean and ready for guests to occupy. Although usually associated with cleaning and sanitizing guest rooms, housekeepers are also responsible for other areas, such as public restrooms, convention space and offices. Housekeeping departments often manage laundry operations, which includes washing linens as well as employee uniforms. At some hotels, housekeepers are responsible for minibar inventory and room service.
- *Types*: Housekeeping departments include a variety of job titles. The department will generally have a director of housekeeping, sometimes called the executive housekeeper. This employee is responsible for managing the department and its employees. Housekeeping departments also have supervisors who inspect work and several types of line staff, including room attendants, laundry attendants, turn-down attendants and public space attendants. In addition, other housekeeping employees run the department office by answering phones and dispatching attendants. In some hotels, the office personnel are responsible for managing lost and found items.
- *Size*: The housekeeping department is often the largest employee

department in the hotel. The number of employees is relative to the size of the hotel, and may be a combination of full-time hotel employees and temporary leased labour. The number of full-time employees is generally based on the average number of rooms one housekeeper can clean in one shift. The housekeeping department's full size is based on the rooms per housekeeper per day formula, but daily scheduling depends on occupied rooms and/or special projects.

- *Schedule*: Hotel housekeeping departments operate 24 hours each day, but the majority of employees work during the day. Day shift housekeepers are typically room attendants who begin cleaning rooms in the morning. The housekeeping schedule revolves around guest occupancy, so housekeeping departments are at their busiest between guest check-out in the morning and check-in in the afternoon. Turn-down attendants are scheduled for evening shifts, so they can perform nightly turn down in guest rooms. Laundry and public space attendants may work any shift.
- *Tools*: Room attendants generally use a cart to hold their tools and supplies so they can bring the necessary equipment with them to each room. Carts are stocked with chemicals and cleaning supplies to clean surfaces in guest rooms and bathrooms. The cart also holds a vacuum cleaner, broom and trash bag. Although not brought to every room, carpet shampooers and ozone machines can be brought to rooms that require extra cleaning attention.

MEANING OF HOUSEKEEPING DEPARTMENT

The Housekeeping Department is one of the busiest sections in the hotel as far as the variety of functions performed, and number of staff working. It is usually situated at the laundry room or any other convenient place close to Housekeeping Supplies.

The Housekeeping Department is responsible for:

- Neatness and Cleanliness of all guest rooms and most public areas
- Maintenance of recycled and non-recycled cleaning inventories

Some of the functions might however be leased to a concessionaire. In this case, hotel shall still have a housekeeping department but to a minimum number of staff! The Housekeeping Department is headed by an Executive Housekeeper.

The procedure of cleaning guest rooms by the housekeeping department can be summarized in the following way:

- Checkout clerk contacts the Housekeeping Department that a room became vacant and needs cleaning!
- Housekeeping Department updates the room status from occupied to on-change and sends a room maid to clean the room

- Room maid cleans the room and contacts the housekeeping department back about the latest status and condition of the room
- If the room is out of order for any reason, then the Housekeeping Department deducts that room from those available for sale, until either scheduled to be extensively cleaned or post to the confirmation from the Maintenance Department that the deficiency was repaired!
- Housekeeping Department sends their inspectors to check whether the stated room has been cleaned to the hotel standards or not!
- If the room is cleaned to hotel's standards, the Housekeeping Department shall update the room status from On-Change to Clean and Available for Sale and communicate this to the Front Office Department!
- If the room is not cleaned to hotel standards, inspectors communicate to the Housekeeping Department that the room shall be cleaned again!

HOTEL HOUSEKEEPING

What Can Happen

Cuts, bruises, sprains, strains, electrocution, Chemical-related injuries, infections etc.

What we Can Do

Watch for things that may cause accidents and report them immediately to your supervisor. Place mops, buckets and other equipment where no one can fall over them.

Practise safe lifting techniques, lift with your legs, not your back. Be careful with cleaning solutions or chemicals read product labels. Store cigarette butts and sharp objects in a separate, metal container. Roll up all linen, rugs and spreads before putting them in the soiled laundry bundle. Wear rubber gloves when using strong cleaning solutions. Push tall or heavy pieces of furniture get help if necessary.

Do not touch light switches or handle electrical equipment when your hands are wet or you are standing on a damp floor Do not stand on the edge of bathroom tubs

Do not mix ammonia and chlorine-based cleaners together, poisonous gas is produced. Do not run up or down stairs, always walk and use the handrail. Do not try to repair machines or equipment, report problems to your supervisor. Do not run your hands along or inside objects unless you have checked first for razor blades, needles, broken glass, etc.

Do not use your hands to compress garbage in a bag, use a stick or plunger. Do not unplug the vacuum cleaner by pulling on the cord, pull on the plug. Housekeeping in a hotel is a very physically demanding job that includes many, varied tasks. Typically, in this case study, housekeepers were responsible for cleaning 16 rooms per shift. The actual amount of work depends on the size of the room and the number of beds. A housekeeper needs between fifteen and thirty minutes to do one room.

A housekeeper carries out the following tasks:

- Making beds
- Tidying rooms
- Cleaning and polishing toilets, taps, sinks, bathtubs and mirrors
- Washing floors,
- Removing stains, and
- Vacuuming

Housekeeping in a hotel is a very physically demanding job that includes many, varied tasks. Typically, in this case study, housekeepers were responsible for cleaning 16 rooms per shift. The actual amount of work depends on the size of the room and the number of beds. A housekeeper needs between fifteen and thirty minutes to do one room.

The main risk factors for repetitive motion injuries (RMIs) in housekeeping are:

Heavy physical workload and excessive bodily motions which are a high risk for back injuries and forceful upper limb motions in awkward positions which are a high risk for neck or shoulder and arm injuries. Space limitations require workers to use many uncomfortable postures.

These are:

- Standing or walking,
- Stooping,
- Squatting,
- Kneeling,
- Stretching,
- Reaching,
- Bending,
- Twisting, and
- Crouching.

A housekeeper changes body position every three seconds while cleaning a room. If we assume that the average cleaning time for each room is twenty-five minutes, we can estimate that a housekeeper assumes 8,000 different body postures every shift. In addition, forceful movements while using awkward body positions include lifting mattresses, cleaning tiles, and vacuuming every shift. Housekeeping is a physically demanding and very tiring job. It can be classified as "moderately heavy" to "heavy" work because the energy required is approximately 4 kilocalories per minute (4 kcal/min.)

Hotel housekeepers work in a unique place. Hotels are usually designed for the comfort of their guests rather than their housekeeping staff. This fact makes it very difficult to improve working conditions for housekeepers by means of better engineering. However, some improvements can be made by selecting more appropriate equipment. Lighter vacuum cleaners (preferably the self-propelling type), and lighter service carts with wheels designed for carpeted floors would ease the workload for their operators providing this equipment is always kept in good repair. When new vacuum cleaners are purchased, low noise emissions should be one of the criteria.

Improving the body postures that pose a major risk for musculoskeletal disorders seems an unachievable task. Again, this fact results from the peculiarity of hotels as a workplace. To attract guests and remain competitive, hotel management pursues a policy that everything should be "so clean it sparkles". Floors, walls, windows, mirrors, and bathroom fixtures might be adequately cleaned with some form of an extension tool to reduce bending and over-stretching. However, the demand for spotless cleanliness and hygiene, management often requires their cleaning staff to spend extra time and effort cleaning by kneeling, leaning, squatting, crouching, slouching and stretching. These postures will in time contribute to new musculoskeletal injuries and aggravate old ones.

New approaches, other than strictly ergonomic ones, need to be investigated. For example, action can be taken from the administrative level.

Options for improvement include:

- Job rotation,
- Job enrichment and job enlargement,
- Team work, and
- Education and training on work practices.

Job rotation is one possible approach. It requires workers to move between different tasks, at fixed or irregular periods. However, it must be a rotation where workers do something completely different. Different tasks must use different muscle groups to allow muscles already stressed to recover.

Another approach is job enlargement. This increases the variety of tasks built into the job. It breaks the monotony of the job and avoids overloading one part of the body. Job enrichment involves more autonomy and control for the worker.

Team work can provide greater variety and more evenly distributed muscular work. The whole team is involved in the planning of the work. Each team member carries out a set of operations to complete the whole product, allowing the worker to alternate between tasks. This reduces the risk of RMI.

A well-designed job, supported by a well-designed workplace and proper tools, allows the worker to avoid unnecessary motion of the neck, shoulders and upper limbs. However, the actual performance of the tasks depends on individuals.

Training should be provided for workers who are involved with housekeeping activities. It is important that housekeeping staff be informed about hazards in the workplace, including the risk of injuries to the musculoskeletal system. Therefore, identification of the hazards for such injury at any given hotel is fundamental.

Individual work practices, including lifting habits, are shaped by proper training. Training should encourage employers and workers to adopt methods that reduce fatigue. For example, it is advisable to plan one's workload and do the heavier tasks at the beginning of the workshift, rather than at the end, when fatigue is at its maximum. When a person is tired, the risk of injuring a muscle is higher.

Training should also explain the health hazards of improper lifting and give recommendations on what a worker can do to improve lifting positions. Training should also emphasize the importance of rest periods for the workers' health and explain how active rest can do more for keeping workers healthy than passive rest. The effect of such training can reach far beyond occupational situations because the workers can apply this knowledge also in their off-job lives.

The Housekeeping department must be the most important. It has the greatest proportion of staffing hours to cover, the most staff, the most hours to cover and it is a cost centre. Unlike the restaurant and bar, which are revenue centres, and as long as they are not overstaffed, the more staff you have the more revenue is generated. The housekeeping department is also the one the customers notice most if anything is wrong. You have to have the right number of staff on duty, or it shows.

The housekeeping department can have the following staff depending on the size of hotel. Housekeeper and assistant housekeepers, room maids, cleaners, staffmaids, cloakroom attendants, houseporters, valets, laundry and linen keeper. The staff hours of cover depend on the hotel and type of customer, business people require different time schedules to people on holiday with children. The staff need to be scheduled accordingly and in a ratio to the number of guests staying in the hotel. Fortunately, most people book ahead and the workload is known well in advance, especially during peak periods.

Your staffing requirement will depend on the occupancy of your hotel. It is possible to get quite good estimates of staff numbers based on average times to do tasks, such as cleaning a room. Then you can allocate 10, or 15, or even 20 rooms to each room maid. It is also quite easy to estimate the total number of staff needed in a year for a task. We have a page about annual hours.

For example, cleaning an occupied room takes 30mins/day, en-suite bathroom 6mins/day, therefore a maid for every 13 occupied rooms. A hotel with 100 rooms(all occupied) needs 8 maids. Then we can sum this up for a year of 365 days, which comes to 2900 maid days per year. We can then divide this by the number of days a maid works per year, say 240, and arrive at a figure of 12 full time maids. Hence we can recruit the 12 maids and start using them on the rooms. I haven't allowed for average occupancy, sickness rates, and a lot of other things which readily come to mind, because at this point, the difficult thing is to find a way of sharing the yearly workload on a day by day basis. This is the difficult part, just how do you allocate the maids so that you have just the right number on every day.

Well, the answer depends on where you are at the moment. An existing hotel staffed, is different to a new hotel unstaffed. If I first deal with a new hotel, then the resultant method is easier. First, don't start from the above yearly totals, use the daily hour totals to tell you how many staff are needed each day. Start Visual Rota, set it up for, say 13 4week periods and name the staff, as RM1, RM2, etc.

Then start to allocate shifts according to your occupancy rates(anticipated). At this stage you can use full time or part time staff, working full shifts, half shifts and split shifts. Give the staff days off, usually in the ratio of for every 5 days they work, they have 2 off. Try to use full time staff as much as possible if they are cheaper, and fill in the blanks with part time staff. Then you can recruit the staff in accordance with your requirements and allocate shifts to the staff weeks in advance, possibly months.

At some stage you need to deal with holidays and staff turnover. All staff take holidays but it is difficult to know in advance when this is going to be. That's why we invented dice. If you look back at your records(difficult if you are a new hotel, I know, then you have to guess) you will see the pattern of absenteeism, sickness and holidays, and even staff turnover. This pattern can be replicated by throwing dice. For instance, if you employ 12 maids and your staff turnover is 50%, then six of your maids leave every year, or one every 2 months. You won't know when exactly and it is difficult for us to be random in our decisions, so throw a dice for each month. If the number is even, a 2, 4,or 6, then a maid leaves that month, if the number is odd, no one leaves that month. Then you can arrange for a new maid to be recruited in line with the throw of the dice. Perhaps not, perhaps what you will do is to include into your budgets the cost of hiring a new recruit and the cost of using an employment agency.

You can use Visual Rota to allocate training days for new staff and existing, or keep records of sickness, absenteeism, lateness, frequency of requests and holidays.

An existing hotel will be using their established working practice for staffing. Visual Rota enables you to analyse this and see if improvements can be made and how much you can save by changing your working practice. Staff need an incentive to change and if you offer part of your savings as a pay increase, that goes a long way to getting the changes accepted. We have regularly improved the way we work by incorporating new pay deals for existing staff and hiring new staff as and when we replaced the staff due to natural wastage on our new terms.

Visual Rota enables you to move your staff around to minimise the effects of peaks and troughs in occupancy levels. You can bring in more staff when needed and give them days off during slack periods. The programme keeps track of their hours and shifts, so everyone gets exactly the right number of hours of work, but your costs are minimised.

Other departments are equally capable of being analysed and scheduled by Visual Rota. It is possible to have one file for the entire hotel, or several files to cover each area, floor or department. Whichever method you use at the moment, you can do the same on the computer, but faster.

There is always a compromise between the number of staff doing a particular job and the cover they provide. If there is only one housekeeper, then the maximum cover would be 40 hours/week, whilst the staff rota would be providing up to 168 hours of cover a week, hence one of the main management functions is to determine how much staffing is provided and at what grade of staff. Fortunately, hoteliers are not subject to staffing levels determined by legislation, and can decide for themselves.

IMPORTANCE OF HOUSEKEEPING DEPARTMENT

- A health club is a part of facilities of most large hotels especially resort hotels this also include swimming pool and spa facilities.
- Accommodation in hotels tend to be the largest part of the hotel, it is the most revenue generating department, the housekeeping department takes care of all rooms is often largest department in hotels.
- Hotel aims to make environment comfortable and offer specialised service to the guest.
- Hotel offer guest the choice of specialty restaurant, coffee shop. The bar also sells liquors which generate the revenue of the hotel. They are available in banqueting, meeting and private party facilities.
- Hotel offer laundry, dry leaning facilities for guest clothes, shoe polishing facilities also.
- Hotels try to make the ambiance as pleasant as possible by nice colour scheme, attractive furnishing and a well kept efficient staff.
- House keeping is the department determine to a large extent whether guests are happy during stay and in turn mankind they return to the hotel.

- Housekeeping is the department that deals essentially with cleanliness and all ancillary service attached to that.
- Revenue can be generated from conferencing, meeting, seminar etc.
- The fine accommodation and service are provided to the guest so they are pleased with the hotel. The guest satisfaction is its primary object and the hygiene factor must always be present in the hotel.
- The rooms in hotels are offered as accommodation to travellers/ guest as individual units of bedroom. Some interconnected rooms are also made which will be helpful to the guest and families. Many hotels offer suits to the guest.
- The standard plays an important role in the reputation of the hotels. One feels comfortable only in the environment which is clean and well ordered, so cleanliness is important for health foremost also for well being.
- These days shopping arcade also found in hotels.

In hotels major part of revenue comes from rooms, rooms which is not sold on any night losses revenue forever and reason for poor occupancy can be anything like hygiene factor, cleanliness, lack of modernizing etc. hence main purpose is to improve whole appeal of the room. A guest spend more time alone in his room than any other part of the hotel, so he can check up the cleanliness he wishes to as some of the guest are more health conscious these days.

He may check up dusting, in-depth cleaning and losses confidence if properly not done *e.g.* If drawers are not cleaned he may generally won't feel like putting his clothes down. Decent room supplies are service like quick laundry and dry cleaning service shows guest that hotel is considering his comfort and wishes to please him. not only this from the cleanliness of lobby, public area, restaurant, cloakrooms, the state and cleanliness of uniform the guest can judge a lot about hotel. it can be positive or negative judgement we can conclude that housekeeping department contributes greatly to all guest impression of the hotel.

FUNCTIONS OF THE HOUSEKEEPING DEPARTMENT

The extension of the housekeeping function outside the hotel bedroom normally includes cleaning of the bedroom floors and may also include the staircases, public cloakrooms and other public areas of the hotel. Many a times outside agencies are involved in cleaning the public areas such as the lobby and the restaurant area as well as the men's and women's restrooms.

This activity is normally carried out at odd hours or at the times when public is not around this area. The standard of the cleanliness needs to be maintained and it's the duty of the executive housekeeper to see that pre-determined standards of cleanliness are maintained in all the areas of the hotel it be if the fire-exit stairwells and goods lifts or any other public area. To ensure this, the day of executive housekeepers begin with a round with assistant housekeeper of all such areas which is visited by the public. For this standards need to be set and once the standards are approved, the department shall strive hard to maintain them.

Other function areas of the housekeeping department includes:

- *Lost and Found Department*: Many a times while cleaning a guest room attendant comes across some personal items of the guest left behind. The value of the personal item can vary from almost nil to thousands of rupees as in the case of Rolex watches, etc. All the objects found while cleanin g the rooms are, thus, handed over by attendants to the floor supervisor, who maintains a list of the found objects against the specific room number.
- *First Aid*: First aid as and when needed by the guests is provided by the housekeeping department which m aintains the first aid kit.
- *Floral Arrangement*: Fresh floral arrangements all over the hotel are maintained by the housekeeping department. The private areas like guest bedroom or the public areas like the restaurants and the lobby floral arrangements are made by housekeeping department.
- *Laundry Services*: The laundry services extended to the guest are usually provided by the housekeeping. The laundry to be washed is collected from the guest room and washed, dried and ironed clothes are supplied back to th e guest room. Earlier, all the hotels had in house laundry services but nowadays many hotels have outsourced this service, both for the hotel linen as well as for the guest laundry.
- *Purchasing*: This is one role of the housekeeping department where a lot of money transactions take place. This is one of the important areas which can affect the profitability of the hotel if various products purchased and supplies are not well managed. The primary areas of purchasing that are under the control of the Executive housekeepers are:
  - Bedroom supplies: *e.g.*, laundry bags, breakfast, cards, shoeshine, etc.,
  - Bathroom supplies: *e.g.*, toiletries,
  - Linen: bed sheets and towelling,
  - Tea and coffee making facilities: *e.g.*, tea/coffee sachets, sugar, milk and biscuits,
  - Working replacements: *e.g.*, shower curtains, crockery, glassware, vacuum cleaners, trolleys, etc.,

- Cleaning supplies: *e.g.*, air freshener, bleach, cleaning product, and
- Uniforms: *e.g.*, for the room attendants/porters.

It is necessary for the Executive housekeeper to ensure that the supplies and their consumption is monitored.

The list of items in the purchasing list can be further classified into:

- *Consumable*: Bedroom supplies, cleaning supplies and TCMF
- *Assets*: Uniforms, working replacement and linen.

The Executive housekeeper would have different policies for these two distinct groups of purchasing. The actual consumption of the first group of purchases can be anticipated in line with the hotel occupancy. It is necessary to maintain a stock of these items so that the staff can put up their requisitions on a daily or weekly basis.

The Executive housekeeper is thus required not only to ascertain the demands but also to control the use of consumable products by maintaining properly the invoices and requisition slips. The consumable products are many and if not properly monitored will obviously affect at large the profit statement of the hotel.

Today, computers are used for the purpose. "Assets", though not in true sense, like uniforms, etc. are not regularly used up and they do not need to be replaced daily.

ATTRIBUTES AND QUALITIES OF HOUSEKEEPING STAFF

HONESTY

This is a very essential attribute for housekeeping staff, especially Room Attendants, who have access to all guest rooms. Guest belongings, sometimes invaluable are often found lying around in the room. The temptations to thieve are great.

It is only the personal quality of discipline and integrity that checks these temptations:

- *Eye for Detail*: It is one of the greatest qualities that house keeping staff must have. It is with this quality that the finer aspects of housekeeping are taken care of and it is what determines a good service from an average one. This quality enables housekeeping staff to take into consideration the minutest details.
- *Co-Cooperativeness*: Housekeeping staff needs to be co-operating with other departments to achieve more efficiency.
- *Briefing and Scheduling of Staff*: Briefing is that process at the beginning of a work shift which is provided by management to facilitate a two-way communication between management and staff. It is the one time during a shift that all housekeeping staff are

together to share information and feelings before they disperse to their work areas.

- Briefing Schedule:
  - i Personal hygiene and grooming.
  - ii Any new policies and procedures introduced by managcl11enL must be made out and explained to the staff.
  - iii At n briefing the duties or each staff member and the areas of accountability are explained. This would mean that staffs are assigned a floor and allotted their number of rooms. The staffs likewise, are told which floors or public areas they are assigned to for cleaning. They are also told which supervisor would be in charge.
  - iv Briefing is a time which can be used as a training opportunity. Simple tasks may be demonstrated so that they can be practiced under supervision at their work place.

CLEANING A ROOM

Prior to reporting on a 11oor the room attendant already knows the status of a room in her given lot of rooms. The room attendant can prioritize room to be attended to first on the basis of immediate needs. Before entering the room knock at the door firmly with the index finger knuckle announcing clearly" Housekeeping".

When there is no answer, repeat the knock after ten seconds announcing yourself as before. If there is still no answer open the door and knock announcing inside the room "Housekeeping".

When there is no reply and one is relatively sure that there is no one in, open the door wide and keep it that way till the entire cleaning cycle in the room is complete.

ROOM CLEANING PROCEDURE

- And centre sashes or windows, close windows.
- Arrange furniture if necessary
- Check the maintenance requirements and report to the department head.
- Clean all the surfaces in single circular motions with a dry cloth. Use a hand dust pan to collect any unwanted matter on the surface without lifting dust in the air Ensure that all surfaces are spotlessly clean. Pay special attention to nooks and corners especially those points that may not obviously be visible to the guests eye.
- Clean lamp shades with a clean dry duster.
- Clean mirror with a dry cloth.

- Clean the bath room.
- Clean the ceiling and air-conditioning vents for cobwebs.
- Collect all loose papers or magazines and stack them neatly on the desk.
- Disinfect telephone mouthpiece with Dettol. Wipe balance of the telephone with a damp cloth, check phone for the dial tone.
- Dust both sides of all room doors, baseboards, window sills, inside and out, bottom
- Dust closet, shelves, hangers and rods. Brush the closet floor.
- Have a last look at the room referring to the checklist for completion of work.
- Switch off the room air-conditioner. Draw all curtains and open the windows for airing the room.
- Switch on the air-conditioning.
- Turn the mattress side-to-side on succeeding days followed by end-to-end turning. Smooth out mattress to air it.
- Use a stiff upholstery brush or vacuum cleaner on upholstered furniture arms, backs and seats.
- Wash the floors.

CLEANING A BATHROOM

- Clean mirror first with dry cloth then with glass cloth and finally with dry cloth.
- Clean the ceiling and air-conditioning vents for cobwebs.
- Cleaning activity starts from the ceiling downwards to the floor.
- Collect all trash in bathroom waste basket and deposit in trash hamper of the maids-cart.
- Finally close the windows shut all lights and close the bathroom doors.
- Floors are cleaned from the wall farthest to the door to the exit.
- Open all exhaust vents.
- Scrub the floor with the prescribed mop and ensure it is dry
- Scrub the toilet bowl and bidet using the special brush or mop and the prescribed sanitizer. The inner rim should be cleaned. Ensure it is dry and spotless inside. Clean the WC from the outside with a sponge till it is sparkling find dry. Clean the lid and toilet seat of the toilet bowl dry and close them.

- Scrub to dry the area next to the wash basin.
- Wipe down tile walls using a sponge or damp cloth. Follow with a dry cloth ensuring that tiles are free of water marks.
- Wipe dry the shower curtain with a sponge.
- Wipe off light bulbs and shades with dry cloth. Check that all bulbs are working.

DIRTY DOZEN

- Air-conditioning ducts and diffuser grills. Under bathroom counters.
- Area above racks
- Behind the WC bowl- the s-trap.
- Beneath the table
- Faucet nozzle filter
- In the toilet roll niche
- Interior surface of drawers
- Rear surface of doors
- Toilet vents
- Top of the door edges and ceiling.
- Top of the picture frames

ROOM MAINTENANCE PROCEDURE

As hose keeping has contact with all rooms and public areas practically in every shift, it is they who detect report and ensure the completion of all maintenance work. This requires close co-ordination with the engineering department.

WEEKLY CLEANING PROCEDURE

In addition to daily cleaning routine, a room attendant normally has some cleaning chores that are of a time-consuming nature. Such items may sometimes be beyond the physical capacity and need the assistance of a skill worker.

Such tasks are:

- Cleaning of window panes
- Polishing of brassware
- Scrubbing of balconies and terraces
- Scrubbing of bathroom tiles
- Vacuuming of under heavy furniture.

JOB DESCRIPTION OF HOUSEKEEPING STAFF

Duties and Responsibilities:

- All Ledgers are to be put up for Joint Directors signature through housekeeping Manager on a quarterly basis.
- Daily use of cleaning agents are to be recorded and the records to be put up for housekeeping managers signature monthly.
- Ensure proper discipline among Housekeepers, Sweepers, Dhobi, and Tailor working in linen department. Make sure that they wear name badges.
- Floor scrubbing Machine is to be taken by other housekeeper only with the permission of the linen housekeeper.
- Floor scrubbing machines are to be chain locked when not in use.
- Any other job given by the housekeeping manager or the senior management staff from time to time.
- Linen and curtains are to be checked for wear and tear quarterly.
- Maintain a sepearate Indent for the cleaning agents used in Laundry and the Indent should be signed by the housekeeping Manager.
- Periodical Maintenance of washing Machine, Ironing Machine, Iron Box, Sewing Machine, and floor scrubbing Machine to be carried out and the record to be maintained.
- Planning and scheduling the standard procedure for cleaning all types of linen to be displayed in laundry and to be followed strictly.
- Responsible for the cleanliness of sweepers uniform.
- Sell all waste materials and deposit the sale proceeds to secretary.
- Supervision and checking the cleanliness of the surrounding area of main hospital.
- Tailoring rates for various items of stitched materials are to be maintained. For any revision in charges prior approval to be taken from secretary.
- Time schedule to be prepared for collection of clean/soiled linen and to be followed strictly.
- Torn or faded linen is to be segregated and to be shown to joint director quarterly. If any item is found unserviceable the same should be written off the ledger getting after the approval of Jt.Director.
- Torn or faded linen is to be used for cleaning purposes.
- Train and Guide the trainees housekeeper posted in linen department.

- Training classes are to be taken for junior housekeepers when required.
- Washing charges for various linen are to be fixed and approval. For any change in the charges, prior approval to be taken from secretary.

Designation – Floor Executive: Housekeeping:

- Control over all keys of all departments in OPDS.
- Disposal of refuse is to be monitored.
- Ensure proper discipline of Housekeepers and sweepers working in out patient department and make sure that they wear name badge.
- Experimenting new techniques and equipments for cleaning.
- Any other job given by the housekeeping manager or the senior management staff from time to time.
- Indenting cleaning agents and equipments and ensure their proper use and keeping records.
- Maintain the Leave list of all sweepers working in main hospital, free hospital, Laico and other supporting areas and day off Roster of sweepers working in OPDs.
- Maintaining the checklist of furniture, electrical plumbing, carpentry and mason work in the OPDs.
- Maintenance details of continuous duties of housekeepers.
- Maintenance of House Keeping department room and attending to phone calls promptly.
- Maintenance of sweepers attendance Register, wage sheets, deployment, control and details for continuous duties.
- Maintenance responsible for the sweepers uniform collected after working hours from the sweepers.
- Make sure the tyre cart is secured and locked after working hours.
- Planning and scheduling the standard procedures in writing for the proper care of all types of floors, walls, windows, furniture, bathrooms, Lavatories and other equipments to be prepared and follows trictly.
- Preparing inventories for furniture and keeping records for their maintenance.
- Reporting and checking of all maintenance work.
- Responsible for the cleaning schedule of freshwater tank, filters, coolers and septic Tanks and the cleaning and due dates are to be displayed in the boards as well as in the Register. The register shall be put up for Housekeeping managers signature every month.

- Supervision and checking the cleanliness of out patient departments and Basement area.
- Supervision of quality maintenance and infection control.
- To develop proper use of cleaning procedures.
- Training and taking classes for juniors

Designation: - Ward Executive: Housekeeping:

- Attending to patients complaints
- Control of all keys of 1st and 2nd Floor
- Development and standardization of newer and improved method of cleaning for better results at lower costs.
- Ensure proper discipline of housekeepers and sweepers in 1st and 2nd floor and make sure the wear name badges.
- Ensure up keep and maintenance of hospital property.
- Any other job that may be assigned by the housekeeping Manager or the senior management staff from time to time.
- Indenting cleaning agents and equipments and ensure their proper use and keeping necessary records.
- Maintain day off roaster of sweepers in 1st and 2nd floor.
- Planning and scheduling the standard procedures in writing for the proper care of all types of floors, walls, windows, furniture, bathrooms, lavatories and other equipments to be placed and to be followed strictly.
- Preparing inventories for 1st and 2nd floor furniture and keeping records for their maintenance.
- Responsible for the sweepers uniform collected after working hours from the sweepers of 1st and 2nd floor.
- Supervision and checking the cleanliness of 1st and 2nd floor.
- Supervision for quality maintenance and infection control.
- Take adequate precautions for controlling cross infections.
- To assist in quality health care and patient care programme.
- Training and taking classes for juniors

Designation – Ward Executive: Housekeeping:

- Attending to patient's complaints.
- Control of all keys of 3rd and 4th floor.
- Development and standardization of newer and improved method of cleaning for better results at lower costs.

- Ensure proper discipline of Housekeepers and sweepers in 3rd and 4th floor and make sure they wear name badges.
- Ensure upkeep and maintenance of hospital property
- Any other job that may be assigned by the housekeeping manager or the senior management staff from time to time.
- Indenting cleaning agents and equipments and ensure their proper use and keeping records.
- Maintain day off roster for sweepers in 3rd and 4th floor.
- Maintaining the checklist of furniture, Electrical, plumbing, Carpenting and Mason works in 3rd and 4th floor.
- Planning and scheduling the standard procedures in writing for the proper care of all types of floors walls, windows, furniture, bathrooms lavatories and other equipments to be placed and to be followed strictly.
- Preparing inventories for 3rd and 4th floor furniture and keeping records for their maintenance.
- Responsible for the sweepers uniform collected after working hours from the sweepers of 3rd and 4th floor.
- Supervision and checking the cleanliness of 3rd and 4th floor.
- Supervision for quality maintenance and infection control.
- Take adequate precautions in controlling cross infections.
- To assist in quality health care and patient care programme
- Training and taking classes for juniors.

Designation – Senior Trainees: Housekeeping:

- Attend all theory and practical classes as per the programme.
- Indenting cleaning agents, equipments and ensure the proper use and maintain their records.
- Planning and scheduling the standard procedures for cleaning in writing and follow strictly.
- Preparing inventories for furniture and keeping records for their maintenance.
- Work under the supervision of executive Linen housekeeper.

CONTROL DESK MANAGEMENT IN HOUSE KEEPING

The housekeeping control desk is the central hub of the housekeeping department. This is the area in the department where all information is received and from where messages are conveyed to housekeeping and other staff present in various parts of the hotel. Thus, the control desk may be considered the nerve centre for to – and – fro communication in the housekeeping department. one of the main functions of the control desk is ensuring smooth coordination between housekeeping and other departments such as maintenance, front office, food and beverages, security, sales and marketing and so on.

The location of control desk is normally adjacent to the Executive Housekeeper's office. This desk is manned 24- hours otherwise the lifeline of housekeeping communication would stop.

ROLE OF CONTROL DESK

- Front office also alerts the desk attendant about the expected and existing crews in the house. So that the rooms can be make ready for the new arriving crew after the departure of existing crew in a very short period of time.
- In most of the hotels, this is the area where housekeeping employees; report for work; collect keys and signing for them; persue the log book get their briefing and at the end of their shift, report back to.
- Its is the control room attendants who receives departure room numbers from the front office and transmits them to the appropriate floor supervisor.
- The control desk attendant receives all the message of the guests such as a request for extra blankets, baby-sitter services, which she transmit to the concerned floor supervisor for further action.
- The control desk receives messages from in house guests over the telephone apart from maintaining the intra and inter –departmental channels of communication. hotel room directories provide the control desk extension number to the guests which they can use if they require housekeeping services.
- The floor supervisor informs the desk attendant once rooms are cleaned and ready for sale and this is updated in the computer so that front office can easily obtain the information o f the status of room.
- The main physical feature visible in most control desk is the key cabinet. On the wall, where all floor masters keys and store keys are kept under lock and key themselves.
- The role of the housekeeping control desk is to facilitate communication to various parts of hotel. this role can be exercised in many forms which are as follows;
- Another common feature here is a large notice board displaying notices like

- Room numbers of the groups in the house
- Room numbers of crews in the house
- Night cleaning schedule
- VIPs in the house
- Weekly cleaning schedules
- Daily roster of supervisors and staff
- Any other significant information relating to in-house guest or the hotel staff.

- One of the most important roles of the control desk is maintaining various important records, registers, forms and formats so that they are available and easily accessible for reference to managers and supervisors.

COORDINATION WITH FRONT OFFICE

The control desk acts as the nerve centre for coordination with the other departments in the hotel. the control desk attendants receives the night report, the arrivals and departures list, VIP list, and the list of crews and groups in the house from the front office.

Based on these documents, the housekeeping department schedules the workers for cleaning, maintenance and servicing of guestrooms and related areas:

- *7. Night report*: This report, prepared each night by front desk attendant, indicates the rooms occupied that night and ones that are to become check-outs the following day. Based on this report, the executive or assistant housekeeper schedules employees for servicing these rooms. Once the rooms have been cleaned and made ready, the floor supervisor calls the control desk or the front desk directly, releasing the room for sale.
- Apart from the communications the front office needs to depend on housekeeping for the provision of clean uniforms to its staff.
- *Crews in the house*: Sometimes the arrival of a crew and the departure of another crew from the same airline may overlap. In such circumstances, it is important for the allotted rooms to be cleaned within a short period of time. Thus for this there should be a effective coordination between front office and housekeeping.
- *Flowers*: sometimes the management extends its compliments to a guest with a special gesture of a flower arrangement in the room as recognition of the importance of a person. This requirement of flower arrangements for certain guests is conveyed to housekeeping by the front office on a daily basis.
- *Groups in the house*: The group rooming list must be provided before

the group's arrival to the housekeeping as groups tends to move together in terms of arrival, departure, sightseeing tours and meals. Their rooms need to be readied together in view of strict time parameters. Group rooming lists enable the hk department to organize their work and have the group's room ready on time.

- It also helps to gear renovations and spring cleaning to low occupancy periods there by preventing loss of revenue.
- The housekeeping and front office department also coordinate with each other for other important information which require special attention like
- There must be coordination between housekeeping and front office department to share information on occupancy levels which helps to forecast occupancy for the year and makes it easier to draw up a budget, establish par stock levels and estimate required staff strength.
- There should be coordination know about the daily room report and housekeeping discrepancy report.
- There should be coordination to clean front office public areas
- To ensure efficient rooming of guests, both housekeeping and front office must inform each other of changes in a room's status. Knowing whether a room is occupied, vacant, on change, out of order under repair, or similar for proper room management
- VIPs in house: this information is essential so that the staff can take a little extra care and keener precautions in cleaning and supervising VIP rooms.housekeeping can take extra care in cleaning the VIP rooms by equipping the rooms with additional amenities as per the policy of the management. These amenities can be; bathrobe; bath slippers; extra soaps; hangers; and glass tumblers.

COORDINATION WITH ENGINEERING DEPARTMENT

The housekeeping control desk have to coordinate with the engineering department for maintenance request that the room attendants registers while servicing the guest room or in the floor.

- A need for urgent repairs is reported to maintenance over telephone and these requests are usually taken into action immediately.
- Boiler work: this is necessary to maintain a supply of hot water to guestroom.
- Electrical work: air conditioning and heating; fused bulbs, lights and lamps that are not functioning; defective plugs and plug points; short circuits; and faulty geysers, refrigerators, and minibar fall under this category.

- Mechanical work: this entails repair or replacement of any faulty equipment, such as vacuum cleaners, ice-cube machines, and so on.
- Plumbing work: this deals with faulty faucets, showers, drainage systems, water closets, and so on.
- The housekeeping department depends on maintenance to keep things in order.
- There are various heads under which maintenance work is done they are:
- While carrying out their scheduled work, housekeeping employees may find some deficiencies in the hotel facilities, such as faulty electrical plugs, dripping faucets, leaking pipes or malfunctioning air-conditioning units etc.

All maintenance requirements needed on floors are entered in the maintenance register kept in the control desk. The control desk attendant notes down the room number, the maintenance work required and the name of the GRA or the supervisor who called attention to the problem. The desk attendant prepares a maintenance slip in duplicate. She retains the second copy in her book and forwards the first copy to the engineering department.

The engineering department then prepares a 'work order slip' and sends the concerned technician directly to the floor. When the job is completed, a copy of tradesperson's completed 'work order ' is sent to the executive housekeeper for acknowledgement of work completed satisfactorily. If this copy is not sent to the executive housekeeper within an appropriate amount of time, housekeeping issues another 'work order', which signals maintenance to provide a status report on the request repair.

KNOWLEDGE IN HOUSEKEEPING MANAGEMENT

KEY CONTROL

Key is a specially shaped and designed piece of metal or plastic/ magnetic card used for opening and closing the lock.it is an essential too for lock. In a hotel, it refers to the door lock key, which is primarily concerned for safety of hotel room contents and guest valuables. The responsibility for handling key of the houseguest has always been with front office and housekeeping department. In all large, hotels the information desk holds the responsibility of issuing, retrieving and controlling room keys. Room attendants also handle room keys to prepare guest bedrooms. Hence, it is essential that strict control of keys is maintained regularly.

MANUAL/MECHANICAL KEY SYSTEM

The standard of manual key system in operation comprises of the following:

- Electronic/ Magnetic Key System

- Emergency key
- Grand master key
- Individual guestroom keys.
- Master key
- Sub master key/floor key

CONTROL OF ROOM KEYS

Maintaining a strict control over the guest room keys is the responsibility of the information part. it is very necessary that a strict control be maintained for averting any mishaps. The information assistant keeps the keys into the correct slots of the key rack/ pigeon hole.

For the security of both guest and the hotel, room keys issuing system must be very efficiently operated and controlled.the theft, loss or unauthorized duplication of keys could have serious security implication.

The system of key control is as follows:

- A logbook or control sheet can be used to monitor the distribution of keys.
- The keys of inter-connecting rooms should be kept secure and scheduled.
- A regular inventory of keys should be carried out, and missing or damaged key should be reported immediately to the concerned authority.
- Guests should be requested to handle their key cautiously.
- Guests should be urged to drop the keys at the 'key drop slot' maintained at front desk each time they leave the premises upon their departure or for their own personal reasons.
- Identification should be sought and verified, if necessary, prior to issuing a key to a guest.
- Key should always be placed in the correct hook/ slot of the rack
- Key should be retrieved from the guests at time of check out.
- Keys should not be handed over to unauthorized personnel.
- Know the different types of keys in circulation within the hotel.
- The master keys, when not in use, should be secured in a safe place.

PEST CONTROL

Pest conrol is a programme of eradicating pests. Pests are removed through pesticides.a pesticide is called a chemical used to control or eliminate pests. Insects are probably the larger pests.many insects transmit diseases such as malaria and typhus.some insects destroy or cause heavy damage to valuable vegetation. Other common pests include bacteria, fungi, rats and such weeds as poison ivy and ragweed.

Manufacturers use various chemicals in making pesticides:

- A pest is any organism that competes with humans, domestic animals. Or desirable plants for food or water.
- Eradication: Destroying an entire pest population.
- Injures humans, domestic animals, desirable plants, structures or possessions
- Pest control goals
- Prevention: Keeping a pest from becoming a problem
- Suppression: Reducing pest numbers or damage to an acceptable level.
- Transmits diseases and annoys humans or domestic animals.

SAFETY AND SECURITY

Safety and security are concepts often used interchangeably, and it should be understood that both are means of safeguarding human and physical assets. The tern 'safety' is with reference to such things as disasters, emergencies, fire prevention and protection, and conditions that provide for freedom from injury and prevent damage to property. The tern 'security' is used with reference to freedom from fear, anxiety, and doubts concerning humans as well as protection thefts of guest, employee, or hotel property.

WORK-ENVIRONMENT SAFETY AND JOB-SAFETY ANALYSIS

The management of any place of work are legally bound to provide a hazard-free environment to their employees. The nature of work that the housekeeping staffs are involved in is such that employees may easily become accident-prone if they are careless with equipment, chemicals, or procedures.

Safety Management Programmes

The overall objective of a safety management programme is to eliminate hazards before they cause any serious accidents.

- Conduct periodic in-house safety inspections.
- Establish a safety committee.
- Investigate and analyses all accidents and injuries.
- Maintain accurate safety records.
- Make departmental heads aware of the nature and variety of hazards.

- Motivate staff members to be safety conscious.
- Practice safety management and monitor follow-ups.
- Review the effectiveness of your own safety management programme.
- Review work procedures and inspect work areas for safety hazards.
- Train staff members to implement safety consciousness.

POTENTIAL HAZARDS IN HOUSEKEEPING

Due to the nature of the work performed by housekeeping staff, they may be exposed to many dangerous and unsafe conditions, or hazards, if they are not careful. To reduce safety risks, all employees should be aware of potential safety hazards.

There hazards may include:

- Faulty equipment;
- Damaged flooring or chipped tiles;
- Slippery floors and spills not mopped up;
- Slippery guest bathrooms;
- Cracked or broken glass;
- Cleaning agents left uncapped;
- Non-adherence to instructions outlined in the materials safety data sheets (MSDS) for the use of cleaning chemicals.
- Handling corrosive cleaning agents with bare hands;
- Worn-out electrical insulation or fittings;
- Overloaded electrical sockets;
- Trailing equipment flexes;
- Worn carpets and rugs;
- Cleaning equipment left lying around;
- Unsafe use of ladders;
- Loose stair treads;
- Mixing certain chemical cleaners, causing undesirable/dangerous reactions;
- Cleaning agents dept in unmarked or wrongly marked containers;
- Incorrect use of trolleys.
- Incorrect methods of bending and lifting;
- Unsatisfactory hygiene and sanitation standards; and
- Incorrect posture.

SAFETY AWARENESS AND ACCIDENT PREVENTION

Safety awareness should be an ongoing programme at all establishments The management of all establishments should be aware of the laws concerning safe work environments and should be provided to all staff in order to raise awareness about safety. All employees should be aware of the potential hazards in their respective departments. All heads of departments must ensure that employees follow safe job procedures, correct unsafe conditions immediately, and take adequate time to do the job so that accidents are not caused due to haste. The executive housekeeper should develop a comprehensive list of safety rules to be followed by all housekeeping employees. This can be part of the'housekeeping safety manual'.

BASIC GUIDELINES FOR THE PREVENTION OF ACCIDENTS

The following guidelines can be followed for the prevention of accidents:

- Always follow instructions when using any cleaning equipment.
- Replace caps on cleaning chemicals immediately and securely after dispensing.
- Label cleaning agents clearly.
- Keep floors clean and dry.
- Place warning and safety signs around the area while cleaning.
- Always dry hands before touching plugs, sockets, and electrical fittings.
- Mark faulty equipment as'out of order'.
- Dispose of rubbish carefully.
- Never place cigarette butts of sharp objects in the trash bag on the room attendants' carts.
- Open and shut doors carefully.
- Clean away broken glass carefully.

PROCEDURES TO FOLLOW IN CASE OF AN ACCIDENT

- When a guest or employee has met with an accident at the hotel, the procedure followed should be as follows:
  - With the help of another person, check if the victim requires any assistance.
  - Report the matter immediately to the manager concerned.
  - Either administer first aid (if you are trained to do so) or get help from trained personnel.

– Transport the victim immediately to a hospital, if required. If the injury is serious, call an ambulance for the same. Follow all necessary first-aid measures until the ambulance arrives.
– Fill in accident report form and hand it over to the manager concerned.

FIRE PREVENTION AND FIRE FIGHTING

To understand fire prevention and fire-fighting, one must know how fires are classified.

Fires may be classified into four groups, based on their source of fuel:

- *Class A*: These are fires with trash, wood, paper or other ordinary combustible material as their fuel source.
- *Class B*: These are fires with flammable or combustible liquids as their fuel source.
- Class C these are fires involving electrical equipment.
- Class D These are fires with certain ignitable metals as the fuel source

Table. Format of an Accident Report form for Employees

Accident Report Form (for employees)
Name of the injured person..
Section...
Supervisor..
Date..............................Time of report..
Exten of injury..
Was hospitalization required?
Nature of the accident
Time..................................Place..
What happened/ cause...
....
Witness 1..
Witness2 ....
Supervisor's remarks..
Supervisor's signature

Prevention of Fire

Fires may be prevented if fire hazards are identified and eliminated.

Some unsafe practices that may lead to fires are as follows:

- Guests smoking in bed.
- The hotel not providing sand urns or sufficient and appropriate ashtrays in rooms as well as public areas.
- Using high-wattage light bulbs in lamps.

- Leaving linen chute doors open.
- Storing rags and cloths with residues of cleaning polish still on them.
- Not unplugging electrical appliances when not in use.
- Using faulty electrical equipment or sockets.
- Leaving magnifying materials that are easily combustible.
- Using furnishing materials that are easily combustible.
- Each establishment must conduct fire drills on a periodic basis and ensure that all staff attend thee drills so that they know what is to be done during a fire emergency.

Fire Warning Systems

These may be electrically powered manually operated systems, automatic fire detection systems, or a combination of both. The usual components of such systems are discussed here:

Fire Alarms

These can be set off by smoke detectors, heat detectors, sprinkler systems, or pull stations. The most common types of fire alarms are the ones operated by pull stations located in corridors, lobbies, and near elevators. The pull alarms themselves are red in colour, with a glass panel that needs to be broken to set off the alarm.

Sprinklers

These are found in most hotel establishments, especially in corridors and rooms. They are situated on the ceiling and automatically spray water when the temperature rises above a certain level.

Smoke Detectors

These are set off by smoke. The two types of smoke detectors available are photoelectric detectors and ionization detectors.

Photoelectric detectors are alarms triggered off when smoke blocks a beam of light emanating from the detector. In the ionization type of smoke detectors, the alarm sounds when the detector senses a shift in electrical conductivity between two plates.

What to do in Case of Fire Emergency

In case a fire breaks out, follow the guidelines given below:

- Immediately switch on the nearest fire alarm.
- If possible, attack the fire with suitable equipment, remembering to direct the extinguishers at the base of the flames. Do not attempt to fight a fire if there is any danger of personal risk.

- Close windows and switch off all electrical appliances, including fans and lights.
- Close the door to the affected area and report to your immediate supervisor for instructions.
- Carry out instructions-for instance, rouse guests in section and direct them to the nearest fire-escape route. Each guestroom should have the route to the nearest fire escape drawn out a displayed in a place where it is most likely to be seen by the guests.
- Report to the departmental fire representative for a roll call. The housekeeper on duty should check the list (in the form of the duty rosters) of the staff who are on duty so that all those on duty can be accounted for.
- Remain at the assembly point until instructed to do otherwise.
- Do not use the lifts.

FIRST AID

The initial assistance or treatment given to a casualty for any injury or sudden illness before the arrival of an ambulance, doctor, or other qualified person is called'first aid'. The notion of'first' aid itself signifies that the casualty is likely to be in need of'secondary aid'.

PRINCIPLES OF FIRST AID

There are certain important principles involved in first aid. These are listed below.

The first aid provider must:

- Act calmly and logically;
- Be in control-both of himself/herself and the problem;
- Be gentle but fire, and speak to the casualty kindly but purposefully;
- Build up trust through talking to the casualty throughout the examination and treatment;
- Explain to the casualty what he/she is going to do;
- Answer honestly and say so in he/she does not know the answer (that is, avoid giving misleading information);
- Never leave the casualty alone and continue to talk to him/her until the ambulance or doctor arrives;
- Continuously reassure the casualty;
- Never separate a child form its parent or guardian;
- Sent the casualty to a hospital or doctor by the quickest means of transport;

- Always inform the police about serious accidents; and
- Inform the relatives of the casualty.

Do not:

- Touch a wound with your fingers or any instrument.
- Put an unclean dressing or cloth over wound.
- Allow bleeding to go unchecked.
- Move a patient unnecessarily.
- Remove clothing unnecessarily.
- Allow a patient with a fracture or suspected fracture to be moved until splints have been applied.
- Neglect shock.
- Risk burning a patient by using an unwrapped hot-water bottle or other hated object.
- Fail to give artificial respiration when needed.
- Fail to remove false teeth, tobacco, or any other eatables form the mouth of an unconscious person.
- Permit air to reach a burned skin surface.
- Wash wounds.
- Try to reduce dislocations, except of the finger and lower jaw.
- Leave a tourniquet on for over 20 minutes without loosening it.
- Forget to send for a physician.

4

Employment Relations in the Hospitality Industry

INTRODUCTION

Three terms denote the relations between managers and workers in the employment relationship-industrial relations, employee relations and employment relations. These terms are often used interchangeably, but can also convey subtle differences of meaning. They may coincide with other fields of academic enquiry and practical activity concerned with'people management', namely personnel management and HRM.

Edwards provides an insightful analysis of the employment relationship, taking as his starting point the distinction made by Fox and Flanders between market relations and managerial relations. At the root is an economic exchange between capital and labour, in which the price of labour is set as a contract of employment. In this economic exchange between the buyer and seller of labour, the parties do not share equal power resources.

In common law the employer has the right to command and the employee has a duty to obey. The commodity at the heart of the bargain is the worker's labour power. The employer will seek to maximize control over that'labour process' in order to generate a surplus as profit. The employment relationship, as an exchange and in recognition of its broader context, has also been termed the effort-reward bargain:'an economic, social and political relationship, for which employees provide manual and mental labour in return for rewards allotted by employers'. Labour only becomes useful if it can be persuaded by management to work, but this is only the beginning. Workers must demonstrate commitment, continue working to the required standards, and not deviate from those standards.

In other words workers must follow'rules', otherwise management may need to deploy corrective or punitive measures via the disciplinary procedure. Bonamy and May argue that a weakening of employment relationships since the 1970s has given rise to the emergence of employment as a service relationship. This relationship demands increased recognition of the professional qualities of the'autonomous' worker, which poses problems of incompatibility with an employment contract built upon subordination. Pay is determined by time worked, whilst idle time due to poor organization and absenteeism is reduced.

This is manifested in new forms of employment contract, externalization of employment to agencies and the sub-contracting of activities. Edwards notes that, if we were starting from scratch, 'employment relations' might be the best label.

Employment relations do not rule out all variants within the employment relationship including:

- Trade unions and formal collective bargaining;
- Individually based management/workforce relations conducted informally;
- Managerialism;
- More democratic and highly participative non-union relations;
- Men, women and disadvantaged groups;
- Employees and workers, including atypical workers and the self-employed.

Further:

- Employment relations is the main term used in the WERS sourcebook;
- Industrial tribunals have been renamed employment tribunals;
- The cornerstone of New Labour's industrial relations policy is the Employment Relations Act 1999.

A necessary departure for this book, as noted earlier, is to relocate the nexus of the employment relationship to include a relatively ignored third actor in the employment relationship-the customer. The notion of the customer in the employment relationship has been increasingly incorporated into the sociology of work, but less so in employment relations. Front-line workers, such as receptionists and servers in bars and restaurants, have to serve two'masters': their superior manager and the customer. Individual workers can have a simultaneous and coterminous employment relationship with the organization and the customer.

Organizations in services are best seen as inverted pyramids, with most workers in direct customer contact. Direct service workers engage directly with customers in an exchange that carries both economic and social connotations.

Their ability to deliver successfully hinges upon a social relationship with indirect service workers, whose actions are also instrumental to the provision of good customer service, *e.g.* an enjoyable meal or clean bedrooms. Indirect service workers are not in regular customer contact, so customer influence may be more economic than social. Hence, customers cannot be excluded from an analysis of the employment relationship.

An earlier definition has been revised:

- Employee relations in hotels and catering are about the management of employment and work relationships between managers and workers and, sometimes, customers; it also covers contemporary employment and work practices.
- Before exploring the facets of the employment relationship, we need to outline why our attitude towards things influences the way in which we see any given situation, and how it.
- Triplets watch a local football match from adjoining seats, getting an almost identical view of the game. The result is United 5 City 1. One triplet is deliriously happy, the second feels very low, while the third is able to provide a balanced analysis of events, conceding that the result was a fair one, although two of United's goals were the result of dubious refereeing and City deserved more than a single goal.
- Why did their particular attitude affect their view of the game?

Fox proposed two frames of reference as a means by which'the problems of industrial relations can be seen realistically and laid more open to solution'. The unitary perspective is a'management ideology' built on the belief that everyone in the organization shares the same goals, and that'conflict' is pathological and derives from deviance. Trade unions are seen as an intrusion, competing with management for worker loyalty.

Fox's main argument was that the unitary perspective was a naive and unrealistic frame of reference that might'distort reality and thereby prejudice solutions'. Yet in reality many managers do perceive their organizations in unitary terms, regarding themselves as the sole source of authority.

Unitarism has underpinned the'human relations school' of management, including Mayo, Likert, McGregor, Schein and Herzberg, and reasserted itself in'managerialism' and HRM. Fox suggested that the more realistic approach to managing people was to recognize that organizations are pluralistic, comprising various groups, each with their own basis of authority and sets of interests.

The'rules' of employment are not just the preserve of management. A new pay rate set by management will not necessarily be seen as fair by workers, creating an issue of potential dispute.

Therefore conflict or differences between individuals and groups are inevitable. Management should recognize this inevitability, and find the ways and means to regulate such differences. An institutional approach-collective bargaining between employers and trade unions, and the development of formal procedures to deal with disputes about pay, grievances and discipline-was considered to be the most appropriate solution. However, this is flawed to the extent that it implies both parties to the bargain have equal power resources at their disposal.

Later Fox revised his thinking and added a third perspective of radicalism, prompted by a wave of'shop floor' discontent and'wildcat' strikes at workplace level. Such worker behaviour was perceived as a reaction against exploitative and oppressive employers whose sole aim was to maximize profit. Conflict was caused by the economic disparity of society as a whole, with the principal disparity between capital and labour-employers who own and manage the means of production and workers who have their capital to sell.

This view underpins the labour process approach. This approach stresses the contradiction of managerial goals, with regulation and control having to be balanced by the need to gain workers' consent. Even today Edwards argues that unitarism cannot be written off as naive and outdated any more than radicalism because of the apparent disappearance of discontent. Ackers' neo-pluralism refocuses the employment relationship beyond the workplace by connecting the old pluralist and voluntary frames of reference with new questions raised by contemporary society. The health of society is put first, encouraging industrial relations policy initiatives that are driven by social concerns, not just a business agenda. Further he argues that the employment relationship bears hidden ethical considerations of trust and responsibility in relation to human beings.

As we shall show, both managers and workers in a variety of work and employment situations in the HI do see their workplaces in unitary terms, but this does not necessarily infer the absence of conflict. Areas of potential dispute, conflict and difference do exist between managers and workers, between managers and other managers, and between workers and customers, demonstrating that workplaces are pluralistic. In cases where workers'fiddle' or'pilfer' from their employer, the nature of their behaviour is more in keeping with a radical perspective.

Thus it is possible to observe facets of unitarism, pluralism and radicalism in the same employment relationship in which management, for the most part, remains the more powerful.

Even so, areas of common interest self-evidently exist otherwise all these relationships would break down. Consent provides the basis for resolving conflict and achieving cooperation. Cooperation is built on trust between individuals engendered at workplace level rather than through elaborate organizational mechanisms. Yet securing workers' consent is neither a straightforward nor certain process. Therefore, a mix of overt and covert conflict and cooperation underpins all employment relationships and, as we shall argue, workplace harmony owes more to pragmatic acceptance and accommodation among the parties in the employment relationship than to ideological belief.

DEVELOPMENT OF EMPLOYMENT RELATIONS

Interest in employment, now the preserve of many individuals, but not all, in western economies, derives from the fact that 'Work dominates the lives of men and women ... the management of employees both individually and collectively remains a central feature of organisational life'. Before beginning an examination of employment relations in the HI, it is useful to outline the historical development of employment relations and their relevance as a field of study, thereby introducing the reader to some of the key terms used throughout the book.

According to Hyman (1989) academic interest in employment relations was prompted when the potential stability of social order was put under threat by militant behaviour among a growing number of unionized industrial manual workers, who were no longer prepared to tolerate very bad terms and conditions of employment.

This challenge to social order, which began in the late nineteenth century, was met by two responses. First, the social welfare reformers, in keeping with their predecessors who had successfully campaigned for health and safety legislation earlier in the nineteenth century, urged legal intervention to improve the conditions under which work was performed and the terms under which it was undertaken. They achieved limited success, notably the introduction of minimum wages in four manufacturing industries in 1906.

The second and main response, which was to characterize public policy on employment relations until 1979, was that voluntary collective bargaining provided the best means to secure order within employer-employee relations. Collective bargaining is a process whereby employers and trade unions negotiate the substantive terms and conditions of employment, such as pay and hours of work, and procedural agreements that facilitate the resolution of disputes between the parties.

Industrial relations, the term in usage at the time, focused on the institutions of collective bargaining in fixing these 'rules' of employment, largely within male-dominated manufacturing environments. Collective agreements were not legally enforceable.

While public services such as the health service, the railways and the coal mines came to assume importance in industrial relations following the mass nationalization programme after the Second World War, private services remained the 'Cinderella' of British industrial relations. Even though the growth of private services such as retailing and hospitality opened up more employment opportunities for women, whose main work opportunities had been in domestic service in the earlier part of the century, unregulated, female service work was deemed not to be part of industrial relations.

Even so, the lack of collective bargaining arrangements prompted the Labour government to extend the scope of minimum wage legislation to embrace these sectors. Thus in 1945 the newly named wages councils, a form of 'state-sponsored' collective bargaining, were able to fix remuneration (any pay including basic pay, overtime and shift premiums) and paid holidays for many 'unprotected' workers in private services.

COLLECTIVE CONSENSUS AND A MORE ACTIVE STATE

Greater state intervention in employment matters was a response by both Conservative and Labour governments to the mounting economic difficulties of the 1960s, e.g. statutory and voluntary incomes policies. State intervention also constituted a response to the perceived failure of voluntary collective bargaining to provide an effective regulatory mechanism for social order and social welfare, notably to protect the interests of the low-paid, many of whom were women. This perceived breakdown prompted the government to appoint a Royal Commission in 1965, the Donovan Commission (1968), to investigate the state of employer- worker relations, in order to recommend how the 'system' could be reformed. The Donovan prescription sought to maintain voluntarism, and placed the onus on employers to improve the rules of employment, and to introduce more formal procedures for the resolution of disputes.

Donovan's prescription was not universal, because it could not be applied to large parts of private services comprising small, informally managed, non-union workplaces, where female and part-time employment was concentrated. A different approach based on legal intervention in employment relations began to develop, based on employment protection for individual employees. Early employment protection rights of the 1960s included the right to a written statement of terms and conditions of employment, statutory redundancy pay and equal pay. Workers lacking the protection of a trade union and with no recourse to formal workplace procedures could resolve employment disputes, which are those in scope of the law, by going to an industrial (now employment) tribunal.

The 1970s represented a significant turning point for legal intervention in employment relations. Britain joined the European Economic Community (EEC) in 1972. This heralded the start of a wide-ranging programme designed to establish a floor of new rights relating to matters including unfair dismissal, maternity leave, sex and race discrimination and health and safety at work. The main beneficiaries were to be those working in private services.

A Challenge to Tradition

Events of the 1980s and early 1990s effectively killed the model of voluntary collective bargaining. In pursuit of an overriding objective to deregulate the labour market and employment, successive Conservative governments systematically dismantled institutions deemed to interfere with the free working of the labour market, notably the trade unions and wages councils. Paradoxically, in spite of the government's antipathy to the EU's social action programme and subsequent opt out of the social chapter, the

EU continued to influence British employment relations in a significant way. Rulings from the European Court of Justice (ECJ) obliged Britain to introduce new legislation, e.g. the transfer of undertakings or the amendment of existing legislation relating to equal pay and sex discrimination. The floor of employment rights was both strengthened and extended.

Managers reasserted the right to manage increasingly flexible and non-standard workers under the banner of 'managerialism', in workplaces that might be labelled 'bleak houses'. An alternative version of management thinking stressed the benefits of 'commitment' over 'control'. Both approaches came to signify the two variants of HRM. 'Soft' HRM emphasized fostering commitment, improving quality and developing the human resource, whereas 'hard' HRM was contingent and calculating in its utilization of the human resource. If organizations were to survive the effects of adverse economic conditions, globalization and increasing competition, the imperative was to integrate HRM within business strategy.

The impact of HRM on industrial relations was widely debated. Other key issues in the wider academic debate included the extent of continuity and change in industrial relations, the sharp decline in trade union membership, the impact of deregulation and whether employment relations could be re-regulated.

Labour

By the mid-1990s individual relationships were catapulted firmly to the forefront of analysis of the employment relationship.

Recognition of this change had been apparent from WIRS in 1990, perhaps most notably within the HI. HI managers are free to exercise a high degree of managerial prerogative in the absence of unorganized labour, termed 'unbridled individualism'.

The election of a Labour government for the first time in nearly 20 years in 1997 raised expectations that there would be a new agenda for employment relations, although Heery's assessment was that 'it is extremely doubtful whether New Labour will issue in a new industrial relations'. New Labour's stakeholder economy is based on fairness and partnership. Fairness at work is to be achieved in two ways.

The government signed up to the EU social chapter and set about introducing a new floor of minimum employment standards, including a National Minimum Wage (NMW), and family-friendly measures. Social partnership between employers and workers is designed to foster a more consensual and cooperative relationship between employers and employees.

The Low Pay Commission (LPC), whose first task was to recommend the initial rate of the NMW, provides an early manifestation of social partnership comprising employer, worker and independent representatives. Although many of the Conservatives' trade union reforms remain in place, the introduction of statutory trade union recognition procedures might help reverse the steep decline in trade union membership.

By the time of WERS in 1998 the system of collective representation had crumbled 'to such an extent that it no longer represented the dominant model'. In reality employment relations could conform to different and diverse patterns. Private service establishments employing 25 or more employees were numerically more important than private sector manufacturing and the public sector put together.

Their share of employment increased from 26 per cent in 1980 to 44 per cent in 1998, reinforcing the point that alternative ways to view and reform employment relations were long overdue, particularly in circumstances of 'bleak house' or 'black hole' employment. Although we find these terms wanting in respect of the HI, they highlight the relevance of the industry as a unit of analysis. Consequently we shall show how these types of workplaces throw up major problems for employment relations reform.

Agenda for the Twenty-first Century

In calling for a new industrial relations paradigm, Ackers (2002) now argues that the new problem of social order focuses on links between employment and society, and that such a link provides an explicit ethical framework for policies like social partnership. He rejects the traditional industrial relations notion of workers as unattached individuals in their out-of-work lives, and argues that industrial relations can no longer ignore issues of work-life balance and corporate social responsibility. Indeed social concerns underpin 'Fairness at Work' and the 'Welfare to Work' programme, and family-friendly issues are a new addition to WERS. Hence a new definition of industrial relations as neo-pluralism:

Employment relations is the study of the social institutions involved in the normative regulation of the employment relationship and business's interaction with other stakeholders in society.

Thus Ackers rejects as inappropriate Kelly's (1997) industrial relations paradigm for the twenty-first century, which derives from a redefinition of Marxism based on socialism, workers' mobilization, economic militancy and strikes, and organized labour.

Edwards (2003a) identifies three pressing issues in contemporary employment relations: 'high commitment' or 'high involvement' work systems, the international context and economic performance. The first, although interesting, is very rarely found anywhere in Britain. Its alternative of 'low skills' and 'low wages' strikes right at the heart of much hospitality employment.

This links to economic performance, where the absence of collective bargaining is likely to have contributed to income inequality and the perpetuation of low pay in the HI, although pay may be subsidized by the state through social security and taxation. The further subsidy of low pay through tips as a defensible employment practice is a matter of conjecture. We shall also explore if particular employment relations practices can be linked to successful performance outcomes. The international context and its implications for employment relations in the HI are considered below.

A fourth pressing issue can be added. Employment relations discourse needs to recognize that prejudice and bias have been built into much of the theoretical and practical analysis, thus distorting its perspective. Gender is not the only example, but may be the most obvious.

In spite of an increasing interest in what may be described as 'women's issues', such as (un)equal pay and employment opportunities, family-friendly policies and sexual harassment, one major barrier to understanding employment relations is an assumption that they are gender neutral. The argument is that adding women's issues to the agenda is simply not good enough.

Management, trade unions and the state are not gender neutral, and therefore we need to recognize the gendered characteristics of the employment relationship and work and integrate this into our understanding of the field of employment relations. Other 'omissions' include age, ethnicity and the role of customers. We shall explore these issues throughout the book where it is possible or relevant to do so.

All these issues were placed under review in The Future of Work Programme launched by the ESRC in 1998. The Programme has supported 27 projects designed to rectify gaps in our understanding and improve the quality of information available to the policy-makers in the UK. Topics under investigation have included the future of unskilled work, business re-engineering and performance, the changing position of ethnic minorities and women in the labour market, the future for trade unions and the changing nature of the employment relationship.

Three terms denote the relations between managers and workers in the employment relationship - industrial relations, employee relations and employment relations. These terms are often used interchangeably, but can also convey subtle differences of meaning. They may coincide with other fields of academic inquiry and practical activity concerned with 'people management', namely personnel management and HRM. Edwards provides an insightful analysis of the employment relationship, taking as his starting point the distinction made by Fox (1966) and Flanders (1974) between market relations and managerial relations. At the root is an economic exchange between capital (the employer) and labour (the worker), in which the price of labour is set as a contract of employment.

In this economic exchange between the buyer (employer) and seller (worker) of labour, the parties do not share equal power resources. In common law the employer has the right to command and the employee has a duty to obey. The commodity at the heart of the bargain is the worker's labour power.

The employer will seek to maximize control over that 'labour process' in order to generate a surplus as profit. The employment relationship, as an exchange and in recognition of its broader context, has also been termed the effort-reward bargain: 'an economic, social and political relationship, for which employees provide manual and mental labour in return for rewards allotted by employers'. Labour only becomes useful if it can be persuaded by management to work, but this is only the beginning. Workers must demonstrate commitment, continue working to the required standards, and not deviate from those standards.

In other words workers must follow 'rules', otherwise management may need to deploy corrective or punitive measures via the disciplinary procedure. Bonamy and May (1997) argue that a weakening of employment relationships since the 1970s has given rise to the emergence of employment as a service relationship.

This relationship demands increased recognition of the professional qualities of the 'autonomous' worker, which poses problems of incompatibility with an employment contract built upon subordination. Pay is determined by time worked, whilst idle time due to poor organization and absenteeism is reduced.

This is manifested in new forms of employment contract (fixed-term and part-time), externalization of employment to agencies and the sub-contracting of activities. Edwards notes that, if we were starting from scratch, 'employment relations' might be the best label.

Employment relations do not rule out all variants within the employment relationship including:

- Trade unions and formal collective bargaining;
- Individually based management/workforce relations conducted informally;
- Managerialism;
- More democratic and highly participative non-union relations;
- Men, women and disadvantaged groups;
- Employees and workers, including atypical workers and the self-employed.

Further:

- Employment relations is the main term used in the WERS sourcebook;
- Industrial tribunals have been renamed employment tribunals;
- The cornerstone of New Labour's industrial relations policy is the Employment Relations Act 1999.

A necessary departure for this book, as noted earlier, is to relocate the nexus of the employment relationship to include a relatively ignored third actor in the employment relationship - the customer. The notion of the customer in the employment relationship has been increasingly incorporated into the sociology of work, but less so in employment relations. Front-line workers, such as receptionists and servers in bars and restaurants, have to serve two 'masters': their superior manager and the customer. Individual workers can have a simultaneous and coterminous employment relationship with the organization and the customer.

Organizations in services are best seen as inverted pyramids, with most workers in direct customer contact. Direct service workers engage directly with customers in an exchange that carries both economic and social connotations.

Their ability to deliver successfully hinges upon a social relationship with indirect service workers, whose actions are also instrumental to the provision of good customer service, e.g. an enjoyable meal or clean bedrooms. Indirect service workers are not in regular customer contact, so customer influence may be more economic than social. Hence, customers cannot be excluded from an analysis of the employment relationship. As shown below and explained later, an earlier definition has been revised:

Employee relations in hotels and catering is about the management of employment and work relationships between managers and workers and, sometimes, customers; it also covers contemporary employment and work practices.

THE RULES OF EMPLOYMENT AND POWER RELATIONS

We have already noted that the employment relationship is underpinned by rules, hence the continuing validity of Clegg's definition of industrial relations as'The study of the rules governing employment' which Edwards explains in more detail: This does not limit the subject to the collective relations between managements and trade unions, for a rule can derive from other sources, and there are rules governing non-union groups; nor does it restrict analysis to one sector, for it covers all paid forms of employment.

A rule is a social institution involving two or more parties which may have its basis in law, a written collective agreement, an unwritten agreement, a unilateral decree or merely an understanding that has the force of custom. In non-union settings, as much as union ones, rules determine rates of pay, hours of work, job descriptions and many other aspects of employment. The subject is about the ways in which the employment relationship is regulated. To regulate means to control, to adapt or adjust continuously or to adjust by rule.

MANAGERIAL ISSUES

While rules may be the substantive rules of employment, *e.g.* pay and conditions of employment, implicit in the notion of rules affecting people is the concept of behaviour. Management's job is to control and direct workers' behaviour to perform work to the desired standards, and thereby ensure that the rules of employment are adhered to.

Four key issues arise:

1. Rules are not always absolute and may be gendered.
2. Managerial control of workers' behaviour is underpinned by a power relationship.
3. This power relationship is unequal and may be gendered.
4. Managers have a choice of means to maximize control.

The first point is that one should caution against perceiving rules in too absolute a sense. At one end of the spectrum rules embodied in the law of the land provide a good example of formal rules. Any breach may incur very severe penalties, *e.g.* health and safety. In a workplace setting rules in practice may derive from informal understandings that can in one set of circumstances be interpreted by the worker as a permissive concession or in a different set of circumstances as something to be observed at all costs. Strawberries as a worker's perquisite during the Wimbledon lawn tennis championship are a good example. Experienced workers know that taking home unwanted strawberries is'permitted' during busy periods. When fewer staff are needed, increased managerial surveillance will be deployed to dismiss staff caught in possession of company property.

Rule-learning is part of what Polanyi refers to as'tacit skills'. As argued elsewhere:

Tacit skills, such as learning to deal with customers, are learnt in and through the very act of doing, often involving trial and error and not from following a body of procedurally-designed rules. They are seen as an interpretive achievement of the user as to how the'rules' fit the task in hand. By mastery of the rules comes the power to extend them. This example embracing the customer provides a developmental point to Edwards' observation that rule-making is difficult, and that rules have to be interpreted in action for them to have any real meaning. Specifically in the labour contract this is because the worker's ability to work is only realised as useful labour in the course of carrying out that work, hence'a rule is a complex social institution'.

In service work physical appearance and'personality', or'aesthetic labour', are an implicit part of the employment contract. Only female flight attendants, not their male colleagues, are subjected to regular weigh-ins to ensure they comply to specified weight: height ratios. This demonstrates clearly how a rule may be gendered. The second point to note is that the very essence of management seeking to control workers' behaviour is underpinned by a power relationship. Power is the capacity to pursue one's own interests individually and collectively, involving the capacity to oppose the actions of others and to pursue one's own objectives, and is embedded in continuing relationships. This does not mean power has to be exercised by either party in an overt sense.

The threat of power may be sufficient to maintain broadly consensual employment relationships, such that any disputes or differences are resolved amicably without recourse to either party seeking to deploy sanctions against the other. The third point assumes a power inequality in the employment relationship. Self-evidently an employer is more powerful than an individual worker. The employer's ability to terminate a worker's services is likely to be more detrimental to the worker than to the employer, in spite of employment protection legislation.

Yet the individual behaviours of workers, such as high labour turnover, may be detrimental to an employer, even though they are not concerted. When workers combine collectively, with or without the backing of a trade union, there is some tilt in the balance of power, because collective sanctions may be imposed against the employer.

Ultimately the outcome of the process by which each side seeks to gain concessions will depend on the relative power of the parties. For example, a plentiful supply of suitable workers in the labour market makes existing workers more readily dispensable and replaceable on the employer's terms. The opposite would be true for workers with scarce skills who can command high wages.

As Wajcman argues, gender relations are power-based and women's subordination in the workforce and workplace owes as much to trade unions as it does to managers. Spradley and Mann provide a graphic account of how the subordination of one group of female workers was brought about by another group of male workers who were the custodians of the male proprietor's trust.

The male bartenders controlled the orders, and sought to make the cocktail waitresses' job difficult by giving orders in an inconsistent and confusing way. Any mistakes became the waitresses' responsibility, even if they had been caused by the bartenders. Such was the power of the bartenders that pleasing them became more important than pleasing the customers. The fourth point is that managers have a choice of means to maximize control over workers. Friedman's'direct control' is a variant of Taylorism.

Management is responsible for planning, designing and organizing the labour process, while cheap, unskilled workers perform standardized, simple repetitive tasks. Fast food is a good case in point, and also epitomizes McDonaldization, a social critique of how contemporary society and culture are being shaped by rationalist scientific management. While Taylorism sought to control the organization of work, McDonaldization is based on rationalization, replication, standardization of products and service, and quantification. In this low trust strategy worker behaviour is controlled through the use of standardized scripts in the service encounter. In Friedman's alternative of'responsible autonomy', a high trust approach, managers delegate control to relatively privileged skilled workers who may already have elements of job control and discretion. The objective is to get workers to identify with the competitive aims of the organization so they will behave responsibly with minimum supervision.

An obvious example of where such an approach might be used is in a luxury hotel, but it is also associated with empowerment and much customer-service work. As we shall argue and implied in the example of cocktail waitresses, these and other similar approaches including'hard' and'soft' HRM provide a useful framework for analysis, but are not necessarily alternatives.

The history of hotel internationalization has been characterized by American chains that secure control and integration through highly standardized procedures and manuals of operational procedures. Yet a'soft' focus on the service encounter as the driver of competitive advantage necessitates developing a culture of customised service. Mass customization illustrated by Burger King's have it your way' slogan as a challenge to McDonald's hold on the market is proposed as an alternative paradigm to McDonaldization.

WORKERS AND CUSTOMERS

Other tensions within the employment relationship impinge upon the rules of employment and power relationships. If management is about the achievement of organizational goals through people it can be argued that managers will be successful to the extent that these goals coincide with the aims and aspirations of those people, be they workers or customers. This'matching' of broadly reciprocal needs between employers and workers may be referred to as a'psychological contract', or set of contracts. It suggests managers and workers can share goals, but this is not at all straightforward. There is not a necessarily clearcut distinction between boss and worker, or a'them and us' scenario. Further we must also account for a psychological contract with customers.

Two key points are noteworthy:

1. Organizations comprise people and are, therefore, social organizations.
2. People, as social animals, may behave in unpredictable ways.

Workers

Human beings do not necessarily behave consistently or predictably, even in the same sets of circumstances. People are citizens and customers as well as employees, and these multiple identities bring different and sometimes conflicting expectations of the organization.

This makes the management of the employment relationship an uncertain process within which there is a blend of contradictory principles around the need to control and to gain the consent of workers. Workers may seek to regain control individually or collectively when they perceive that management has operated outside the rules.

At that point workers' consent has been withdrawn and management will need to find ways to restore order and regain consent. In Lucas workers' individual response to organizational rules is seen in three main ways-to conform or be deviant in employment, or to terminate their employment. These responses are similar to Marchington's'getting on','getting by' and'getting back'.

These are behaviours deployed in circumstances where customer care and service quality are dependent on workers' use of their tacit skills, which contain both technical and attitudinal elements. Limiting the definition of tacit skills to employer-employee relations is too narrow. Marchington overlooked how workers exhibit their tacit skills in ways other than in respect of their relationship with the employer, notably the customer. The point that'getting back','getting by' and'getting on' are as much resistance strategies in the labour process as coping mechanisms is developed.

At workplace level personal relationships are likely to be closely connected to morale and success. Managers often'muck in' when required. In small workplaces the existence of a single leader, often the owner, may serve to inspire loyalty from the workforce, but it is not a one-way process, as workers' respect has to be earned.

Is it realistic to suggest that Mina, Jo and Sadie, who wait on table in the restaurant, share all the same goals as their boss? The hotel may not be doing very well, so there may be mutual concern for the survival of the business. Yet these ladies' main goal may be to serve their customers cheerfully and effectively, while at the same time enjoying some social banter among themselves and with their customers in the process of earning a reasonable wage.

Customers

Within the triadic employment relationship a simultaneous and coterminous relationship with the organization and the customer directly impinges on how workers carry out their work, and such interactions may be rewarding or stressful. The consequent effect on workers' performance may have positive or negative implications for the rules of employment: what they can earn, their prospects of promotion or actually keeping their job. Unequivocally the worker-customer relationship affects the rules governing employment and workplace behaviour.

But so do employer-customer relationships, hence the employment relationship embodies a triadic set of power relations. This relationship embodies a socio-economic exchange, and is not simply an economic exchange around the price of labour. Fox provides a useful starting point, since he noted that organizations are social organizations and how people behave is a crucial issue in the employment relationship. Even Edwards' point that'a rule is a complex social institution' does not adequately encapsulate our position. The main justification for widening the scope of this relationship derives from the fact that the service encounter is the interaction of the producer and consumer of services, and is a more complex phenomenon where financial considerations are interwoven with social ones. In hospitality the social function of service work derives from the provision of a'home away from home'.

The service encounter entails'emotion work'-the assumption of a social-self, which effectively masks the individual's own personal dispositions to act, including the need to smile and be pleasant in an uninvolved way. We have already noted that'aesthetic' and sexual labour may also be inherent in service work. It is the'normalizing' social role of service labour that distinguishes it from other wage labour. Service work cannot be understood in terms of economic rationality alone.

Examination must be based on the supposition that service work is the intended outcome of a necessarily social process in which some social interaction occurs between one or more producers and one or more consumers. The relations between three groups of people-managers, workers and customers-embody the potential for contradiction between, on the one hand, uncertainty, unpredictability, conflict and difference and, on the other hand, consent, team effort and concerted performance.

The practical benefit this book seeks to convey accrues from an understanding of the nature and scope of the rules of employment in this triadic employment relationship, and how it is regulated, primarily at workplace level.

EMPLOYMENT MANAGEMENT STYLE IN THE HOSPITALITY INDUSTRY

It is widely accepted that managers' approach to employment relations, often referred to as management style, is the result of choices that are influenced by certain constraints. The nature of the product and labour markets, organizational status and structure, including size of workplace, and culture are chief among the factors thought to place constraints on managers. Managers, as much as workers and customers, are never truly free agents. We have already noted how economic, technical, social, legal and political factors external to the workplace provide boundaries that may constrain managers' behaviour and actions. We also discussed how managers' personal frame of reference will inform the choices they make about the strategies, policies and practices they pursue, and why power relationships are integral to this process. Of particular note here is the virtual absence of trade unions to act as a countervailing force to counteract managerial power. The HI sustains a mere 2 per cent trade union density.

Managers must be able to exercise choice otherwise we would not be able to account for variations in management style among similar types of firm. In seeking to control events managers may be constrained by their own rational thinking of what is good and bad, failing to recognize that opposites are often very closely related and may even coexist simultaneously. The right to manage is so deeply ingrained into behaviour and thinking that it may dominate over their tacit acceptance of a more pluralist ethos.

Hence 'a constant underlying pressure within management both to resist any extension of joint regulation and to restore unilateral regulation wherever and whenever circumstances allow'. HRM is often seen as unitarist and a reassertion of managerial prerogative, especially the 'hard' version, even though the 'soft' variant contains some positive attributes.

While we can debate the extent to which particular constraints affect the choices that particular managers make in particular circumstances, this approach still implies a rationality that does not account for pragmatism, opportunism and reacting to events. This approach is beginning to emerge as an alternative.

That said, we take as a universal truth that all HI employers place high priority on seeking to control labour costs. As we shall argue this is achieved predominantly through 'low road' practices that may be both intentional and/ or the result of pragmatism or opportunism. This approach is so successful that managers have no incentive to take the 'high road'. Organizations that focus on quality in the service encounter exceptionally approach the management of employment by the 'high road' using more sophisticated and developmental HRM practices, but not necessarily in respect of the workforce as a whole.

CONSTRAINTS AND CHOICES

To cope with market uncertainties managers can opt for the external regulation of employment matters, choose to develop their own internal responses, or use a combination of both. Grimshaw et al. (2001) argue that internal and external market pressures mutually interact to shape employment strategy, generating a wide range of possibilities for different workforce groups. The weakening of national regulatory and collective bodies in the UK, and the accompanying widening of scope for managerial prerogative, has made managing an even more uncertain process.

Marchington and Parker (1990) suggest that stable product markets will encourage the development of 'high road' practices based on partnership, job security, systematic recruitment, selection, training and development, two-way communications and formal procedures. Turbulent market conditions, which affect large parts of the HI, militate against long-term policies, even in larger companies. They will drive 'low road' practices based on hire and fire, ad hoc recruitment, selection, training and development, low pay, one-way communication, if any, from management, and lack of procedures, reinforcing a culture of macho management.

If the economic climate deteriorates firms may be forced to change route towards 'low road' practices, graphically illustrated by the case of British Airways (BA). Keenoy (1997) identifies a wide-ranging programme of 'soft' measures, including improvements to communications and leadership, while maintaining a 'hard' approach to headcount. In respect of cabin crew, Boyd (2001) argues that 'soft' HRM in the form of a sanctimonious mission and policy statement may have provided a smoke screen for short-term, costrational HRM leading to work intensification.

Case study research has identified a more complex pattern of highly firm specific policy solutions in response to a variety of different internal and external pressures. Contradictory outcomes emerge as new policies capitalize on changing external conditions at the expense of organizational demands. New policies may be unsustainable where on aggregate they fail to develop workforce skills or fulfill career expectations. Considerable emphasis on recruitment and training in hotels, which is symptomatic of labour flux, militates against uptake of new HRM initiatives of a longer-term nature.

Organization status and structure, including size of workplace will also serve to constrain the extent to which managers can exercise choice. Not all managers own and control their own business, and in larger hotel companies, restaurant and public house chains, and contract catering firms, managers are themselves also workers reporting to a more senior manager. Managers' choices are constrained by organizational policies, as well as by the actions of other managers and subordinates.

Management is necessarily a messy business. Achieving organizational goals through people is a complex and political process, political in the sense that it involves choosing how to reconcile differences among colleagues of different status and power who may be senior managers, peers or subordinate workers. Some large HI organizations comprise many small workplaces, so we cannot necessarily generalize their management style to singlesite workplaces.

Owner managers of small firms have more freedom to make rules on the 'hoof', as there are no precedents or constraints from any higher authority. Surplus labour supply of amply skilled labour, and the simple division of labour are conducive to an ad hoc management style within the economic determinism approach of externalization. As Riley et al. (2000) note, productivity is largely a matter of matching supply to demand in the short term, because of the almost instantaneous impact of customer trends on labour supply.

This dynamic instability based on stochastic demand creates and continually reinforces a short-term perspective where small unit structure creates a style of management that is good at improvising. Reliance on a plentiful supply of unskilled labour from the labour market and hire and fire serve to enhance managerial power. The manager may be aware of the constraint of unfair dismissal legislation. By making a simple risk assessment, the manager will calculate that a fired worker will probably not bother to make a claim, if eligible, because alternative work is easily secured (and a replacement easily obtained). If the worker does proceed to employment tribunal, at worst there will be a cheap out-of-court settlement, because of the worker's low pay and short service.

Culture can be considered on three levels - organizational, national and occupational - with some crossover between the first two in the case of MNCs. Two American Case study 3.1 Workplace structure in the Australian hotel industry

Hotels may appear to be structured bureaucracies under the control of a general manager, but are essentially organic structures within which departmental managers have considerable autonomy and responsibility. Each department is a unique entity controlled by a manager skilled in that work who hires and fires, and determines the categories of labour to be used, the tasks to be performed and the timing of work.

The autonomy and responsibility invested in departmental managers encourages an informal management style and a system of rule-making that shapes the pattern of labour use (initial engagements tend to be casual), and encourages the growth of informal work practices between manager and worker designed to engender loyalty and commitment. Departmentalization and labour flexibility forms part of the hierarchy of control, shifting transaction costs (of uncertainty) to the worker, protecting the hotel from unfair dismissal litigation, and using behaviour and discipline to determine permanent employment status.

Weak and low-status HRM within hotels militates against participation in new HRM practices, such as multi-skilling, because managers fear other departments may poach good staff. This acts as a barrier to strong internal labour markets, so the external market becomes a significant mechanism for the allocation of skill.

MNCs, McDonald's and Disney, have been hailed as 'influential models of excellence in the development of particular organisational cultures or systems of production and job design with their respective implications for management and the conduct of employee relations'. International chains display more sophisticated HRM, e.g. in Greece. Larger units and those owned by foreign chains appear to veer towards the 'best practice' models of HRM.

Organizational culture encapsulates 'the way we do things around here'. Culture and values underpin the organization's identity and core purpose and new initiatives in employment relations and HRM may entail programmes of culture change, especially where there is a conscious shift towards a service quality (SQ) culture. Redman and Mathews (1998) argue that the traditional dichotomy between the 'high road' and the 'low road' has been increasingly challenged by effective quality management systems resulting in both improved quality and reduced costs. This reflects a new approach to corporate management. 'Organisational culture is rooted in the future and change' whereas work-based culture is rooted in the here and now. Occupational culture may be more readily identifiable within skilled occupations such as chefs, and may create adversity in the employment relationship where professional values conflict with commercial values. Employment relations systems reflect the society in which they operate.

Case study : Effects of Institutional Change on Large Hotels in New Zealand

A major change in the law in 1991 was designed to shift employment relations from a highly regulated environment to a minimalist and market led regime. In spite of the opportunity presented for firms to innovate on the basis of high commitment work practices, there was neither any evidence of a complete displacement of the traditional pattern of collective relations nor any indication of HRM practices designed to secure workforce commitment. Rather, any changes made to improve communications did not diminish the level of managerial control typical of the industry.

People in different countries approach work in different ways. Interestingly many of the countries discussed in this book (Australia, Canada, Britain, New Zealand and the US) display 'Anglo' characteristics - a belief in equality, acceptance of uncertainty, emphasis on personal initiative and achievement, and the right to a private life. Money and material standards are important.

By contrast European countries, largely in relation to geographical location, fall into four groups and are more diverse. Approaches that may work well in one country do not necessarily transplant well to other countries. Local managers may resist the incursion of expatriate managers who are socialized in a different culture. The application of western practices to transitional economies such as Bulgaria, and Russia may be difficult to achieve, particularly in Slovakia where there are few MNCs. Differences in national institutional arrangements and the extent to which employment systems rely on detailed regulation and labour codes contribute to national cultural differences. Changes to national institutions have not necessarily impacted upon employment relations practices.

Models and Maps

Models and maps of employment relations have developed from the constraints and choices approach in an attempt to depict variations in the management style of employment relations. A useful start point is Purcell and Sisson's (1983) five ideal types of industrial relations management:

- Traditionalists are hostile to trade unions, exploit their workforce and believe in management's right to manage.

- Sophisticated paternalist/human relations embodies strong management, but with concern for employees' welfare. Unions are kept at bay by giving employees good pay and terms of employment.
- Sophisticated moderns accept trade unions as a positive force, and there is strong emphasis on developing and maintaining informal and formal procedures for resolving disputes. There are two types of sophisticated moderns. 'Consulters' accept unions but also deploy techniques designed to enhance individual commitment. 'Constitutionalists' place more emphasis on collective agreements.
- Standard moderns take a pragmatic approach to industrial relations with recognized trade unions, with line managers taking the lead.

In reviewing management styles we have discounted any model that embraces trade unions and a collective approach because, to all intents and purposes, these are not relevant to the HI in Britain. Indeed Streeck's (1987) system of industrial governance without trade unions bears a remarkable resemblance to the way in which many HI managers have traditionally 'done business'.

The managerial line of command and authority is the only institution necessary to maintain control in highly uncertain market conditions, hence the perceived legitimacy of a unitarist form of employment relations. While we do not include the McDonaldization model here, we can note that managers often display a management style derived from an individualist and unitarist approach. HRM is dealt with separately.

Of course models and maps are not absolute constructs, as Kessler and Purcell note:

- Style is a preferred way of managing employees that may be amended in practice.
- Firms may have no real style, being essentially opportunistic in reaction to events, and cannot be depicted.
- Styles may differ in relation to different groups, notably managers, highly skilled workers and peripheral workers.

We can add a fourth point - management styles may be gendered. Rutherford's (2001) study of male and female managers in an airline confirms differences in their approach to management. Men tend to follow a more command and control style with a distancing of personal self, while women are more communicative and caring, with more emphasis on people skills such as listening rather than mere performance of the task. That said the business function is the most important determinant of management style.

The locus of management style for employment relations in the HI is best identified as falling somewhere within the models and maps of non-union relations. All authors, with the exception of Scase (1995), attribute directly or implicitly their particular approach as applicable to the HI. We should note that Lucas's (1996a) and Sisson's (1993) approaches were based on WIRS3.

Approaches to non-union employment relations

'Traditional' cost-minimization/no collectivism (Kessler and Purcell, 1995)

- Labour is a cost and factor of production
- Employee subordination part of the natural order
- Fear of union interference '! opposition or kept at arm's length
- Low pay and no job security
- Little or no training

'Fraternal autocracy'

- High financial rewards to obtain short-term commitment from skilled workers
- Owner-managers work alongside employees
- Managerial prerogative conditioned by weak market position of most employees who are unskilled
- Low pay, poor working conditions
- Non-union

'Bleak house'

- Unorganized conflict (high labour turnover and accidents)
- No grievance and health and safety procedures
- No communications and employee involvement
- No consultative committees
- Lack of employment security, including temporary contracts
- High rate of dismissals

'Black hole'

- No HRM or industrial relations
- Small privately owned organizations
- Pragmatic and authoritarian cost-cutting approachs
- Low-skill, short-service marginal workers
- Low pay and insecure conditions of employment
- Little employee involvement

'Unbridled individualism'

- High degree of managerial prerogative in the absence of organized labour
- Employers regard workers as a commodity to be controlled and constrained

- Low pay
- High employee quit rates, sickness, absence, injury, and use of grievance procedure
- High use of disciplinary sanctions and dismissal
- More limited opportunity for employees to challenge management
- Little consultation, especially on health and safety, or employee involvement

'Determined opportunism'

- High degree of managerial prerogative in the absence of organized labour
- Workforce structuring includes high reliance on so-called casuals with no contract
- Majority of workforce ('peripheral' unskilled) are subject to more 'hard' form of HRM
- Not constrained in dismissing workers, failing to comply with many minimum legal requirements, or observing the law in spirit
- Extreme instance of 'retaining control/cost-control' management

Doherty (2002) argues that the way in which the state of employment management in the HI is perceived depends on how it is benchmarked, either as industrial relations/personnel management or HRM. She suggests that the measure of HRM may invite more positive conclusions, especially in larger organizations and workplaces.

There may be some truth in this where the issue of service quality has been embraced, predicated on a redefinition of organizational purpose and a programme of culture change that embraces a clear strategy for long-term success and competitive advantage. Here there is some considerable interest in HRM within hotel and restaurant chains cite the case of a luxury hotel in New Zealand where a distinct set of HRM practices introduced in support of the strategic decision towards quality enhancement demonstrated very positive outcomes against key performance indicators, especially overall guest satisfaction and financial performance. Indeed Hoque (1999a) asserts that hotels are more interested in HRM than manufacturing firms. Conversely do not find a clear relationship between business strategy and the approach to HRM in designer restaurants.

However, there are two problems with Doherty's argument. All been developed explicitly as an alternative to the trade union/collective industrial relations paradigm. Second, her conclusion that HRM is about managerial control gained through indirect and direct methods is not necessarily a good deal for the workers. Indeed one major piece of evidence she cites in support of this comes from research about management development, which suggests that managers may be the beneficiaries of 'soft' HRM, but not the workers, reaffirming that this variation of HRM is directed only at managers. Rather it infers a cost-minimization route for the majority, and is symptomatic of McDonaldization where labour flexibility and work standardization militate against the development of strategic HRM systems and internal labour markets.

In discussing the role of HRM in the management of employment, we begin with an overview of key issues that encapsulate the way in which HRM has emerged and become established in mainstream thinking. Not everybody subscribes to a new HRM model and orthodoxy of 'people management', notably those maintaining the broadly personnel management tradition. Even then among both camps there is a considerable divergence of view as to what HRM (or personnel management) is and means, how it can be operationalized and its effects measured, and its relationship with corporate performance. As Woods (1999) suggests HR(M) is a paradox that has never really been mastered. We then turn in more detail to issues that have most relevance to the management of hospitality employment, notably to account for a psychological contract and service work.

Key Issues in HRM Discourse

HRM is a phenomenon of the 1980s when, according to Streeck (1987), the key issue for management was to find ways of managing in an unprecedented degree of economic uncertainty, which derived from a need for continuous rapid adjustment to an increasingly turbulent market. Hence the imperatives that HRM issues should be integrated with business strategy, and that HRM should be able to demonstrate its contribution to business performance (from the expectancy model, see high performance practices below).

Issues such as commitment, quality, flexibility and adaptability became important. And so HRM was born. HRM also stresses the importance of the devolving the ownership and delivery of HR initiatives from specialist HR managers to line managers.

Others deny that HRM represents anything different or new. Armstrong claims HRM is a 'construct largely invented by academics and popularised by consultants', yet Grant and Oswick (1998) found a majority of practitioners agreed that HRM was different from personnel management. Gennard and Kelly (1995) and Torrington et al. (2002) are among those who regard HRM as the next stage in the evolution of personnel management. Equally there has been a growth in the proportion of specialists using HR in their title. These specialists are better qualified, more involved in strategic planning, more likely to use HRM practices than their counterparts using the title 'personnel', and most likely to be found in foreign-owned firms. One outcome has been a realignment of the personnel/line manager relationship, with more personnel work being devolved down the line. Yet in the more cost-conscious and value-added environment line managers are making more, not less, use of their specialist personnel advisers. The personnel function does contribute to corporate objectives by being delivered in many different but flexible forms. It is not necessarily the case that an organization not acting strategically will mean that the workforce is not managed in a strategic way. Hence strategic management of people is not purely within the domain of the HR department, and can be diffused throughout the organization and owned and directed by the line.

The emphasis within HRM discourse has remained largely managerialist because of the emphasis on management's cost and performance concerns, hence a management practice research agenda. The management of employment also tends to be discussed in terms of bipolar opposites in and around the metaphors of 'hard' and 'soft'. Key instances include high and low trust work practices, direct control vs. responsible autonomy, control vs. commitment and 'high road' vs. 'low road'. Here managers may exercise strategic contingency choice in terms of which approach best fits their organization.

In some respects these divergences are symptomatic of some of the differences between personnel management and HRM. Within personnel management people are more likely to be recognized and treated as human beings, whereas in HRM they are treated as people in the 'soft' variant and resources in the 'hard' variant.

A further criticism of HRM is that it is not gender neutral, with Townley (1994) being an exception in making gender more visible within her analysis. Dickens (1998) argues HRM policies and practices perpetuate rather than challenge gender inequality.

In terms of securing employee commitment assumptions about women being less committed than men will affect the shape of the core-periphery, and determine which jobs are full-time or part-time. Cost-cutting 'hard' HRM has underpinned existing sex segregation. Wajcman (2000) echoes these observations, pointing out that men are most likely to be found in occupations where management is convinced of a high quality strategy, whereas women are most likely to be found in low-skill jobs where management feels competition on costs is the most viable option.

High Road' or 'low road' HRM

There are two broad approaches to HRM, both of which have been found wanting. The first, a 'high road' version, is generally agreed to comprise a list of tangible practices, with 'best practice' HRM or 'bundles' of practices having the greatest impact on performance. Two groups of practices can be identified:

Some practices may be core requirements, e.g. selection, training, communications and reward. Others are more marginal because they do not necessarily have general application, e.g. family-friendly policies, profit-related pay and share ownership. An alternative approach stresses that HRM may be contingent, with 'best fit' HRM differing according to the stage in the business life cycle, the strategy-structure configuration and the business strategy being pursued.

Schuler and Jackson (1987) identify three alternative 'best fit' strategies - innovation, quality enhancement and cost-reduction - but acknowledge that organizations may pursue two or more competitive strategies simultaneously. Hence 'best fit' may embrace both 'high road' and 'low road' approaches. Espousal of the 'best practice' approach suggests that the 'sophisticated paternalist' and 'consultative' models of industrial relations management (Purcell and Sisson, 1983) triumph over 'bleak houses' and 'black holes', in effect denying them legitimacy when they undoubtedly exist. Legge (1995b) proceeds from the basis that HRM has never been anything but 'hard'. 'Some managements have always preferred a unitarist approach and have exploited their workers - HRM may have provided a language to justify that approach but was not responsible for it'.

Marchington and Grugulis (2000) point out that the rhetoric of HRM disguises the way in which it reinforces managerial control, sometimes against workers' interests or wishes.

Indeed the rhetoric of 'best practice' HRM can be turned on its head to depict 'low road' HRM as the following examples show:

- The practice of teamworking can be regarded as a means to replace over the shoulder managerial control by peer surveillance.
- Empowerment is about getting workers to take more responsibility with no commensurate increase in reward.
- Using the management chain to cascade information simply denies employees any voice in what is going on around them.

In support of the contingency approach Cappelli and Crocker-Hefter (1996) caution against 'best practice' and benchmarking, suggesting each organization should develop its own set of core competencies to reflect its own distinctiveness. Conversely others have observed that international pressures have driven countries and companies to adopt similar HRM concepts, regulations and practices.

Purcell (1999) considers that a 'best practice' prescription is a cul-de-sac, while contingency and 'best fit' HRM are a chimera. Both are predicated upon the logic of rational choice and neglect other organizational processes at work.

Importantly they fail to identify circumstances in which particular HRM practices are successful. Others share Purcell's scepticism, denying that HRM can exist in the diametrically opposite forms of 'soft' and 'hard'. Policies are always both 'hard' and 'soft', e.g. McDonald's provides all the support that employees need to perform to the required level, yet it deploys a 'no excuses' policy if they do not conform. Legge (1995b) sees the implementation of

Walton's soft model of mutuality being restricted to knowledge-based industries seeking value added. Even though the majority of employees may fall within this larger than normal privileged core, there may still be a minority for whom harder conditions exist.

Keenoy's (1999) metaphor of HRM as a hologram, or virtual image, usefully encapsulates why the HRM debate has become somewhat sterile. As a hologram HRM changes its appearance as we move around its image, and appears different each time we look at it. It is akin to quality, something that is always in the process of becoming (a continuous and never-ending process).

The paradox remains why so few American (Milkman, 1998) and British workplaces take the 'high road' to employment management. While the UK historical tradition does not favour this approach, it is also likely to have been undermined by the devolution of HR activities and associated budgets, which are necessary to measure the contribution of HRM. Thus line managers' HR actions will be driven by adherence to short-term financial targets, and working to budgets will drive a short-term employment relations agenda, encouraging a deterioration towards 'low road' practices.

Ultimately people are always expendable. Labour costs may be a significant proportion of operating costs, and are always far easier to trim than other fixed costs. BA cannot cut the cost of fuel or new aircraft, so it is cheaper to sack and re-employ sizeable numbers of workers because re-employment costs are lower than exit costs. It is hardly surprising, then, that the overall conclusion from WERS was that the broad approach to employment relations management in Britain was 'one of retaining control and doing what they could to control costs'.

As the HI product is highly diverse and ever-changing, there is no reason why 'high road' HRM should be effective, and there will be circumstances in which other HRM strategies, including cost-control will be effective. Indeed support for this comes from contingency models of HRM. In new businesses the personal influence of the founder and an entrepreneurial spirit will predominate over a clearly defined organization or HRM structure. As organizations mature and become more complex quality assurances, standardization, systems, structures controlling costs and increasing efficiency begin to emerge.

These are heightened where there are plans to expand a chain under franchises. Concurrently more attention is given towards systematic 'people management', including motivating managers, spreading values and developing a service culture, in order to sustain the business. In short there is a mix of 'hard' and 'soft' measures that conforms to Lashley's 'promise of control and commitment'.

A Psychological Contract

A further problem with the 'best practice' approach is that it does not take account of employees' view of HRM within the psychological contract. Renewed interest in the psychological contract and taking account of employees' expectations has become an increasingly important dimension of HRM. The concept of the psychological contract, where employees' needs are necessarily satisfied to ensure commitment to organizational objectives that will translate into business success, has remained the keystone of Torrington's philosophy of HRM as an emergent version of personnel management.

Grant (1999) identifies two approaches. The first derives from Argyris (1960) and Schein (1978) who focus on employer-employee perceptions to the exchange implied by the employment relationship within the broader context of social processes. Alternatively perceptions are shaped in the mind of the employee.

All approaches draw from expectancy theory, where the state of the psychological contract is influenced by our desired goals and outcomes, while the experience we have of these goals and outcomes determines our motivation to work and our behaviour at work. Two types of contract can be identified:

- Transactional - characterized by short-term security with most emphasis on financial reward.
- Relational - where long-term employment security is based on a mixture of loyalty, commitment and financial reward.

The nature of the contract following recruitment appears to be linked with new recruits' career motivations and intentions to stay. In transactional contracts workers may perceive regular job change as a prerequisite to career development, a point frequently noted in respect of hospitality workers. Consequently they may expect less from their employer in terms of consultation, appraisal and job security in the knowledge that they will be moving on.

While in one sense 'soft' HRM is implied in a relational contract, and 'hard' HRM is implied in a transactional contract, Grant (1999) questions the extent to which HRM policies and practices viewed across these dichotomies have led to a change in the nature of the psychological contract. Indeed employees may experience both types of psychological contract simultaneously, as noted in the case of part-time students, but it is important to emphasize that their financial reward is relatively poor.

Employees draw on past and current employment experience in order to rationalize and create their own sense of reality in relation to work. A satisfied employee will adopt and believe the prevailing HRM rhetoric. Gibb (2001) also argues that bringing employees into the equation will help to shed light on whether HRM leads to real benefits or exploitation and injustice. Fears that employees are more likely to display a preponderance of negative work attitudes have not been borne out by the WERS findings of general employee satisfaction at work. Employees are generally appreciative and positive about HRM systems, while unhappy employees may still experience effective HRM.

NATURE OF THE HOTEL INDUSTRY

Hotels and other accommodations are as diverse as the many family and business travellers they accommodate. The industry includes all types of lodging, from upscale hotels to RV parks. Motels, resorts, casino hotels, bed-and-breakfast inns, and boarding houses also are included. In fact, in 2004 nearly 62,000 establishments provided overnight accommodations to suit many different needs and budgets.

Establishments vary greatly in size and in the services they provide. *Hotels* and *motels* comprise the majority of establishments and tend to provide more services than other lodging places.

There are five basic types of hotels—*commercial, resort, residential, extended-stay,* and *casino*. Most hotels and motels are *commercial* properties that cater mainly to business people, tourists, and other travellers who need accommodations for a brief stay. Commercial hotels and motels usually are located in cities or suburban areas and operate year round. Larger properties offer a variety of services for their guests, including a range of restaurant and beverage service options—from coffee bars and lunch counters to cocktail lounges and formal fine-dining restaurants.

Some properties provide a variety of retail shops on the premises, such as gift boutiques, newsstands, drug and cosmetics counters, and barber and beauty shops. An increasing number of full-service hotels now offer guests access to laundry and valet services, swimming pools, and fitness centres or health spas.

A small, but growing, number of luxury hotel chains also manage condominium units in combination with their transient rooms, providing both hotel guests and condominium owners with access to the same services and amenities. Larger hotels and motels often have banquet rooms, exhibit halls, and spacious ballrooms to accommodate conventions, business meetings, wedding receptions, and other social gatherings.

Conventions and business meetings are major sources of revenue for these hotels and motels. Some commercial hotels are known as conference hotels—fully self-contained entities specifically designed for meetings. They provide physical fitness and recreational facilities for meeting attendees, in addition to state-of-the-art audiovisual and technical equipment, a business centre, and banquet services.

Resort hotels and *motels* offer luxurious surroundings with a variety of recreational facilities, such as swimming pools, golf courses, tennis courts, game rooms, and health spas, as well as planned social activities and entertainment. Resorts typically are located in vacation destinations or near natural settings, such as mountains, the seashore, theme parks, or other attractions. As a result, the business of many resorts fluctuates with the season.

Some resort hotels and motels provide additional convention and conference facilities to encourage customers to combine business with pleasure. During the off season, many of these establishments solicit conventions, sales meetings, and incentive tours to fill their otherwise empty rooms; some resorts even close for the off-season.

Residential hotels provide living quarters for permanent and semi permanent residents. They combine the comfort of apartment living with the convenience of hotel services. Many have dining rooms and restaurants that also are open to residents and to the general public.

Extended-stay hotels combine features of a resort and a residential hotel. Typically, guests use these hotels for a minimum of 5 consecutive nights. These facilities usually provide rooms with fully equipped kitchens, entertainment systems, ironing boards and irons, office space with computer and telephone lines, fitness centres, and other amenities.

Casino hotels provide lodging in hotel facilities with a casino on the premises. The casino provides table wagering games and may include other gambling activities, such as slot machines and sports betting. Casino hotels generally offer a full range of services and amenities and also may contain conference and convention facilities.

In addition to hotels and motels, *bed-and-breakfast inns, recreational vehicle (RV) parks, campgrounds,* and *rooming and boarding houses* provide lodging for overnight guests. *Bed-and-breakfast inns* provide short-term lodging in private homes or small buildings converted for this purpose and are characterized by highly personalized service and inclusion of breakfast in the room rate. Their appeal is quaintness, with unusual service and decor.

RV parks and campgrounds cater to people who enjoy recreational camping at moderate prices. Some parks and campgrounds provide service stations, general stores, shower and toilet facilities, and coin-operated laundries. While some are designed for overnight travellers only, others are for vacationers who stay longer. Some camps provide accommodations, such as cabins and fixed campsites, and other amenities, such as food services, recreational facilities and equipment, and organized recreational activities. Examples of these overnight camps include children's camps, family vacation camps, hunting and fishing camps, and outdoor adventure retreats that offer trail riding, white-water rafting, hiking, fishing, game hunting, and similar activities.

Other short-term lodging facilities in this industry include *guesthouses,* or small cottages located on the same property as a main residence, and *youth hostels*—dormitory-style hotels with few frills, occupied mainly by students traveling on limited budgets. Also included are *rooming and boarding houses,* such as fraternity houses, sorority houses, off-campus dormitories, and workers' camps. These establishments provide temporary or longer term accommodations that may serve as a principal residence for the period of occupancy. These establishments also may provide services such as housekeeping, meals, and laundry services. In recent years, hotels, motels, camps, and recreational and RV parks affiliated with national chains have grown rapidly. To the traveller, familiar chain establishments represent dependability and quality at predictable rates. National corporations own many chains, although many properties are independently owned but affiliated with a chain through a franchise agreement.

Many independently operated hotels and inns participate in national reservations services, thereby appearing to belong to a larger enterprise. Also, many hotels join local chambers of commerce, boards of trade, convention and tourism bureaus, or regional recreation associations in order support and promote tourism in their area.

Increases in competition and in the sophistication of travellers have induced the chains to provide lodging to serve a variety of customer budgets and accommodation preferences. In general, these lodging places may be grouped into properties that offer luxury, all-suite, moderately priced, and economy accommodations. The numbers of limited-service or economy chain properties—economy lodging without extensive lobbies, restaurants, or lounges—have been growing. These properties are not as costly to build and operate. They appeal to budget-conscious family vacationers and travellers who are willing to sacrifice amenities for lower room prices.

While economy chains have become more prevalent, the movement in the hotel and lodging industry is towards more extended-stay properties. In addition to fully equipped kitchenettes and laundry services, the extended-stay market offers guest amenities such as in-room access to the Internet and grocery shopping. This segment of the hotels and other accommodations industry has eliminated traditional hotel lobbies and 24-hour front desk staffing, and housekeeping is usually done only about once a week. This helps to keep costs to a minimum.

All-suite facilities, especially popular with business travellers, offer a living room or sitting room in addition to a bedroom. These accommodations are aimed at travellers who require lodging for extended stays, families traveling with children, and business people needing to conduct small meetings without the expense of renting an additional room.

Increased competition among establishments in this industry has spurred many independently owned and operated hotels and other lodging places to join national or international reservation systems, which allow travellers to make multiple reservations for lodging, airlines, and car rentals with one telephone call. Nearly all hotel chains operate online reservation systems through the Internet.

HOSPITALITY AND LOADGING

Organizing, the process of structuring human and physical resources in order to accomplish organizational objectives, involves dividing tasks into jobs, specifying the appropriate department for each job, determining the optimum number of jobs in each department, and delegating authority within and among departments. One of the most critical challenges facing lodging managers today is the development of a responsive organizational structure that is committed to quality.

The framework of jobs and departments that make up any organization must be directed toward achieving the organization's objectives. In other words, the structure of a lodging business must be consistent with its strategy. Managers give structure to a hotel and lodging through job specialization, organization, and establishment of patterns of authority and span of control.

There are as many degrees of job specialization within the lodging industry as there are types of organizations—and there are many types of organizations. One extreme is the case of a hotel where the owner/operator is responsible for checking in the guests, servicing their needs, taking care of the housekeeping for the guest rooms, maintaining the building and grounds, and checking out the guests. There is, to be sure, much to recommend this method of work. It is rewarding to have total control over a project from beginning to end, and many people find it motivating to see the results of their efforts.

However, as the demand for additional products or services increases (i.e., if additional rooms are added or another hotel is purchased), it becomes more and more difficult for an individual to do his or her job well. One benefit of the increased workload is increased revenue, which would enable the individual hotel operator to add housekeeping staff, one or more front desk agents to check in and check out the additional guests, and engineering and maintenance personnel to care for the building and grounds.

As a general rule, specialization increases worker productivity and efficiency. On the other hand, delegating jobs increases the need for managerial control and coordination. Someone has to make sure that housekeeping staff come in after the painters have repainted a room (and that the paint is dry), not before! A crucial element of hotel and lodging management is coordinating the many specialized functions within hotels so that the organization runs smoothly.

Specialization has its own set of problems; it can result in workers performing the same tasks over and over again. A point can be reached where the degree of specialization so narrows a job's scope that the worker finds little joy or satisfaction in it. Signs of overspecialization include workers' loss of interest, lowered morale, increasing error rate, and reduction in service and product quality.

One solution to this problem is to modify jobs so that teams can perform them. Instead of a single guest room attendant being assigned to a group of rooms, a work team in a hotel housekeeping department might clean all of the rooms on a particular floor. Some establishments use teams regularly throughout the organization; others use teams more selectively. Teams can be directed by a manager or can be self managed. The idea behind self-managed work teams is for workers to become their own managers, which increases their self-reliance as well as develops a talent pool.

A concept called the quality circle is based on the belief that the people who actually do the work, rather than their managers, are the ones who are best able to identify, analyze, and correct problems they encounter. The idea originated in Japan in 1962.

The quality circle is a group of employees, usually fewer than ten, who perform similar jobs and meet once per week to discuss their work, identify problems, and present possible solutions to those problems. For example, a quality circle might be formed among front desk agents. The group forwards its findings and proposals to management for evaluation and action. Quality circles are most successful when they are part of an organization- wide improvement effort. American business picked up on the quality circle concept in the mid-1970s.

The Lodging Establishment

As their facilities grow in size, lodging managers are faced with the need to group certain jobs in order to ensure efficient coordination and control of activities. These job groupings are usually called departments. In general, departments might be grouped as front of the house (those departments in which employees have guest contact, such as front desk), and back of the house (where employees have little guest contact, such as accounting). However, separating departments by function is the most common method of organizing a hotel or a lodging business.

The limited-service hotel, a full-service hotel with under 500 rooms, and a full-service hotel with over 500 rooms. There may be as few as 2 or as many as 50 employees in a particular department. In a very small lodging business, such as a bed-and-breakfast, the owner can supervise each department. However, as the lodging business increases in size, it is most effective to create managerial positions within departments.

Typically, the rooms department (called the front desk department in a limited-service facility) includes reservations, the front office, housekeeping, and telephone or PBX. In smaller full-service hotels, security and engineering might also be included in the rooms department. Responsibilities of the rooms department include reservations, guest reception, room assignment, tracking the status of rooms (available or occupied), prompt forwarding of mail and phone messages, security, housekeeping of guest rooms and public spaces such as lobbies, and answering guests' questions.

To perform these many duties effectively, the rooms department may be divided into a number of specialized subunits. To complicate matters, in many instances these subunits are also referred to as departments. For example, the laundry department. Because of its specialized function, little of the knowledge and skills required to manage a laundry operation is transferable to other areas of hotel operations. The front office is one of the most important departments in a hotel, as it often offers the only contact between guests and staff.

A hotel's front office is where guests are greeted when they arrive, where they are registered and assigned to a room, and where they check out. Usually, the telephone operator, other guest communications functions, and the bell staff or those employees responsible for delivering luggage and messages and attending to special guest requests also fall under the front office umbrella. The reservations department takes and tracks the hotel's future bookings. The housekeeping department is responsible for cleaning guest rooms and public spaces. Because of their specialized nature, the security and engineering departments are discussed in separate sections.

A great deal of interdependence exists among the subunits of the rooms department. For example, reservations must inform the front office of the number of presold rooms each day to ensure that a current inventory of salable rooms is always available. On the other hand, the front office must let reservations know whenever walk-in guests (those who do not have reservations) register. A similar level of cooperation is required between the front office and housekeeping. When a guest checks out, the front office must inform housekeeping so that the room may be cleaned.

Once a room is cleaned, housekeeping must inform the front office so that the room may be sold. Certain tasks within the rooms department must occur in a specific order.

For example, housekeeping cannot properly provision a guest room if the laundry does not supply enough clean towels or bed sheets. Engineering cannot replace a defective light switch in a guest room if housekeeping does not report the problem. Effective management of this busy department calls for standardized plans, procedures, schedules, and deadlines, as well as frequent direct communication between the executives who manage the key operating units of the rooms department.

Security

The hotel and lodging business is vulnerable to security and safety problems. Problems can be created by guests, employees, or intruders. Security breaches can result in embezzlement, theft, arson, robbery, and even terrorism. Depending on the size of a hotel or a lodging establishment, the security function may be handled by a fully staffed department on site, contracted to an outside security company, or assigned to designated staff members or on-premises supervisory personnel in the rooms department. In a larger, full-service hotel, the director of security may report directly to the general manager.

In smaller hotels, the security function might become a task of the rooms department.

Engineering

Typically, the engineering department's responsibilities include preventive maintenance; repair; replacement; improvement and modification to furniture, fixtures, and equipment (FFE); and ensuring uninterrupted provision of utilities (gas, electricity, water). Preventive maintenance involves routine checks and inspection of the key components of all equipment. Maintenance of recreational facilities may be part of the engineering department's responsibilities. In particular, swimming pools require extensive maintenance to ensure proper filtration and to prevent the accumulation of algae and other conditions unsuitable for swimming.

Prompt repair minimizes loss of productivity in other hotel operating departments and inconvenience to hotel guests. When a particular FFE has reached the end of its useful life and repair is no longer cost-effective, replacement is indicated. Improvement projects enhance the existing operation or reduce operating costs of the facility. Modification projects alter the existing operation to accommodate one or more new functions.

One hotel might have a large engineering staff that includes plumbers, carpenters, painters, electricians, and other technicians. Another might have maintenance personnel who have general knowledge and understanding of the hotel's operations but rely on outside contractors for specialized jobs. In larger, full-service hotels, engineering may be a separate department, with a director who reports directly to the resident manager.

The primary function of the food and beverage department is to provide food and drink to a hotel's guests. In earlier times, when an inn had a single dining room that could hold a limited number of guests, this was a fairly simple task. Today, however, providing food and drink is much more complicated.

A large hotel might well have a coffee shop, a gourmet restaurant, a poolside snack bar, room service, two banquet halls, and ten function rooms where food and beverages are served. It might also have a lounge, a nightclub, and a lobby bar. On a busy day (or night), it's quite likely that functions will be booked in many outlets at the same time. In addition, some outlets may have multiple events scheduled for a single day. As you can see, there is great diversity in the types of activities performed by a food and beverage department, requiring a significant variety of skills on the part of its workers.

Patterns of Authority

The delegation of authority creates a chain of command, the formal channel that defines the lines of authority from the top to the bottom of an organization. The chain of command consists of a series of relationships from the highest position in the organization to the lowest. The chain of command specifies a clear reporting relationship for each person in the organization and should be followed in both downward and upward communication.

Following the chain of command enables each new employee, no matter what his or her position, to know exactly for whom and to whom he or she is responsible.

When designing an organizational structure, managers must consider the distribution of authority. Defined simply, authority is the organizationally sanctioned right to make a decision. Authority can be distributed throughout an organization or held in the hands of a few select employees. Decentralization is the process of distributing authority throughout an organization.

In a decentralized organization, an organization member has the right to make a decision without obtaining approval from a higher-level manager. Centralization is the retention of decision-making authority by a high-level manager. Traditionally, hotel and lodging management has been very centralized, probably due to its roots in small, owner-operated lodging. In recent years, as the hotel and lodging industry has expanded, decentralization has become a more frequent style of operation.

Decentralization has several advantages. Managers are encouraged to develop decision-making skills, which help them advance in their careers. The autonomy afforded by this style of operation also increases job satisfaction and motivation. When employees are encouraged to perform well, the profitability of the organization increases. Many hotel and lodging organizations have begun to empower employees and supervisors to make decisions that typically have been made by managers. One example that we have already discussed is the use of the quality circle. For example, if a front desk agent determines that a guest's bill is incorrect, in a decentralized organization the agent has the power to make the correction immediately. If that same front desk agent determines that a guest's stay has been unsatisfactory, he or she has the power to reduce the guest's bill by an amount previously specified by management.

Additional challenges, control of the process, and quality assessment become part of everyone's job, and each employee is given the authority to take positive actions that will lead to high quality and improved performance.

Span of Control

Span of control refers to the number of people who report to one manager or supervisor. A wide span of control results in a flat organization— that is, a large number of employees reporting to one supervisor. A narrow span of control results in a tall organization, in which a small number of employees report to a supervisor, necessitating a larger number of supervisors. No formula exists for determining the ideal span of control. The following factors determine the most appropriate span of control: task similarity, training and professionalism, task certainty, frequency of interaction, task integration, and physical dispersion.

When a large number of employees perform similar tasks, the span of control can be increased. When the employees perform very different tasks, the supervisor must give each subordinate more individual attention in order to keep in touch with the different types of tasks; this requires a narrower span of control.

For example, the rooms department manager might easily manage the front desk agents and housekeepers until the brand standards for check-in or checkout of a guest increase in complexity and the standards for the various types of rooms and their cleaning procedure increase in detail. At this time, the rooms department manager's span of control must be narrowed. The better trained and more skilled a subordinate is, the less supervision is required. For example, a front desk agent might require a higher level of training and skill than a room service waiter. Thus, a front desk supervisor can supervise more employees (wider span of control) than the room service supervisor (narrower span of control).

Task certainty refers to the predictability of a task. Routine tasks allow management to devise standard procedures for subordinates to follow, minimizing questions about the job and widening the span of control. On the other hand, close supervision is called for when tasks are ambiguous and uncertainty is great. For example, the task of checking a guest in or out of the hotel can be documented and standard procedures can be created, so the front desk manager can have a relatively wide span of control over the front desk agents.

However, because of the diversity of customers the sales manager encounters, the tasks of a hotel sales manager are less certain. The director of sales is responsible for coaching the sales managers, observing sales calls, and ensuring deal closings; these tasks require a hands-on approach that limits the number of employees the director of sales can handle, narrowing the span of control.

If the supervisor-subordinate relationship requires frequent interaction, the span of control must be narrow. If interaction is infrequent, the span of control can be wide. For example, the hotel controller must review regularly the status of collections and payments with staff.

In contrast, the frequency of interaction between the chief engineer and his or her subordinates is directed by written work orders in most circumstances and thus requires less direct communication, enabling a wider span of control.

If the supervisor must integrate and coordinate the tasks of subordinates, the span of control narrows. For example, in the production of a meal for one table of four guests with different appetizers, salads, and entrées, the chef must have a narrow span of control to ensure that each component of the meal is assembled correctly and delivered to service personnel on a timely basis. The span of control of the executive housekeeper can be much wider because the procedure for cleaning and preparing each guest room is similar, if not exactly the same, for every room.

Physical dispersion refers to the distribution of employees within the lodging establishment. For example, if the executive housekeeper has guest room attendants on 20 floors in two buildings and the front desk manager has all front desk agents located in one place, the span of control would narrow for the executive housekeeper and widen for the front desk manager.

The ideal number of people that one person can supervise depends on a variety of factors. Consistent with trends in organizational structure such as teams, quality circles, and employee empowerment, many hotel and lodging organizations are widening their span of control. The objective behind these trends is to develop a flatter, more responsive organizational structure in which employees can make decisions without going through several levels of management.

Functional Organization Design

The most important strength of a functional organizational design is efficiency. The performance of common tasks allows for work specialization, which increases overall productivity. Workers develop specialized skills and knowledge more rapidly. Training is easier because of the similarity of tasks and the resulting opportunities for inexperienced workers to learn from experienced workers. This helps new employees quickly learn the kinds of behaviour that lead to success and promotion. Coordination of activities within functional departments is easier than in more broadly based organizations.

A functional organization fosters efficiency, teamwork, and coordination of activities within individual units. However, the functional organization's most important strength is also the source of its greatest shortcoming. The success of a hotel as a business is measured by its overall performance and not by the performance of any one department. A hotel with spotless guest rooms will not be successful if guests' front desk experiences are not up to par. Even if guests' dining experiences are superb, the hotel will fall flat on its face if its rooms are dismal. It is sometimes difficult for each department to fully appreciate its role in the overall success of the organization. It is vital that each department keep in mind the hotel-wide goals of customer service and profitability rather than focus narrowly on its own concerns. Some means must be found to coordinate the activities of functional departments and to set hotel-wide strategies and goals. A hotel's functional organization demands strong leadership.

New initiatives in hotels often require cooperation and coordination between functional departments. New ideas tend to be stillborn if department heads lack a hotel-wide perspective or have difficulty coordinating their activities. The tendency to concentrate on doing things right often overshadows the organization's ability to do the right thing.

The GM, as the chief executive of the hotel, emerges as the single person capable of providing the overall organizational direction, decision making, coordination, and arbitration needed to make a hotel's functional departments work together effectively. A hotel simply cannot run itself from the departmental level. Thus, the GM must be a strong leader to be effective.

Meetings and Committees

An organizational chart is useful in identifying the formal reporting and authority relationships of a hotel or a lodging enterprise. However, it is not of much help in coordinating administrative units at the department and subdepartment level.

Consider this scenario. If the director of sales increases group bookings without consulting other hotel departments, a disaster is in the making. If the reservations department is not consulted, the sales department might guarantee more rooms to a group than are actually available at a price lower than the reservations department's quarterly goal. If the convention services manager is not consulted, necessary meeting rooms might not be available. If the food and beverage department is not consulted, the group might be sold a banquet that exceeds the hotel's capabilities. If the accounting department is not consulted, credit terms might be extended that violate the credit manager's policies. If the front office is not consulted, the group might experience lengthy delays at check-in (groups are usually preassigned rooms and keys).

The executive operating committee (EOC) of a hotel, made up of the general manager and senior executives from each department, is designed to increase the level of coordination between departments. There is no standard membership for this committee, but it usually comprises those executives who report directly to the general manager. The EOC is also responsible for a hotel's major budgetary units, such as the food and beverage and housekeeping units. EOC functions depend on how the hotel GM chooses to use the group, the GM's style, and the structure of other management meetings in the hotel.

Typically, the EOC meets weekly, focusing on matters ranging from day-today operational issues (daily function schedules and labour and food cost control) to comparing budgets with actual operating results. Many hotels increase communications through an elaborate structure of additional committees and meetings, including some or all of the following: operations, staff, sales forecast and marketing, departmental, subdepartmental, credit, safety, energy conservation, and employee meetings.

The operations committee comprises the general manager, department heads, front office manager, manager on duty, and representatives from housekeeping, security, engineering, and food and beverage. This committee might meet four or five times per week for 15 to 20 minutes to review upcoming activities and assess the results of previous activities.

The staff committee might include the GM, department heads, and all subdepartment heads who report to the department heads. This committee, which might meet weekly for one or two hours, reviews the prior week's performance, the current week's activities, the next week's plans, and special projects. The staff committee also presents performance awards to employees.

The sales forecast and marketing committee might meet one to four times per month for several hours so the GM and department heads can review room demand for the coming 90 days and devise strategies to increase room nights (and thus bring in more revenue) and to increase average daily rates by up-selling potential guests to higher-rated rooms with perhaps more amenities or services.

The departmental committee consists of the department head and his or her subdepartment heads, managers, and supervisors. Meeting once or twice per month for an hour or so, the group reviews departmental issues. Similarly, subdepartment committees meet monthly for about an hour so the subdepartment head, managers, and supervisors can address issues unique to their subdepartment, such as the selection of a new type of floor cleaner by the housekeeping department or a more energy-efficient light bulb by the engineering department.

The credit committee includes the general manager, the controller, sales, the front office, reservations, catering, and the credit manager. Meeting monthly for an hour, the committee reviews those guests and clients of the hotel who were granted credit but have not settled their account. The safety committee typically comprises representatives from human resources, food and beverage, housekeeping, and engineering. Meeting monthly for an hour or so, the committee reviews safety programs and safety records, addresses problems, and discusses the implementation of new safety regulations.

In some full-service hotels, an energy conservation committee includes the chief engineer, resident manager, food and beverage staff, human resource representatives, rooms staff, and housekeeping representatives. The committee typically meets monthly for an hour to discuss strategies and programs for controlling energy costs. Most full-service hotels convene a monthly meeting or at least an annual meeting of all hotel management and employees to review performance and to distribute awards. This event ranges from an hourlong meeting to a company-wide celebration lasting several hours.

The Future Organization

As new business practices are evolving as fast as our technologies, resistance to change has become a primary cause of business failure. The future success of a hotel will be driven in large part by the ability to foresee and capitalize on change. As we go through global transitions, the successful hotel will examine the key factors that will not only define success but also the ability to survive in coming years. These key organizational trends must be acknowledged by the successful hotel organization: visionary leadership, globalization, diversity, flexibility, flat structure, customer focus, zero defects, network orientation, and being in the information fast lane.

The organization must be able to respond to increasingly globalized sales, the movement to maintaining sales offices in many countries and hotel properties across the globe, and an increasingly globalized labour market. Intercontinental Hotels Group recently introduced a new organization structure to more efficiently use regional and global resources to drive higher levels of innovation, customer focus, and revenues.

Diversity means the organization must respond to a workforce that is heterogeneous sexually, racially, and chronologically; innovation and conflict/ communication issues; and different styles of interaction, dress, presentation, and physical appearance. Flexibility in the modern hotel organization means assuring that systems, processes, and people can respond differently to different situations; fewer detailed rules and procedures; greater autonomy and encouragement of initiative; customizing employment relationships to include telecommuting and job-sharing; and lifetime employability rather than lifetime employment.

The trend toward flatness in hotel organizations means fewer levels of management, workers empowered to make decisions, and fewer differences in responsibility. The organization's employees need to believe in a sense of entrepreneurship that reacts proactively to market diversity. Traditional organizations that follow well-documented rules must give way to leaders who can balance a sense of discipline with one of flexibility.

If the customer is king or queen in the 21st century, hotel organizaions will be best served by focusing less on their hotel assets as measures of success and more on their customers. This involves a fundamental shift from viewing the real estate asset as the wealth creator to seeing the customer as the key to building shareholder wealth. A customer focus must reflect business decisions at all levels of developing and operating a hotel organization. Pursuing such a course will inevitably impact shareholder wealth.

The Japanese concept of zero defects in products and services can yield tremendous benefits for a hotel business organization. In practical terms, the hotel industry finds it extremely difficult to meet the standard of zero defects in service. Hotel services are based primarily on people, not on computers or other equipment. Twenty years ago, a business executive did not expect a consistent and predictable level of service wherever he or she traveled. Today that is the standard, not the exception, as is the expectation of sophisticated technology in hotel rooms to support business needs. With customer discrimination so acute, it is not surprising that brand loyalty is a diminishing commodity in the hotel industry.

Today's hotel organization must recognize the need for visionary leadership. The old command-and-control model of leadership is giving way to a focus on leadership in ideas, information, inspiration, vision, and teamwork. A failing hotel organization is overmanaged and underled. The networked hotel organization can facilitate direct communication across unit and property boundaries, ignoring the chain of command; cross-unit team structures; outsourcing and downsizing; strategic alliances with competitors and others; customization; and decentralization. Being in the information fast lane is critical. The traditional role of information technology as a back office support for accounting and bookkeeping has clearly moved to front and center stage. Information technology today influences all aspects of business from corporate strategies to organizational structure.

Technology was once viewed as a way to reduce costs by replacing people. That attitude has been firmly supplanted by the idea of seeking information technology support for the creative work all organizations must pursue. Information technology must enable organizations to react more speedily to market needs and, of course, produce the fulfillment of customer demands both quickly and accurately. To do this it must operate on a decentralized basis. Information technology delivers, but it has to deliver the right information to the right people at the right time.

5

Hotel Management and Advertisement

STRATEGIC MANAGEMENT OF HOTEL

Strategic management is that set of managerial decisions and actions that determines the long-run performance of a corporation. It includes environmental scanning, strategy formulation, strategy implementation and evaluation and control.

An organization's strategy must be appropriate for its resources, environmental circumstances, and core objectives. The process involves matching the company's [internal resources (eg IT) and capabilities (eg quality management)] to the external business environment the organization faces.

Strategy formulation involves:

- Doing a situation analysis: both internal and external; both micro-environmental and macro-environmental.
- Concurrent with this assessment, objectives are set. This involves crafting vision statements (long term view of a possible future), mission statements (the role that the organization gives itself in society), overall corporate objectives (both financial and strategic), strategic business unit objectives (both financial and strategic), and tactical objectives.
- These objectives should, in the light of the situation analysis, sugsgest a strategic plan. The plan provides the details of how to achieve these objectives.

This three-step strategy formulation process is sometimes referred to as determining where you are now, determining where you want to go, and then determining how to get there. These three questions are the essence of strategic planning. SWOT Analysis: I/O Economics for the external factors and RBV for the internal factors.

Strategy Implementation involves:

- Allocation of sufficient resources (financial, personnel, time, technology support)

- Establishing a chain of command or some alternative structure (such as cross functional teams)
- Assigning responsibility of specific tasks or processes to specific individuals or groups
- It also involves managing the process. This includes monitoring results, comparing to benchmarks and best practices, evaluating the efficacy and efficiency of the process, controlling for variances, and making adjustments to the process as necessary.
- When implementing specific programmes, this involves acquiring the requisite resources, developing the process, training, process testing, documentation, and integration with (and/or conversion from) legacy processes.

Strategy formulation and implementation is an on-going, never-ending, integrated process requiring continuous reassessment and reformation. Strategic management is dynamic; It involves a complex pattern of actions and reactions. It is partially planned and partially unplanned. Strategy is both planned and emergent, dynamic, and interactive. Some people (such as Andy Grove at Intel) feel that there are critical points at which a strategy must take a new direction in order to be in step with a changing business environment. These critical points of change are called strategic inflection points.

HOTEL MANAGEMENT SYSTEM

Every company must be able to satisfy and retain customers. That is the key to its business performance. Your job—as an executive in charge of improving quality, customer satisfaction, or loyalty—may be to enable others to act through training and support. Alternatively, if you're in the quality, customer assessment, or development areas of your company, your job may be to do the work directly—to collect, analyze, or use customer data to improve quality, satisfaction, and retention. Whether you are an enabler or a doer, customer satisfaction and retention are your responsibility. Providing high-quality products and services builds strong relationships with customers and ensures future revenue streams.

Even though you may agree about the importance of customers in driving performance, an important question remains. Does your company align its activities to satisfy and retain customers? Too often the answer is either "no" or "not so well." To help understand the problem, consider how a customer focus has evolved in recent decades.

In the 1970s, quality gurus argued that "quality is free." That is, a tireless pursuit of improvement should not only increase efficiency but also increase customer satisfaction in the process, saving enough on costs and bringing in enough new and repeat business to more than cover any expenditures on quality. This was an underlying concept in the success of many Japanese companies. In the 1980s the experts began to focus more directly on increasing customer satisfaction as an explicit goal. Satisfying and keeping customers, it was argued, is simply less expensive than constantly replacing them. More recently, quality and satisfaction have been viewed as not sufficient by themselves. Companies boast of moving "beyond" quality and satisfaction to focus directly on customer loyalty as the key to profitability.

Yet to argue that quality, or satisfaction, or loyalty is what matters misses the point. These factors form a chain of cause and effect, building on each other so that they cannot be treated separately. They represent a system that must be measured and managed as a whole if you want to maximize results.

An example from our teaching experiences underscores the nature of the problem and why companies need to take a systems approach to customer measurement and management. Back in 1993 an executive seminar participant from a Fortune 100 company introduced himself as the "customer satisfaction manager" for his organization.

This prompted one of the authors to ask, "What happened to the quality manager?" The participant replied that quality was passé, and that customer satisfaction had become the hot topic in his organization. In fact, being the quality manager had become the "kiss of death" from a career standpoint—a dead-end job! Five years later, a seminar participant from the same company introduced himself as the "customer loyalty manager" for the organization. Again the natural question arose, "What happened to the customer satisfaction manager?" "Oh, him?" It turned out that the satisfaction manager was now the one with the dead-end job.

Many business organizations are beginning to recognize the need to avoid this "Book of the Month Club" mentality and to view customers from a systems perspective. They want explicit linkages that extend from internal processes to customer perceptions to customer satisfaction to loyalty—and ultimately to bottom-line performance.

The framework in this book will give executives hard numbers and not just persuasive theories to show that the connection is real and that improving satisfaction and loyalty really does improve profits. And those on the front lines—the quality engineers and service providers—will get specific guidance on what to improve and how to improve it to get the optimal response from customers.

This book will show you how to create an integrated customer measurement and management system that will help you allocate resources and increase profits. To create such a system, you must first understand your company's entire system for generating profit, from internal quality through to business performance. A systems approach acts on the basis of collected and interpreted customer data—but then you have to use the data to allocate resources and create change in the system or else you merely waste time and money.

With an effective customer measurement and management system, you can build organizational value. To do so, you will continually pursue three key activities that underlie a customer orientation: (1) gather customer information, (2) spread that information throughout the organization, and (3) use the information to maintain, improve, or innovate in products and processes.

You need solid information about the concrete product and service attributes or features that customers value, the more abstract consequences and benefits these attributes provide, and ultimately the personal values they serve. The purpose is to understand what your customers want not only in today's products and services but in tomorrow's as well. When you understand your customers at the various levels that motivate their behaviour, you can see their present needs and predict their future needs as well.

To maintain a customer orientation throughout your organization, you need to make sure that customer information gets to everyone who is involved—either directly or indirectly— in improving quality and value and satisfying customers. This both prepares the entire organization for change and provides benchmarks by which to monitor its performance. Finally, you need to prime the organization to act on the customer information to improve product and service offerings so as to increase satisfaction, loyalty, and profitability. This makes it essential to clarify the links among these three factors and understand how your company delivers a compelling product to its customers.

Creating a customer measurement and management system is central to the pursuit of all three of these activities. With such a system in place, you have your customer information in a form that can serve as a basis for both incremental and more revolutionary product and service improvements. The system also makes it easier to share customer information throughout an organization, enhancing its ability to follow through on that information to make product and process changes. It is essential to view customer measurement from a systems perspective that encompasses multiple areas of measurement and expertise (from engineering and design through market research and strategy to finance and accounting) so that you pick up both concrete and abstract details— both what the customers like and dislike and why they react that way—and develop information that will be genuinely useful.

Now you may well be saying, "But we already do a good job of gathering customer information, spreading it, and acting on the voice of the customer." The question is whether you really adopt the "lens of the customer" in this process or fall into the trap of relying on the "lens of the organization."

The lens of the customer shows you your products and services—and the benefits they provide—from your customers' perspective. You see them as they really are in the marketplace, rather than the different and potentially misleading picture you're likely to get from the lens of your own organization. For example, if you run a convenience store chain you may be inclined to view the chain's stores as providing customers with people (service), products (from soft drinks to gasoline), and operations (such as opening hours), each under the management of a different department or business function. The problem is that customers may not share this perspective. Customers view products and services from the standpoint of the benefits they provide and problems they solve, which may not align well with individual business process areas. In this case, customers are looking for safety, convenience, and cleanliness, which are benefits that are not uniquely provided by specific business process areas. Rather, they cut across the people, products, and operating policies of the stores.

Aside from providing a more accurate picture of the drivers of satisfaction and loyalty, adopting the lens of the customer has other advantages. It blurs functional boundaries and provides a common basis and language for communication. The forging of concrete links from area to area within a company is also a key to effective implementation. When an organization reaches a consensus on the importance of customer benefits that are not defined along functional or business process lines, it finds it much easier to engage in the cross-functional activities required to truly innovate and implement change.

We emphasize the word *framework* here. Our aim is to show just what links and models are possible.The actual elements and links in any model vary tremendously from company to company and context to context. After describing the framework, we will illustrate this point using two very different cases in which companies (Volvo and Sears) have developed models to become more customer focused.

The framework includes four general areas: internal quality, external quality and satisfaction, customer loyalty and retention, and financial performance. *Internal quality* encompasses various production and maintenance processes. In the case of a manufactured product, it includes everything from manufacturing processes to the physical characteristics and attributes that describe the product. In a service and retailing context, it includes the service offer, the physical surroundings, and the satisfaction of employees and the resulting service quality they provide.

External quality and satisfaction encompasses what customers see in the purchase and consumption experience: the attributes and benefits that products and services provide and the costs they impose, and the conclusions the customers draw about the company. In the area of customer loyalty and retention, *loyalty* is a customer's intention or predisposition to buy, while *retention* is the behaviour itself (as when a customer returns to a restaurant, comes back to buy the same brand of car, or purchases another financial instrument from the same institution). Although we will use the term *loyalty* at times to encompass both intended loyalty and actual retention, it is important to understand the distinction. When actual retention information is available, it proves extremely valuable in sorting out the drivers of financial performance. When it is unavailable, as it often is, you can use loyalty measures as a proxy for retention.

Quality, satisfaction, and loyalty ultimately affect financial performance, both directly and indirectly. The framework illustrates this point and highlights the possibility that there may be a tension between direct and indirect effects. Consider first the impact of internal quality. Producing a high-quality product or service at an attractive price indirectly affects financial performance through its effect on external customer perceptions of the purchase-consumption experience.

But internal quality may also have a direct effect on costs and revenues. According to the "quality is free" argument, improvements in internal quality can increase productivity and lower internal costs and thus directly increase profitability. Recent research suggests, however, that this link is likely to be more positive for products and less positive or even negative for services. Why the difference? Services are produced and delivered at a time and place that is typically dictated by the customer. Thus improving service quality often requires an increase in personnel and operating or contact hours, which raises operating costs.

The external quality, value, and customer satisfaction component of the framework also has both direct and indirect effects on costs and revenues. Indirectly, a positive overall experience predisposes customers to stay loyal toward a product, service, or provider, which generates future sales. Satisfaction thus contributes to financial performance through its effect on loyalty and retention. But satisfaction also has direct effects, independent of loyalty.

The cost of maintaining a customer account—or fixing a product—is a direct function of how happy the customer is. Satisfied customers are less likely to demand expensive product repairs or replacements or to invoke service guarantees. Also—even outside the world of TV commercials—people do talk about the products and services they buy, and your company's entry into that stream of word-of-mouth publicity is through perceived quality and satisfaction rather than through loyalty. Satisfaction is *news*—something to talk about—while loyalty is a background state that goes without saying unless something happens to damage it.

The direct effects of loyalty and retention on performance include revenues from repeat purchases, reduction in costs of finding new customers (to replace lost customers), and revenues generated through cross-selling. Another direct effect is the price premium that loyal customers often pay. Because loyal customers are not actively shopping for alternatives, they tend to be insulated from price incentives and offers such as coupons, price cuts, and free merchandise. The recent turnaround at Volvo Car Company provides a good example of how a durable goods manufacturer views the links described in our framework.

In 1991, Volvo was performing poorly in the global automotive market. It ranked as low as twenty-sixth out of thirty-four brands in the J. D. Power Initial Quality Study in the United States, and sales and profitability were suffering.

In its comeback effort, Volvo began to develop a customer orientation from a total quality management foundation. Formerly, Volvo had emphasized changing internal quality to improve productivity and reduce costs. Its management realized, however, that just focusing on internal quality was insufficient. Internal improvements had to matter to the customers before they could create improved external quality, customer satisfaction, and loyalty.

Volvo's approach is just one example of the variety of tailored models that are consistent with the framework. Like Volvo, Sears has attempted to radically transform itself into a more customer-focused organization. But since Sears is a retailer that competes primarily on service, its model has evolved quite differently. Internal quality at Sears is primarily about its people and the service they provide. The Sears model draws directly on a service-profit chain that links internal quality (including employee satisfaction and loyalty) to service quality, and the satisfaction generated by service quality to loyalty and financial performance.

In developing its model, Sears has discovered both direct effects of satisfaction on financial performance and indirect effects through loyalty, which is consistent with our framework. A quantitative employee-customer-profit model at Sears has helped the company to establish very specific links that have enabled it to improve financial performance. The model shows, for example, that a 5-point improvement in employee attitudes (on a 0 to 100 scale) drives a 1.3-point improvement in customer satisfaction, which in turn drives a 0.5 percent improvement in revenue growth.

The Volvo and Sears models share a common logic, but each model is uniquely tailored to the organization's own situation. Both models link internal quality through to profitability. At the same time, each reflects the nature of a specific company, its customers and offerings, and the contexts involved. When you look at your own company, you will see that the same logic will work for you when you develop a similar understanding of your own customers and what you can offer them.

The best measurement system can only provide information— it can't make decisions for you. People make decisions, whether it is the convenience store executive who sets corporate priorities, the front-line service manager who translates these priorities into policies and procedures, or the service worker who translates policies and procedures into concrete actions. At all three levels, decision makers are much more likely to choose to do something that will help the store chain succeed if they understand what matters to customers and how the job at hand can enhance that value.

The process of moving from information to decisions draws heavily on *importance-performance analysis.* According to this analysis, the most cost-effective areas of product and service performance to improve are those that are important to customers *and* on which, at the same time, the company is performing poorly. Executives and managers must identify these priority areas of high importance and low performance. As an output of this selection process, they can categorize and display the drivers of satisfaction and loyalty using a strategic satisfaction matrix.

The matrix identifies four categories of performance drivers with different market action implications. Again, the aspects to improve first are those where impact or importance is high and performance is weak. This focuses resources and quality improvement efforts likely to have the greatest impact on satisfaction and thus on loyalty and profitability. Those aspects where performance and impact are both high reflect a firm's competitive advantage. It is essential to maintain if not improve performance on these drivers. When impact and performance are both weak, on the other hand, there is no need to waste resources on improvement.

More interesting is the low impact–strong performance category. This may be an area where resources have been wasted in the past because the benefits and attributes are not important to customers. Alternatively, this category may contain drivers of satisfaction that customers see as basic and necessary—so much a part of the product or service that they ignore it as long as it's there when they want it, like electric power or water on tap.

Although such drivers are important in an absolute sense, they have little to no impact on satisfaction because there is little variance in their performance. The danger is that a reduction in performance quality would increase the impact on satisfaction (this danger is often referred to as a "slippery slope"). Another possibility here is to find a new target market segment for the product or service. For example, if the quality of an electrical system is so constant that it has no impact on satisfaction in one application, the system might be used in applications where minor fluctuations in this quality are more important and therefore likely to have a real impact on satisfaction.

There is also a danger that something in this category may become important in the future. For example, few customers considered "environmental friendliness" to be an important factor until recently, but more and more people are beginning to pay attention to this aspect of the goods and services they buy. In a growing variety of fields, companies that predicted the importance of this area and prepared their business accordingly clearly have an advantage over those that did not. The circular nature of the process reflects the continuous nature of a customer orientation. Customer needs, competitive offerings, and business technologies change constantly, so customer focus is an ideal of constant growth rather than static achievement. The cycle in is thus a continuous process of planning, researching, analyzing, deciding, implementing, and learning. This includes identifying the system's purpose or goals within a more balanced set of corporate performance measures (including financial goals, employee satisfaction goals, process improvement goals, knowledge and learning goals, and so forth). The chapter explores the key customer and market segmentation issues upon which the system is based, including the distinction between internal and external customers.

Chapter Three tells how to conduct qualitative research to guide the development of the measurement system. Conducting interviews and focus groups and observing customers provides you with the lens through which customers view products and services. This lens is the basis for your quality-satisfactionloyalty modeling.

Chapter Four tells how to use the lens of the customer to develop a customer monitoring system. It discusses ways to develop and administer surveys that assess the attributes and benefits your products and services provide and the overall levels of customer satisfaction and loyalty that result. The goal is to customize the measurement of quality, value, satisfaction, and loyalty for a particular customer segment, company, and context.

Chapter Five tells how to analyze satisfaction and loyalty data to provide the information you will need to set priorities for improvement. Again, the purpose is to identify both the relative importance and performance of key satisfaction and loyalty drivers. It provides guidelines for identifying the area or areas where importance is high and performance is low, which offer the most potential return on quality improvement efforts. We develop a statistical approach to help you estimate your system or model linking quality to loyalty and financial performance. We also provide concrete examples.

Chapter Six tells how to evaluate system outputs to make decisions. As emphasized earlier, management must take part in categorizing the output of a customer analysis into a strategic satisfaction matrix. Just where boundaries are set between highversus low-impact drivers and strong versus weak performance depends on a variety of factors, including what you can achieve in the time available, your cost structure, and your overall strategy. Interpreting model outputs also requires appropriate bench for evaluating both performance and importance. We will end Chapter Six by describing how to translate customer priorities into their means of accomplishment.

Who should collect your customer data, analyze it, and use it to set priorities and allocate resources? It often seems logical to delegate the satisfaction and loyalty measurement operation to outside research firms and consultants. This is especially true early in the process of becoming a customer-oriented organization, because outside specialists offer specific skills related to collecting and analyzing customer data that you do not have. Unfortunately, if you delegate the system, your company does not take ownership of it, and you and your people may fail to learn or acquire the skills necessary to measure and manage customer data on your own. The consultant's bills, heavy as they are likely to be, are only a small part of the cost of handing off a customer information system.

Bear in mind that when customer information is the key to strategy, it should reside within the company. Your best teachers about what is right and wrong with your products and services are your own customers. Direct contact with customers and customer data is a critical part of learning what it takes to satisfy customer needs. No matter how good the consultants are, they will always function as filters.

An important part of establishing a customer orientation as a core competency is creating, over time, internal specialists to measure, model, and manage quality, satisfaction, and loyalty. Early in the process, external experts are apt to be a necessity. They can provide the interviewing, surveying, data warehousing, statistical analysis, and interpretation skills that you may lack or not yet want (or be able) to invest in. Over time, however, continued reliance on external specialists becomes costly and also fails to develop customer measurement and management as a core competency. Internalization of the process allows you to adapt to changing market needs and competitive environments in a cost-effective fashion. More important, your organization accepts ownership of the process and the data—and the decisions that emerge.

This is not to say that all parts of the process should be brought in-house in all cases. You may not want to try to run a survey that involves computer-aided telephone interviews or a Web-based system with highly specialized personnel (such as trained interviewers) and potential economies of scale. Even in the most customer-savvy organization, it may be best to outsource certain parts of the process. At the same time, a truly customer-oriented firm should own rather than rent the ability to observe and to talk to customers, formalize survey instruments, analyze and interpret customer data, and use the output to make resource allocation decisions.

Over the last three decades business organizations have evolved from a focus on quality to a focus on customer satisfaction, and onward to a focus on loyalty as a means of creating value. A customer measurement and management system views each of these areas as an indispensable link in a chain of causes and effects that runs from internal quality through to profitability.

The goal of this book is to help you and your organization create an integrated customer measurement and management system for making effective resource allocation decisions and increasing profitability. In the process of building a system, organizations develop internal specialists capable of gathering, analyzing, and interpreting customer data. Truly customer-oriented companies should, over time, add these skills to their core competencies. A systems approach to customer measurement and management also requires that you tailor the system to your unique purpose, customers, and contexts. As an illustration, Volvo's model incorporates the positive effects of improving internal quality on both productivity and customer perceptions of quality, satisfaction, and loyalty. In contrast, a major retailer such as Sears incorporates the central role that satisfied employees play in delivering quality and value to customers.

These measurement systems and models are not substitutes for decision making. Rather, they provide the information you need to make resource allocation decisions and manage the process. The system provides information on how the company and its competitors are performing in different areas and how important the areas are to customers.

When combined with cost and strategy considerations, the system allows both enablers and doers to create organizational value through a continuous focus on customers. To maximize the value generated by the system, make sure your company's own staff perform the bulk of the work of collecting and interpreting customer data, so that you get the full benefit of the insights generated by the effort.

Before you dive in and start conducting customer interviews or surveys, you must know how your measurement system will be used. This chapter focuses on the strategy and planning for such a system. Since a customer orientation builds on internal quality, we'll start with a brief overview of quality management and its role in driving company strategy and customer measures. We'll then discuss two related approaches to translating strategy into action: policy deployment and balanced performance measures. Then we'll focus on the process of getting started on developing a customer measurement and management system—or improving an existing one—which involves taking a look at the breadth and depth of the proposed system and the role of market segmentation in it.

In our customer satisfaction framework, internal quality is the first in the chain of events that drives financial performance. It's important not to underestimate the role of *total quality management* (or TQM, also known as *company-wide quality management*, CWQM, and as *total quality control*, TQC)—nor to exaggerate it. For longterm survival, businesses have been forced to improve their abilities to change and innovate. But internal quality management is not in itself sufficient to assure success. Internal quality improvements must be linked to improvements in external quality, satisfaction, loyalty, and financial performance. And the links must be established in an environment of constantly evolving customer preferences, markets, competitors, and technologies.

The broad principles and methods of quality management apply directly to the development of a customer measurement system. The concept of quality should unify all of a company's activities. After all, only your customers can ultimately define quality for you! In the end, it doesn't matter how well the production system works, how well marketing functions are performed, or how good the company's strategy is. If no one buys, there will be no revenues.

Quality experts emphasize three basic strategies for successful quality management: use reference models or benchmarks, set priorities for quality improvement, and focus your resources.

Do not try to do things completely on your own. Instead, make use of reference models or benchmarks when they're available. Benchmarking is particularly important in developing a customer measurement and management system.

Process benchmarking—finding out how things are done— works as well in developing a customer measurement and management system as in any other area of business. When you can manage it, arrange visits to firms with strong reputations to gauge their practices and learn what they are doing, see how they are doing it, and understand what is possible. Devote some time to reverse engineering their products as well.

And don't limit the benchmarking to competitors—in a general area such as customer measurement, you'll find individuals or organizations in many fields who excel in areas that you are interested in improving. Benchmarking on their processes can help you to learn how to conduct better customer interviews, develop and administer more effective surveys, and analyze customer data in more productive ways—and they're likely to be much more willing to share information with you if you're not trying to sell the same offering to the same customers.

For *output* or *performance benchmarking,* you will measure your product or service against direct or indirect competitors on various dimensions such as internal or technical quality, external or perceived quality and value, and overall customer satisfaction, loyalty, and retention. As noted in Chapter Six, external benchmarks will help you interpret your findings regarding your own customers and decide just where to devote your resources to get the most mileage from your improvement efforts.

STRATEGIES IN MARKETING

Marketing strategy is a powerful process that gives an organization a competitive advantage in the marketplace. While just defining a marketing strategy will not automatically create a competitive advantage, it will allow the organization to concentrate its (always limited) resources on the greatest opportunities to increase sales and achieve a sustainable competitive advantage.

The word strategy comes from the Greek word strategos meaning general. Strategy is what generals use to win battles. Thus properly understood, marketing strategy is a high-level exercise involving the "generals" of the organization in determining how to build on the firm's strengths while (ethically) taking advantage of competitors' weaknesses. Marketing strategy is most effective when it is a vital component of corporate strategy, defining how the organization will engage customers, prospects and the competition in the market arena for consistent success.

A marketing strategy also serves as the foundation of a marketing plan. A marketing plan contains a set of specific actions required to successfully implement a specific marketing strategy. For example: "Use a low cost product to attract consumers. Once our organization, via our low cost product, has established a relationship with consumers, our organization will sell additional, higher-margin products and services that enhance the consumer's interaction with the low-cost product or service."

A strategy is different from a tactic. While it is possible to write a tactical marketing plan without a sound, well-considered strategy, it is not recommended. Without a sound marketing strategy, a marketing plan has no foundation. Marketing strategies serve as the fundamental underpinning of marketing plans designed to reach marketing objectives. It is important that these objectives have measurable results. A good marketing strategy should integrate an organization's marketing goals, policies, and action sequences (tactics) into a cohesive whole. The objective of a marketing strategy is to provide a foundation from which a tactical plan is developed. This allows the organization to carry out its mission effectively and efficiently.

Marketing strategies are partially derived from broader corporate strategies, corporate missions, and corporate goals. They should flow from the firm's mission statement. They are also influenced by a range of microenvironmental factors. Marketing strategies are dynamic and interactive. They are partially planned and partially unplanned.

Commercial Planning

In the modern world of business, it is useless to be a creative original thinker unless you can also sell what you create. Management cannot be expected to recognize a good idea unless it is presented to them by a good salesman. The success of a new product depends not only on the idea behind the product, but also on the marketing of the new product before, during and after the product launch. Commercializing a product is commonly known as Commercial Planning. No concrete methods are currently available for New Product Launching (NPL). However, several articles are published about NPL and the essential activities, to launch a new product. This article describes a set of activities and products, that are essential for launching a new product. New Product Launching is part of the New Product Development method.

Strategic Management

Strategic management operates on several time scales. Short term strategies involve planning and managing for the present. Long term strategies involve preparing for and preempting the future. Marketing strategist Derek Abell (1993), has suggested that understanding this dual nature of strategic management is the least understood part of the process. He claims that balancing the temporal aspects of strategic planning requires the use of dual strategies simultaneously.

Strategic Management is actually a solid foundation or a framework within which all the functionning managerial operations are bundled together. This is the highest level corporate activity that sets the terms and goals for a company that it should follow for prosperity.

Strategic management techniques can be viewed as bottom-up, top-down, or collaborative processes. In the bottom-up approach, employees submit proposals to their managers who, in turn, funnel the best ideas further up the organization.

This is often accomplished by a capital budgeting process. Proposals are assessed using financial criteria such as return on investment or cost-benefit analysis. The proposals that are approved form the substance of a new strategy, all of which is done without a grand strategic design or a strategic architect. The top-down approach is the most common by far. In it, the CEO, possibly with the assistance of a strategic planning team, decides on the overall direction the company should take. Some organizations are starting to experiment with collaborative strategic planning techniques that recognize the emergent nature of strategic decisions.

In most (large) corporations there are several levels of strategy. Strategic management is the highest in the sense that it is the broadest, applying to all parts of the firm. It gives direction to corporate values, corporate culture, corporate goals, and corporate missions. Under this broad corporate strategy there are often functional or business unit strategies.

Functional strategies include marketing strategies, new product development strategies, human resource strategies, financial strategies, legal strategies, and information technology management strategies. The emphasis is on short and medium term plans and is limited to the domain of each department's functional responsibility. Each functional department attempts to do its part in meeting overall corporate objectives, and hence to some extent their strategies are derived from broader corporate strategies.

Many companies feel that a functional organizational structure is not an efficient way to organize activities so they have reengineered according to processes or strategic business units (called SBUs). A strategic business unit is a semi-autonomous unit within an organization. It is usually responsible for its own budgeting, new product decisions, hiring decisions, and price setting. An SBU is treated as an internal profit centre by corporate headquarters. Each SBU is responsible for developing its business strategies, strategies that must be in tune with broader corporate strategies.

The "lowest" level of strategy is operational strategy. It is very narrow in focus and deals with day-to-day operational activities such as scheduling criteria. It must operate within a budget but is not at liberty to adjust or create that budget. Operational level strategy was encouraged by Peter Drucker in his theory of management by objectives (MBO). Operational level strategies are informed by business level strategies which, in turn, are informed by corporate level strategies. Business strategy, which refers to the aggregated operational strategies of single business firm or that of an SBU in a diversified corporation refers to the way in which a firm competes in its chosen arenas.

Corporate strategy, then, refers to the overarching strategy of the diversified firm. Such corporate strategy answers the questions of "in which businesses should we compete?" and "how does being in one business add to the competitive advantage of another portfolio firm, as well as the competitive advantage of the corporation as a whole?"

Since the turn of the millennium, there has been a tendency in some firms to revert to a simpler strategic structure. This is being driven by information technology. It is felt that knowledge management systems should be used to share information and create common goals. Strategic divisions are thought to hamper this process. Most recently, this notion of strategy has been captured under the rubric of dynamic strategy, popularized by the strategic management textbook authored by Carpenter and Sanders. This work builds on that of Brown and Eisenhart as well as Christensen and portrays firm strategy, both business and corporate, as necessarily embracing ongoing strategic change, and the seamless integration of strategy formulation and implementation. Such change and implementation are usually built into the strategy through the staging and pacing facets.

Management by Objectives (MBO) is a process of agreeing upon objectives within an organization so that management and employees buy in to the objectives and understand what they are. Management By Objectives term was first popularized by Peter Drucker in 1954 in his book 'The Practice of Management'.

It is all too easy for managers to fail to outline, and agree with their employees, what it is that everyone is trying to achieve. MBO substitutes for good intentions a process that requires rather precise written description of objectives (for the period ahead) and timelines for their monitoring and achievement. The process requires that the manager and the employee agree to what the employee will attempt to achieve in the period ahead, and (very important) that the employee accept and buy into the objectives (otherwise commitment will be lacking).

For example, whatever else a manager and employee may discuss and agree in their regular discussions, let us suppose that they feel that it will be sensible to introduce a key performance indicator to show the development of sales revenue in a part of the firm. Then the manager and the employee need to discuss what is being planned, what the time-schedule is and what the indicator might or might not be. Thereafter the two of them should liaise to ensure that the objective is being attended to and will be delivered on time.

Organizations have scarce resources and so it is incumbent on the managers to consider the level of resourcing but also to consider whether the objectives that are jointly agreed within the firm are the right ones and represent the best allocation of effort. Also, reliable Management information systems are needed to establish relevant objectives and monitor their "reach ratio" in an objective way.

MBO is often achieved using set targets. MBO introduced the SMART criteria: Objectives for MBO must be SMART (Specific, Measurable, Agreed, Realistic, and Time-Specific).

However, it has been reported in recent years that this style of management receives criticism in that it triggers employees' unethical behaviour of distorting the system or financial figures to achieve the targets set by their short-term, narrow bottom-line, and completely self-centered thinking.

MARKETING THROUGH ADVERTISING

Marketing is a social and managerial function that attempts to create, expand and maintain a collection of customers.

It attempts to deliver demand satisfying output through profitable exchanges:

- Marketing, as suggested by the American Marketing Association, is "an organizational function and a set of processes for creating, communicating and delivering value to customers and for managing customer relationships in ways that benefit the organization and its stakeholders".
- Philip Kotler, in his earlier books, defines marketing as: "human activity directed at satisfying needs and wants through exchange processes". Still another marketing definition, coined by Brian Norris: "The process of repeatedly moving people closer to making a decision to purchase, use, follow, refer, upload, download, obey, reject, conform, become complacent to another person's, society's or organization's value. Simply, if it doesn't facilitate a "sale" then it's not marketing."
- Identifying needs/wants and finding and implimenting solutions that satisfy those needs and wants.
- Add to Kotler's and Norris' definitions, a response from the Chartered Institute of Marketing (CIM). The association's definition claims marketing to be the "management process of anticipating, identifying and satisfying customer requirements profitably". Thus, operative marketing involves the processes of market research, market segmentation, new product development, product life cycle management, pricing, channel management as well as promotion.

- Marketing-"taking actions to define, create, grow, develop, maintain, defend and own markets".
- An approach to business that seeks to identify, anticipate and satisfy customers needs.
- Al Ries and Jack Trout defined marketing as simply "war" between competitors.
- Any activity that connects producers with consumers.
- At a macro level, marketing is the process of raising the standards of living, by identifying the existing problems and unsatisfied needs of people and then satisfying that need with a product/service that delivers value to the customer.

The practice of marketing is almost as old as humanity itself. Whenever a person has an item or is capable of performing a service, and he or she seeks another person who might want that item or service, that person is involved in marketing. A Market was originally simply a gathering place where people with a supply of items or capacity to perform a service could meet with those who might desire the items or services, perhaps at a pre-arranged time.

Such meetings embodied all the aspects of today's marketing methods, although in an informal way. Sellers and buyers sought to understand each other's needs, capacities, and psychology, all with the goal of getting the exchange of items or services to take place. Open air markets throughout the world, with buyers and sellers freely mingling, are today's example of this basic activity. Today's New York Stock Exchange had its humble beginnings as an open air market located at Wall Street in New York City.

The rise of Agriculture undoubtedly influenced markets as the earliest means of 'mass production' of an item, namely foodstuffs. As agriculture allowed one to grow more food than could be eaten by the grower alone, and most food is perishable, there was likely motivation to seek out others who could use the excess food, before it spoiled, in exchange for other items.

Prior to the advent of market research, most companies were product-focused, employing teams of salespeople to push their products into or onto the market, regardless of market desire. A market-focused, or customer-focused, organization instead first determines what its potential customers desire, and then builds the product or service. Marketing theory and practice is justified on the belief that customers use a product/service because they have a need, or because a product/service has a perceived benefit. Two major factors of marketing are the recruitment of new customers (acquisition) and the retention and expansion of relationships with existing customers (base management).

Once a marketer has converted the prospective buyer, base management marketing takes over. The process for base management shifts the marketer to building a relationship, nurturing the links, enhancing the benefits that sold the buyer in the first place, and improving the product/service continuously to protect her business from competitive encroachments. Marketing methods are informed by many of the social sciences, particularly psychology, sociology, and economics. Anthropology is also a small, but growing, influence. Market research underpins these activities. Through advertising, it is also related to many of the creative arts.

For a marketing plan to be successful, the mix of the four "Ps" must reflect the wants and desires of the consumers in the target market. Trying to convince a market segment to buy something they don't want is extremely expensive and seldom successful. Marketers depend on marketing research, both formal and informal, to determine what consumers want and what they are willing to pay for.

Marketers hope that this process will give them a sustainable competitive advantage. Marketing management is the practical application of this process. The offer is also an important addition to the 4P's theory. Within most organizations the activities encompassed by the marketing function are led by a Chief Marketing Officer, or an equivalent executive. Most often the CMO position reports to the Chief Executive Officer.

The big debate in the marketing discipline is whether marketing is an art or a science. Marketing is a technology or set of technologies. Marketing can be neither an art nor a science because arts and sciences only seek to explain natural phenomena.

The objective of marketing is to manipulate and influence natural phenomena to create practical unnatural outcomes, specifically to manufacture, grow, sustain and defend markets. Marketers use their knowledge of economics, psychology, sociology, anthropology and strategy to arrange and control the external environment to their advantage and lock in profit. To understand what marketing is one must understand that marketing operates on three different levels.

Corporate Level Marketing

Marketing at the corporate levels asks this question as 'What business should we be in and what opportunities should we pursue?' This is marketing before we even have a business, idea or product. This is what is known as entreprenuership. This level of marketing strategy is where the Ted Turners, Bill Gates' and Michael Dells of the world make market changing decisions. This level is also where corporate management of existing companies decide to branch off into new uncharted territories and opportunities.

Business Level Marketing

Marketing at the business level asks this question as 'How are we going to compete against the competition?' When Jack Trout says that marketing is 'the war between competitors' and 'the conflict between companies' what he is really doing is defining marketing at the business level. Business level marketing deals with high level strategic marketing concerns. This level deals with long term sustainable advantages and business models.

Functional Level Marketing

Marketing at the functional level (also known as the operating level) ask this question as 'How do we create and keep customers?' This level deals with marketing tactics and the '4ps' of the marketing mix. This level of marketing defines and develops products, prices them, promotes them and then distributes them in a way that helps a company create and sustain demand for their products.

In popular usage, "marketing" is the promotion of products, especially advertising and branding. However, in professional usage the term has a wider meaning which recognizes that marketing is customer centered. Products are often developed to meet the desires of groups of customers or even, in some cases, for specific customers. E. Jerome McCarthy divided marketing into four general sets of activities. His typology has become so universally recognized that his four activity sets, the Four Ps, have passed into the language.

The four Ps are:

- Product: The Product management and Product marketing aspects of marketing deal with the specifications of the actual good or service, and how it relates to the end-user's needs and wants.
- Pricing: This refers to the process of setting a price for a product, including discounts.
- Promotion: This includes advertising, sales promotion, publicity, and personal selling, and refers to the various methods of promoting the product, brand, or company.
- Placement or distribution refers to how the product gets to the customer; for example, point of sale placement or retailing. This fourth P has also sometimes been called Place, referring to the channel by which a product or service is sold (e.g. online vs. retail), which geographic region or industry, to which segment (young adults, families, business people), etc.

These four elements are often referred to as the marketing mix. A marketer can use these variables to craft a marketing plan. The four Ps model is most useful when marketing low value consumer products. Industrial products, services, high value consumer products require adjustments to this model. Services marketing must account for the unique nature of services. Industrial or B2B marketing must account for the long term contractual agreements that are typical in supply chain transactions. Relationship marketing attempts to do this by looking at marketing from a long term relationship perspective rather than individual transactions.

As a counter to this, Morgan, in Riding the Waves of Change (Jossey-Bass, 1988), adds "Perhaps the most significant criticism of the 4 Ps approach, which you should be aware of, is that it unconsciously emphasizes the inside–out view (looking from the company outwards), whereas the essence of marketing should be the outside–in approach". Even so, having made this important caveat, the 4 Ps offer a memorable and quite workable guide to the major categories of marketing activity, as well as a framework within which these can be used.

As well as the standard four Ps (Product, Pricing, Promotion and Place), services marketing calls upon an extra three, totalling seven and known together as the extended marketing mix.

These are:

- People: Any person coming into contact with customers can have an impact on overall satisfaction. Whether as part of a supporting service to a product or involved in a total service, people are particularly important because, in the customer's eyes, they are generally inseparable from the total service. As a result of this, they must be appropriately trained, well motivated and the right type of person. Fellow customers are also sometimes referred to under 'people', as they too can affect the customer's service experience, (e.g., at a sporting event).
- Process: This is the process(es) involved in providing a service and the behaviour of people, which can be crucial to customer satisfaction.
- Physical evidence: Unlike a product, a service cannot be experienced before it is delivered, which makes it intangible. This, therefore, means that potential customers could perceive greater risk when deciding whether or not to use a service. To reduce the feeling of risk, thus improving the chance for success, it is often vital to offer potential customers the chance to see what a service would be like. This is done by providing physical evidence, such as case studies, or testimonials.

As well as the other 7 Packaging has been added to this list by some people. The rationale is that it is very important how the product is presented to the customer, and the packaging is often the first contact that a customer has with a product. Although some disagree because packaging is seen as a subfield of promotion.

"Philosophy" is the potential 8th P of marketing. Products (or services) should reflect the underlying philosophy or ethos of the organization. It should also be clear what the philosophy behind the introduction of the particular product is, as well. In his book, "Meeting Need", Ian Bruce explains this concept as it relates to marketing for charities. It also applies to other products and services

Business Models

Marketing in the past focused mainly on basic concepts like the 4 Ps, and primarily on the psychological and sociological aspects of marketing. Competitive advantage was created by directly appealing to the needs, wants and behaviours of customers, better than the competition. Successful marketing was based on who could create the better brand or the lowest price or the most hype. Marketing in the future will be based on a more strategic approach to competitive marketing success. Marketers will consciously build and allocate resources, relationships, offerings and business models that other companies find hard to match.

Companies with a greater amount of resources than their competitors will have an easier time competing in the marketplace. Resources include: financial (cash and cash reserves), physical (plant and equipment), human (knowledge and skill), legal (trademarks and patents), organizational (structure, competencies, policies), and informational (knowledge of consumers and competitors). Small companies usually have a harder time competing with larger corporations because of their disadvantage in resource allocation.

Success in business, as in life, is based on the relationships you have with people. Marketers must aggressively build relationships with consumers, customers, distributors, partners and even competitors if they want to have success in today's competitive marketplace.

Most companies sell a mix of products and/or services. Today's marketplace is often too competitive for "one-trick ponies". Companies that sell the right mix products and services can have a competitive advantage over companies that sell just one product or service.

The concept of product vs. product in competitive marketing is dying. It's slowly becoming business model vs. business model. Business model innovation can make the competition's product superiority irrelevant. Business model innovation allows a marketer to change the game instead of competing on a level playing field.

Customer Focus

Most companies today have a customer orientation (also called customer focus). This implies that the company focuses its activities and products on ever changing consumer demands. Generally there are tthree ways of doing this: the customer-driven approach, the sense of identifying market changes and the product innovation approach.

In the consumer-driven approach, consumer wants are the drivers of all strategic marketing decisions. No strategy is pursued until it passes the test of consumer research. Every aspect of a market offering, including the nature of the product itself, is driven by the needs of potential consumers. The starting point is always the consumer. The rationale for this approach is that there is no point spending R&D funds developing products that people will not buy. History attests to many products that were commercial failures in spite of being technological breakthroughs.

The next big thing is a concept in marketing that refers to a product or idea that will allow for a high amount of sales for that product and related products. Marketers believe that by finding or creating the next big thing they will spark a cultural revolution that results in this sales increase.

Product Focus

In a product innovation approach, the company pursues product innovation, then tries to develop a market for the product. Product innovation drives the process and marketing research is conducted primarily to ensure that a profitable market segment(s) exists for the innovation. The rationale is that customers may not know what options will be available to them in the future so we should not expect them to tell us what they will buy in the future. However, marketers can aggressively over pursue product innovation and try to overcapitalize on a niche.

When pursuing a product innovation approach, marketers must ensure that they have a varied and multi-tiered approach to product innovation. It is claimed that if Thomas Edison depended on marketing research he would have produced larger candles rather than inventing light bulbs. Many firms, such as research and development focused companies, successfully focus on product innovation. Many purists doubt whether this is really a form of marketing orientation at all, because of the ex post status of consumer research. Some even question whether it is marketing.

Other Aspects:

- An emerging area of study and practice concerns internal marketing, or how employees are trained and managed to deliver the brand in a way that positively impacts the acquisition and retention of customers (employer branding).
- Diffusion of innovations research explores how and why people adopt new products, services and ideas.
- A relatively new form of marketing uses the Internet and is called internet marketing or more generally e-marketing, affiliate marketing or online marketing. It typically tries to perfect the segmentation strategy used in traditional marketing. It targets its audience more precisely, and is sometimes called personalized marketing or one-to-one marketing.
- With consumers' eroding attention span and willingness to give time to advertising messages, marketers are turning to forms of Permission marketing such as Branded content and Reality marketing.
- The use of herd behaviour in marketing.

Some aspects of marketing, especially promotion, are treated as the subject of criticism. It is especially problematic in classical economic theory, which is based on the assumption that supply and demand are independent. However, product promotion is an attempt coming from the supply side to influence demand. In this way producer market power is attained as measured by profits that would not be realized under a free market. Then the argument follows that non-free markets are imperfect and lead to production and consumption of suboptimal amounts of the product.

Critics acknowledge that marketing has legitimate uses in connecting goods and services to the consumers who want them. Critics also point out that marketing techniques have been used to achieve morally dubious ends by businesses, governments and criminals. Critics see a systemic social evil inherent in marketing. Marketing is accused of creating ruthless exploitation of both consumers and workers by treating people as commodities whose purpose is to consume.

Most marketers believe that marketing, like any other technology, is amoral. It can be used for good or evil purposes, but the technique itself is ethically neutral.

The Observer's survey among 1'206 UK adult consumers in 2001 highlighted some of the stark changes our society has gone through in the last two decades. This raises a question on the effectiveness of the CIM's definition of marketing (anticipating, identifying and satisfying customer needs profitably), mainly in consumer marketing. There are similar concerns in industrial markets, also known as business-to-business or B2B.

Core marketing elements such as segmentation, targeting and positioning are still relevant in the modern (or post-modern) world. However, they are complex topics that need a high level of effort, intelligent thinking as well as resources to be implemented successfully. A definitive statement cannot be made whether the conventional marketing concept is applicable in today's environment. Its relevance is very much situational and depends on many factors such as the product, the segment, time, location, political and economic conditions and the inner workings of a company.

However, some scholars such as Stephen Brown challenge the marketing concept in an extreme language. Their statements, though self-contradicting and sometimes unfair, are relevant, which is why Post Modern Marketing 2 was chosen as a key reference point for this chapter.

On the one hand Brown makes positive statements about marketing, e.g. marketing is endowed with considerable personal charm and has enjoyed more than its fair share of conquests; and indeed, the increasing academic attention that is being devoted to marketing and consumption-related phenomena by non-business disciplines such as sociology, anthropology and history; far from being the second-hand rose of the scholarship, marketing is now something of a fashion leader. On the other hand, he condemns marketing by saying "marketing has to decide whether to expose its intellectual nakedness or press itself against the searing heat of postmodernism"; and using quotes such as "mid-life crisis"; "in decline; failing; anachronistic; being abandoned; no longer appropriate; in an unprecedented state of crisis; delivered nothing of value; failure; confusion; misunderstanding; occasional inexplicable hitting of the jackpot".

This apparent love-hate relationship is proof in itself that even a sceptic Mr. Brown cannot deny the contribution that marketing has made and can make to customer satisfaction and economic value. It has contributed to both customers' and suppliers' quality of life by selecting profitable customer satisfaction as its sole objective.

The marketing concept, together with other business disciplines, helped the UK to make the transition from a 19th-century manufacturing economy to a modern model of success in the service industry, creating an economic growth period never seen in UK history before.

It is marketing that has helped create value through customised products, no-questions-asked refund policies, comfortable cars, environmental attention, shopkeepers' smile, and guaranteed delivery dates. Even some government departments address the public not as 'the Queen's subjects' or 'the applicants' any more but as 'customers'. Of course all of the above is done for economic or political gain, for better or worse. Despite all this achievement, to dismiss marketing as a failure is unfair.

Marketing also helps companies avoid unnecessary R&D, operational and sales costs by helping to develop products because customers want them, not for the sake of innovation. Another success is the now commonly implemented value-pricing principle, whereby a product or service is sold for the price the customer is willing to pay, not on a cost-plus basis. This way, both suppliers and customers get a fair deal.

In the context of segmentation, Brown suggests that "the traditional, linear, step-by-step marketing model of analysis, planning, implementation and control no longer seems applicable, appropriate or even pertinent to what is actually happening on the ground". If Mr. Brown had studied "the ground" before making his statement, he would have realised that companies are successful the world over precisely because they implement this model.

They segment their markets, relate their products and services to them, define their value proposition and serve their customers accordingly. Examples are GE, HSBC, PriceWaterhouseCoopers, Smiths Aerospace, BAE Systems, BOC Edwards, Weir Group and BT to name but a few. A brief visit to their websites can make this point clear.

Brown also has a constructive suggestion: "I reckon we need more passion in marketing, not less; it is time we banished banishing passion from works of marketing scholarship". This refers mainly to promotion, which is only one element within the marketing concept. The truth is that marketing today leads the way in segmentation, innovation, pricing, product management, distribution, and last but not least, promotion.

After all the contribution as well as further potential, to deny its successes and try to reduce it to only promotion is a great injustice to the marketing profession as well as to academic insight. Contrary to Brown's suggestion in his final paragraph, we need objectivity, rigour, quantification, models, relationships, paradigm shifts and (some application of) science.

Marketing is not full of holes, but a management process that has helped generate wealth and satisfied millions of customers for the most part of the 20th century. It can do even better in the 21st provided practitioners and scholars do not loose faith and focus. Kotler is not dead, but very much alive, and still kicking.

APPLIED MODERN ACCOUNTANCY IN HOTEL

The first book on accounting was written by a Croatian merchant Benedetto Cotrugli, who is also known as Benedikt Kotruljeviæ, from the city of Dubrovnik. During his life in Italy he met many merchants and decided to write, Della Mercatvra et del Mercante Perfetto (On Trade and the Perfect Merchant) in which he elaborated on the principles of modern, double-entry book-keeping. He finished his lifework in 1458. However, his work was not published until 1573, as a result of which his contributions to the field have been overlooked by the general public.

For this reason, Luca Pacioli, also known as Friar Luca dal Borgo, is credited for the "birth" of accounting. His Summa de arithmetica, geometrica, proportioni et proportionalita (Venice 1494), a synthesis of the mathematical knowledge of his time, includes the first published description of the method of keeping accounts that Venetian merchants used at that time, known as the double-entry accounting system. Although Pacioli codified rather than invented this system, he is widely regarded as the "Father of Accounting". The system he published included most of the accounting cycle as we know it today. He described the use of journals and ledgers, and warned that a person should not go to sleep at night until the debits equalled the credits! His ledger had accounts for assets (including receivables and inventories), liabilities, capital, income, and expenses — the account categories that are reported on an organization's balance sheet and income statement, respectively. He demonstrated year-end closing entries and proposed that a trial balance be used to prove a balanced ledger. His treatise also touches on a wide range of related topics from accounting ethics to cost accounting.

The first known book in the English language on accounting was published in London by John Gouge (or Gough) in 1543. It is described as A Profitable Treatyce called the Instrument or Boke to learn to knowe the good order of the kepyng of the famouse reconynge, called in Latin, Dare and Habere, and, in English, Debitor and Creditor.

A short book of instructions was also published in 1588 by John Mellis of Southwark, in which he says, "I am but the renuer and reviver of an ancient old copie printed here in London the 14 of August 1543: collected, published, made, and set forth by one Hugh Oldcastle, Scholemaster, who, as appeareth by his treatise, then taught Arithmetics, and this booke in Saint Ollaves parish in Marko Lane." John Mellis refers to the fact that the principle of accounts he explains (which is a simple system of double entry) is "after the forme of Venice".

A book described as The Merchants Mirrour, or directions for the perfect ordering and keeping of his accounts formed by way of Debitor and Creditor, after the (so termed) Italian manner, by Richard Dafforne, accountant, published in 1635, contains many references to early books on the science of accountancy. In a chapter in this book, headed "Opinion of Book-keeping's Antiquity," the author states, on the authority of another writer, that the form of book-keeping referred to had then been in use in Italy about two hundred years, "but that the same, or one in many parts very like this, was used in the time of Julius Caesar, and in Rome long before."

An early Dutch writer appears to have suggested that double-entry book-keeping was even in existence among the Greeks, pointing to scientific accountancy having been invented in remote times.

There were several editions of Richard Dafforne's book - the second edition in 1636, the third in 1656, and another in 1684. The book is a very complete treatise on scientific accountancy, beautifully prepared and containing elaborate explanations. The numerous editions tend to prove that the science was highly appreciated in the 17th century. From this time on, there has been a continuous supply of literature on the subject, many of the authors styling themselves accountants and teachers of the art, and thus proving that the professional accountant was then known and employed.

The requirements for entry in the profession of accounting vary from country to country. Accountants may be licensed by a variety of organisations, such as the British qualified accountancy bodies including Association of Chartered Certified Accountants (ACCA) and Institute of Chartered Accountants, and are recognized by titles such as Chartered Certified Accountant (ACCA or FCCA) and Chartered Accountant (UK, Australia, New Zealand, Canada, India, Pakistan, South Africa), Certified Public Accountant (Ireland, Japan, US, Singapore, Hong Kong, the Philippines), Certified Management Accountant (Canada, U.S.), Certified General Accountant (Canada), or Certified Practising Accountant (Australia). Some Commonwealth countries (Australia and Canada) often recognise both the certified and chartered accounting bodies.

The majority of "public" accountants in New Zealand and Canada are Chartered Accountants; however, Certified General Accountants are also authorized by legislation to practise public accounting and auditing in all Canadian provinces, except Ontario and Quebec, as of 2005. There is, however, no legal requirement for an accountant to be a paid-up member of one of the many Institutes and other bodies which are effectively a form of professional trade union. Unlike the Law Society, which can legally stop a solicitor from practising, accountancy institutes do not have such authority. However, auditors are regulated.

Before the Enron and other accounting scandals, there were five large firms and were called the Big Five. Since Arthur Andersen's assurance practice split (after the firm was found guilty in the Enron scandal), with a plurality joining KPMG in the US and Deloitte & Touche outside of the US, Arthur Andersen left from the group. Previous to this there were also groupings referred to as the "Big Six" (Arthur Andersen, plus Coopers & Lybrand before its merger with Price Waterhouse) and the "Big Eight" (Ernst and Young prior to their merger were Ernst & Whinney and Arthur Young and Deloitte & Touche was formed by the merger of Deloitte, Haskins and Sells with the firm Touche Ross).

Enron turned out to be only the first of a series of accounting scandals that enveloped the accounting industry in 2002. This is likely to have far-reaching consequences for the U.S. accounting industry. Application of International Accounting Standards originating in International Accounting Standards Board headquartered in London and bearing more resemblance to UK than current US practices is often advocated by those who note the relative stability of the UK accounting system (which reformed itself after scandals in the late 1980s and early 1990s). Accounting reform of a far more comprehensive sort is advocated by those who see issues with capitalism or economics, and seek ecological or social accountability.

According to Accountancy Age's 2005 league table, fee income amongst the Top 50 accounting firms in the UK rose from £6.3bn to £7.0bn. This followed two successive years in which fee income had declined, largely a result of the sale by some of the larger firms of their consultancy arms. Fee income in most business areas - audit, tax, corporate finance and consultancy - rose in the 2005 survey, with insolvency and wealth management being the only segments where revenue fell. PricewaterhouseCoopers remains the largest firm with fee income totalling £1,780m followed by Deloitte (£1,350m), KPMG (£1,066m) and Ernst & Young (£945m). The combined revenue of the Big Four accounted for £5.0bn, 72% of the fee income of the Top 50, down from 78-79% in the years up to the 2002 survey and the third year in succession a decline in their share has occurred (Chart 1). Ernst & Young's fee income is the smallest of the largest four firms, but still over three times that of the next largest firm, Grant Thornton. The amount of fee income tapers off amongst the mid-tier firms so that in total there were only 25 firms that each generated more than £15m of revenue in the 2005 survey.

Management Accounting

Management accounting is concerned with the provisions and use of accounting information to managers within organizations, to provide them with the basis in making informed business decisions that would allow them to be better equipped in their management and control functions. Unlike financial accountancy information (which, for the most part, is public information), management accounting information is used within an organization (typically for decision-making) and is usually confidential and access to which is only available to a select few.

According to CIMA, The Chartered Institute of Management Accountants, Management Accounting is "the process of identification, measurement, accumulation, analysis, preparation, interpretation and communication of information used by management to plan, evaluate and control within an entity and to assure appropriate use of and accountability for its resources. Management accounting also comprises the preparation of financial reports for non management groups such as shareholders, creditors, regulatory agencies and tax authorities".

Aims:

1. Formulating strategies;
2. Planning and constructing business activities;
3. Making decisions;
4. Well use of resources;
5. Supporting financial reports preparation; and
6. Safeguarding assets.

In the late 1980s, accounting practitioners and educators were heavily criticized on the grounds that management accounting practices (and, even more so, the curriculum taught to accounting students) had changed little over the preceding 60 years, despite radical changes in the business environment. Professional accounting institutes, perhaps fearing that management accountants would increasingly be seen as superfluous in business organizations, subsequently devoted considerable resources to the development of a more innovative skills set for management accountants.

The distinction between 'traditional' and 'innovative' management accounting practices can be illustrated by reference to cost control techniques. Traditionally, management accountants' principal technique was variance analysis, which is a systematic approach to the comparison of the actual and budgeted costs of the raw materials and labour used during a production period.

While some form of variance analysis is still used by most manufacturing firms, it nowadays tends to be used in conjunction with innovative techniques such as life cycle cost analysis and activity-based costing, which are designed with specific aspects of the modern business environment in mind. Lifecycle costing recognizes that managers' ability to influence the cost of manufacturing a product is at its greatest when the product is still at the design stage of its product lifecycle (i.e., before the design has been finalised and production commenced), since small changes to the product design may lead to significant savings in the cost of manufacturing the product. Activity-based costing (ABC) recognizes that, in modern factories, most manufacturing costs are determined by the amount of 'activities' (e.g., the number of production runs per month, and the amount of production equipment idle time) and that the key to effective cost control is therefore optimizing the efficiency of these activities. Activity-based accounting is also known as Cause and Effect accounting.

Both lifecycle costing and activity-based costing recognize that, in the typical modern factory, the avoidance of disruptive events (such as machine breakdowns and quality control failures) is of far greater importance than (for example) reducing the costs of raw materials. Activity-based costing also deemphasizes direct labour as a cost driver and concentrates instead on acitivities that drive costs, such as the provision of a service or the production of a product component.

The most significant recent direction in managerial accounting is throughput accounting, which recognizes the interdependencies of modern production processes and provide managers with a tool that will allow them to measure the contribution per unit of constrained resource for any given product, customer or supplier.

A seldom expressed alternative view of management accounting is that it is neither a neutral or benign influence in organizations, rather a mechanism for management control through surveillance. This view locates management accounting specifically in the context of management control theory.

There are several related professional qualifications in the field of accountancy including:

- Management Accountancy Qualifications
  - CIMA
  - CMA
  - Institute of Cost and Works Accountants of India
  - AAFM
- Other Professional Accountancy Qualifications
  - Chartered Certified Accountant, (ACCA)
  - Chartered Accountant, (CA)
  - Certified Public Accountant, (CPA)

Accounting Management (Business) is the practical application of management techniques to control and report on the financial health of the organization. This involves the analysis, planning, implementation, and control of programs designed to provide financial data reporting for managerial decision making. This includes the maintenance of bank accounts, developing financial statements, cash flow and financial performance analysis. Accounting management is a mandatory knowledge module of any MBA programme. Accounting is often referred to as billing management. The goal is to gather usage statistics for users.

Using the statistics the users can be billed and usage quota can be enforced.

Examples:

- Disk usage
- Link utilisation
- CPU time

For non-billed networks, 'Administration' replaces 'Accounting'. The goals of Administration is to administer the set of authorized users, by establishing users, passwords and permissions; and to administer the operations of the equipment such as by performing software backup and synchronization.

Activity-based Costing

Activity-based costing (ABC) is a method of allocating costs to products and services. It is generally used as a tool for planning and control. This is a necessary tool for doing value chain analysis.

The concepts of ABC were developed in the manufacturing sector of the U.S. during the 1970s and 80s. During this time, the Consortium for Advanced Manufacturing-International, now known simply as CAM-I, provided a formative role for studying and formalizing the principles that have become more formally known as Activity-Based Costing. Robin Cooper and Robert Kaplan, proponent of the Balanced Scorecard, brought notice to these concepts in a number of articles published in Harvard Business Review beginning in 1988. Cooper and Kaplan described ABC as an approach to solve the problems of traditional cost management systems. These traditional costing systems are often unable to determine accurately the actual costs of production and of the costs of related services. Consequently managers were making decisions based on inaccurate data especially where there are multiple products.

Instead of using broad arbitrary percentages to allocate costs, ABC seeks to identify cause and effect relationships to objectively assign costs. Once costs of the activities have been identified, the cost of each activity is attributed to each product to the extent that the product uses the activity. In this way ABC often identifies areas of high overhead costs per unit and so directs attention to finding ways to reduce the costs or to charge more for costly products.

Activity-based costing was first clearly defined in 1987 by Robert S. Kaplan and W. Bruns as a chapter in their book Accounting and Management. They initially focused on manufacturing industry where increasing technology and productivity improvements have reduced the relative proportion of the direct costs of labour and materials, but have increased relative proportion of indirect costs. For example increased automation has reduced labour, which is a direct cost, but has increased depreciation, which is an indirect cost.

Traditionally cost accountants had arbitrarily added a broad percentage onto the direct costs to allow for the indirect costs. However as the percentages of overhead costs had risen, this technique became increasingly inaccurate because the indirect costs were not caused equally by all the products. For example one product might take more time in one expensive machine than another product, but since the amount of direct labour and materials might be the same, the additional cost for the use of the machine would not be recognised when the same broad 'on-cost' percentage is added to all products. Consequently, when multiple products share common costs, there is a danger of one product subsidising another.

Like manufacturing industries, financial institutions also have diverse products which can cause cross-product subsidies. Since personnel expenses represent the largest single component of non-interest expense in financial institutions, these costs must also be attributed more accurately to products and customers. Activity based costing, even though developed for manufacturing, can therefore be a useful tool for doing this. This extended use of ABC to financial institutions was presented in 1990 in an article appearing in the Journal of Bank Cost and Management Accounting (Volume 3, Number 2) by Richard Sapp, David Crawford and Steven Rebishcke.

Direct labour and materials are relatively easy to trace directly to products, but it is more difficult to directly allocate indirect costs to products. Where products use common resources differently, some sort of weighting is needed in the cost allocation process. The measure of the use of a shared activity by each of the products is known as the cost driver. For example, the cost of the activity of bank tellers can be ascribed to each product by measuring how long each product's transactions takes at the counter and then by measuring the number of each type of transaction.

Even in activity-based costing, some overhead costs are difficult to assign to products and customers, for example the chief executive's salary. These costs are termed 'business sustaining' and are not assigned to products and customers because there is no meaningful method. This lump of unallocated overhead costs must nevertheless be met by contributions from each of the products, but it is not as large as the overhead costs before ABC is employed.

Although some may argue that costs untraceable to activities should be "arbitrarily allocated" to products, it is important to realize that the only purpose of ABC is to provide information to management. Therefore, there is no reason to assign any cost in an arbitrary manner. Management accountants can be creative in finding other ways to represent these costs on internal reporting statements.

EVOLUTION OF ADVERTISING

In the nineteenth century a substantial part of advertising consisted of what would now be termed announcements and of items we now find in the classified advertising section of newspapers. In addition to these, however, the advertising agencies sold a quantity of space to the "patent medicine" business. During the period around 1870, modern medicine was in its infancy. As a result there was a considerable field for the sale of all sorts of remedies. These accounts, which almost any agency would frown on today, were perhaps the backbone of the early agency business.

Those were the days of rugged individualism, not of professional ethics. It was the pioneering period. There was no social legislation and, looking backward, it appears that there was little conscience or application of a moral standard in most business. Thus it was natural that the advertising agency seldom investigated the merits of the product it advertised. Actually, it can scarcely be said that the agency was responsible for the advertising that it sold and placed. In most cases, the advertiser and not the agency prepared the copy for the advertisement. All the agent did was to sell the space, forward the advertising copy and instructions to the publisher, and collect for the advertisement.

In addition to the classified and patent medicine advertising, the early agency placed what we today might consider legitimate advertising, including local notices and the advertising of farm implements and a few other products. Mail-order houses and manufacturers of farm products, books and machinery were some of the first industries to use advertising as a sales tool. The 1870 advertisement is a far cry from the elaborately designed advertisement for the same store today; while the 1911 advertisement for the Buick Motor Company shows that the trend was beginning to change into what is used in present-day styles of advertising.

The nature of the advertising agency business, as it was first constituted, was bound to cause trouble. Nearly all agencies were committed for large amounts of space in the publications which they represented. Consequently, it was profitable for them to urge their clients to use those particular papers. This, of course, was not economically sound. In addition, if the advertiser wanted to use space in periodicals that the agency did not have direct representation for, it was necessary for the agent to try some makeshift negotiations for the space. Agencies were in constant competition with each other in an effort to secure the space that an advertiser wanted. At the best, the agencies' basis of operations was not conducive to creating confidence between the advertiser and the agent since it was never clear to whom the agency was responsible. This confused state of affairs finally stimulated a clarification of the business, and toward the close of the nineteenth century the agencies began to give up the position of space jobber by instituting what was called the open contract.

The Open Contract

Under the open contract plan, the agency became the representative of the advertiser. The open contract provided that the advertiser have free access to all of the information available to the agency. The agency promised to buy the space needed by the advertiser at the lowest possible rates, and in return charge a commission for its services. The agency began to promise the advertiser unbiased recommendations concerning circulation, population, general reputation of the paper, etc.

The open contract clearly was the beginning of the system existing today for remunerating advertising agencies through a commission paid by the publication.

In 1891, George Batten opened an agency in New York City. From the very beginning, he adhered to the new principle of buying space for the advertiser at the lowest possible cost. To this cost he added fifteen percent for his services. In contrast to the questionable speculative profit that agencies had received when they jobbed space, this new basis provided a reasonable profit margin. It placed the agency in a more secure position and enabled it to develop services for the advertiser. As agencies throughout the country began to adhere more and more to the open contract system, two important developments occurred:

1. They had made their decision to work for the advertisers' interests exclusively.
2. In addition to buying space for the advertiser at the lowest possible cost, they began to provide additional services and to be known as service organizations.

It is during this period that we first hear of "copywriters." Simultaneously with this development in the advertising agency business, publishers began to stabilize their rates so that those agencies which still acted as space brokers had difficulty in buying space below the market. By about 1890, many newspapers had arranged to pay advertising agencies a commission of fifteen percent on the space placed. National magazines at that time were paying agencies a commission of ten percent. During the period from 1890 to about 1930 when agencies were making the transition from space brokers to service organizations, there were many agencies and advertisers who still were wedded to the old idea of buying space below the market. This brought about the vicious practice of price cutting, which the agencies accomplished by rebating a part of their commissions to the advertisers. In 1910, out of twenty-five reasonably large advertising agencies doing business with the Curtis Publishing Company, ten were suspected of rebating commissions. In 1920, six of these ten price-cutting agencies were still in business, but by 1930 only one of them remained.

During the period from 1890 to 1930, publishers began to see that the advertising agency was a valuable tool for legitimately creating advertising business. There was a real incentive for them to protect the agency from price cutting and unsound competition, for the publisher wanted the advertiser to get his money's worth. Since the publishers were not in a position to conceive the advertising campaign, select the media, prepare the copy and visualize the art work, the advertising agency was the perfect answer to their problem.

In 1893, the American Newspaper Publishers' Association adopted a resolution which provided that agencies' commissions be paid only to advertising agencies and that no similar price reduction be allowed to advertisers. The Curtis Publishing Company in 1901 put into effect a new contract arrangement with advertising agencies. This new contract provided for a commission of ten percent to approve advertising agencies. To be approved the agencies agreed to charge advertisers the full card rate, less only the cash discount for prompt payment. The agreement provided that in the event an agency quoted space in the Curtis publications for less than the published rate, such a quotation would be considered a violation of the contract. The contract provided that upon a second violation, the agent would be dropped from the approved list of advertising agencies.

Gradually, all publishers and other media fell in line with the commission system which stabilized advertising rates and the income of the advertising agencies. Magazine publishers increased the commission basis first from ten to thirteen percent. In 1918, the American Association of Advertising Agencies sought to increase the commission basis of magazines from thirteen to fifteen percent, with an additional two percent cash discount for prompt payment. Today, the fifteen percent agency commission is standard with only inconsequential exceptions.

On various occasions from 1890 to the present time, publishers and advertisers have questioned both the commission system itself and the rate of commission paid; but since 1925, it has been more or less standard practice for the advertising agencies to receive a fifteen percent commission allowed by the publishers and other advertising media.

CHECKING ADVERTISING

The purchaser of an article wants to be sure he receives it and wants to verify the quantity and quality before he pays for it. Printed advertising is purchased in accordance with definite terms and conditions as to quantity, quality and time of publication. Before the agency makes payment to the publisher, it is desirable to check the advertising to determine whether it meets the specifications in accordance with the contract and order. In most agencies one or more persons are assigned the job of checking the advertising. This is a routine job and usually follows a more or less standard pattern.

News Papers

A copy of each newspaper insertion order is sent to the checking department. Newspaper orders are filed by state and city in which the paper is published. Upon receipt of publications, agencies usually sort them in the same manner in which insertion orders are filed. Then, by referring to the insertion order bearing the same name as the publication, the checker is able to determine what advertising to look for. For example, if the checking department receives a copy of the Chicago *Sun*, the checker then looks in the file under "Illinois, Chicago, *Sun*" A copy of the insertion order covering the advertising should be filed there.

If the title discloses an insertion order for "Illinois, Chicago, *Sun*" covering an insertion in a particular edition on a specified date, the checker then looks at the order further to find the name of the advertiser and the product, after which he runs through the paper to locate the advertisement. When this is located, the checker examines it for quality and correctness. Assuming that the correct advertisement has been published and that the quality of printing is acceptable, the checker then measures the advertisement to determine the amount of space occupied by it.

Newspaper space is usually sold in lines or inches. Daily papers usually sell space by lines; the small papers and weekly papers usually sell it by inches. An inch represents fourteen lines of "agate" type. The insertion order indicates whether the space is purchased by lines or inches. The checker is furnished with a rule calibrated in both.

A line of space is the depth measure, a column is the width measure. In other words, if an advertisement occupies three columns in width and ten lines in depth, the space measurement would be thirty lines. The same rule holds true when the unit is inches instead of lines; that is, if an advertisement is three columns wide and three inches deep, the measurement would be nine inches.

Some agencies have established the practice of rating the various positions in which advertising appears in newspapers. The purpose of such a rating system is to determine whether or not a particular newspaper is giving the advertiser reasonably good positions in the paper. Generally, advertising which appears on the first few pages of a newspaper is considered to be more effective than that appearing far back in the paper. Advertising appearing in the upper right-hand corner of a page generally may be considered more effective than advertising appearing on the left bottom corner, etc.

After advertisement positions are rated, position reports are prepared to show the number of advertisements that secured the best position, the number that secured the second best position, etc. With these reports, the space buyer is in a position to determine which papers have been giving the advertiser reasonably good advertising positions and which have not. He can then call the representative of the paper that is not giving the advertiser reasonably good advertising positions and can demand greater consideration in the future.

Where the agency rates the positions of advertising, the key or code for such positions is noted on the insertion order at the time the checker examines and measures the advertisement. The position indication would be as follows: Date of Insertion Ad Number Space Ordered Space Used Position.

Magazines and Trade Papers

Checking magazine and trade-paper space is considerably simpler than checking newspaper space. Space in magazines is usually purchased in units of pages or fractions thereof, although occasionally magazines arid trade papers sell space by columns or inches. The usual magazine advertisement occupying a page, half-page, quarter-page, etc. is not subject to shrinkage. This is because electrotypes and half-tones are used instead of mats. These are built to occupy the exact amount of space ordered. The checker, then, needs to inspect a magazine advertisement only for quality of print and position.

Some agencies, in addition to checking the appearance of advertising for quality and quantity, wish to determine the position secured in either a paper or a magazine.

There are different methods of rating the comparative position of advertisements, but among the most important factors to be considered are:

1. The page number on which the advertisement appears.
2. The section in which the advertisement appears (such as buyer's guide, society section, financial section, etc.).
3. The position on the page.
4. Whether or not the advertisement appears adjacent to competitive copy.

Where the agency is interested in rating the position of the advertising, the checker usually is furnished with a code for this purpose. The code is entered on an accounting record from which the agency can prepare a report showing the various positions secured from the different publications.

Radio

The checking of radio advertising is, obviously, a different matter from checking printed advertising. Usually the broadcasting station sends the agency an affidavit certifying the fact that each message or programme was actually broadcast. Such affidavits are required by agencies before bills for broadcasting are paid. At times, advertising agencies have attempted to listen to each broadcast to check the message or programme, but this practice was never general. Most agencies rely on the honesty of the broadcasting stations and on other reports secured from the advertiser or his distributors in each town where a programme is broadcast. These distributors, of course, are acquainted with the facts concerning the advertiser's programme. Since the advertising is important to the distributor, it may be expected that the distributor would report any omissions or other defects in the radio advertising campaign.

In addition, there is a radio checking service available on both the East and West Coasts. Clients are furnished with actual recordings of what is said on the air waves on a particular programme, product or topic, or, occasionally, with programme scripts. There is available, also, a spot-checking service, with listeners or monitors in several hundred cities. Agencies and advertisers are advised whether the spots were actually used at the time they were scheduled; what the adjacencies were; the caliber of the presentation; and other pertinent data bearing on the effectiveness of the spot message.

Other Media

It is not a general practice for agencies to check the appearance of outdoor advertising and car cards. Lithographs or other material are sent to the outdoor advertising plants, which certify the actual placing and appearance of the advertising. It would be extremely difficult for an agency to check the posting date and the quality of the posting of each outdoor sign. The cost of such checking would not be warranted. For this reason, agencies do little or no checking of outdoor advertising space.

The National Outdoor Advertising Bureau does render a valuable service in this regard. In addition to checking the appearance of outdoor advertising, the Bureau furnishes other services.

One agency checked every outdoor location to determine the date on which each billboard was posted and the quality of the posting. In addition, for several years, this agency made intensive studies to determine the comparative value of the locations used. This practice was discontinued by the agency after a few years when it was found that the outdoor plants billed correctly for the space used and that the statistics furnished by the plant owners were reliable. This, they concluded, made independent checking and study of little value. Checking the appearance of advertising in the manner discussed is a service that the agency renders to the advertiser in consideration of the commissions received from the advertising media. No special or extra charge is made for such service.

Advertising Materials, Publicity and Miscellaneous

Certain materials are necessary to produce a printed advertisement. These are called mechanical production or advertising materials. They include art work, photography, typography, engravings, half-tones, electrotypes, mats, stereos, Photostats, etc.

6

Customer Relationship Management

INTRODUCTION

Customer relationship management (CRM) covers methods and technologies used by companies to manage their relationships with clients. Information stored on existing customers (and potential customers) is analyzed and used to this end. Automated CRM processes are often used to generate automatic personalized marketing based on the customer information stored in the system.

Customer relationship management is a corporate level strategy, focusing on creating and maintaining relationships with customers. Several commercial CRM software packages are available which vary in their approach to CRM. However, CRM is not a technology itself, but rather a holistic approach to an organisation's philosophy, placing the emphasis firmly on the customer.

CRM governs an organization's philosophy at all levels, including policies and processes, front-of-house customer service, employee training, marketing, systems and information management. CRM systems are integrated end-to-end across marketing, sales, and customer service.

A CRM system should:

- Identify factors important to clients.
- Promote a customer-oriented philosophy
- Adopt customer-based measures
- Develop end-to-end processes to serve customers
- Provide successful customer support
- Handle customer complaints
- Track all aspects of sales
- Create a holistic view of customers' sales and services information

There are three fundamental components in CRM:

- Operational - automation of basic business processes (marketing, sales, service)

- Analytical - analysis of customer data and behaviour using business intelligence
- Collaborative - communicating with clients

Operational CRM provides automated support to "front office" business processes (sales, marketing and service). Each interaction with a customer is generally added to a customer's history, and staff can retrieve information on customers from the database as necessary.

According to Gartner Group operational CRM typically involves three general areas:

- *Sales force automation (SFA):* SFA automates some of a company's critical sales and sales force management tasks, such as forecasting, sales administration, tracking customer preferences and demographics, performance management, lead management, account management, contact management and quote management.
- *Customer service and support (CSS):* CSS automates certain service requests, complaints, product returns and enquiries.
- *Enterprise marketing automation (EMA) :* EMA provides information about the business environment, including information on competitors, industry trends, and macroenvironmental variables. EMA applications are used to improve marketing efficiency.

Integrated CRM software is often known as a "front office solution", as it deals directly with customers. Many call centers use CRM software to store customer information. When a call is received, the system displays the associated customer information (determined from the number of the caller). During and following the call, the call center agent dealing with the customer can add further information. Some customer services can be fully automated, such as allowing customers to access their bank account details online or via a WAP phone.

Analytical CRM

Analytical CRM analyses data (gathered as part of operational CRM, or from other sources) in an attempt to identify means to enhance a company's relationship with its clients. The results of an analysis can be used to design targeted marketing campaigns, for example:

- Acquisition: Cross-selling, up-selling
- Retention: Retaining existing customers (antonym: customer attrition)
- Information: Providing timely and regular information to customers

Other examples of the applications of analyses include:

- Contact optimization
- Evaluating and improving customer satisfaction
- Optimizing sales coverage

- Fraud detection
- Financial forecasts
- Price optimization
- Product development
- Programme evaluation
- Risk assessment and management
- Strategic Marketing
- Operational marketing

Data collection and analysis is viewed as a continuing and iterative process. Ideally, business decisions are refined over time, based on feedback from earlier analyses and decisions. Most analytical CRM projects use a data warehouse to manage data.

Collaborative CRM

Collaborative CRM focuses on the interaction with customers (personal interaction, letter, fax, phone, Internet, e-mail etc.)

Collaborative CRM includes:

- Providing efficient communication with customers across a variety of communications channels
- Providing online services to reduce customer service costs
- Providing access to customer information while interacting with customers

Driven by authors from the Harvard Business School (Kracklauer/Mills/Seifert), Collaborative CRM also seems to be the new paradigma to succeed the leading Efficient Consumer Response and Category Management concept in the industry/ trade relationship.

In its broadest sense, CRM covers all interaction and business with customers. A good CRM programme allows a business to acquire customers, provide customer services and retain valued customers.

Customer services can be improved by:

- Providing online access to product information and technical assistance around the clock
- Identifying what customers value and devising appropriate service strategies for each customer
- Providing mechanisms for managing and scheduling follow-up sales calls
- Tracking all contacts with a customer
- Identifying potential problems before they occur
- Providing a user-friendly mechanism for registering customer complaints

- Providing a mechanism for handling problems and complaints
- Providing a mechanism for correcting service deficiencies
- Storing customer interests in order to target customers selectively
- Providing mechanisms for managing and scheduling maintenance, repair, and on-going support
- Scalability: the system should be highly scalable, as the volume of data stored in the system grows over time
- Communication channels: CRM can interface with a variety of different channels (phone, WAP, Internet etc.)
- Workflow - a company's business processes need to be represented by the system with the ability to track the individual stages and transfer information between steps
- Assignment - the ability to assign requests, such as service requests, to a person or group.
- Database - the means of storing customer data and histories (in a data warehouse)
- Customer privacy considerations, such as data encryption and legislation.

Improving Customer Relationships

CRM applications often track customer interests and requirements, as well as their buying habits. This information can be used to target customers selectively. Furthermore, the products a customer has purchased can be tracked throughout the product's life cycle, allowing customers to receive information concerning a product or to target customers with information on alternative products once a product begins to be phased out.

Repeat purchases rely on customer satisfaction, which in turn comes from a deeper understanding of each customer and their individual needs. CRM is an alternative to the "one size fits all" approach. In industrial markets, the technology can be used to coordinate the conflicting and changing purchase criteria of the sector.

The data gathered as part of CRM raises concerns over customer privacy and enables persuasive sales techniques. However, CRM does not necessarily involve gathering new data, but also includes making better use of customer information gathered as a result of routine customer interaction.

The privacy debate generally focuses on the customer information stored in the centralized database itself, and fears over a company's handling of this information. For example, there is virtually no way a consumer can determine if the company shares private (personally identifiable) data with third parties. Furthermore, companies may not always accurately declare to the consumer the types of information collected by CRM systems and the specific purposes for which the information is used.

CRM is also important to non-profit organizations, which sometimes use the terms "constituent relationship management", "contact relationship management" or "community relationship management" to describe their information systems for managing donors, volunteers and other supporters. salesforce.com, a popular CRM service that is on demand, offers its products for free to nonprofit organizations.

UNDERSTANDING THE CUSTOMER

To understand the customer is to understand your business. To understand the customer's perspective is basic to defining a business. The first obvious q7uestion is, who is the customer? If the firm defines the customer too narrowly or without context, any subsequent analysis is flawed. Firms either focus on their end users as packaged-goods firms tend to do, or as in the case of industrial firms, the focus is on the immediate customer.

Both cases reflect a narrow view and a lack of understanding of the context. To determine who the customer is, the question to ask is, how does what we produce or provide add value to the client's value creating process? Most important, what do customers see as the value we are providing to their value creation process? This point is central to what we know as the "value chain" concept.

An understanding of customers requires an understanding of the customers' value chain that includes the set of their value consumption activities. If the value created by the immediate customer creates value for a subsequent customer, that customer is also an indirect customer of the firm. We really need to identify the customer as a first step to determine whose perspective we should take and to understand the customer value that we are providing.

Performing the analysis of the customer sometimes forces the redefining of the customer. For Bright Horizons, a workplace child care and early education service company, it made a huge difference in how they went about their business when they viewed employers, and not parents, as their primary customers. The company could now tap into the financial and other resources of corporations and gain access to a much wider pool of parents. The value they were providing to the employer became the focus of the company. Chase Manhattan, for example, figured that its child care centre was yielding 110 percent return on investment through reduced absenteeism. Similarly, Merck found that its employee retention rate among those who were young parents went up dramatically.

The customer-focused perspective blurs the boundaries between entities in the value chain. Take the case of Aramark Corp., a firm that caters special events and runs cafeterias for big corporate clients. Nancy Naatz, resident district manager for business services for Aramark, has an office in the premises of her customer, Sears, in Chicago. Since Ms. Naatz is on location at her client's company, she is able to observe and interact with the local vendors Aramark has contracted to supply and serve Sears. Ms. Naatz is able to understand Sears executives' and employees' nutritional needs and interact with the vendors to ensure that the appropriate choices are made available. In this case, Aramark matches the food vendors' solution with the needs of the Sears employees who are the real customers.

So, who is the customer? The perspective of *which* customer I inspect and analyze, so as to help determine the business of my business, is the question. This question also raises the fundamental marketing decision of what or who our target market should be. It is a logical place to start before making any marketing or operations decision.

Of all the potential customers that make up the market, which particular type of customer is most appropriate for our solution? The analysis involves segmentation, and the decision involved is one of targeting. We are able then to determine which particular type of customer from the universe of all customers for this product would find most value in what our value-creating assets can produce. We thus segment the market and target those segments for whom our value-creating assets can provide differentiation and a cost advantage. To know who the customer is necessitates an understanding of the typical customer in that segment at a general or aggregate level.

Traditionally, customer profiles have come out of the segmentation exercise. Segmentation variables in the B2C context have included demographic, psychographic, and behavioural variables. For customer-focused management we need information on all of the characteristics of the need or problem or use-situation that the customer is involved in, encompassing all of the activities of the customer that the product is a part of. Consequently, the question, who is the customer? takes on different shades and meanings.

You want to know how the customer purchases and uses the product. Similarly, the profile of the customer in a B2B context involves understanding the business of the organizational customer. For either the B2C or the B2B context, an understanding of the customers requires analysis of their use-situations, and the contexts within which a product helps them in what they do. Of what value are you to them? Now we begin to hint at the notion of what customer value really is. The answers lie in the *consumption* of the product, not in its production.

MANAGING THE CUSTOMER

Since the customer is part of the process and some degree of interaction with the customer is necessary and inevitable, managers of services must find ways to educate customers on their roles. If the customer fails in playing the appropriate coproducer role, it could ruin the process and the outcome quality. A clear understanding of the steps in the process and how, where, and when customers interact with the process is a must. Doctors, nurses, and pharmacists provide directions and instructions for patient roles.

Banks and other financial institutions have specific protocols for various financial transactions. A key question to ask is how the customer should participate in the process and whether you have the appropriate instructions for your customer. Differences in customer willingness and ability to participate in the production of the process force the issue of segmentation on the service delivery process.

Thus, restaurants have self-service, take-out, or drive-through options. Automatic teller machines are an early example of self-service in banking services. Hotels have express check-in and check-out facilities. Airlines have electronic ticketing options. Self-service checkout facilities have become a standard option at grocery stores in the United States and elsewhere.

It is clear as we think about these issues that not all services are alike. While all services face all these challenges to some degree, the challenges manifest themselves differently in different services. In fact, the management solutions presented are more applicable in some and inappropriate or impossible in others. There is a systematic way of addressing these differences among services by examining characteristics that differentiate services from one another. A service that shares characteristics with another service exhibits similar challenges and opportunities.

In employing the service orientation, every manager needs to understand that there are different types of services in every product, each with its own manifestations of the fundamental characteristics of services. The nature of these manifestations in different services implies different situations for the customer and the manager. While all services are fundamentally intangible, inseparable, perishable, and variable, services differ from each other along dimensions peculiar to their category. These category characteristics provide the manager with an insight into the specific situations that they have to deal with in their particular service category.

Christopher Lovelock demonstrated that this sort of categorizing is necessary and powerful as a means of understanding the managerial situations specific to each type of service. Service managers should look toward other services that share similar characteristics and expect to find similar challenges and transferable solutions to those challenges. Consider for example that hospitals provide executive-style rooms for the businessperson who is a patient.

They learned this from hotels that have executive-style suites for the businessperson. Now consider the service characteristics that are shared between hospitals and hotels. In both cases, the customer comes to the factory and frequently requires an overnight stay. In both situations, the executive is likely to be away from an office with all its business support for an extended period of time. Both services are similar in the type of customer interactions, even though they are in two completely different service sectors. An analysis as depicted earlier represents the benefits of learning from the successes of services that share certain specific service characteristics.

Managers of services can understand the specific challenges and opportunities presented by the characteristics of their product and corresponding situations by examining a number of characteristics that profile a service category. Here are a few characteristics to examine:

- Tangible or intangible act
- Person or thing as recipient of the act
- Type of interaction between provider and customer
- Service delivered by people or equipment
- Extent of customization or standardization

What are the tangible and intangible acts involved in the services that you are providing? Is the service act delivered on a person or a thing? For example, if you are an entertainment electronics repair and service provider, you perform tangible acts on a DVD player and intangible acts with the customer as you obtain information on what problems the customer has experienced with the DVD player. Now, examine the nature of the acts and the impact on the customer. When you are working on the DVD player, the customer needs not be present and the process that you employ need not be visible to the customer. However, you do interact with the customer at a number of points, from the initial customer call to the final interaction at delivery or pickup of the DVD player.

Similarly, you might analyze your service about the nature of interaction of with the customer. Is it face-to-face or arm's length, via telephone or the Internet? Do you visit the customer or does the customer visit your premises? How much technology is involved in the interface with the customer? Sometimes the customer does not even interact with a person. How much standardization is built into the service? Are there options provided to customers who require a customized interaction? What benefits does this analysis provide the manager?

The challenges and opportunities discussed earlier as fundamental are common to all service managers. By understanding the characteristics of their specific category of services, the manager can find ways to take advantage of the opportunities and address the challenges of their specific situation. Additionally, in understanding how the fundamental characteristic of intangibility manifests itself in their particular situation, managers can understand customers' perceived risk and use the tangibles in the customer experience to reduce the risk that customers perceive. By understanding the nature of the interaction, managers are in a better place to manage the roles of customers and recognize opportunities for customization and standardization to improve the customer experience and, therefore, customer value. What is most interesting is that you may find that service businesses in a different industry sharing certain characteristics may offer you innovative ideas to meet these challenges and capitalize on opportunities to better serve customers in your business.

MANAGING CUSTOMER INTERACTIONS

The process of delivering value is a tricky and detail-rich exercise; it requires careful planning, using techniques such as blueprinting to visualize the entire customer experience. From the customer perspective, some service encounters are critical incidents requiring more attention than others. All service encounters must be staged for a customer-focused experience just as in the production of theater.

Why does Kimberly-Clark manage the discount retailer Costco's inventory of its diapers? The firm has a salesperson live near the Costco headquarters, and a data analyst responsible for overseeing stock at 155 Costco stores in the western United States. Similarly, Procter & Gamble stations 250 people near Wal-mart's headquarters in Bentonville, Arkansas. Large retailers are asking suppliers to more actively manage the movement of products from factory to retail store shelves. P&G estimates that stock-outs amount to 11 percent of an average retailer's annual sales. When firms like Kimberly-Clark pay more attention to how its immediate customers—the retailers—create value to their customers, they demonstrate that they are being customer focused. In fact, the Kimberly-Clark salesperson passed on information on how customers place packages in their shopping cart that played into package design for diapers. Wayne Sanders, chairman and CEO of Kimberly-Clark, attributes this change to the information age.

Prior to the industrial revolution, a service orientation and the individual-to-individual interaction was the predominant mode of competitiveness. Assembly-line production distanced the firm from the customer due to the sheer number of customers and the physical distance between the customers and the firm brought about by the wonders of modern transportation. Manufacturing goods became the engine of individual and collective (national) economic growth. Mechanization far outpaced services and replaced producer-customer interaction, relying instead on intermediary institutions to provide a specialized set of competencies that the producing firm lacked. Businesses lost sight of the customer. Now, information technology has brought this full circle, back to the customer.

We call it the information age because what has changed in our time is that new technology has revolutionized the way information is handled. Another equally significant revolution is the change in the customer's domain. Customers not only have access to more information on products and service offerings, they also have the ability to interact with the providers of products and services in ways not previously possible. Providers can also present enhancements to customer experiences from the functionalities presented by technology. Service providers must, however, also manage customer participation when they utilize technology. When firms take advantage of online marketplaces, it might be necessary to make changes in organizational structure so that value creation and delivery processes are adjusted to the addition of the online delivery. Two key technologies underlie this information age technology phenomenon: the Internet and wireless communications. What customer access to these technologies has done is to bring customer interactions to a new level and to the front and centre in how a firm deals with the customer. These interactions are essentially service encounters with the customer.

Much has been said about the service encounter—customer interactions with the firm. In a way, all customer relationship management (CRM) solutions are basically technology support to ensure that the firm maximizes returns from customers by enabling customer-focused interactions. The service encounter is truly "where the rubber hits the road"—where the prospects of customer loyalty are materialized or lost.

It is where promises made in advertising are honored or reneged on, and where expectations of customers are disappointed or met. It is where all the assets of the firm need to be brought to bear. Service encounters with the customers are also laden with the challenges of a product that is produced and consumed in real time, where failures are bound to happen. When the firm designs the value creation process with the customer in mind, it will be prepared for all predictable eventualities.

When the service fails, smart firms have smart processes, that recover and learn from the failure. They have service recovery and knowledge management processes in place. As firms compete more and more on services, the management of the customer interaction becomes critical to ensure superiority in customer value.

As the core product is a commodity, and most facilitating services approach the commodity state, the competitiveness comes from how the customer is treated by the firm at each and every encounter. This chapter discusses a method for designing the value delivery process with special attention paid to the service encounter and the critical incidents in the value creation and delivery process. A framework for designing the service encounter based on the theatrical metaphor is offered as a way to examine the customer focus of value creation and delivery.

Analyzing customer interactions can be very rewarding. Amazon constantly tracks the reasons for every customer contact. It has made numerous changes to its value creation and delivery process based on customer input. The customer service function at Amazon is considered a research lab for ways to improve the Amazon customer experience. We can turn to the unique characteristics of services to obtain a clear understanding of what is involved in a customer interaction. Something intangible is always exchanged in the interaction (intangibility).

Without a customer, there is no interaction and the separation of production and consumption is irrelevant (inseparability). To conduct the interaction, the firm has the resources and infrastructure in place that "perish" when not utilized (perishability). Each interaction is unique (variability). From these characteristics, emerge situations that are challenges and opportunities typical to the service firm.

We need to keep these in mind as we design the process of creating and delivering customer value. At the most general level, all customer interactions occur in a certain place (or space), at a certain time, for a certain duration, between certain entities, in a certain manner for a certain purpose. Consider these as ingredients in a customer interaction and categorize them into elements of structure, content, and process. When the customer interaction is mapped onto the consumption activity cycle, the objective of the interaction becomes the driving force behind the design of the interaction in terms of its structure, content, and process.

- Structure relates to who or what entities are involved in the interaction.
- Content relates to the subject, the task, and its significance in the interaction.
- Process relates to the sequence of steps in the interaction.

The primary decisions that would configure the structure of the interaction involve the nature of the interaction—what entity should represent the firm, should the interaction be face-to-face or not, what technology can be utilized, where should it occur, and so forth. As a complementary question about the customer: What entities from the customer's domain are involved in the interaction?

Similarly, decisions determining the content of the interaction should centre around the task and include what information should be required in the interaction, what should transpire between the parties, and what value should be created and consumed in the interaction. Decisions about process would include a script of the interaction and the roles of both parties in the interaction.

Any of these decisions must be based on the information that the firm has about the customer's consumption cycle and on preferences regarding these dimensions of the interaction. For example, technology may provide the firm with scale economies, but the customer may want to disengage from the script and interact with a person instead. Ultimately, the important question is what value is being created in the interaction.

As we saw earlier the execution of the product concept as the delivery of the product involves a process, a sequence of activities. Therefore, designing the product must necessarily include a design of the delivery process. Lynn Shostack proposed a technique called "blueprinting" to detail the process design in the delivery of services.

The service blueprint is a map or flowchart as a visual representation of the process of service delivery. Essentially, the blueprint design is diagramed in three steps. In the first step, all types of customer interactions with the firm are listed. Next, these interactions are arranged in sequence of occurrence. In the final step, processes within the firm that are required to create and provide each customer interaction are mapped. How and what information, materials, facilities and equipment, and people are processed must be included in the service blueprint.

The customer-focused blueprint is one that is designed with the customer in mind. With the activities in the customer's consumption cycle in mind, processes within the firm need to be designed in such a way that the desired value added in the solution is reflected at each and every encounter with the customer. Commerce Bancorp, for example, encourages its employees to make suggestions in streamlining the service delivery process. Commerce Bancorp employees receive a fifty-dollar reward for finding something about a process that does not contribute to customer value and instead is an impediment to serving the customer; the bank immediately adjusts its operations.

Even as a simple representation of the value creation and delivery process, the service blueprint has a variety of important strategic, analytical, and diagnostic uses. In designing the delivery of the product, it can be used to determine the uniqueness of the service process. When compared with competitive blueprints, where and at which points in the process the firm derives its competitive advantage and superiority in customer value become evident. Thus, the service blueprint can be used in a strategic analysis of the differentiating features and benefits of the service delivered by the firm. Only with such comparative analysis of the service blueprint is it possible to ensure that the value creation and delivery processes are commensurate with the superior customer value planned in the product concept and operations design.

The service blueprint has two major dimensions that characterize the nature and scope of the service delivery process: complexity and divergence. The complexity dimension reflects the number of steps or activities in the process. A highly complex service process has a great variety of activities during the series of customer interactions. Some of these activities occur in the front stage and some in the back stage, away from the customer's view. A so-called line of visibility determines what the customer sees or does not see. The customer-focused firm will need to examine everything that the customer sees and experiences to determine whether the service delivery at the service encounter is contributing to or detracting from customer value. The divergence dimension reflects the degree of flexibility at each customer interaction. The greater the divergence, the greater the customization built into the service—the greater the number of options the customer is given to choose from at each interaction. Therefore, supplementary product benefits such as customization must be mapped into the service delivery process. Complexity and divergence decisions will determine the position of the firm's offering compared to competitive offerings. Competitive blueprints can be compared to determine how competitive value bundles differ from each other. It becomes clear that the positioning of each competitive offering is reflected in the service blueprints.

The patient experience is very carefully orchestrated to support the entire concept of the "Shouldice Method." The surgical procedure itself is probably the least sophisticated element of the whole process. The recovery process is more important than the surgery. Every step in the blueprint is designed for a speedy recovery and an overall "enjoyable" experience—despite the anxiety and pain of the surgery. The method is known for a very low recurrence rate and high customer satisfaction. The hospital even has patient reunion parties each year that are sometimes attended by as many as a thousand former patients. For this service, its critical steps are not in the surgical procedure but in in the recovery process and the total customer experience.

All customer interactions depicted in the blueprint are not of equal importance in terms of criticality toward customer value—some are more important to the customer than others. It is imperative that the firm employ its knowledge of customer expectations so that the critical interactions are highlighted for priority when allocating resources of the firm. This is the primary application of the blueprint technique.

Jan Carlson, CEO of the SAS airline, popularized the notion of the "moment of truth" in services. While each customer interaction is a moment of truth, those product features and customer encounters with the firm that are considered critical to the satisfaction of the customer are considered *critical incidents.* The critical incident technique has been applied in the managing of services to understand what can make or break the customer's experience. The method was initially developed for the U.S. Air Force in simulations to help in cockpit design and pilot training.

A simple question to the customer soliciting a verbal description of a typically satisfying and a typically dissatisfying experience with the product and firm would yield valuable information on what might constitute a critical incident. The incidents to which the customer attributes a satisfying or dissatisfying experience are those that are critical to customer satisfaction. When a particular point in the service delivery process keeps recurring in customer descriptions of satisfying and dissatisfying experiences, it becomes clear that it is a critical incident. These incidents can also uncover "failpoints"—points in the process that are especially likely to fail to perform as desired. Some are internal to the firm and cannot be obvious to the customer, while others occur during direct interactions with the customer. For each of these, the design of the process should ensure "fail-safe" methods and have a system recovery process in place. Fail-safe processes require a metric that triggers the recovery processes. Thus, benchmarking the performance at the failpoints is critical to the successful implementation of the product concept and operations design to deliver the desired customer value.

For firms that rely on intermediaries to bring the product to the customer, critical incidents may lie outside the firm's control. Consider, for example, what Handspring, Inc. does to make sure the customers of its products are served well at the retailer. The firm sends its employees from channel marketing posing as customers to retailers such as CompUSA and ensures that its product is stocked and well displayed and that the floor salespeople are presenting the product to the customer in the way Handspring had instructed them to do. Microsoft hands out a free Casio pocketPC to every sales rep who completes its training. These examples show an awareness that customer interactions at these intermediaries are failpoints and need to be monitored.

Critical incidents help in assigning the appropriate level of resources within the firm. Thus, the service blueprint is useful from a quality control perspective. Customer evaluations of a firm's service can be linked to specific customer encounters in the blueprints and all processes directly affecting or affected by the critical incidents must be monitored for quality. Customer-focused quality control efforts can be focused on critical variables that can be controlled. Service recovery procedures must be designed into the process at these points.

Interactive technologies provided by the information age revolution are now an integral part of the design of the value creation and delivery process. These technologies work through the three primary productive components of customer value—the people, the infrastructure in facilities and equipment, and processes and systems of value creation and delivery. Consider all the ways in which the customer can interact with a firm. Each touch-point can be made by the converging technologies of today. For example, in some interactions the location of either buyer or seller becomes irrelevant. Customers can interact by wireless or wired means, which can be by voice, video, or text, initiated by either party; they are constantly getting cheaper and better in features and functionality.

The basic difficulty with any of this newer interactive technology is that the objective and role of the technology can be lost sight of and the technology itself become the focus. The final measure is whether the technology is contributing toward sustainable profits for the firm by improving customer value. The benefits of interactive technology come in the form of efficiency and efficacy. Efficiency is reflected in increasing productivity and efficacy is reflected in improved customer value. Both of these outcomes contribute to the bottom line of the firm. For a firm competing on service, interactive technology is critical to sustain profits because of what it can do to customer value. Maximize the return from interactive technologies by deploying it at the critical points; prioritized by its customer value-creating power. For example, a common source of dissatisfaction and irritation to the customer is the length of waiting time before being served. Any point in the process where there is likely to be a wait is a potential critical incident requiring the firm's express attention. If there are interactive technologies that can be used to effectively manage the customer in these situations, customer value is not threatened.

All the service components in the total product, being susceptible to the inherent characteristic of being produced and consumed in real time, force customers to the experience of "wait." Demand and supply need to be matched as closely as possible.

To avoid idle capacity, services adopt the queuing (and scheduling) approach to processing customers, resulting in a certain amount of wait before the process begins. In multi-stage processes, which many services are, in-process waits are common as well. The problem of course is that no one wants to wait. Customers will wait for a certain amount of time that is reasonable to them as per their expectations. What is reasonable is a very subjective judgment, of course—one that requires analysis of the factors that determine the perception of waits.

Maister's work on the psychological cause and effects of wait suggests a way to reduce the negative consequences where wait is a given.

- Preprocess waits feel longer than in-process waits. Allow the customer to begin the process by completing the first step in the value delivery process.
- Unoccupied waits feel longer. Keep the customer in wait occupied with activities, preferably related to the product or service.
- Uncertain waits feel longer. Keep the customer informed about how long the expected wait is to likely to be.
- Unexplained waits feel longer. Keep the customer informed about why they are having to wait.
- Inequitable waits feel longer. Serve customer based on priority, determined by what is considered just in the ambient society.
- Value of the service. Ensure that the customer value you are providing is clearly superior to any alternative.

The most important common thread through all of these suggestions is that they all have to do with managing the customer perceptions. The firm is better placed if the customer perceptions can be influenced favourably by managing customer role and expectations in the value creation and delivery.

To varying degrees, customers play a role in the production of products and not just in the consumption. Firms that realize this have paid serious attention to how the customer fits in the organization. In services, the role of the customer is abundantly evident. Customers engage in a coproduction role. In services or in the service component of the product, customers are coproducers in self-service configurations.

All services as we saw earlier involve some kind of customer participation, as in the case of providing required information to the tax preparer, for example. Even when placing the order with the provider, the customer is essentially contributing to the production of the product by providing input into product specifications. When the customer is interacting with the firm and this interaction has some relevance to the production of the product, by definition we have the customer engaging in coproducing the product.

Service firms instinctively manage the role of the customers in their participation in the service. Restaurants have menus, professors have syllabi, airlines have their method of emplaning passengers according to a certain priority, etc. Sometimes managing customer roles may be in the form of a complementary service. For example, Universal is experimenting with a calming zone adjunct to its roller-coaster rides, for people who need help with coaster-phobia before they get on the ride. UPS and other package delivery firms instinctively accommodate special customer requests as to where their packages should be deposited if the customer is not at the location of delivery.

It is a matter of perspective. If we take the notion of value creation a step further, we could argue that even in the case of packaged goods, the value hasn't really been created to the customer until the customer actually begins to use the product. Value creation and value consumption are both inextricably interwoven into a continuous and overlapping set of activities. This is an important issue in a service orientation.

In the case of services, customer interaction is a given. And the firm must include the customer in the design of its operations. The customer-focused firm by always keeping the customer in central view manages the role of the customer in the value creation and the value consumption activities. For example, providing excellent product assembly instructions improves the value created for the customer in an "easy to assemble yourself" product. Conversely, even with a well-engineered product, poor instructions reduce customer value.

Recent product innovation studies have shown that some firms are equipping customers with the tools to design and develop their own products, ranging from minor modifications to major new innovations. PTC (formerly Parametric Technology) is a world leader in computer-assisted-design (CAD) technology, whose software solutions bring suppliers and customers together so that a client can use the software during product development to virtually interface with upstream and downstream players.

Ultimately, anything that the firm can do to manage the customer's role in the value creation as well as value consumption process is an imperative for the customer-focused firm. As mentioned earlier, Procter & Gamble is recruiting families to allow a team of their ethnographer-filmmakers to observe their daily routines to get a better sense for how their customers use household products. The actual use situation says a lot about how a product should be designed. It would also be a way to learn how the customers should be instructed in the appropriate use of the product.

How does a firm take a systematic approach to managing the customer? First, the firm identifies all the activities that the customer enacts in the value creation as well as value consumption blueprint. Next, the firm scripts the role for the customer at each activity.

Firms then have to determine how best to communicate and educate the customer in playing the appropriate role. Customers' performance of their roles will depend on their ability and inclination to perform those roles. The consumer's ability will depend on consumption skills that the customer's past experience may have provided. The customer's inclination will depend on the personal characteristics of the customer. Familiarity with the service and service provider could affect the ability and the inclination of the customer in the role performance.

In the case of services and the service components of a product, customer role is managed by the service provider. The service provider's production skills and motivation could affect the way in which the service provider manages the customer's role. The service provider's familiarity with the segment and the specific customer will influence the service provider's skills and motivation in managing the customer's role performance. The service provider's production skills are reflected in its operations and customer interaction skills. The personal characteristics of the service provider can affect the service provider's motivation. When designing the service delivery process, it is important that the firm incorporate these factors on the customer's role performance.

MANAGING CUSTOMER RELATIONSHIPS

The task of creating and delivering superior customer value must be complemented with the selection of the appropriate customers and the effective management of relationships with those customers. Managing customer relationships should be guided by an understanding of what the customer's equity is to the firm. Customer equity, the value of customer to the firm, improves as superiority in customer value improves. Since customer equity is perhaps the firm's most valuable asset, the firm must continually seek to improve customer value for it best customers. A firm's potential return on customer equity should determine the investment it makes in customers. For its most valuable customers, the firm must guarantee superior service quality and customer service, with special attention to recovering from inevitable product failures when they occur.

Maximizing long-term profitability comes from maximizing customer equity—firms must maximize the lifetime value of the customer, including revenues, referrals as well as costs of serving the customer. Customer acquisition and retention efforts must be guided by the worth of the customer to the firm.

Maytag provides premium service to its premium customers—those who purchase the Neptune line of laundry machines. Neptune customers get a dedicated staff, a separate toll-free number and fast response on service calls. This is an example of the common business practice where firms allocate resources by the profitability and value of the customer. They utilize the opportunity in directly interacting with individual customers to determine customer profitability and allocate assets accordingly. And what are the benefits of the practice of differentiating among your customers?

Broadly referring to the practice as CRM can sometimes defeat its purpose by losing sight of the basic meaning of the term: managing customer relationships. Managing customer relationships would mean actively planning, organizing, directing, and controlling a firm's business relationships with its customers.

The term might be "new" in its current usage, but the business practice of managing relationships with customers is certainly not new. What has prompted the increased attention to CRM is new technology: how well firms can practice CRM has been advanced by information technology in the new economy. Technology brings with it the risk of missing the benefits of huge investment costs if used inappropriately, however. The benefits can seem so attractive that the costs are rationalized until the technology fails to deliver.

The American Customer Satisfaction Index, a measure of customer attitudes toward about 200 companies from over 30 different industries, has actually shown a decline, while at the same time CRM technology investments had grown about five times.

When used with a fundamental understanding of CRM's purpose, the benefits of CRM technology enabling the business practice of managing customer relationships are clearly powerful. Siebel, Peoplesoft, Oracle, and other CRM technologies are really customer information management or customer knowledge management systems. These systems gather data and convert it to knowledge that will help firms in their customer relationship management activities.

The most significant contribution of CRM technology to the practice of business is not the technology itself, of course. It is in what the technology does to the practice of managing customer relationships. Because technology has now made it easy to do all the tasks of gathering and analyzing customer information, firms have been able to discover and realize the incredible benefits in proactively managing customer relationships. For example, Continental Airlines' customer information system allows its staff to mine data on passenger profitability and is also able to suggest remedies and perks for special requests or complaining customers.

Customer benefits from relationships with firms have been conceptualized under three categories: social, psychological, and customization benefits, in a two-part study using interviews and surveys. Financial services such as brokerage and banking are heavy users of CRM technology. Deregulation and information technology have effectively blurred the boundaries between those two once-different financial institutions. They have had a heavy reliance on information because these are primarily knowledge businesses. "Signature"-level customers at Charles Schwab wait no longer than fifteen seconds to reach a customer service person, whereas other customers can wait ten minutes or more. Some banks have coded their customers so that customer service reps can decide on rates and fees depending on the customer's profitability code. Centura Banks rates its customers on a profitability scale of 1 to 5. The most profitable customers get service calls from staff and an annual call from the CEO.

Attrition rate at the bank is down 50 percent in four years, and—more interesting—the percentage of unprofitable customers has gone down from 27 percent to 21 percent. The hospitality industry was able to slash 50 percent of its promotion programs and increase response rates by 20 percent with a good database of response behaviour from its mailing list. CRM systems have provided firms with the data they need to determine the revenues and costs to serve at the individual customer level, allowing firms to prioritize their allocations of value-creating assets and resources to the more profitable customers.

According to AMR research, the CRM market grew from $200 milllion to $1.1 billion between 1994 and 1997, and is expected to reach as much as $16 billion—an indication of how much firms want this technology to manage customer relationships. A firm's knowledge about its customers has allowed it to adjust customer value based on the profitability of the individual customer.

Just as with power, information technology has to be used judiciously. Discriminating against less profitable customers can seem unreasonable to all paying customers and could backfire with publicity. AT&T withdrew its minimum usage charges for its basic-plan customers who were unprofitable. GE Capital tried to charge credit-card users who were not accruing a minimum level of interest charges and ended up having to sell its credit card business. When used appropriately at the individual level, information technology can be very rewarding. Capital One's senior vice-president for domestic card operations, Marge Connelly, says, "We look at every single customer contact as an opportunity to make an unprofitable customer more profitable."

CRM systems are not just about profiling customers and loyalty programs. To derive maximum benefits, one must broaden the thinking about CRM technology. The technology should be viewed as knowledge-based systems that seek to prioritize commitment of a firm's assets and resources to the more profitable customers while enhancing the relationships with ALL (right) customers.

Pricing may not be the appropriate means to deal with the unprofitable customer. CRM systems give the firm access to information that may reveal other ways to manage the unprofitable customer. *Enabling* the managing of customer relationships is the goal of the CRM system. Managing customer relationships is about selecting, acquiring, retaining, and enhancing relationships with customers by using an intimate knowledge of the customer's consumption domain to maximize the return on the firm's assets. With CRM systems, firms have the knowledge and the technological capability to identify, retain and enhance more desirable customer relationships.

This chapter covers issues regarding which customers to acquire and retain for maximum sustainable profits. How do you assign value to customers and what is involved in that evaluation? Who is the right customer? Who should be in your customer portfolio? Firms look at customers as investments. How do you value these investments? Or, What is the equity of your customers?

SELECTING THE RIGHT CUSTOMER

Markets consist of customers with diverse needs and differences in customer profitability. When serving multiple groups of customers, the goal must be to maximize the profitability of the combination of segments. When different segments are targeted, the firm essentially has a portfolio of customer segments—just as investors have an investment portfolio that maximizes returns at a certain level of risk, firms manage customer portfolios for maximum profits. In other words, this is the selection of customers at any point in time, compared to other segments, from which the firm can generate maximum profits. Firms must attract these most profitable customers and then must establish systems and procedures to retain them.

Most firms serve different segments depending on how the definition of segment is aggregated. The "segment-of-one" used in common business parlance to refer to customization at the individual level is really a maximum disaggregation of a market segment. As we saw in the preceding chapter, most firms facing fluctuating demand and experiencing peak, shoulder and low periods of demand find it inevitable that, at different times, different segments must be served. Of course, each of these segments must have a compatible fit with the overall corporate image as well as a compatible fit with the products, services, employees and other customers. The question is, are they selected based on their combined long term value to the firm? Most firms forecast the volume and revenues from various segments at certain price points at different times in the purchase cycle. In the typical firm, sales and communications efforts follow these underlying assumptions in pricing and in messages targeting sales prospects.

The typical firm then attempts to formalize advertising campaigns to reach as many people as possible in the case of packaged goods. In the case of business-to-business services, the salespeople focus on making a sale. Most firms then struggle to orchestrate all these messages for acquisition of the customer in a coordinated fashion. Much less attention is paid to the retention of the customer. Barring the well-run operation, common business practice for many firms is short-term oriented. On the contrary, a customer-focused firm begins by approaching sales as acquiring the right customer. The customer-focused firm also approaches the acquisition of customers as only the first step in managing the relationships with its customers. Once acquired, the customer must be retained. But, not always retained at any cost—a necessary condition is that the benefits outweigh the costs of acquiring *and* retaining that customer.

Customer-focused firms align all their activities and processes in acquiring and retaining the right customer. They see their value-creating assets as most profitably leveraged by focusing on the most valuable customers. In principle, the value of the customer is determined by contribution to the firm's objectives over the lifetime of the customer.

CUSTOMER VALUE

Customer value is what the customer thinks he or she is getting in return for what the customer has to part with, reflecting an implicit comparison akin to "give and receive." It has been described as the quotient of quality over price. Understanding the customer is about understanding customer value. Customer value is a complex concept and measuring it is complicated. But in the exercise of trying to understand customer value, the manager benefits from a better understanding of the customer and of the opportunities for a superior solution.

Here are some characteristics of customer value that any manager should examine in an analysis of the firm and its activities: Customer value:

- Is what the customer believes that a product or service provides in a certain use situation.
- Is an implicit comparison between what the customer receives from the provider and what the customer provides in time, effort, and money. The frame of reference is not just the price tag on the product, but also the ease and convenience in the acquisition and use of the product and the whole interactive experience the customer has with the firm.

- Is the customer's rather than the provider's perspective. It has to do with customer perceptions of the product and the firm, and not the provider's perspective of what the firm is delivering.
- Is dynamic, in that it can change over time before, during, and after the purchase, use, over repeated use of the product, and during all the various stages in the relationship with the providing firm.
- Can vary over different use situations. Your automobile may provide less or more value in transporting a group of kids to the ballpark compared to taking the spouse to the boss's house for a party.
- Can be shaped by attitudes, opinions, and behaviours of others, such as friends, family, media, the providing firm, and other competitors in the industry as well as in substitute industries.
- Determines customer satisfaction and the likelihood of brand or firm loyalty. This cause-effect relationship could be affected by comparisons with competitors and other substitutes.
- Is hard to measure and keep track of. Customers may find it hard to articulate all the different dimensions of customer value and firms may find it a rather onerous task to keep track of all the manifestations of customer value.

In order to determine what business a firm is in, therefore, the fundamental and imperative exercise is to understand customer value. Let us begin the analysis with the question, what exactly does customer value consist of? It is not easy to determine what the customer is getting as value from a product or service. To understand customer value, you really need to get into the customer's way of thinking about products. In a recent *Harvard Business Review* article, Chase and Dasu urge the use of behavioural science to get into the head of the customer, to understand their total experience with the product or service. Only then can you grasp all the components of customer value.

Examining the components and determinants of customer value is a critical step in the analysis. It requires analysis of the benefits as well as costs to the customer. The benefits seen are evident in the perceptions of the product performance. Perceptions of product performance are framed in the context of customer expectations.

The expectations are shaped by past experience with the product and by messages about the product received from a variety of sources such as friends and family as well as from the marketer. From an analytical perspective, product performance comes from functional (core) benefits and supplemental benefits. Functional benefits arise from the core attributes of the product. For instance, you buy a set of golf clubs. How the golf clubs affect your game is a core and functional benefit, as in the primary benefit from the product. The prestige of the brand image, the product return policy, and other customer service features would translate into supplemental benefits. Every customer value analysis requires that we identify and examine core and supplemental benefits.

Similarly, we need to identify the costs to the customer—both monetary and non-monetary costs. Monetary costs include costs incurred in the acquisition, use, and disposition of the solution. Non-monetary costs could include the time and effort in acquiring and benefiting from the solution and the opportunity costs where the product failed. Tom Wright, Buy.com's vice president of operations called his company's old way of handling returns "almost embarrassing.

To return a product that a customer bought from Buy.com, the customer had to telephone Buy.com to generate a return authorization, which led to a shipping label from the package delivery firm (UPS) to be mailed to the customer, who then used that label to send the product back to Buy.com. It was weeks before the customer got credit for the product return!

Imagine the non-monetary cost of aggravation to that customer. Many firms that focus on acquiring customers do not retain customers because of their shallow understanding of customer value. Customer value includes interactions with the firm before, during, and after the consumption of the product. Smart firms are focusing on the whole customer and defining their business in terms of market spaces. The market space is the actual set of customer solutions defined by the consumption activities to which the firm caters.

In recognizing that customer value is dynamic, we need to place this analysis in the context of different use situations and how they are changed over time by various influences. Customers' concepts of what to expect from a provider change with each consumption experience. They learn from their own experiences with the product as well as vicariously from others. Competitor offerings and marketing messages continually shape their expectations. Therefore, implicit in the assessments made by the customer is a comparison with expectations based on the alternative—that is, the competition. Customer value analyses can be performed at a qualitative level and with some difficulty can be quantified as well.

Data-driven representations of monetary worth of what a firm does for a customer are what Anderson and Narus called "customer value models." Such models are useful in assessing the customer value of your product and comparing it with the competition to determine whether you are providing superior customer value or not. The next fundamental question is, Can you provide this superior customer value at a sustainable profit by commanding revenues to cover costs and profits?

Just as the customer value analysis requires an examination of the benefits versus the costs, the firm makes a similar analysis to determine the profit potential. In providing the customer value, what does the firm get in return? How do the monetary and no monetary benefits from the customer compare with what it cost the firm to provide that solution to that customer? Can we sustain these profits in the long term?

A firm creates value for itself by creating value for the customer. In many ways, the value of a firm is reflected in the profits it provides its investors and the value of the customer to the firm is reflected in the profits that the customer provides the firm. The greater the value of the customer to the firm, the greater are the profits.

This means that the surplus from the revenues after costs is greater if you can attract and retain profitable customers in the long run. Part IV in this book covers the valuation of the customer by the firm. Firms can attract and retain customers if they can provide superior value. It could boil down to, Can we command a premium on our solution? If you can, it turns out that the margins are not in the commoditized part of the product, it is in the services provided by the firm. The margins increase when you are able to extend your role in the customer's space. This may come in the form of "cross-selling" or "up-selling." It may be the case that the total solution provides such value to the customer that the customer is better off with you than with the competition.

As the firm gets more valuable to the customer, the customer gets more valuable to the firm. The value from a customer is derived not only from purchases. Customers can become advocates for the firm, the benefits of which are frequently less understood. The value of the customer in terms of purchases and referrals over the lifetime of the customer should be an imperative calculation for firms who are focused on the customer. It appears that in the final analysis, it is the customer-focused firm that can provide a complete solution through a service orientation that succeeds in providing superior customer value and in return enjoys sustainable profits. So, how is it that a firm is able to provide superior customer value? What gives them a sustainable competitive advantage, such that the firm has sustainable profits?

What characterizes firms that can provide *superior* customer value? To answer this question, we have ample evidence from research on such firms. Every firm in any industry provides some customer value. The firm that provides superior customer value is the one that has a sustainable competitive advantage.

Firms compete with each other on differentiable aspects of the total solution. If we can conceptualize that every product has parts that are commodities and parts that differentiate it from others, superior value is in the augmented product, not in the conceptual core. For example, all airlines provide transportation from point A to point B. But the total solution includes aspects other than the physical transportation of the person itself, such as amenities on the airplane. A firm must seek opportunities to differentiate itself from the competition in ways that are meaningful and relevant to the customer. How do firms find opportunities to differentiate themselves in a way that it is sustainable?

Consider how CDW creates superior customer value. CDW is the leading B2B e-commerce firm selling technology equipment to small and medium-sized firms. Wall Street analysts claim that the firm uses a "clicks and people" strategy. Supposedly, their competitive advantage is superior customer service and lower customer acquisition costs. The firm's Web site is tailored to each specific customer as a "custom extranet." How are they able to sustain this competitive advantage? Their own chief financial officer, Harry Harczak, notes that retaining people is key. In his experience, the productivity difference between an employee who has been at the firm six months versus one there three years is a factor of six. CDW values employee commitment.

What are the generalizable characteristics of firms that create superior customer value? A team of Harvard Business School researchers set out to discover exactly this and concluded that successful firms such as BancOne, Intuit, Southwest Airlines, ServiceMaster, USAA, Taco Bell, and MCI made employees and customers paramount. These researchers modeled the findings from their case studies into a framework they called "the service profit chain." Their cases provided data to establish powerful relationships between profitability, customer loyalty, and employee satisfaction, loyalty, and productivity. Evident in the whole model is the focus on the customer and the service orientation of satisfied employees, and the implications on investors and other stakeholders of the firm.

As firms focus on customer needs and become service oriented to deliver satisfaction, there are favourable ripple effects throughout the firm. Consistent delivery of customer satisfaction persuades customers to be loyal because perceived risk in buying a product from that firm is substantially reduced. When providers of solutions to customer needs are able to consistently deliver expected value, customers are more likely to be consistently satisfied. By way of their continued patronage, they become more valuable to the firm.

When customers are loyal to the provider by choice, it is also in their best interest to support the provider because the prosperity and longevity of the provider is beneficial to the customer. Similarly, with regard to employees, research has shown that when employee satisfaction is high employees are more likely to be loyal to the company. When employee loyalty is high, employees are likely to be more productive and to be providing quality products and service.

Neither employees nor customers are likely to be loyal unless their expectations are met and they are satisfied. Therefore, customer satisfaction and employee satisfaction are inherently tied to each other, in that, when employees are loyal to the firm, they provide superior performances driving customer loyalty. When employees are productive and customer loyalty is high, the firm is successful and can command a premium. With increased profitability and growth prospects, investors are attracted to the firm, which in turn makes more resources available to the firm. With more resources available to the firm, capital is available to continuously improve value-creating assets (people and processes) and to produce consistently superior customer value in its products and service. This sequence of events, presented as the "loyalty circle", contributes to profitability and growth and requires that people and processes are aligned to deliver superior customer value. Delivering superior value should be a relentless endeavor for the firm.

LOOKING FOR CUSTOMER VALUE OPPORTUNITIES

An understanding of the role that the firm's product plays in the customer's value chain could open up value-creating opportunities. A customer-focused firm has a detailed picture of the customer's consumption domain.

When a firm views value consumption activities, it can see if there are other value creating opportunities that it can leverage from its assets. The watchmaker Swatch, for example, offers wrist watches with the technology that allows them to function as electronic passes at ski resorts in Switzerland or for public transportation in Finland. Wrist gadgets can now serve not only the function of telling time, but also making phone calls, playing music and videos, browsing the Internet, or sending email.

This example defies categorization of product. What is the product? It is a wallet or a pocketbook, as well as a telephone, a personal stereo, a personal VCR, and an Internet communications device! The exercise of determining what revenue opportunities Swatch's value-creating assets would offer forces a complete redefinition of the product.

As we saw the (product) solution is conceived to take advantage of opportunities to meet the needs in the customer's life with the assets that the firm has. Swatch has found a way to provide value to a recreational activity—skiing—and a functional activity—public transportation. It is contributing to the "customer access" components of the ski resort's and public transportation's product. By enabling customer access, information technology provides a whole range of supplementary benefits to a variety of products.

Contrast this with the example of a firm that does not understand the value of complementary product components and the customer's value chain. A customer came out of a movie theater in Kendall Square, Cambridge, and experienced a 40-minute ordeal trying to leave the theater's parking lot. She spent 30 minutes standing in line in frigid weather to pay the $2.50 parking fee and a further 15 minutes to exit the parking lot.

When complaining to the management of the movie theater, she asked if she could pay the parking fee as she bought the movie ticket. She was told that the parking lot was owned by a different company and the theater would not take responsibility for the customer's bad experience at the parking lot.

In contrast, the airline SAS has been known to provide an annual dinner to taxicab drivers in Stockholm because the SAS management wants the drivers to treat passengers on the way to and from the airport with professional courtesy and respect. Clearly, firms that are customer-focused conceive their product differently from other firms, because of their intimate knowledge of the customer's consumption activities.

Information about the customer's consumption cycle, therefore, is a key prerequisite to exploring the opportunities that might be tapped. An understanding of how the customer actually benefits from the solution and the information of how, when, where, and with whom the customer consumes the product should provide some interesting revelations of what the firm is doing and can be doing in the composition of the total product solution for customers.

Thus, Procter & Gamble sends its researchers to homes to observe how people actually use laundry detergent. When Samsung was trying to break into the microwave business in the late 1970s and early 1980s, their design engineers observed homemakers shopping for microwaves at the retail store. You can stay ahead of the curve by offering value through supplementary product that your customer information tells you customers will be willing to pay for. Even if the value-producing feature or activity cannot be priced separately, you may be able to command a premium for your superior customer value. Being customer-focused is critical in identifying opportunities for establishing superiority in customer value.

All decisions about the product and, therefore, the value-creating activities of the firm are based on an understanding of the value-consumption activities of its customers. What are the decisions and what are the issues to be considered in determining the total product by a firm? The three major decisions constituting the product strategy are: the product concept, the operations design, and the value creation and delivery process alredy—displayed. The product concept defines the customer to be served and what value is to be provided. The operations design defines the productive assets of the firm required to create and deliver that value for that customer. Together, the product concept and the operations design define the scope and configuration of the productive assets that can be leveraged to produce the specific customer value that maximizes profits to the firm.

The *value creation and delivery process* executes the product concept with the operations design. In developing the product strategy, the firm makes a fundamental decision in answering the question of how the product will be positioned among all potential solutions to the customer's need.

This positioning question poses an asset- and market-based decision that comprises two perspectives:

- The *market-based perspective* looks outward at the market and asks what customer needs can be most profitably served by the firm.

- The *asset-based perspective* looks inward, at the firm's assets, and asks what assets of the firm can be most profitably leveraged by the firm.

The market-based perspective drives the product concept and the asset-based perspective drives the operations design. Thus, the initial step in developing product strategy involves two critical analyses. The product concept requires analyses of the various segments in the marketspace, while the operations design requires analyses of the firm's productive factors. These two sets of analyses are essential to determining what value-creating activities the firm should engage in to generate the maximum revenue from its assets.

A market analysis to determine what would be the most profitable segment mix for a configuration of the productive assets of the firm is the foundation for product strategy. First you need to identify the segments and the solutions that are currently available to the segments. The target market selection or the selected market segments to be served can be based on the profitability and size of each segment that the firm's assets are best positioned to serve. Here, a formal comparison of all the current solutions from the customer's perspective is necessary. Based on this analysis, the firm is able to determine what it can provide better than the alternative available to the appropriate target market, thus framing the firm's competitive advantage. Only after such customer needs analysis is it possible to specify what would be the desired customer value in the product offering.

The intended customer value in the product offering can now be translated into a detailed picture of the product concept—what the core and supplementary product ought to be. Remember that the customer value also reflects the customer's implicit assessment of the firm's solution compared to competitive offerings and, indeed, all solutions that are available to customers in the segment. To ensure that the product concept can effectively be superior customer value, the core product should combine the imperatives that have become commodities in the product category with the appropriate features in the supplementary product to reflect superiority in customer value. Thus, the product concept embodies the product differentiation and the superiority in customer value.

The operations design decision rests on how best the assets of the firm can be most profitably leveraged and follows a sequence of questions that pertain to the productive assets and capabilities of the firm and how they should be deployed: What people, facilities, equipment assets are needed to create and deliver the product? Which employees' skills and knowledge would be needed? When and where would specific human capital be needed and for how much time? Similar questions are asked about the facilities and equipment of the firm. Of course, when the asset or resource is not available within the firm, it seeks suppliers or outsources that part of the value creation. Ultimately, the question is what competitive advantage the firm is capable of and how the assets needed should be configured.

The process decisions are about determining the specific activities of the value creation and delivery. The process of making the product and delivering it to the customer must be detailed. The value creation and delivery activities required are set in a specific sequence. The firm must deliberate on the structure, content, and process of creating and delivering the product to the customer.

No product differentiation from supplementary product can be seen in isolation. If the total benefits from the product are not worth the costs that the customer incurs in acquiring and using the product, the product is likely to fail. The more carefully the firm designs the process with the customer in mind, the more likely the process ensures ease, convenience and quality for the customer. Thus, the customer-focused firm designs the creation and delivery process with the customer's percep tion of benefits and costs in the value consumption process.

Firms must also recognize that since customer value is dynamic, they need to continually monitor and improve this customer value. Ignorance of the need to innovate to sustain competitive advantage is a common mistake committed by the complacent firm. The argument is sometimes made that the firm's priority of customer focus minimizes the attention to innovation. Customer focus and innovation are not contradictory, an either/or strategic decision.

Indeed, to be customer-focused would mean that the firm is continually looking for new ways and solutions to meet customer needs—and to be aware that customer needs evolve as well. Now we can know what the firm needs to do to ensure that it is creating and delivering customer-focused value that can be sustained.

To sustain superiority in customer value the firm must ensure that management continually assess its market and its assets to ensure that the choice of customer and the value being created and delivered by the firm maximizes the profit goals of the firm. How well is the customer value in the product concept translated to the operations design and the value creation and delivery process? Is the superiority in customer value being executed. The answer lies in the customer's judgment. Customer-focused firms will let the customer decide whether the firm's value creation and delivery is customer-focused.

Continual customer satisfaction assessment information needs to be available for the customer-focused firm to improve by changing the product concept, the operations design, and the value creation and delivery process, or to continually reassess whether its assets and capabilities are being leveraged to realize the maximum profit potential.

To ensure customer-focused value creation and delivery, firms must assess customers' perceptions of the benefits they receive as well as the costs incurred by them.

As an ongoing assessment of customer value, firms must continually assess customer needs and customer satisfaction. As customer needs change, the value bundle needs to be reviewed in terms of its product concept, operations design and delivery. An assessment of customer satisfaction presents an opportunity to improve customer value. The smart firm will continually monitor customer satisfaction to understand what customers perceive as the benefits they are getting from product compared to the costs that they incur. Based on customer satisfaction, does the value bundle need to be modified and redesigned? Are the assets and capabilities of the firm being leveraged for maximum sustainable profits? If the expected customer value cannot be delivered with the existing value-creating assets, then the firm has two choices. Either it acquires or outsources the required value-creating assets and capabilities, or it determines that the target market decision needs revisiting.

BENEFITS OF CUSTOMER KNOWLEDGE MANAGEMENT

Scholars have implored managers to "spend a day in the life of your customer" and to "get inside the lives of your customers, " so as to obtain a deeper understanding of customers. The quality of the knowledge on the customer is much greater because of direct observation. Obtaining that knowledge is only the first step.

The basic skill of listening involves competence in sensing, evaluating *and* responding. A study of 500 new car buyers found customer perceptions of these three dimensions of listening to be strongly linked to trust in the salesperson.

There are also benefits within the firm when the practice of listening to customers is emphasized by senior managers. Senior managers at First Chicago discovered that in emphasizing listening to the customer they found a cultural change within the organization. Customer knowledge gained from firsthand customer contact is very persuasive. Smart CEOs at firms like IBM, Cisco, and EMC intuitively realize this, and their senior managers contact their major customers on a regular basis. These firms also act on that information to improve relationships with those important customers.

The benefits of customer knowledge management have concentrated at the individual level. For example, Dreyfus, like other mutual fund firms, keeps track of client activity, claiming that they can predict when a client is going to shift money out of their mutual funds. Clients receive a call from a Dreyfus representative, who wants to know how the client feels about the investment and if his or her goals are being met.

If Dreyfus is able to track clients at all stages of the consumption process, then the firm has a better chance of retaining the customer. A number of CRM- and ERP-type software programs allow companies to track processes in the life of a specific sales order from order entry all the way to delivery to customer. Of course, FedEx introducing package tracking is a well-known example from years ago. There are a number of benefits of information technology for firms of any size.

Siebel software allows Honeywell to spot problems and opportunities by tracking and analyzing all customer interactions; and at Marriott, Siebel empowers sales reps to respond more quickly to customer needs by integrating customer information from different departments. Lexmark International used Microstrategy software to help build what they call a data warehousing solution that accomplished a reduction in product delivery time by 70 percent, a threefold improvement in being able to deliver a customer's order on the desired date, and a 60 percent reduction in the information costs. Package delivery firm UPS's selfservice tracking system, built by IBM, saved the company $450,000 a day in customer service expenses; and, the Clarify call centre software helped payroll-processing firm ADP improve customer retention rate by 5 percent and increase revenues by $100 million in 1999 simply by providing its customer service reps with customer information on its 8000 clients.

There are numerous such examples of technology-based customer information management systems having a profound impact on a firm's productivity and in customer retention. Both outcomes are the basis for achieving and sustaining profits.

The marketing research practice has undergone a major transformation in recent years. A primary function of marketing research activities is to collect and analyze customer information. Technology has enabled all phases of the marketing research process ranging from sampling and data collection to analysis and reporting.

With newer technologies and faster cycle times, firms conduct research at all stages of the product life cycle and not just at the product development stage or the test marketing stage. This is at the aggregate level, whereas there is another change in research on the customer at the individual level, where technology is enabling customers to interact with the firm in a multitude of different ways not previously possible. These interactions can now occur during all stages of consumption. At every interaction with the customer, a firm has the opportunity to acquire valuable customer information, as well as to process and utilize the information for creating and delivering superior customer value.

Once the data is available, the challenge is to provide the user of the information and decision maker with targeted information. Enter rulesbased approaches, which are simply programs that make sense of data using preconceived models. Sadly, the majority of CRM and ERP packages fail the firm not for lack of data, but simply because the firm does not have the appropriate understanding and appreciation of the fundamentals of customer-focused management. The rules for decision-making should be founded on customer-focused management principles. The better the understanding of the customer and the utilization of that knowledge, the more customer focused the rules are.

The best technology is only as good as what you tell it to do. CRM and ERP packages are really knowledge management software, tools to manage knowledge of the customer and enable the processes within the firm that are working to meet specific customer needs. To be more effective with these tools, firms need to gather the information, analyze and process it to obtain a good understanding of the customer, and utilize it at every opportunity in the value-creation and delivery process. Therefore, for a thorough understanding on how to manage customer information, it is important to understand the principles of knowledge management, in general.

What is knowledge management? To answer this question, we have first to deal with a more fundamental question: what is the difference between data, information, and knowledge? Are these terms just synonyms that are interchangeable?

No, they are not! The simplest way to understand the differences among these terms is to picture a continuum. As we add value to data, it becomes information; and as we add value to information, information becomes knowledge. When we interpret data in a context, we convert that data into information that has some meaning. When we categorize and elaborate on that information with explanations, then we have added more value and the information can now be considered knowledge. Thus, *knowledge management* is the management of data and information so that a firm can optimally capture, process, and utilize its knowledge for effective decision-making and operation.

Customer knowledge management is the management of the acquisition, processing, and utilization of customer information for effective customer-focused decision making. Knowledge management practice has been studied in the context of how organizations learn. Before we discuss the methods of managing customer knowledge, it would be useful to understand knowledge management and, specifically, information processing from the perspective of organizational learning.

Organizational learning can be broadly depicted as a three-stage process:

- Information acquisition or generation
- Information transmission or dissemination
- Information analysis or interpretation

Studies have demonstrated that a customer-focused firm has a formal and systematic method for gathering, interpreting and using customer information. To be customer-focused, therefore, firms need to be committed to the importance and value of customer information and to the use of customer information in guiding the creation and delivery of customer value.

Thus, recognizing information's value to the firm and realizing when and where it is accessible is a prerequisite for knowledge management.

Richard Schulze, CEO of Bestbuy, the runaway success in electronics retailing, says: The best way to find out whether a store is running smoothly is by asking the cashier. "The cashier really understands where the problems lie. They're the last people to see the customer. "To consider all of the sources of customer information we also need to first identify the natural state of the information.

Customer information is available as tacit and as explicit knowledge. The explicit knowledge is present in the databases of the firm or as documented information. Customer information files in databases are usually quantitative data. More and more firms are also using qualitative data when the technology is used to accommodate that type of data. Otherwise, most of this rich information remains as hidden knowledge. This information that is not recorded is the tacit knowledge that is usually resident with the employees and managers of the firm.

For example, records of customer service interactions capture the actual transaction, complaint, or feedback from the customer. At the same time, employees, based on their prior experience, will unconsciously record and bring to bear their judgments of the situation, which are not necessarily documented. The knowledge that employees have that is not recorded anywhere is deemed the tacit knowledge of the firm.

While at the individual level information is available from customer information files in the firm's databases, other types of information at the aggregate level may be gathered during the course of product development activities and other specific projects and reside in research reports. There is information on the customer at several locations within the firm, from sales to customer service, to name the most obvious areas. As we know besides this explicit knowledge, there is a wealth of information at both the aggregate and the individual levels.

Wherever the firm has interfaced with the customer, the "touch-points, " there is information on the customer. It immediately becomes apparent that several product and service delivery contact points within the firm have access to customer information, but not all are part of the customer information management system.

CRM software packages enable the firm to capture all of the information gathered at each touch-point into a central database and make it available at any touch point. To determine all of the opportunities for gathering information on the customer, firms can develop a blueprint of the order delivery or customer service processes depicting all of the touch-points from the consumption cycle when the customer interacts with the firm. Knowledge gained on the customer from each and every customer interaction when recorded and made available can be valuable in improving the customer focus of any of the firm's decisions or actions. The major sources for customer knowledge are discussed below.

Table. States and Forms of Customer Information

	Individual level	Aggregate level
Explicit - Documented knowledge	Customer Information Files	Research Reports
Implicit - Tacit knowledge	Knowledge held by employees and intermediaries about individual customers that are not recorded	Knowledge held by employees and intermediaries about groups of customers that are not recorded

Table. Customer Information Sources Based on Consumption Stages

	Sources of Information Salespeople
Preconsumption	Channel intermediaries Referral data Frontline service personnel
Consumption	Service delivery personnel Service failure and recovery data Customer satisfaction surveys
Postconsumption	Customer complaints Customer service logs Frequent user profiles

Customer Information Files are typically transaction-related and purchase-related individual-level customer data found in sales records, customer interaction records, and customer service incident records. What is perhaps not in these files, which needs to be considered as a necessary component of individual customer profiles where available, is information related to the activities of preconsumption, consumption, and postconsumption.

Research Reports have segment-level aggregate data that are found in product development reports, advertising research reports, sales and marketing reports, and customer service reports. What needs to be seen is whether research on market segments is an ongoing pursuit of the firm—to indicate that the firm is proactively assessing customer value being delivered by the firm.

Knowledge held by employees and managers: Tacit knowledge of the customers—is by definition not completely identified and its utility not realized. If there is no formal process to regularly capture and utilize this information, a wealth of knowledge resident in the firm is being ignored.

Upstream and downstream sources: When suppliers and intermediaries are regularly included in discussions of value-creation and delivery decisions, there is an opportunity to discover information on market trends, technology, ideas for product improvement, and so on that are useful at the aggregate level. At the individual level, where there are (downstream) intermediaries, if it is possible, it would be highly valuable to obtain individual customer level information.

Now let us look at opportunities that may be missed by firms that are not proactive in looking for customer information. For example, how many firms capture and utilize data on referrals? If it is appropriately captured and analyzed, firms can use this information to proactively stimulate referrals. Firms can identify customers who could be bringing in new customers. Firms can determine what incentives would be effective in stimulating referrals.

From the referring and referred customers, firms can learn what messages are being conveyed about the firm and which messages are most effective in stimulating product trial from new customers. Firms can learn what types of customers are most liable to switch from their current patronage based on word of mouth.

Firms can track and follow the patronage behaviour of these new customers and nurture their loyalty and referral behaviour. Firms can also find out from these new customers valuable information on the competition as well. Similarly, what about prospective customer queries? How well is this information captured and utilized? What would such information contain? They are a good source of what customers look for in a product, a reflection of their choice criteria. How many firms systematically record information on complaints and praises? This type of information would be very helpful in understanding how the firm is faring on creating and delivering customer value. It could highlight failpoints in the value-creating processes and provide input into frontline evaluation and motivation activities.

Many firms have loyalty programs to reward the frequent user. What sort of frequent-user data do these firms maintain? How many firms really use the frequent-purchase data? Some firms who know their customers well recognize the importance of sorting out the most profitable customers from their customer base and treating them differently. Some customers are indeed more equal than others! Most firms use frequent-purchaser data for targeting specials and promotions. However, this data can also provide invaluable information on customer value and customer profile information to align the firm's value-creation and delivery processes.

Traditionally, firms have gathered routine customer information only at purchase and when a customer returns a product for a refund or mechanisms. Feedback forms and customer surveys are administered on a regular basis in some firms. However, most often the information gathered from these efforts is worthless because of faulty designs and worse, sometimes even result in misdirected decisions because of flawed survey methodology. More often than not, the surveys are neither reliable nor valid. While reliability and validity as statistical measures of the psychometric stability of a scale are important for a scientific, unbiased study, management can improve the utility of customer surveys with a rather simple analysis. Examine the design, administration, and use of any survey along the dimensions of structure, content, and process. Structural features such as length and the time it would take the respondent to fill out the survey, the layout of the various questions in the survey, and the response format for the questions affect the effectiveness of the survey.

Content decisions, such as the categories of information sought from the respondent and information identifying the type of respondent filling out the survey, affect the utility of the survey, which will only be as good as the effectiveness of its administration and its usability. Thus, the process of survey delivery, customer response delivery mechanisms, and the customization of the reports to the decision maker and user of the information in their value-creating and delivery roles is critical to the success of the customer feedback exercise.

There are other sources of customer information that the firm has access to and may not fully utilize. The systematic way of determining what these sources might be is to list all the possible touch-points where customers interact with the firm and placing them in sequence in the three phases of consumption. In the preconsumption phase, customers may interact with salespeople or customer service or other frontline personnel. Recognizing what these touch-points are and what kinds of information is shared between the firm and the customer is an important step. Firms must decide what data needs to be captured at the touch-points and how it is to be used in guiding decisions and activities.

CUSTOMER SERVICE BY CUSTOMER RECOVERY

Acquiring the right customers is only the first step in managing customer relationships. A large percentage of new customers—up to 50 percent in some sectors—was found to defect before their third anniversary with an e-commerce site. Once acquired, firms must do everything possible to keep that customer or prevent itself from doing things that force or even allow the customer to switch.

When a customer switches to another firm, not only do you lose the remainder of that customer's lifetime value, but you also incur the costs of attracting a new one to replace the lost customer. The costs of serving a customer are high in the initial stages, as the firm sets up procedures for the new customer and becomes familiar with the needs and situations of that customer. As time goes by, the costs of serving that customer go down.

To replace a lost customer, the firm has to incur all these costs again before costs to serve the customer go down. So adding the cost of attracting new ones and bringing them to the same level of profitability as the old ones doubles the cost of losing a customer. When you consider the *total cost* to the firm in terms of the opportunity cost of lost customers, it behooves firms to pursue the retaining of customers as a relentless endeavor. The first step in retaining customers is to understand why they would want to switch in the first place.

Most firms have established procedures to recover from product failures. Typically, these customer recovery procedures are a part of customer service, a business function that is generally relegated to the status of a necessary evil. It is typically associated with unpleasant situations like product complaints, product returns and refunds. With the way firms are organized, it might fall upon the customer service department to ensure that these processes are in place and that they work properly. Product-focused firms may be focused on their core product and may view complementary services of the product as customer service. But service is not customer service. Facilitating services such as customer service is just one of the various services that a firm might offer its customers as part of the total solution.

The customer service function is a significant factor in the efforts to retain customers. Firms may see it as a function to handle customers' special requests or complaints. However, customer service from a customer's point of view is more broadly defined than from the firm's point of view. Some scholars have defined customer service as all customer interactions that enhance the core product other than proactive selling.

Even in its narrowest definition, customer service as complaint management is very beneficial for the firm. Not only does it provide the mechanism to make amends to the customer for a botched job, it also provides information to the firm for service design improvements. When the firm goes out of its way to compensate the customer for its failures, it creates an opportunity to obtain a lifelong customer.

Traditionally designed for complaint handling and refund/exchange for product returns, customer service as a function serves other important uses. If one takes the perspective that customer service is at the tactical level of customer retention, there is a very important by-product from these customer retention efforts. It can be a powerful research source to obtain information on the customer and on customer value delivered by the firm. This information can be used as input for product and service design improvements. We know that that the customer service process and what many firms struggle to do with it.

The customer complaint management process discussed is generalized for any firm. When a customer complaint is received by the front line in any firm, it is important to take the approach that a dissatisfied customer is an opportunity—an opportunity to alleviate the customer distress and compensate for it in such a way that the customer is impressed with the service recovery and is satisfied with the process. A first step in the whole process of customer service is to acknowledge and apologize to the customer. If the customer is in the presence of other customers, it is important to isolate the complaining customer so as not to disrupt the service delivery process for other customers. Let the unhappy customer vent and explain the nature of the product failure. Fully document the customer's complaint and explore the likely actions that the firm and the customer may have committed to cause the unfortunate situation.

Customer-focused firms will want to gain as much information as possible about the situation and to indicate to the customer that the firm is taking the problem seriously. A commitment to customer satisfaction from a customer-focused firm is also evident in the firm asking the customer for suggestions on how the customer may be compensated and how the product and service may be improved for other customers in the future. The firm then initiates remedial action and promises to rectify the situation for the customer and make product and process improvements such that it will not happen again.

Finally, it is important that the firm follow through with its promises and follow up with the customer to ensure that the recovery process met with the customer's satisfaction. It is also a powerful message to the customer if the firm is able to inform the customer about what it has done to prevent such product failures from happening again. Such would be the case when the product failure has indicated a systemic problem with the firm's operation. An important outcome of this whole customer service process is that valuable information has been obtained, recorded, and utilized for permanent product and service improvements to improve customer value created and delivered by the firm.

The TARP study concluded that only 4 percent of dissatisfied customers complain; dissatisfied customers share their story with about 9 or 10 other people. If a complaint is satisfactorily handled, about 70 percent of them will continue to do business with the firm, and if resolved quickly, this figure goes up to 95 percent and they will tell about 5 people about their fair treatment. Thus, it is safe to say that what the firm does in its complaint handling has serious consequences for customer equity. Many firms seem to offer customers avenues to provide feedback.

The customer-focused firm will even proactively encourage customers to complain. The Bank of New Zealand, for example, has complaint procedure brochures available at every teller window that show the customer what to do step-by-step if they need to complain. There are instructions on who to call or write to if the problem is not resolved at the first service encounter. If not resolved by senior management, it lists the address and phone number of the CEO for good measure!

Customers will act when they are emotionally charged, either because of the importance of the solution to their need situation or because of the degree of their dissatisfaction. If the product failure was avoidable, customers are more likely to act. Customer action may be in the form of a customer complaint or defection without complaint. The recovery is likely to be effective if the firm has provided the frontline personnel dealing with the complaint or customer action with the appropriate skills and motivation. Effective recovery requires customer knowledge and freedom to exercise the discretion they require to satisfy the complaining customer and remedy the consequences of the product failure. Customers are likely to forgive the product failure if the firm demonstrated a customer-caring attitude in its handling of the complaint and if the recovery options offered the customer were appropriate. Nevertheless, preventing dissatisfied customers from defecting to a competitor is a challenge.

Why do customers switch? A study of 526 responses covering 45 different service industries, using the critical incident technique to explore the question, found eight main reasons for customer switching behaviour. These were categorized under price, inconvenience, core product failures, service encounter failures, failed employee responses to service failures, competitive issues, ethical problems, and involuntary factors.

The study found that even satisfied customers switch providers for reasons such as price, competitive issues, convenience, or access. The bottom line is that managers need to develop customer retention strategies or customer defection management programs to preempt customer switching, and to minimize or eliminate systemic reasons for customer switching behaviour. They need to understand why their customers switch.

Firms need to be able to identify those customers who are at risk of switching. It is imperative that they set up alerts and remedial mechanisms to reach those customers to prevent them from switching to a competitor. Ensuring a high retention rate must be a treated as a constant endeavor for the customer-focused management. Striving to sustain long-term profitability means ensuring a stable and growing customer base. Growing the customer base by targeting the right customer is only the start of customer relationship. Enhancing the value of each customer to the firm presumes that the customer is retained by the firm. Retaining the customer base requires a close monitoring of how each customer is feeling and behaving in terms of product purchase and consumption.

The defection management system should comprise of a means:

- To assess customer value changes so that it can alert the firm about the possibility of customer defections,
- To assess the extent of long-term revenues at risk, and
- To determine and execute the appropriate recovery methods for each type of customer.

Customers switch when the customer value they receive at the individual or segment level is inferior to an alternative. Thus, it is necessary to conduct a continual assessment of customer value as the critical first step. Failpoint data on customer experiences is a metric that could serve as a barometer for customer value changes. Customers who have experienced the service when failpoints have failed are at risk of switching. The firm has failed to deliver the expected customer value for these customers. Customer defection management is proactive—its purpose is to identify customers who are at risk of switching and to initiate an assessment of the status of customer value to the firm, followed by an analysis to determine how to increase customer value to those customers.

One of the functionalities required in a good customer knowledge system is to alert its users when there might be a problem with a customer, and to provide the information necessary to rectify that problem. Customer defection management begins with designing into the customer information system alerts that are triggered by customer switching indicators. These alerts can be based on thumb rules suggested by the information on successful and unsuccessful customer recovery captured and stored. Thus, any time there is a change in the customer's situation, a thumb rule-based trigger sets off a defection alert that indicates the customer is at risk of switching.

As we saw earlier, customers switch for a number of reasons. Customer-focused firms with good customer information systems would have identified reasons for switching behaviour in their customer base. Causes of switching behaviour can be grouped into firm-induced reasons or environmentally induced reasons. Firm-induced reasons are really customer value changes that could be from price changes, product failures, service encounter failures, or problem resolution failures.

Environmentally induced reasons can be those that are customer life events. For the individual consumer it could be events such as change in professional or marital status, income changes, relocation, or change in lifestyle—or in other words, change in need situation in general. For the business customer it could be change in value creation and therefore consumption of productive factors or change in value creation processes, including change in the buying centre, a change in the buying process or criteria, or individuals making the buying decision.

Environmentally induced reasons could also include competitor actions that have changed the relative worth of customer value in the firm-such as a price change or a product feature change by a competitor making the firm's own customer value less attractive than the competitor's promise of customer value. Legal, social, or technological factors in the environment could also result in customer switching. Wherever possible, the firm must attempt to integrate alerts into the customer knowledge for system for when any firm-induced or environmentally induced changes occur portending a negative change in customer value.

Once a defection alert is activated, whether related to a specific customer encounter or not, the firm initiates an analysis of whether the customer is in fact at risk of switching. If the customer is at risk, the firm must now determine if this customer is worth the effort, so to speak. If the loss in customer equity outweighs the retention costs, then the firm must attempt to employ the means necessary to alleviate the switching triggers. Incidentally, this thumb rule could apply at the segment level or to a specific customer. When the switching triggers are related to a specific encounter with a customer, it usually involves a critical incident, a product failure of some kind. Either the core product has failed or there was a service encounter failure or a failure to resolve a problem for the customer. For any of these reasons, a service recovery procedure needs to be in place to retain the customer. Customer-focused firms should consider it a functional requirement from investments made in any CRM technology that it is able to power a rich recovery database. The recovery database should yield costs and benefits of the various recovery options for this particular customer either based on segmentspecific information or information related to this specific customer.

A recovery database is utilized to determine possible recovery programs, where specific retention options are assessed along with customer input. Once the retention plan is selected and implemented, it needs to be assessed for effectiveness and employed until the point where customer equity does not exceed retention costs. The recovery database must consist of all the information regarding customer switching behaviour and recovery successes as well as failures.

Customer switching behaviour information should contain the reasons for customer switching obtained from customer satisfaction surveys, from exit interviews, and from customer research in general. All methods of recovery that have been tried need to be recorded for their effectiveness. A matrix developed to record what recovery procedures worked and didn't work for each switching trigger should determine a recommended retention programme.

To accomplish this, retention reports from each customer recovery experience will need to be recorded, analyzed, and stored in the recovery database. The analysis would deal with the costs of the retention programme and the effectiveness assessment of the programme. Each customer switching trigger needs to be calibrated so that when a segment or customer is at risk the defection alert will move the firm to act with its recovery procedure. A well-planned customer recovery procedure is crucial to a sound customer defection management system. Customer service is considerably enhanced by such a knowledge-based decision support system.

Corporate strategy is about core competencies being leveraged to meet corporate goals. When analyzed into its parts, corporate strategy is about how the core competencies are leveraged in the operations and marketing strategies. Customer service is lost in the shuffle and usually ends up in neither strategy, primarily as a consequence of misplaced definition. Customer service has its unfortunate connotations because of its history and original intent as a business function, and the label does it a tremendous disservice. Customer service is where most of the interactions with the customers occur for a manufacturing firm, whereas for a service firm not all customer interactions need be customer service.

There are interactions whose task is the value creation and delivery of the core product. If firms find that customer service is where most of the customer interactions occur, then customer service should be the most crucial business function for the firm in managing customer relationships. Wherever there is a customer interaction, there is an opportunity to gather information about the customer and how the product meets the customer's needs. The knowledge of the customer's experience with the product in a customer database, if properly utilized, could serve to improve the product.

With improved quality and customer value, customer loyalty is nurtured. With the knowledge about specific customers, firms can become intimately familiar with specific preferences of each customer, allowing for customization where possible.

Customers can also provide knowledge about how the firm is doing compared to the competition in the customer's eyes. They provide an access to market information not otherwise possible. Firms develop market competence in understanding their competitive advantage and seek the loyalty of the customer by employing this knowledge. As summarized earlier, any manager should be able to look at the good sense in incorporating customer service in the overarching task of managing customer interactions and customer relationships.

Generally, in firms that are not customer focused, customer service has not transcended its image of a necessary evil involving a firm's obligations to take care of the annoyance of product failures. Customer-focused firms elevate customer service to a strategic level by placing it in the context of customer retention and giving it the prominence in the firm that it deserves, alongside customer acquisition, an integral part of customer relationship management.

Elevating the status of customer service function within the firm to a strategic level requires senior managers to practice and perform customer service as well. MBNA requires its senior management to handle four hours of customer service phone calls each month. Folklore in Freeport Maine has it that the founder of L.L. Bean had piped in customer service phone calls to his home!

The customer-focused firm makes customer service the responsibility of everyone in the firm. Ritz-Carlton says to its employees, if you are the one to receive a customer complaint, you own it—follow that complaint's resolution process to its conclusion. It is a good practice to regularly involve the backstage personnel in handling customer service. Firms need to construct integrated knowledge management systems that obtain and utilize information from customer service experiences to improve the design and delivery of its value-creating processes. All customer touchpoints in the firm need to be involved in the planning and control functions of the product and service design and delivery.

The customer-focused firm needs to have several things in place to be able to implement a strong retention programme. It needs to have a rich recovery database, the processes to implement the retention programme and the people appropriately trained in recovery procedures. As we will see later, the best-designed processes will not work unless the people involved in the execution of these processes are empowered not only with the knowledge, support, and skills but the motivation and inclination in a customer-focused climate.

Operationally, retention programs and the actual customer service activities must prioritize attention for its most valuable (customers) relationships so that all assets of the firm are dedicated at all times to maximum long-term profitability. The problem is that not all firms are proactive in their management of customer relationships. As a result, customer defections go unnoticed and customer service is the only desk at the firm that handles a customer defect risk. Customer service as an operation of the firm needs to be viewed as within the scope of customer relationship management. It should participate in the firm's retention activities with a much broader scope and higher status. A key consideration is what status the firm has given its customer service function.

Customer-focused quality, when combined with customer-focused productivity, ensures that the firm views operations with a customer focus for an outside-in view of the firm. Productivity is defined differently—not in quantity of customers handled but in quality of their lifetime value. Customer service productivity should not be measured by how many complaints were handled in a certain amount of time, but in terms of how effective it was in retaining customer equity. Costs and efficiencies are measured in terms of customer lifetime value.

A short-term orientation is discarded in favour of acquiring and retaining the more profitable customers for the long term. Short-term losses in a customer relationship are accepted if the long-term relationship with that customer will yield large and sustained profits over the duration of the relationship with that customer.

No customer-focused management decision can be executed without the appropriate customer-focused culture within the firm. The people in a firm, its managers and employees, should be provided with a customer-focused environment. The commitment begins with the CEO. The task of creating and delivering superior customer value must be complemented with the selection of the appropriate employees and the effective management of relationships with those employees. Employee equity, the value of the employee to the firm, should be linked to customer value by valuing an employee based on the individual's contribution to customer value and sustainable profits. Strategies and tactics that are discussed from the customer-focused perspective are not deliverable unless there is the right kind of environment within the firm. Ultimately, for all of this to work, the people and indeed the corporate culture need to be customer focused and service oriented.

John Chambers runs CISCO Systems, one of the most successful among the largest firms in the world. Rated among the top firms as a "most admired company" and "best company to work for, " by *Fortune* and *Financial Times,* Cisco has grown to over 35,000 employees from about 3,000 when Chambers assumed leadership in 1995. During the same time, sales increased from $2 billion to $22 billion in fiscal 2001. When asked about how he manages growth, Chambers ranked "make your customers the centre of your culture" at the top of his list.

To demonstrate the CEO's focus on the customer, Chambers regularly reviews customer satisfaction data and has a daily critical list of customers for whom the firm's products are in jeopardy of failure. He has access to a customer knowledge system that allows him, as he says, to explode critical information on each customer. Chambers focuses on recruiting, developing, and retaining the leadership team that can implement his customer-focused strategy. He ties manager and employee compensation to customer satisfaction.

Over and over again, it is very clear that the successful firm focuses on its people and ensures that new hires fit its corporate culture.

Southwest Airlines' director of field employment says: "We hire for attitude and train for skill." Candidates are put through a rigorous interview process, taking as much as six weeks sometimes. After that, the training period rejects 20 percent of the new hires because they don't fit into the corporate culture. Like CISCO, Southwest has a culture of teamwork and cooperation.

This final chapter is about the glue that keeps the entire firm collectively focused on the customer and on delivering a service-oriented customer value that is superior to the competition. Each chapter in this book thus far has outlined and discussed the critical business decisions and processes in the customer-focused firm. The success of the firm in executing and delivering on the goal is predicated upon the ability of its people, managers and workers, to make it happen. Without the employees, workers, and managers, individually and collectively sharing and believing in a cohesive culture or climate conducive to performing as a customer-focused firm, none of what has been covered in this book would have any meaning.

The CEO sets the tone for the climate within a firm. Senior managers take their cue from the CEO. You can tell how strong the culture is by observing how senior managers refer to their CEO. If you have had the opportunity to hear or watch Jeff Bezos, CEO of Amazon, you will have noted his playful nature and "we can make it" attitude. This attitude is also evident in how the people in his firm approach their tasks. Another CEO credited for his firm's customer-focused culture is Fred Smith, of FedEx, who says: "Customer satisfaction begins with employee satisfaction." Lou Gerstner talked about changing IBM's culture as critical to competing in the information age. By most accounts, he appears to have succeeded. GE's Jack Welch, one of the great CEOs of our time, talked about shared values as critical to realizing his vision.

If the culture is not customer focused, the firm cannot be customer focused. The German ERP software company SAP almost disappeared into oblivion until its CEO, Hasso Plattner, who founded the company around an engineering-focused corporate culture, began to heed customers who had been asking for changes in the way its product was configured and were demanding a Web-enabled interface for the product. When CEOs who have been successful in getting a firm to the top or keeping the firm at the top of their industry are asked about how they did it, there is always some mention of the attention they gave to the culture of the firm.

The importance of culture in the performance of a firm comes to the fore following mergers and acquisitions. In a survey of 1,200 adults, Andersen Consulting (now called Accenture) reported that customers of recently merged firms compared to other customers in the three telecom sector players—cable companies, Internet service providers, and phone companies—felt that service was worsening.

The telecom industry had been and is still going through some pretty significant series of takeovers, mergers, and consolidations, causing the customers, even the goldplated and special ones, to suffer from lack of customer focus. CEOs who have been successful in leading a firm through a merger are likely very good at also shaping cultures. Such CEOs are much sought after and financially well rewarded by firms going through dissolution, turnaround, consolidation, acquisition, a merger, or some other form of asset reorganization. The clash of cultures is perhaps the most important challenge for this CEO.It takes a capable CEO who understands the importance of corporate culture and renders it prominent attention to successfully lead and shape the culture of the firm.

To ensure a customer-focused culture, the CEO must commit his attention to it. Fleet bank CEO Chad Gifford pledged $75 million in 2002 "to improve the overall customer experience, " recognizing the severity of the customer service problems it had after its merger with BankBoston. Through a number of mergers, Bank of America's CEO, Kenneth Lewis, said he has been insistent on "one culture" and feels that he has succeeded in bringing the previously disparate entities with their respective cultures into one single culture.

A major cornerstone of his efforts was the six-sigma programme and the "Spirit to Serve" customer service training at the bank. As of this writing the jury is still out on how successful Carly Fiorina, CEO of Hewlett Packard, is with her reorganization and change, involving everything from strategy, structure, and culture to compensation, following their controversial merger with Compaq in 2002. It had only been a few short years since Compaq itself had acquired Digital Equipment Corp. Even Wall Street has not been kind to its darling, HP. The challenge is tremendous and the rewards are huge. The task of shaping culture is perhaps the most important and fundamental challenge for any CEO. For a successful corporate culture that emphasizes a focus on the customer, the commitment has to begin at the top and be reflected in how the CEO runs the shop.

How an organization behaves depends on what Peter Drucker calls its "theory of the business." He says that the assumptions that a firm makes about its markets, about its technology, and about the strengths and weaknesses of the firm are what define its behaviour. He draws evidence from IBM creating the computer industry in the 1950s, Apple bringing personal computers to the household in the 1980s, and GM inventing lifestyle segmentation in the 1990s.

These companies had the right theory of their business because the assumptions they made about the world around them were the right ones. The characteristics that define a customer-focused firm align closely with the assumptions that Drucker is talking about. Drucker's three assumptions centre around markets, technology, and firm. In customer-focused management terms, these relate directly to customers and to the firm's value-creating assets. Firms must understand their customers and be open-minded about the technology of the value creation and delivery in their business to leverage its core competencies toward superior customer value.

The strategic decision making process begins with assessments of markets and firm to determine the customer value that can be created profitably from its productive assets. These assessments serve to define the customer in terms of consumption activities and to define the solution or value bundle it will provide the customer through the core and supplementary product. Value-creating and delivery processes are designed according to these definitions of customer and product.

What follows from the definition and analysis of the customer is the estimate of the lifetime value of all customers or more appropriately the long-term profits of the firm. In parallel, the product definition will guide the asset and resource allocation toward the more profitable products. Firms seek to maximize the value to the firm by serving the most profitable customers with the most profitable value bundle that can be produced with its assets.

The strategic decision-making process incorporates a customer focus to guide value creation and delivery decisions. As developed and emphasized throughout this book, the principles of customer-focused management are the following:

- Obtaining and utilizing information about customers, especially with respect to their consumption cycle

- Designing value creation and delivery strategy and processes that are based on that customer knowledge
- Implementing the strategy and processes that provide superior value to customers so as to meet the firm's goals

To make any of this work, the entire firm has to get behind believing in these principles of customer-focused management. To become customer focused, the firm must really change the way it thinks and behaves, such that the customer is always the centre of the value creation and delivery. The firm must have in place the appropriate people with the appropriate attitude. When the goals, structures, processes, and rewards are also in place, the culture and climate should follow for the firm to become customer focused. Two underlying fundamental concepts defining organizational behaviour become evident here in the processes and people requirement: organizational structure and corporate culture. *Organizational structure* refers to how firms define the roles and relationships between the various functions or processes and the individuals responsible for and given the authority to fulfill them. *Corporate culture* refers to the values and beliefs held in the firm that dictate how the firm operates.

Value creating and delivering processes may be designed so that firms can be customer focused. But if the culture does not provide the climate, the firm cannot be customer focused. Just about everything in the firm from the office and building design to social hours can affect the culture of the firm. Nokia, the wireless devices giant from Finland, went so far as to instruct its building designers to design and construct an environment where individuals are immersed in the corporate culture and can interact with the company and fellow employees on a variety of levels. Notice the company's slogan: "Connecting People." Citibank has "pulse lunches" at its banks where managers have a weekly lunch with employees and listen to their concerns and then act on them. These are two examples of how climate can be created for the firm to be customer focused.

7

Food, Beverage and Service Management in Hotel Industry

FOOD AND BEVERAGES

While U.S. hotels have enjoyed a strong increase in room revenue during the current recovery period, growth in hotel food and beverage sales, while improving, lacked the same kind of sizzle, according to an recent study by a leading hospitality consultant. Fortunately, tight cost controls by management have enabled food and beverage profitability to keep pace with the profit growth of other operating departments.

In 2004, hotel food and beverage (F&B) revenues grew 6.7 percent, the result of a 6.9 percent increase in food sales and a 5.5 percent bump in beverage sales. The 6.7 percent growth rate is certainly very healthy, but it does fall short of the 8.6 percent growth in rooms revenue, and 7.6 percent increase in total hotel revenues achieved during the same time period.

Table. Mix of Food and Beverage Revenues 2004

Banquet Food	38.2%
Food Outlets / In Room	25.0%
Other	15.5%
Beverage Outlets / In Room	11.1%
Banquet Beverage	6.1%
Banquet Meeting Room Rental	4.1%

"While the magnitude of the increase in food and beverage revenue may have fallen short, the pace of profit growth equaled that of the other operated departments within a hotel. This can be attributed to good expense control practiced by F&B management," Woodworth concluded. In 2004, food and beverage departmental expenses grew 6.2 percent versus and an average of 6.9 percent for all other operated departments. The bottom- line was an 8.1 percent growth in food and beverage profits for 2004. This equals the increase in total Operated Department Income for all hotels. Food and beverage revenues and expenses are just some of the 200 discrete hotel revenue and expense items captured in 2005 Trends in the Hotel Industry report. The 2005 report marks the 69 th annual review of U.S. hotel operations conducted by PKF. This year's sample draws upon year-end 2004 financial statements received from more than 5,000 hotels across the country. Hotel managers use the PKF Trends report to benchmark the performance of their hotel's revenues, expenses, and profits.

Revenue Gains

The growth in food and beverage revenues appears to be driven more by increased guest and customer counts, as opposed to increases in pricing. While food and beverage revenues measured on a per-available-room basis grew 6.7 percent in 2004, food and beverage revenue measured on a per-occupied-room basis grew 2.3 percent. "The implication from these two statistics is that the increase in F&B revenue was more attributable to the fact that there were 4.3 percent more rooms occupied, as opposed to any substantial increase in the F&B expenditures per occupied room. Of course, another reason could be a boost in food and beverage patronage from local residents.

When looking at the sources of food and beverage business for the typical hotel in PKF's sample, revenues from banquet events account for 44.3 percent of the total sales.

This compares to 36.1 percent of the total sales volume that comes from the restaurants, lounges, and room service. The remaining 19.6 percent is derived from the rental of meeting and banquet rooms, as well as other miscellaneous sources. When looking at growth by the revenue source, we found sales emanating from restaurants and lounges increased 6.1 percent in 2004, while banquet and catering related revenues grew 7.0 percent.

Expense Controls

For hotel food and beverage departments, the "prime costs" are Labour and cost of goods sold. In 2004, the cost of food and liquor purchased for re-sale averaged 25.6 percent of total food and beverage revenue. Salaries, wages, and employee benefits combined for another 56.1 percent of the dollars spent in the department.

Like most other departments in a hotel, labour costs are the biggest expense item. In 2004, F&B labour costs rose 6.1 percent. This compares Favourably to the 6.3 percent overall growth rate in Labour costs throughout the hotel. It also looks like the chefs and bartenders did a good job in the back-of-the- house limiting food and beverage cost increases to only 4.9 percent."

As a result of the tight cost controls, food and beverage department profit margins improved from 30.4 percent in 2003 to 31.0 percent in 2004. While food and beverage sales accounted for 26.2 percent of total hotel revenues in 2004, F&B department profits were only 11.1 percent of total Operated Department Income for the year.

INDUSTRIAL FOODSERVICE

The industrial segment of the foodservice industry is composed of

- Corporations
- Companies
- Factories

and any other type of business that employs enough people to warrant the need for an in-plant foodservice operation. For the menu planner to plan a successful menu within the industrial segment of the foodservice industry, the following factors must be taken into consideration:

1. Management's reasons for having a foodservice operation inhouse
2. The food preferences of the employees to be fed
3. The type of work the employees are doing
4. The time allotted for meals
5. The amount of money the employees have to spend on meals

Profit

Management will spend money to make money. How does an industrial foodservice operation make a profit for management? It does so by keeping employees at or near their working stations during their meal period. Most employees are given a half-hour or an hour for their meal period. Employees will slow down or quit production five to ten minutes before eating, and many workers are five to ten minutes late in returning from eating when a business does not have a cafeteria or a foodservice operation in-house. Keeping the employees on the grounds of the business for meals helps to reduce the number of workers who return late from lunch, which increases production and, in turn, increases profits.

Operating Methods

The two methods of operating an industrial foodservice operation are for management to contract with a professional foodservice company to manage the operation or to take full responsibility of controlling the feeding system as a part of the business.

Contracting an outside professional foodservice company to handle the responsibility of feeding employees is popular and, in most cases, a profitable choice. There are several methods of feeding employees for which management may contract:

1. Computerized vending units
2. Full table service
3. Cafeteria service

4. Coffee-deli shops
5. Fast-food service

The two most important factors in choosing industrial foodservice establishments are offering fast service and providing menus that fit the needs of the employees.

Pricing

When pricing an industrial foodservice menu, management has a choice of setting the price in one of three ways:

1. Setting a large profit percentage (10 to 15 percent)
2. Setting a small profit percentage (1 to 2 percent)
3. Setting a break-even price (food is sold at a price that covers only the cost of the food, Labour, and overhead, and the company does not make a profit)

Food Preferences

The menu planner must be familiar with employee food preferences in order to be able to plan a successful menu. A food survey should be conducted to determine employees' preferences in foods. Some employees may prefer a nutritional menu that includes poultry, fish, salads, fruits, and vegetables rather than a menu that includes hamburgers, hot dogs, sandwiches, and French fries. The survey should be conducted every three months in order to accommodate employee turnover and also because attitudes and tastes can change over time.

Type of Work

The menu planner needs to know the type of work that employees do. Are employees involved in physical activity, or are they sitting at their desks all day? This information helps to determine food portions, the amount and variety of foods to offer, and whether the items should be hearty and of a heavy calorie count. With jobs that require physical Labour, employees are burning large amounts of calories, so the menu should offer a selection of foods that will replace lost calories. When employees do limited physical work, the menu selections should be light in calories and smaller in portion size.

Time

Knowing the amount of time allotted for the meal period is an important consideration. Food items that take a long time to prepare should not be included on the menu. Most employees are given only a half hour or an hour to eat. If an item takes too long to produce, employees will not have enough time to finish their meals and will feel rushed. Thus, employees will be dissatisfied with the foodservice operation.

Price

The amount of disposable income that an employee has or is willing to spend for a meal on a daily basis may be limited. Disposable income is income that is available for the employee's use after federal, state, and city taxes, and personal bills have been paid. The menu planner should not select foods that have a high food cost and offer them at an even higher cost, because the average employee cannot afford to buy that product on a daily basis. The average employee does not want to spend more than $5 on each meal. The menu planner needs to offer food items that are of good quality and that are reasonably priced.

COMMERCIAL FOODSERVICE

The commercial segment of the foodservice industry includes:

- Hotels
- Restaurants
- Clubs
- Diners
- Fast-food operations
- Specialty shops
- Cafeterias
- Catering businesses
- Vending businesses
- Dinner theaters
- Delicatessens

In each of these foodservice operations, the menu planner must know management's point of view on the following:

1. How the operation is run
2. The type of clientele that management would like to attract (also known as the market)
3. Check average
4. Decor
5. Profit margin
6. Competition
7. Market trends

How the Operation Is to Run

Although there are many philosophies on how to operate a foodservice operation, there are three basic approaches: fast food, family, and fine dining. Management must recognize and have a full understanding of an operation's philosophy in order to achieve a maximum profit. Management must be completely dedicated to the philosophy selected and should avoid mixing different philosophies that would only serve to confuse the market.

Fast-Food Operation

Characteristics of the fast-food philosophy and operation are as follows:

- Low check average: $4 to $8
- High turnover of capacity and high volume of sales: the National Restaurant Association indicates a $1,000 to $5,000 sales amount per hour as high volume
- Limited square footage per person for dining: 7 to 9 square feet
- Bright lights: almost a shadowless lighting scheme
- The use of bold, bright, and loud primary colors: red, blue, and yellow
- Rapid employee movement, which tends to affect the customer's pace
- Limited seat comfort: the use of plastic nonmoveable seats provides less comfort than a cushioned, unfixed seat
- High noise (decibel) level: the use of nonacoustic materials (made from a hard substance, such as stone, brick, ceramic tile, or stainless steel)
- The use of styrofoam cups and plates, and paper napkins
- Limited menu: the selection of food items on the menu is limited to no more than 30 items, to reduce the time it takes for customers to read the menu and to decide on their orders

With this philosophy, the goal is to create an atmosphere that will allow the customer to eat and leave the foodservice operation as quickly as possible, usually within a 30-minute time period. Management must design the entire building (interior and exterior), in order to allow for rapid movement (flow) of customers. Every detail is geared toward getting the customer in and out of the foodservice operation as quickly as possible, without making the dining experience an uncomfortable, rushed, or negative one for the customer.

Family Operation

The objective of the family philosophy is designed to appeal to the market that falls between the fast-food and the finedining market. The term "family" indicates that management must take into consideration the desires of a wide range of customers—from grandchildren to grandparents.

Characteristics of the family philosophy are as follows:

- Moderate check average: $8 to $15 per person
- Moderate turnover rate: one-and-a-half to two-and-a-half times per hour with a 100-seat capacity
- Square footage per person: 12 to 14 square feet
- Illumination (lighting) level: balanced, not dim or bright, but adequate
- Color scheme that incorporates a blend of pastel and bright colors
- Employee movement: prompt, not slow or too rapid
- Seating that is moderately comfortable; good quality chairs used
- Noise (decibel) level: ranges from 60 decibels (calm conversation) to 90 decibels (a loud argument), with a balanced use of acoustic and nonacoustic material
- Menu selections include 45 to 150 items: of all the types of menus, this type of menu takes the longest time to read, because graphics (such as photographs) accompany the description of the food products

This philosophy incorporates objectives from both the fast-food and fine-dining philosophies. The objective of not rushing customers is borrowed from the fine-dining philosophy, while the goal of not allowing the customer to take two hours to dine stems from the fast-food philosophy.

Fine Dining

The fine-dining philosophy is, in many ways, the opposite of the fast-food philosophy. The objective of the fine-dining philosophy is to provide the customer with a relaxing and pleasant dining experience.

Characteristics of this philosophy include:

- High check average: $45 to $100 per person
- A low turnover rate: a 100-seat capacity foodservice operation will have a three-quarter to one-and-a-half turnover capacity
- Square footage per person: 24 to 30 square feet to provide greater room and privacy, which allows the customer to be more relaxed
- Illumination level (lighting): low
- Colors selected are relaxing: pastel and earth-tone colors, such as tan and beige
- Employee movement in the dining room is not so rapid as to give a rushed impression and not so slow as to suggest indifference
- Seating is very comfortable: the use of fabric-padded seats provides more comfort

- Noise (decibel) level: a quiet, relaxing level of 30 to 70 decibels, facilitated by the use of soft acoustic material (wood, plants, carpets, fabric wallpaper, or other materials that absorb sound waves)
- Menu selections that are extensive (60 to 125 items) or limited (20 to 45 items), with more of a description accompanying the food items so as to enhance a person's appetite (when done correctly)
- High-quality interior decor: an atmosphere that encourages customers to relax, enjoy themselves, and spend money It is important that a foodservice operation select only one philosophy.

A combination of two or three philosophies during various hours of operation will only serve to confuse the customers and to deter them from identifying who you are and what you are all about. Very few foodservice operations can successfully combine philosophies and achieve a profitable margin.

Clientele

It is critical that the menu planner know the type of clientele for whom the menu is being planned. In the commercial segment, the primary motive for going into business is profit. To generate a maximum profit, the menu must satisfy the clientele. The menu is one of management's ways of meeting the demands of the clientele. The menu needs to reflect these demands through food selections, price, and creativity.

Check Average

The *check average* is used to indicate the amount of money that people are spending. Foodservice managers use this information to evaluate and to set financial goals. If a foodservice operation sets a $12.50 check average per person as a goal prior to opening and is achieving only a $9.50 check average per person after it has opened, this information allows management to analyze why the check average is $3 short and to make the necessary changes. If management does not use this information, it will fall short of its financial goals, which could lead to indebtedness or failure.

Décor

The decor, or decoration, of a foodservice establishment should project an image with which the market can identify. All of the exterior and interior design (such as landscaping, painting of the building, color of the menu, the type of artwork, the wallpaper, the style of windows, the size and shape of the parking lot) must be done to accommodate the taste and style of the market. The first impression of the interior is derived from the appearance of the exterior of a property. A littered parking lot reflects a negative image—one of messiness and filth that is certainly not appealing or attractive to the customer who has never been to the establishment. To know what the market is looking for, you must do a market survey.

Profit Margin

Profit margin is the amount of money made on a food or beverage product. All food and beverage products generally have different profit margins, even if they have the same food cost percentage. The profit margin is calculated when the food and beverage product is marked up from a preliminary selling price to a final selling price. For example, a slice of apple pie may cost $.35 to make. To make a profit, the slice of pie is sold for $1.75.

The difference between $.35 and $1.75 is $1.40, which will pay for the ingredients, the cost of Labour, the cost of the equipment, and the energy to make the pie, and will also contain a percentage for profit. When the price of the pie is increased to $2.25, the true margin of profit increases. If the price is lowered to $1.50, the margin of profit is lowered. Management will always make a profit on the piece of apple pie if it is priced correctly. The question is, how much profit? The answer is determined by how much the market is willing to pay for the slice of pie. If the market will pay $3.50 for the slice of apple pie, then management can price it at $3.50 on the menu.

Competition

Competition in the foodservice industry, as in all business endeavors, keeps operations at a competitive edge. Management must keep its standards high or the customer will go elsewhere. Competition does the following:

1. It keeps the prices of menu items under control and competitive. A food operation will not overprice a product such as coffee, which is common among all operations.
2. It decreases advertising costs. If an independent foodservice operation locates next to a national foodservice chain organization, the independent operation can reduce spending on advertising, since the chain operation brings customers into and next to the independent foodservice operation.

Market Trends

The market is always changing. To be successful, the menu in a commercial foodservice operation needs to keep pace with the changes in the market. The menu planner and management must accurately forecast the demands of the market.

This task is not simple. The following items must be considered:

1. New developments in food products, menu styles, decor concepts, as well as a variety of other trends occurring in the foodservice industry;

2. The economy and how it is affecting the market; and
3. The social needs of the market.

FOOD AND BEVERAGE SERVICES

Food and beverage services are among the most visible locations at ski areas, and a ski area's environmental commitment is often judged by the environmental practices within these establishments. Food and beverage services at ski areas range from fine dining establishments to bars and cafeterias. Numerous programs exist for the food and beverage service industry that help restaurants and their customers minimize environmental impacts. These programs have established systematic approaches to help restaurants reduce their environmental impacts. Involvement in environmental programs is a good way for a restaurant to learn more about environmental best practice opportunities.

Food and beverage serving and related workers are the front line of customer service in restaurants, coffee shops, and other food service establishments. These workers greet customers, escort them to seats and hand them menus, take food and drink orders, and serve food and beverages. They also answer questions, explain menu items and specials, and keep tables and dining areas clean and set for new diners. Most work as part of a team, helping coworkers to improve workflow and customer service.

Waiters and waitresses, the largest group of these workers, take customers' orders, serve food and beverages, prepare itemized checks, and sometimes accept payment. Their specific duties vary considerably, depending on the establishment. In coffee shops serving routine, straightforward fare, such as salads, soups, and sandwiches, servers are expected to provide fast, efficient, and courteous service. In fine dining restaurants, where more complicated meals are prepared and often served over several courses, waiters and waitresses provide more formal service emphasizing personal, attentive treatment and a more leisurely pace. They may recommend certain dishes and identify ingredients or explain how various items on the menu are prepared. Some prepare salads, desserts, or other menu items tableside. Additionally, they may check the identification of patrons to ensure they meet the minimum age requirement for the purchase of alcohol and tobacco products.

Waiters and waitresses sometimes perform the duties of other food and beverage service workers. These tasks may include escorting guests to tables, serving customers seated at counters, clearing and setting up tables, or operating a cash register. However, full-service restaurants frequently hire other staff, such as hosts and hostesses, cashiers, or dining room attendants, to perform these duties.

Bartenders fill drink orders either taken directly from patrons at the bar or through waiters and waitresses who place drink orders for dining room customers. Bartenders check identification of customers seated at the bar, to ensure they meet the minimum age requirement for the purchase of alcohol and tobacco products. They prepare mixed drinks, serve bottled or draught beer, and pour wine or other beverages. Bartenders must know a wide range of drink recipes and be able to mix drinks accurately, quickly, and without waste. Besides mixing and serving drinks, bartenders stock and prepare garnishes for drinks; maintain an adequate supply of ice, glasses, and other bar supplies; and keep the bar area clean for customers. They also may collect payment, operate the cash register, wash glassware and utensils, and serve food to customers seated at the bar. Bartenders usually are responsible for ordering and maintaining an inventory of liquor, mixes, and other bar supplies.

The majorities of bartenders directly serves and interact with patrons. Bartenders should be friendly and enjoy talking with customers. Bartenders at service bars, on the other hand, have less contact with customers. They work in small bars often located off the kitchen in restaurants, hotels, and clubs where only waiters and waitresses place drink orders. Some establishments, especially larger, higher volume ones, use equipment that automatically measures, pours and mixes drinks at the push of a button. Bartenders who use this equipment, however, still must work quickly to handle a large volume of drink orders and be familiar with the ingredients for special drink requests. Much of a bartender's work still must be done by hand to fill each individual order.

Hosts and hostesses welcome guests and maintain reservation or waiting lists. They may direct patrons to coatrooms, restrooms, or to a place to wait until their table is ready. Hosts and hostesses assign guests to tables suitable for the size of their group, escort patrons to their seats, and provide menus. They also schedule dining reservations, arrange parties, and organize any special services that are required. In some restaurants, they act as cashiers.

Dining room and cafeteria attendants and bartender helpers assist waiters, waitresses, and bartenders by cleaning tables, removing dirty dishes, and keeping serving areas stocked with supplies. Sometimes called backwaiters or runners, they bring meals out of the kitchen and assist waiters and waitresses by distributing dishes to individual diners. They also replenish the supply of clean linens, dishes, silverware, and glasses in the dining room and keep the bar stocked with glasses, liquor, ice, and drink garnishes.

Dining room attendants set tables with clean tablecloths, napkins, silverware, glasses, and dishes and serve ice water, rolls, and butter. At the conclusion of meals, they remove dirty dishes and soiled linens from tables. Cafeteria attendants stock serving tables with food, trays, dishes, and silverware and may carry trays to dining tables for patrons. Bartender helpers keep bar equipment clean and wash glasses. *Dishwashers* clean dishes, cutlery, and kitchen utensils and equipment.

Counter attendants take orders and serve food in cafeterias, coffee shops, and carryout eateries. In cafeterias, they serve food displayed on steam tables, carve meat, dish out vegetables, ladle sauces and soups, and fill beverage glasses. In lunchrooms and coffee shops, counter attendants take orders from customers seated at the counter, transmit orders to the kitchen, and pick up and serve food. They also fill cups with coffee, soda, and other beverages and prepare fountain specialties, such as milkshakes and ice cream sundaes. Counter attendants also take carryout orders from diners and wrap or place items in containers. They clean counters, write itemized checks, and sometimes accept payment. Some counter attendants may prepare short-order items, such as sandwiches and salads.

Some food and beverage serving workers take orders from customers at counters or drive-through windows at fast-food restaurants. They assemble orders, hand them to customers, and accept payment. Many of these are combined food preparation and serving workers who also cook and package food, make coffee, and fill beverage cups using drink-dispensing machines.

Other workers serve food to patrons outside of a restaurant environment, such as in hotels, hospital rooms, or cars.

Food and beverage service workers are on their feet most of the time and often carry heavy trays of food, dishes, and glassware. During busy dining periods, they are under pressure to serve customers quickly and efficiently. The work is relatively safe, but care must be taken to avoid slips, falls, and burns.

Part-time work is more common among food and beverage serving and related workers than among workers in almost any other occupation. In 2004, those on part-time schedules included half of all waiters and waitresses, and 40 percent of all bartenders.

Food service and drinking establishments typically maintain long dining hours and offer flexible and varied work opportunities. Many food and beverage serving and related workers work evenings, weekends, and holidays. Many students and teenagers seek part time or seasonal work as food and beverage serving and related workers as a first job to gain work experience or to earn spending money while in school. Around one-fourth of food and beverage serving and related workers were 16 to 19 years old—about six times the proportion for all workers.

There are no specific educational requirements for food and beverage service jobs. Many employers prefer to hire high school graduates for waiter and waitress, bartender, and host and hostess positions, but completion of high school usually is not required for fast-food workers, counter attendants, dishwashers, and dining room attendants and bartender helpers. For many people a job as a food and beverage service worker serves as a source of immediate income, rather than a career. Many entrants to these jobs are in their late teens or early twenties and have a high school education or less.

Usually, they have little or no work experience. Many are full-time students or homemakers. Food and beverage service jobs are a major source of part-time employment for high school and college students.

Restaurants rely on good food and quality customer service to retain loyal customers and succeed in a competitive industry. Food and beverage serving and related workers who exhibit excellent personal qualities—such as a neat clean appearance, a well-spoken manner, an ability to work as a member of team, and a pleasant way with patrons—will be highly sought after.

Waiters and waitresses need a good memory to avoid confusing customers' orders and to recall faces, names, and preferences of frequent patrons. These workers also should be comfortable using computers to place orders and generate customers' bills. Some may need to be quick at arithmetic so they can total bills manually. Knowledge of a foreign language is helpful to communicate with a diverse clientele and staff. Prior experience waiting on tables is preferred by restaurants and hotels that have rigid table service standards. Jobs at these establishments often offer higher wages and have greater income potential from tips, but they may also have stiffer employment requirements than other establishments, such as prior table service experience or higher education.

Usually, bartenders must be at least 21 years of age, but employers prefer to hire people who are 25 or older. Bartenders should be familiar with State and local laws concerning the sale of alcoholic beverages.

Most food and beverage serving and related workers pick up their skills on the job by observing and working with more experienced workers. Some full-service restaurants also provide new dining room employees with some form of classroom-type training that alternates with periods of actual on-the-job work experience. These training programs communicate the operating philosophy of the restaurant, help establish a personal rapport with other staff and instill a desire to work as a team. They also provide an opportunity to discuss customer service situations and the proper ways of handling unpleasant circumstances or unruly patrons with new employees. Additionally, managers, chefs and servers may meet before each shift to discuss the menu and any new items or specials, review ingredients for any potential food allergies, or talk about any food safety concerns, coordination between the kitchen and the dining room, or any customer service issues from the previous day or shift.

Some employers, particularly those in fast-food restaurants, use self-instruction or on-line programs with audiovisual presentations and instructional booklets to teach new employees food preparation and service skills. Some public and private vocational schools, restaurant associations, and large restaurant chains provide classroom training in a generalized food service curriculum. All employees receive training on safe food handling procedures and sanitation practices.

Some bartenders acquire their skills by attending a bartending or vocational and technical school. These programs often include instruction on State and local laws and regulations, cocktail recipes, proper attire and conduct, and stocking a bar. Some of these schools help their graduates find jobs. Although few employers require any minimum level of educational attainment, some specialized training is usually needed in food handling and legal issues surrounding serving alcoholic beverages and tobacco. Employers are more likely to hire and promote based on people skills and personal qualities rather than education.

Due to the relatively small size of most food-serving establishments, opportunities for promotion are limited. After gaining experience, some dining room and cafeteria attendants and bartender helpers advance to waiter, waitress, or bartender jobs. For waiters, waitresses, and bartenders, advancement usually is limited to finding a job in a busier or more expensive restaurant or bar where prospects for tip earnings are better. Some bartenders, hosts and hostesses and waiters and waitresses advance to supervisory jobs, such as dining room supervisor, maitre d'hotel, assistant manager, or restaurant general manager. A few bartenders open their own businesses. In larger restaurant chains, food and beverage service workers who excel at their work often are invited to enter the company's formal management training program.

BEER PROCESSING SYSTEM

Some historians speculate that grain and water was used to make beer even before our prehistoric ancestors learned to make bread. Beer has been made with different ingredients in different cultures and regions throughout the world for millennia, with the first commercial enterprises developing in Germany, Austria and England in the 1200s. In colonial North America, it is said that the Pilgrims landed at Plymouth Rock because they were running low on beer supplies. Mind you, beer had been made by North American Indians with corn and black birch sap long before hops and grains were introduced by the European settlers.

Prior to taverns being built and becoming the communal hub of every town, many colonial households had a malt house attached to their homes, just like a kitchen. One reason cited for this necessity: fear of drinking the water in this new world! Everyone from babies to elderly women drank beer, from breakfast onward throughout the day. This was, ostensibly, before the discovery that the same process of boiling water to make beer also made water potable!

While most of us don't have beer for breakfast anymore, for many, beer continues to be a very enjoyable, thirst-quenching beverage that we imbibe on a regular basis. The joy of producing your own beer, experimenting with different varieties and tastes while avoiding the chemicals and additives in commercial beer, can be a very satisfying, healthful and economical hobby that may develop into a passion.

Beer processing goes through different methods. Pasteurisation is a process by which a liquid is heated for a brief time to kill microbes that may be in the liquid. Pasteurisation has also been used for many years to keep milk safe for drinking due to bacteria that may be present. Sterile filtration, in which the beer is passed through a mechanical filtration system which removes anything larger than 0.5 micrometres. This removes any yeast or hops that may still be in the beer which would continue to react with it. Bottle conditioning allows yeasts to remain in the beer after it is bottled.

This helps prevent some oxidation of the beer. Freshness longevity affects the time it takes a beer to become stale. Some of this depends on the type of beer ingredients included. If the beer has more hops and more alcohol than otherwise, it will stay fresh longer than those that are not as strong. Filtered beer is beer which has been cleaned of significant contact with yeast.

FILTERING METHODS

There are several methods used for clearing yeast from beer.

Some methods involve filtration media such as sheets or candles, while others use a fine powder made of, for example, diatomaceous earth, also called kieselguhr, which is introduced into the beer and recirculated past screens to form a filtration bed.

Filters range from rough filters that remove much of the yeast and any solids (e.g. hops, grain particles) left in the beer, to filters tight enough to strain color and body from the beer. Normally used filtration ratings are divided into rough, fine and sterile. Rough filtration leaves some cloudiness in the beer, but it is noticeably clearer than unfiltered beer. Fine filtration gives a glass of beer that you could read a newspaper through, with no noticeable cloudiness. Finally, as its name implies, sterile filtration is fine enough that almost all microorganisms in the beer are removed during the filtration process.

Sheet (pad) Filters

These filters use pre-made media and are relatively straightforward. The sheets are manufactured to allow only particles smaller than a given size through, and the brewer is free to choose how finely to filter the beer. The sheets are placed into the filtering frame, sterilized (with hot water, for example) and then used to filter the beer. The sheets can be flushed if the filter becomes blocked, and usually the sheets are disposable and are replaced between filtration sessions. Often the sheets contain powdered filtration media to aid in filtration.

It should be kept in mind that pre-made filters have two sides. One with loose holes, and the other with tight holes. Flow goes from the side with loose holes to the side with the tight holes, with the intent that large particles get stuck in the large holes while leaving enough room around the particles and filter medium for smaller particles to go through and get stuck in tighter holes.

Sheets are sold in nominal ratings, and typically 90% of particles larger than the nominal rating are caught by the sheet.

Kieselguhr Filters

Filters that use a powder medium are considerably more complicated to operate, but can filter much more beer before needing to be regenerated. Common media include diatomaceous earth, or kieselguhr, and perlite.

Cold Filtering

A method that is gaining popularity is cold filtering in which the beer is chilled before or during a sheet filtering process. When beer is chilled the protein molecules tend to clump together and so are easier to filter out.

Beer can also be filtered by allowing the yeast to settle to the bottom of the container and the clear or *bright* beer is then decanted off the sediment. The period spent allowing the beer to settle is known either as lagering or as conditioning. With ale conditioning finings are used to assist in clearing the beer.

BRIGHT BEER

The term used by brewers for beer which has been cleaned of yeast is bright beer; such beer is usually held in *bright tanks* before bottling or additional treatment.

PASTEURISATION

An additional process that is sometimes done to filtered beer is pasteurisation in which the beer is flash heated to kill off any bacteria. Because this process is known to have an adverse effect on the flavour of the beer the practise is declining in most breweries, though some British regional breweries still pasteurise.

BREWERY CONDITIONED

In the UK a beer which has been filtered in the brewery is known as *brewery conditioned* beer. A brewery conditioned beer may just be filtered, or it may also be pasteurised. The term is used to differentiate such beers from those which are still in contact with the yeast which are known as bottle conditioned, cask conditioned or real ale.

CHINESE BEVERAGE AND FOOD

The industrial value added to RMB 629.995 billion in China food industry in 2005, increasing 18.08% year-on-year; the sales rate was 98.6% and the total pretax profit was RMB 336.5 billion, increasing 21.6 year-on-year; the total import and export was USD 44.97 billion, increasing 13.7% year-on-year; and employees in this industry reached 4.53 million.

China has taken the leading position in some major food and beverage products. For example, the total production of edible vegetable oil, beverage and gourmet power each hit 16.12 million ton, 33.8 million ton and 1.36 million ton in 2005.

Food expenditure took largest ratio of about 40% of the total consumption expenditure in 2005. Chinese food structure has changed a lot. Expenditure on self-efficient food is gradually lowered down while demand for nutritious, convenient and green leisure food is in great potential. Traditional food is now developing towards cleanness, nutrition and health. Chinese major convenient foods market is in perfect competition and monopolistic competition, relatively the former takes priority, which is decided by their characteristics of primary products processing, low industrial added value and low market entry threshold.

Chinese beverage expenditure is still out of basic consumption needs, with an average consumption amount far less than the world average level. It can be predicted that still great potential is to be explored in the market and the developing prospect is optimistic. Chinese beverage has developed from single drink to a variety of drinks including carbonated soft drink, fruit juice and vegetable juice. In 2005, the production of soft drink in China was 33.8 million ton, increasing 24.08% year-on-year. The total product value and sales revenue was RMB 109.079 billion and RMB 113.950 billion, increasing 25.82% and 24.97% respectively.

While in the alcoholic drinks market, beer production in China increased 10.3% year-on-year in 2005 to 30.61 billion liter, thus took the world leading position for the fourth successive year. White wine production amounted to a total of 3.4937 billion liter, increasing 15.03% year-on-year. The economical benefit in wine realized a sudden growth. Sales revenue of large-scaled white wine manufacturers added up to RMB 72.265 billion. In 2005, grape wine industry kept a rapid development too. The total production of grape wine reached 434.3 million liter and realized a profit of RMB 1.256 billion, increasing 25.40% and 58.78% year-on-year respectively.

Chinese food and beverage market maintain rapid growth in 2006. In H1 2006, the listed companies overall realize an income of RMB 50.637 billion from major business, increasing 16.85% year-on-year; they achieved a profit of RMB 15.056 billion, increasing 22.11% year-on-year; their major business rate was 29.73%, slightly increasing 1.28% year-on-year. During this period the cost rate lowered down by 0.8%, and the overall net benefit increased 77.47% year-on-year. The production and sale volume of China food and beverage industry keeps rising and it is forecasted that in the next few years such rise will continue at even a higher speed. Investment opportunities lie in this industry once investors see the tendency clearly and work out feasible risk-resistance policies to follow. As for the sub-industries, the first half of 2006 saw a rapid growth resumed in white wine and beer industry.

Especially in white wine industry, both output increase and growth rate appeared a rising tendency. In addition, rate of return on sales (pretax) saw an obvious increase. While domestic grape wine industry was impacted by the imported grape wine thus decelerated the sales. But we still take an optimistic attitude toward Chinese grape wine market in the long run.

Prices of white wine generally raise a lot. Dairy products thus confront great pressure from cost. Dairy manufacturers one by one enhance their production ability of good yoghourt to earn more profit. Beer industry keeps a rise of about 16%, slightly declined compared to the growth in last year and the growth of industry revenue. The competition is still fierce despite a moderate relaxation.

This report explains and analyses the status quo, the changes of various economical indicators, the development status of related industry, market status of key regions, leading enterprises, consumer strategies and competition strategies of China food and beverage industry, based on National Bureau of Statistics of China, Light Industry Statistics Bureau, China Beverage Organization, and China Economics Information Center. It also makes prudent judgments towards the development trend of the industry and seeks new growth points for investors.

In addition, it objectively comments on the common benefits and possible risks. It is of great reference value if you are trying to decide when, what, how and how much to invest in China food and beverage industry. It is forecasted that the investment opportunities will still lie in the beverage production industry, mainly in alcohol production from 2006 to 2007. Investment opportunities in beverage production are far more than in food processing and food production. Attention should be paid to big companies at the same time much care should also be given to the opportunities in segmented market.

This report examines China's macroeconomic trends, investment environment, food and beverage additives industry structure and capacity, production and demand, end-use market consumption trends, distribution channels and principal industry participants. Long-term forecasts for major food and beverage additives production and demand are included. Key producers are profiled. Top Chinese food and beverage additives, food and beverage producers are listed in the producer directory section.

Most primary and secondary research were done in China in order to access up-to-date government regulations, market information and industry data. Data was collected from the Chinese government publications, Chinese language newspapers and magazines, Chinese chemical industry associations including Chinese rubber industry associations, local governments' chemical industry bureaus, food and beverage additives industry publications, and our inhouse databases. Interviews were conducted with Chinese industry experts, university professors, and food and beverage additives producers in China.

Historical data include 1995, 2000 and 2005. Longterm development trends are projected to the years 2010 and 2015. Economic models and quantitative methods are applied in this report to project market demand and industry trends. Metric system is used and values are presented in either yuan (RMB, current price) and/or US dollars. Exchange rate for 2000 is based on the annual average rate (8.1 yuan per US dollar). The word "demand" is used interchangeably with "consumption". Totals may not add due to rounding.

THE PERCEIVED VALUE OF A SERVICE

Most Hospitality Operators use the term "Quality" somewhere in their advertising and promotion. What exactly does that mean? One would compile multiple responses, as Management tried to define "Quality". The same would be said for their Staff, and, just as importantly, the Guest. We all have different perspectives. Hospitality invites a Quality Experience, but, if expectations are not met, you have a disappointed Guest, reduced Revenue, unhappy employees and a deteriorating reputation.

So, what is the Value of Quality: the Concept, the Experience and Reward, and how does this relate to your Hospitality Business?Recent research has revealed that few leisure providers integrate marketing techniques into programming efforts and that "leisure service agencies have long attempted to serve diverse and, at times, non-responsive populations". A marketing perspective would suggest leisure and tourism providers analyze the needs and desires of their participants, in order to develop the most appropriate delivery methods. In doing so, leisure/tourism programmers may benefit by attracting more responsive and possibly more loyal participants.

Quality is a Process. There are Performance Standards created, communicated and implemented. The Standards are reviewed constantly to stress Continual Improvement. Success Stories are heralded. Problem Areas are immediately addressed. Steady "feed back" is required. This is not a one day exercise. Quality must become integral to your Business Performance.

Does your definition of Quality translate to the Guest's expectations? Hospitality Operations are boldly diverse. We present to the Consumer various locations, architecture, ambiance, price, amenity, and activity. When they make a reservation – book a room, a table, or a ticket – the Guest has an Expectation. Now, we must deliver and not create a disconnect, because we may be at cross purposes with our Guest and their concept of Quality.

How do we create a "common ground" to meet these expectations and avoid the false steps in fully serving our Guest? The Quality Process begins with recognized, reasonable Hospitality Performance Standards. All parties understand cleanliness. The environment you represent must be clean and not assault the five senses. We need to feel safe and secure. We require certain "creature comforts". We look for our needs to be attended with some courtesy, accuracy, speed and pleasant attitude. Finally, we expect the facility to present an acceptable appearance / condition. These elements are how you will be judged by your Guest. They represent the Benchmarks for a memorable Quality experience or not. These Performance Standards are the foundation, and the Guest needs to know you are serious and sincere. Particularly for those Destinations which are Family oriented, recognize that the greatest influence on where the Family will stay, dine and recreate is the Mother, and she holds Quality Standards dearly.

The success of a Process needs to be measured – a Performance Evaluation. Where do you rate with these Hospitality Standards? Do you deliver, and, just as importantly, does your Staff? Your Quality message must be communicated daily. Your Staff must abide by your Message. Clear guidelines, need to be in place, practiced and assessed.

Attention to detail and meeting the Guest's needs are the Mantra. There are many means to evaluate your Performance: the personal relationship you have with your Guests; in-house mechanisms, like Comment Cards; Mystery Shop Services; Assessment Companies; and formal Guest Satisfaction Systems. They are all meaningful. Further, many leisure and tourism providers would benefit by obtaining a more consistent participant base as it has been shown that it is six times less expensive to plan marketing strategies for retaining consumers, than it is to attract new consumers.

In the field of marketing, the construct of perceived value has been identified as one of the most important measures for gaining competitive edge, and has been argued to be the most important indicator of repurchase intentions.

Yet, in regards to leisure and tourism services, repurchase intentions and consumer loyalty are often predicted solely by measures of consumer satisfaction, and/or service quality. Woodruff (1997) states, "if consumer satisfaction measurement is not backed up with in-depth learning about customer value and related problems that underlie their evaluations, it may not provide enough of the customer's voice to guide managers where to respond".

Further, just because a consumer is "satisfied" with a product/service, does not necessarily mean the product/service is a good value. It is quite possible a consumer who is very satisfied with a product or service, may consider it a poor value if the costs for obtaining it a re perceived to be too high. On the contrary, a moderately satisfied consumer may find a service to have good value, if they believe they receive good utility for the price paid.

Since perceived value has been found to be an important indicator of repurchase intentions it is believed leisure/tourism providers could benefit from refined measures of the construct. Valid and reliable measures of perceived value would allow for comparison of value between leisure/tourism programmes, and would allow individual leisure/tourism providers the ability to identify the dimensions of perceived value in which they perform well or poor.

While recent multidimensional scales have been created for measuring the perceived value of tangible products, a multi-dimensional scale for the measurement of perceived value of intangible products (services) does not exist. Thus, the purpose of the current study is to develop a multidimensional scale for the measurement of perceived value of a service.

Perceived value has been defined as "the consumer's overall assessment of the utility of a product based on perceptions of what is received and what is given". Within this definition, Zeithaml (1988) identified four diverse meanings of value:

(1) Value is low price,

(2) Value is whatever one wants in a product,

(3) Value is the quality that the consumer receives for the price paid, and

(4) Value is what the consumer gets for what they give. The majority of past research on perceived value has focused on the fourth definition.

A fundamental base for the conceptualization of perceived value of a service was developed by Zeithaml. Her research utilized focus groups and in-depth consumer interviews to explore the relationships between consumers' perceptions of price, quality and value. The focus groups were utilized to determine the salient attributes and variables related to perceived value, while the interviews were utilized to reveal the causal links among product attributes, quality and value. Open ended questions were then used to examine the information needed to make judgments about quality and value (i.e., advertising and packaging).

Results of her study showed that perceived quality leads to perceived value, which leads to purchase intentions. Both intrinsic (i.e., how the purchase makes you feel) and extrinsic attributes (i.e., reputation of the product/service), as well as price, were found to be positively related to perceived quality. Moderating variables of perceived value included perceived sacrifice (non-monetary price), extrinsic attributes and intrinsic attributes. Overall, Zeithaml reported quality, price (monetary and non-monetary), reputation of the product/service and how the product/service makes one feel (emotional response) were dimensions related to perceived value.

Similarly, the Profit of Impact Marketing Strategies (PIMS) study conceptualized value as the relationship between quality and price. They ascertained competitive success is obtained through "perceived relative value" of the total package of products and services that influence customer behaviour. Relative value, is the value received from one product/service, in comparison to similar offerings.

According to Bojanic: "the notion of relative perceived value results in three possible value positions: (1) offering comparable quality at a comparable price, (2) offering superior quality at a premium price, or (3) offering inferior quality at a discounted price." Perceived value may thus be altered if management changes what they are doing, a competitor changes what they are doing, or if consumer's desires or needs change.

More recently, Parasuraman and Grewal (2000) conceptualized perceived value as a dynamic construct consisting of four value types: acquisition value, transaction value, in-use value and redemption value. They define acquisition value as the benefits received for the monetary price given, and transaction value as the pleasure the consumer receives for getting a good deal. In-use value is the utility derived from utilization of the product/service, while redemption value is the residual benefit received at the time of trade-in or end of life (products) or termination (for services). Utilizing these definitions, the relevance of each of the four dimensions are different during varying times of the product/services life (i.e., acquisition and transaction value are most salient during purchase, while in-use value and redemption value are more pertinent after purchase).

While all of these theorized frameworks aid in the understanding of perceived value, they do not offer measures for collecting perceived value data. Perceived value is most commonly measured by using a self-reported, unidimensional measure asking respondents to rate the value they received for their purchase. The problem with a one-dimensional measures is that it assumes that consumers have a shared meaning of value. Zeithaml states, "quality and value are not well differentiated from each other and from similar constructs such as perceived worth and utility."

Thus, it has been argued that one-dimensional measures of perceived value lack validity. Another inherent problem is unidimensional measures result in the knowledge of how well one is rated for value, but give no specific direction on how to improve value.

It is believed that a formal measurement tool for the perceived value of a service, would allow comparisons similar to comparisons of service quality that are now available due to Parasuraman, Zeithaml and Berry's (1988) SERVQUAL scale and Cronin and Taylor's SERVPERF scale. With the use of reliable and valid multi-dimensional measures, leisure and tourism providers should be able to identify the dimensions in which they are succeeding and/ or failing in regards to both their own past measures and those of their competition.

Current efforts to measure perceived value have shown it is difficult to quantify perceived value. Kantamneni and Coulson focused on the development of a multi-dimensional measure of perceived value of a product.

They utilized undergraduate business students to identify potential measurable dimensions of a product's perceived value. Results identified the distinct factors of societal value, experiential value, functional value and market value.

Societal value was termed to be the product's benefit/value to society. Experiential value was related to the senses: if the product feels, smells and looks good, while functional value was related to whether or not the product is reliable and safe. The final factor, market value, was the product's worth regarding price for value. Another multi-dimensional scale for the measurement of perceived value of a product was presented by Sweeney, Soutar and Johnson.

Utilizing exploratory factor analysis of 29 items generated from a literature review, the factors of quality, emotional response, price and social emerged as dimensions of perceived value of a product. Quality referred to how well the product was made, and emotional response to how a product made the consumer feel. Price was operationalized as whether or not the money paid for the product was reasonable, and social as the impression that the purchase of the product had on others.

While the aforementioned studies show promise for the measurement of perceived value of tangible products, there is need for a different scale to be developed for measuring the perceived value of a service. Past research has shown that scales developed for measuring a product's perceived value are difficult to use when measuring perceived value of a service. Further, the dimensions inherent in a service differ from those of a product. Lovelock argued that services differ from products in that they are intangible, perishable, variable and inseparable. Thus, multi-dimensional measures of a service must consider these properties.

Following the theoretical model conceptualized by Zeithaml, current conceptual frameworks, and the properties of a service, multiple dimensions of perceived value of a service can be identified. Most researchers agree that perceived value is a comparison of what a consumer "receives," with what the consumer "gives" for the attainment of a product or service. Perceived price is what a consumer gives up or sacrifices in order to obtain a product.

While some consumers may know the exact price of the service purchased, others may only remember (encode) that their purchase was expensive or inexpensive in relation to past purchases. Still others may not encode a price at all. Consumers also evaluate non-monetary costs in their determination of quality received for price paid. Non-monetary costs include such things as time, search costs, brand image and convenience. It is therefore a combination of both perceived monetary and non-monetary costs that equate to consumers' overall perceived sacrifice which, in turn, affects their perception of product or service value. In regards to what a consumer "receives" past research has identified emotional response, or the joy received from purchase, and quality as dimensions of perceived value of a product/service. Further, the product/

services reputation has been identified as an influence on consumer's perceived quality, and perceived value. Thus it could be argued that dimensions of what a consumer receives from the purchase of a service include: the emotional response to the service, quality received from the service, and the reputation of the service rendered. While the dimensions related to what is given, consist of monetary and non-monetary (behavioural) price.

Utilizing these dimensions, a hypothetical model of one of the roles that perceived value plays in the assessment of a service. It is suggested that the perceptions of service quality leads to the purchase and experience rendered by the service. This experience results in the perception of the value received from the service. It is further postulated that perceived value influences intention to reinvest in the service experience, and how positively or negatively individuals talk to others about their service experience.

This process then effects future assessments of the quality of a service. While it has been postulated that perceived value changes during different stages of a purchase, the proposed scale will only measure perceived value after completing a purchase. Thus the role that perceived value plays in the decision-making processes of the current conceptualization can only occur after service has been rendered.

Instrument Development

The operational definition of the construct of perceived value that was used to guide development of the scale was "the consumer's overall assessment of utility of a product based on perceptions of what is received and what is given. Further, perceived value was a priori conceptualized as a multi-dimensional construct, including the dimensions of quality, emotional response, monetary price, behavioural price, and reputation. Since reliability has consistently been found to be the most important dimension of quality for recreation and tourism managers, quality was defined as a consumer's judgment about a product or service's overall excellence or superiority.

Emotional response was defined as a descriptive judgment regarding the pleasure that a product or service gives the purchaser. The definition utilized for monetary price was the price of a service as encoded by the consumer. Behavioural price was defined as the price (non-monetary) of obtaining a service, which included the time and effort, used to search for the service. Finally, reputation was defined as the prestige or status of a product or service, as perceived by the purchaser, based on the image of the supplier.

The initial pool of items was accumulated from various scales developed by others relating to the construct of perceived value. Fifty-two items were acquired from a review of both scientific and popular literature.

In order to examine the scale's external validity and generalizeability it was administered to samples on two different seven-day Caribbean cruises, on board the same vessel. To ensure that cruise passengers taking back-to-back cruises were not sampled twice, the two samples were taken three weeks apart. One questionnaire was distributed to each cabin on board the vessel that was accommodated by a paying cruiser on the second to the last evening of the cruise. A letter was included with the questionnaire explaining that only one member in the room was to complete it, and that it was to be returned to their cabin steward.

The scale was operationalized by asking participants to rate each item on a scale from 1, definitely false, to 5 definitely true for their cruise on board the vessel. The survey also included single-item measures of overall perceived value and overall satisfaction. Overall perceived value was measured by asking respondents to rate the value received for their money when purchasing their cruise. The single item, 10-point scale, was anchored by extremely poor value and extremely good value.

A total of 591 questionnaires were distributed during the first cruise, and 592 during the second. Of these 394 (66.7%) and 398 (67.2%) completed questionnaires were returned from the first and second sample respectively. Among passengers who participated, the average age was 51.6, the median household income was $75,000 to $99,999, 58.7% were female and, on average, respondents had taken 8.1 cruises in their lifetime.

Eight expert judges, from four different universities (all faculty members with Ph.D.'s and expertise in service marketing), were selected to refine and edit the initial 52 items for content validity. The judges were given the following operational definition of perceived value: the consumer's overall assessment of a product, or service's utility based on the perceptions of what is received and what is given. They were also given operational definitions for the proposed dimensions of quality, emotional response, perceived monetary price, behavioural price and reputation.

Consistent with Zaichowsky and Lee and Crompton (1992), each of the judges were first asked to rate each of the 52 items as either clearly representative, somewhat representative or not representative of the perceived value construct. The judges were also asked to assign each of the items as either "clearly representative" or "somewhat representative" to one of the five proposed dimensions of perceived value. They were further asked to identify if any items were representative of more than one dimension.

Following the same criteria utilized by Lee and Crompton, a series of rules were established in order to determine whether or not each item was to be discarded. An item was also discarded if less than five of the eight-member panel assigned it to the same dimension. This process resulted in 25 of the 52 items being eliminated.

The judges were further asked to: a) edit and improve the items to improve their clarity, readability and content, b) identify any items which they believed may be objectionable to respondents and c) offer any suggestions they felt might improve the study. This process resulted in the slight rewording of one item, and the removal of two others. The items removed were due to the judges' belief that the items were too similar to others in the scale. In both cases, the item with the weakest rating by the panel of judges was removed.

The resultant scale consisted of 25 items. Of these items, four were assigned to the dimension of "quality", six to "perceived monetary price", and five each to "emotional response", "behavioural price" and "reputation".

To examine dimensionality and internal reliability of the scale items, a convenience sample of 344 undergraduate students was used. Students were selected from two undergraduate tourism classes, and three undergraduate marketing classes. All students who attended the class periods on the date the questionnaire was administered were asked to complete a questionnaire. To enable a majority of the students to be familiar with the service context, respondents were asked to rate each of the 25 items as they related to lunch at a well-known fast food restaurant.

Respondents were further asked the last time that they had experienced a lunch at the restaurant. Only respondents who had been to the restaurant within the last month were included in the study. Of the respondents included in the study (n 278), approximately one half (51%) were female. Respondents had visited the restaurant 3.6 times on average in the last month.

In order to validate the a-priori assignment of the 25 items to their respective dimensions (as assigned by the expert panel), confirmatory factor analysis (CFA) was employed. The analyses were conducted with the use of the SAS System's proc calis procedures and followed guidelines suggested by Hatcher. Fit indices were chosen following recommendations by Hu and Bender. Fit indices included in the current investigation are the Bender comparative fit index, or CFI, Bender and Bonett, normed fit index, or NFI, and Joreskog and Sorbum root-meansquare residual, or RMSR.

Both the CFI and NFI may range in value from 1.0 to 0.0. According to Bender (1989), a fit index of 0.0 is associated with a "null" model (one specifying that all items are uncorrelated), while a fit index of 1.0 represents a "saturated" model (a model with zero degrees of freedom that perfectly reproduces the original covariance matrix). Values greater than 0.9 indicate a good fit of the data, while values higher than 0.95 indicate an excellent fit of the data. Conversely, An RMSR of less than .10 suggests a good fit of the data.

Since both the CFI and NFI are greater than 0.90, and the RMSR is less than .10, results suggest that the model is a good fit of the data. This finding further suggests, that each item is uniquely related to the factor to which it was assigned. A review of the resultant Wald and Lagrange tests did not suggest any conceptually sound changes to the model. Therefore, the proposed model was tentatively accepted, pending further tests to examine its reliability and validity.

The resultant standardized path coefficients are displayed. The t-tests investigating the null hypothesis that each of the coefficients are equal to zero were all significant, suggesting that all paths were assisting in the prediction of their assigned factors. These results provided evidence supporting the convergent validity of the indicators. Composite reliability is analogous to coefficient alpha, and reflects the internal consistency of the indicators measuring each CFA factor. Results show that all five factors have composite reliability scores greater than 0.70. Utilizing the criteria set for the current analysis, this suggests that each of the factors are reliably measuring their respective constructs.

Combined, these findings support the reliability and internal validity of the hypothesized model. Since the model was found to be a good fit of the data and all paths were found to be significant, it is suggested that the proposed scale effectively measured the pretest subjects' perceived value. Thus, the scale was tentatively accepted, pending further examination and given the name SERV-PERVAL scale.

In order to further test the reliability of the 25 item SERV-PERVAL scale, separate confirmatory factor analyses (CFA) were conducted on the two samples of cruisers. The analyses were conducted utilizing the procedures described previously. Since the CFI and NFI fit indices for both samples are greater than 0.90 and the RMSR scores are less than .10, results suggest that both models are good fits of the data.

This finding also suggests, that each item is uniquely related to the factor to which it was assigned. Further, review of the resultant Wald and Lagrange tests did not suggest any conceptually sound changes. Therefore, the models were tentatively accepted, pending further tests to examine their reliability and validity.

The resultant standardized path coefficients are displayed. The t-tests investigating the null hypothesis that each of the coefficients were equal to zero were all significant, suggesting that all paths are assisting in the prediction of their assigned factors. These results provide evidence supporting the convergent validity of the indicators.

Results show that all five factors from both samples have reliability scores greater than 0.90. Utilizing the criteria set for the current analysis, this suggests that all of the factors are reliably measuring their respective constructs for both data sets. Combined, these findings support the reliability and validity of the hypothesized models.

Since the model was found to be a good fit of the data and all paths were found to be significant, it is suggested that the proposed scale effectively measured the proposed factors of perceived value for both samples. To further validate the scale, the perceived value factors were tested for criterion validity (sometimes called predictive validity).

According to Babbie, criterion validity is demonstrated if scores from the developed scale show expected relationships with one or more external variables that provide direct measure of the construct measured. It would be expected that each of the five factors would be positively related to an overall measure of perceived value. Thus, Pearson's correlations were employed to examine the relationships between each of the factors of perceived value, and overall perceived value. All five factors correlated positively and significantly to overall perceived value for both samples.

To further examine criterion validity, multiple regression with overall perceived value as the dependent variable, and the factors of perceived value as independent variables was employed. It would be expected that the five factors would explain a majority of the variance in perceived value. The regression analysis predicting perceived value was significant and explained 63.5% of the variance in the model.

Therefore results suggest that the proposed five factors of perceived value are related to the construct of perceived value (have criterion validity). Further validation of the scale was completed by testing the factors of perceived value for discriminant validity. Discriminant validity can be examined by comparing the inter-correlations of the constructs to the square root of the average variance extracted. The square root of the average variance for each of the factors is greater than any of the inter-correlations of the constructs. This finding suggests that the factors of perceived value have discriminant validity.

Results demonstrated a valid and reliable five dimensional scale for measuring perceived value. With the use of a panel of experts, the scale was judged to have content validity. The scale consisted of five interrelated, but unique dimensions: quality, emotional response, monetary price, behavioural price and reputation.

Utilizing CFA on the data from a pretest, and two separate samples, the generated items were found to saliently load uniquely on their predicted factors. Further, all of the resultant standardized path coefficients were found to significantly assist in the prediction of their assigned factors. This finding provided evidence of the convergent validity of the proposed indicators.

In order to confirm the reliability of the five factors, composite reliability scores for each of the factors were computed. All reliability scores for the three samples were deemed acceptable, suggesting that each of the factors were reliably measuring their respective constructs. Criterion validity was investigated by examining the correlations between perceived value and each of the factors. It was found that perceived value was positively and significantly related to each of the five factors. Finally, discriminant validity was investigated by comparing the inter-correlations of the constructs to the square root of the average variance for each of the factors. It was revealed that discriminant validity was found for each of the factors of perceived value.

While the current methods were thorough, the study was limited to a specific context. More research is necessary to determine how generalizeable the scale is across service sectors. Also, the future research should examine interrelationships between each of the factors. While the identified dimensions are unique, the causal paths between each dimension would assist in theoretical development of the construct of perceived value. It is believed that this knowledge would assist leisure and/or tourism management in better understanding the role each of the dimensions play in consumers' decision making processes. It is also recommended that future research examine the redundancy of items in the scale.

Redundant items could thus be removed to make the scale more succinct, and less taxing on respondents. Further, it is possible that potential dimensions of perceived value were not identified in the final instrument and the items included were not exhaustive of the five dimensions identified. Thus, it is suggested that future research examine the potential addition of both different factors and different items.

As suggested by Havitz, marketing literature, while seldom utilized in leisure research, is consistent with many of the important "perspectives within the leisure literature". It is thus postulated that the adaptation of tools in the field of marketing, for the fields of recreation and tourism may have far reaching benefits for leisure and tourism providers.

Since there are currently no multidimensional measures of perceived value of a service, and evaluations of perceived value of a service have been found to differ from evaluations of products, it is believed that the current conceptualization is important to leisure and tourism providers. Further, it has been suggested that current perceived value measures are difficult to quantify, though perceived value has been recognized as one of the most salient determinants of purchase intentions and repeat visitation. Thus it is hoped that, similar to the Parasuraman et al., the scale offered here will facilitate comparison of value within, and across services.

Since the seminal work of Chandler, the notion of a linkage between strategy and structure has become widely accepted-that is, if an organization is to implement its strategy most effectively, it needs the appropriate structure and support systems. At the same time, it needs the flexibility to exploit strategic options that arise from environmental changes. However, at least in the short run, a firm cannot easily change its organizational structure, and this may be a major impediment to its ability to change its strategy.

In an increasingly globally integrated world, firms attempting to become major players in their industry need to cope with and exploit environmental changes and adjust their organizational structure to create what Bartlett and Ghoshal (1989) termed "transnational" organizations. In other words, firms need to be able simultaneously to achieve local responsiveness, global efficiency. and the creation of knowledge (learning).

Chandler based his conclusions on a study of four of the largest corporations in the United States — General Motors, Dupont, Standard Oil, and Sears Roebuck — of which only Sears Roebuck was a service organization. Indeed, much of the literature on both the strategy of multinational firms and organizational structure has emanated from studies of large and powerful manufacturing firms, notwithstanding the ever-increasing importance of large multinational firms in service industries. While some of these service industries have more in common with MNEs producing goods, others are quite different. The purpose of this chapter is to explore the effects of globalization on the organizational structures and systems of service firms in general, and professional service firms in particular. The paper postulates certain relationships between key success factors in multinational professional service firms and the structure and systems of these firms. The resulting propositions help provide the basis for a contingency theory of organizational structure and systems.

In the first section, some of the contributions to organization design theory and to organizational taxonomies are briefly surveyed. In the second section, some of the relevant theories on the organizational structure of multinational enterprises are reviewed. The third section discusses the globalization of services, while the fourth proposes a taxonomy of multinational service firms by the key factors contributing to their success, and it hypothesizes on the implications for organizational design.

This analysis is offered as preliminary to devising a contingency theory of organizations for service multinationals' particularly professional service multinationals. Organization theory is a positive theory focused on understanding organizations. On the basis of its findings, the organization focuses its design on normative solutions, that is, on the optimal means of creating an organization to achieve given goals and missions. Organization theory has moved a long way from the belief prevailing at the beginning of the century in immutable general laws of organization design or in the classical depiction of a "machine" organization.

March and Simon summarized the state of the art as follows: "Much of what we know or believe about organizations is distilled from common sense and from the practical experience of executives. The great bulk of this wisdom and lore has never been subjected to the rigorous scrutiny of scientific methods". Many assertions have since been tested to check whether or not they are supported by the facts. In addition, the importance of such factors as information, motivation, power, conflict. and innovation have been subjected to much scrutiny.

Moreover, different theses have also been tested in a variety of national and cultural contents. The organizational structure of the firm has been shown to be a reflection of its operating environment. Lawrence and Lorsch examined the firm's differentiation and integration characteristics in three industries. By differentiation, they meant orientations toward goals, time, and interpersonal relationships, as well as toward the degree of formality of the structure; by integration, they meant the degree of collaboration among departments working on common projects.

They demonstrated that these characteristics depend on the degree of turbulence in the environment: in a highly stable environment, organizations tend to be much more integrated, whereas in a turbulent environment, differentiation becomes more necessary. In Lawrence and Lorsch's model, complex tasks are performed through increased task specialization and subsequent coordination.

The different needs in different stages tn an organizational evolution have also been recognized. Child called attention to the importance of growth as a means of meeting the aspirations of the participating members of the organization. Kimberly argued for a dynamic perspective — researching the different stages in the life cycle of organizations — from creation to transformation to maturity and then decline. Pfeffer and Salancik distinguished between internally generated growth, to achieve individual or organizational goals, and growth based on biological systems limited by constraints and resources. They saw growth as a purposeful response to external constraints.

Mintzberg developed a taxonomy of organizational structures in different categories of organizations — the entrepreneurial, bureaucratic (machine and professional), divisional, adhocracy, and matrix. He suggested that, as organizations grow. they undergo structural changes — from the entrepreneurial to bureaucratic. divisional, and finally matrix structures. An organization can be bureaucratic without being centralized. This happens when professionals are needed because of the complexity of tasks, but the tasks themselves can be perfected through standardized operating programmes. The result is the professional bureaucracy structure.

Structural changes, therefore, correspond to both internal requirements and environmental demands. They arc contingent on quite a large number of factors.

Organizations must change and adapt to internal political conditions, to external changes in the environment, and to technological changes and the opportunities they create. Integration mechanisms are needed to achieve coordination and these needs also depend on situational variables such as the competitive market structure or the stage of the life cycle. Although empirical research has failed to lend unequivocal support to the hypothesis that strategy follows structure, the implementation of any strategy must be based on a certain structure and on systems, including rewards.

Organizations are basically information-processing entities, and must match the demand for information processing with the capacity of the firm to do it. The information required depends on the environment, on technology, and on other variables such as size and complexity. Nowadays, firms can create significant competitive advantage on the basis of sophisticated use of information systems.

New information technologies are facilitating new forms of organizations and different structures, allowing greater integration across national borders.

The increased power of personal computers, for example, is profoundly affecting both structures and systems. Computers have also allowed service firms to achieve both low-cost positions and customized services. All these new developments arc allowing new types of structures, such as the "infinitely flat" organization.

New telecommunications capabilities have eroded the boundaries between firms and their suppliers, as well as between geographic territories; and organizations can run borderless networks connected by electronic data interchange (EDI) and electronic mail with very little formal hierarchy. Moreover, in a knowledge-based society, the ability to tap all possible knowledge to achieve the task is crucial.

Much of the needed knowledge cannot be maintained in books on standard operating procedures, but is tapped by professionals communicating with each other. Professional workers must be willing to cooperate across tasks, professions, and geography to implement the strategy of the firm. This kind of cooperation has been achieved by professionals such as engineers and consultants. However, when a firm needs to trim its staff, self-preservation, fear, and frustration may lead individuals to be much less cooperative.

The organization of the future is sometimes portrayed in terms of project management and flat structures. This type of structure is perhaps more appropriate to expert organizations such as consulting firms or CNN (Cable News Network), with their prima-donna "star" performers, than to organizations that can standardize their operation to allow a machine bureaucracy as the optimal mode.

Indeed, companies such as CNN, EDL, and McKinsey & Co. are organized around many small teams carrying out shifting project assignments. They employ mainly bright, aggressive, though not arrogant, individuals who are unwilling to abide by too many arbitrary rules and standard operating procedures, but are happy to do all it takes to get the job done. These organizations focus on solutions to customers' problems, which they achieve at a much greater speed than the older, hierarchical bureaucracy.

Much in the way of theoretical contributions and empirical evidence is available on the relationships between structure and contextual factors. A survey of the organization theory literature certainly shows a diverse and sometimes inconsistent set of rules related to the organizational structure of firms.

In many cases, the number of variables to be taken into account is quite large. Duncan, for example, suggested a decision tree for structures based on three possible dimensions of the environment: complexity, change, and segmentation. Robbins discusses environmental hostility, positing that greater hostility necessitates greater centralization. Perrow discussed the impact of technology, while considered the impact of size.

If one combines all these variables with Mintzberg's (1979) basic configurations (simple, functional, divisional, matrix, machine bureaucracy, professional bureaucracy, ad hoc), a very large number of possible combinations emerge. Organization theory guides managers in choosing those configurations that allow fit between the organization and various parameters, such as environment, strategy, size, technology, and management style.

These variables may or may not be different in an international context. Bartlett and Ghoshal in particular stressed the role of overseas operations (as well as the development and diffusion of knowledge) in creating unique configurations for international operations.

8

Hospitality and Food Management

HOTEL OCCUPATIONS

The owner, chairman, or CEO of a hotel or hotel group is known as a hotelier. A comfortable room, good food, and a helpful staff can make being away from home an enjoyable experience for both vacationing families and business travellers. While most lodging managers work in traditional hotels and motels, some work in other lodging establishments, such as camps, inns, boardinghouses, dude ranches, and recreational resorts. In full-service hotels, lodging managers help their guests have a pleasant stay by providing many of the comforts of home, including cable television, fitness equipment, and voice mail, as well as specialized services such as health spas. For business travelers, lodging managers often schedule available meeting rooms and electronic equipment, including slide projectors and fax machines.

Lodging managers are responsible for keeping their establishments efficient and profitable. In a small establishment with a limited staff, the manager may oversee all aspects of operations. However, large hotels may employ hundreds of workers, and the general manager usually is aided by a number of assistant managers assigned to the various departments of the operation. In hotels of every size, managerial duties vary significantly by job title.

General managers have overall responsibility for the operation of the hotel. Within guidelines established by the owners of the hotel or executives of the hotel chain, the general manager sets room rates, allocates funds to departments, approves expenditures, and ensures expected standards for guest service, decor, housekeeping, food quality, and banquet operations. Managers who work for chains also may organize and staff a newly built hotel, refurbish an older hotel, or reorganize a hotel or motel that is not operating successfully. In order to fill entry-level service and clerical jobs in hotels, some managers attend career fairs.

Resident or hotel managers are responsible for the day-to-day operations of the property. In larger properties, more than one of these managers may assist the general manager, frequently dividing responsibilities between the food and beverage operations and the rooms or lodging services. At least one manager, either the general manager or a hotel manager, is on call 24 hours a day to resolve problems or emergencies.

Assistant managers help run the day-to-day operations of the hotel. In large hotels, they may be responsible for activities such as personnel, accounting, office administration, marketing and sales, purchasing, security, maintenance, and pool, spa, or recreational facilities. In smaller hotels, these duties may be combined into one position. Assistant managers may adjust charges on a hotel guest's bill when a manager is unavailable.

An Executive Committee made up of a hotel's senior managers advises the general manager, assists in setting hotel policy, coordinates services that cross departmental boundaries, and collabourates on efforts to ensure consistent and efficient guest services throughout the hotel. The Committee may be comprised of the department heads for housekeeping, front office, food and beverage, security, sales and public relations, meetings and conventions, engineering and building maintenance, and human resources. Executive committee members bring a different perspective of guest service to the total management objective reflecting the unique expertise and training of their positions.

Executive housekeepers ensure that guest rooms, meeting and banquet rooms, and public areas are clean, orderly, and well maintained. They also train, schedule, and supervise the work of housekeepers, inspect rooms, and order cleaning supplies.

Front office managers coordinate reservations and room assignments, as well as train and direct the hotel's front desk staff. They ensure that guests are treated courteously, complaints and problems are resolved, and requests for special services are carried out. Front office managers may adjust charges posted on a customer's bill.

Convention services managers coordinate the activities of various departments in larger hotels to accommodate meetings, conventions, and special events. They meet with representatives of groups or organizations to plan the number of rooms to reserve, the desired configuration of the meeting space, and banquet services. During the meeting or event, they resolve unexpected problems and monitor activities to ensure that hotel operations conform to the expectations of the group.

Food and beverage managers oversee all food service operations maintained by the hotel. They coordinate menus with the Executive Chef for the hotel's restaurants, lounges, and room service operations. They supervise the ordering of food and supplies, direct service and maintenance contracts within the kitchens and dining areas, and manage food service budgets.

Catering managers arrange for food service in a hotel's meeting and convention rooms. They coordinate menus and costs for banquets, parties, and events with meeting and convention planners or individual clients. They coordinate staffing needs and arrange schedules with kitchen personnel to ensure appropriate food service. Sales or marketing directors and public relations directors oversee the advertising and promotion of hotel operations and functions, including lodging and dining specials and special events, such as holiday or seasonal specials. They direct the efforts of their staff to purchase advertising and market their property to organizations or groups seeking a venue for conferences, conventions, business meetings, trade shows, and special events. They also coordinate media relations and answer questions from the press.

Human resources directors manage the personnel functions of a hotel, ensuring that all accounting, payroll, and employee relations matters are handled in compliance with hotel policy and applicable laws. They also oversee hiring practices and standards and ensure that training and promotion programmes reflect appropriate employee development guidelines.

Finance (or revenue) directors monitor room sales and reservations. In addition to overseeing accounting and cash-flow matters at the hotel, they also project occupancy levels, decide which rooms to discount and when to offer rate specials.

Computers are used extensively by lodging managers and their assistants to keep track of guests' bills, reservations, room assignments, meetings, and special events. In addition, computers are used to order food, beverages, and supplies, as well as to prepare reports for hotel owners and top-level managers. Managers work with computer specialists to ensure that the hotel's computer system functions properly. Should the hotel's computer system fail, managers must continue to meet the needs of hotel guests and staff.

Living in Hotels

The American billionaire Howard Hughes lived much of his life in hotels. He moved with his entourage from hotel to hotel and from Beverly Hills to Boston before deciding to move to Las Vegas and become a casino baron. Less than a month after his November 27, 1966 arrival , Hughes made a public offer to buy the Desert Inn. The hotel's 8th floor became the nerve center of his empire and the 9th floor penthouse became Hughes's personal residence. Hughes moved to the Bahamas, Vancouver, London and several other locations — always taking up residence in the top floor penthouse of the hotel. Between 1966 and 1968, he also purchased several other hotel-casinos from the Mafia: Castaways, New Frontier, The Landmark Hotel and Casino, Sands and Silver Slipper.

Coco Chanel made the Hôtel Ritz in Paris her home for more than thirty years, until the day of her death, at 87, in a suite now named "Coco Chanel Suite". King Peter II of Yugoslavia spent much of the Second World War at Claridge's, a hotel in London. His son, Aleksandar Karaðorðeviæ, was born in the hotel. Prince Felix Yusupov lived in the Hotel Vendôme in Paris. Alois

Brunner, Austrian Nazi war criminal, is believed to have lived in the Meridian Hotel in Damascus, Syria, under the name Georg Fischer. Sultan Said Bin Taimur of Muscat lived at Dorchester Hotel in London after he was deposed by Qaboos of Oman in 1970, He died in the hotel in 1972. Eleftherios Venizelos, Greek statesman and diplomat, lived in the Hôtel Ritz Paris while he was in exile in France from 1935-1936.

FOOD INDUSTRY

The food industry is the complex, global collective of diverse businesses that together supply much of the food energy consumed by the world population. Only subsistence farmers, those who survive on what they grow, can be considered outside of the scope of the modern food industry.

The food industry includes:

- Regulation: local, regional, national and international rules and regulations for food production and sale, including food quality and food safety, and industry lobbying activities
- Education: academic, vocational, consultancy
- Research and development: food technology
- Manufacturing: agrichemicals, seed, farm machinery and supplies, agricultural construction, etc.
- Agriculture: raising of crops and livestock, seafood
- Food processing: preparation of fresh products for market, manufacture of prepared food products
- Marketing: promotion of generic products (e.g. milk board), new products, public opinion, through advertising, packaging, public relations, etc
- Wholesale and distribution: warehousing, transportation, logistics
- Retail: supermarket chains and independent food stores, direct-to-consumer, restaurant, food services

OVERVIEW

Essentially, the food industry involves the commercial movement of food from field to fork. The modern food industry is the result of technological and cultural changes that have occurred over the last 150 years. Traditionally, over thousands of years, food production was centered around two activities:

1. Labour-intensive agricultural activities, the farming of grain, produce and livestock;
2. Personal food preparation, where individuals and families acquire raw and minimally processed ingredients, and prepare them for their own consumption.

A significant percentage of the population was directly involved in farming, and in the process, many people actually fed themselves, from field to table. By contrast, the modern food industry relies far more on technology, particularly on mechanization and biochemistry, than on human and animal labour.

In this way, food is raised, manipulated, preserved and moved around, resulting in a food industry that is to a great degree global in nature, with food and related resources travelling great distances. For example, farm machinery and parts from Europe and agrichemicals from the US may routinely travel to farms in South America, where farm products are raised and shipped to North America for fresh market consumption, or for use in processed foods which may then travel to further points around the world. The point at which foods are gathered and prepared has also become fragmented: much of what we eat has already been assembled for consumption.

This modern food system relies heavily on technology, transportation, management and logistics for physical fulfillment, and on marketing and government regulation for maintaining an efficient consumer market. An incredibly wide range of businesses and individuals are employed by and profit from all aspects of this huge and complex system. A tremendous amount of governmental regulation and administration is also involved in this continual flow of materials, food products, and related information.

DEFINITIONS

Food industry is not a formally defined term, however, it is usually used in a broadly inclusive way to cover all aspects of food production and sale. The Food Standards Agency, a government body in the UK, describes it thus:

"the whole food industry – from farming and food production, packaging and distribution, to retail and catering."

The Economic Research Service of the USDA uses the term food system to describe the same thing:

"The U.S. food system is a complex network of farmers and the industries that link to them. Those links include makers of farm equipment and chemicals as well as firms that provide services to agribusinesses, such as providers of transportation and financial services. The system also includes the food marketing industries that link farms to consumers, and which include food and fiber processors, wholesalers, retailers, and foodservice establishments."

Industry Size

Processed food sales worldwide are approximately US$3.2 trillion (2004). In the U.S., consumers spend approximately US$1 trillion annually for food, or nearly 10 percent of the Gross Domestic Product (GDP). Over 16.5 million people are employed in the food industry.

Agriculture

Agriculture is the process of producing food, feed, fiber and other desired products by the cultivation of certain plants and the raising of domesticated animals (livestock). The practice of agriculture is also known as "farming", while scientists, inventors and others devoted to improving farming methods and implements are also said to be engaged in agriculture. More people in the world are involved in agriculture as their primary economic activity than in any other, yet it only accounts for four percent of the world's GDP.

Wholesale and Distribution

A vast global transportation network is required by the food industry in order to connect its numerous parts. These include suppliers, manufacturers, warehousing, retailers and the end consumers.

Retail

With populations around the world concentrating in urban areas, food buying is increasingly removed from all aspects food production. This is a relatively recent development, taking place mainly over the last 50 years. The supermarket is a defining retail element of the food industry, where tens of thousands of products are gathered in one location, in continuous, year-round supply.

Food preparation is another area where change in recent decades has been dramatic. Today, two food industry sectors are in apparent competition for the retail food dollar. The grocery industry sell fresh and largely raw products for consumers to use as ingredients in home cooking. The food service industry offers prepared food, either as finished products, or as partially prepared components for final "assembly".

FOOD INDUSTRY TECHNOLOGIES

Sophisticated technologies define modern food production. They include many areas. Agricultural machinery, originally led by the tractor, has practically eliminated human labour in many areas of production. Biotechnology is driving much change, in areas as diverse as agrichemicals, plant breeding and food processing. Many other areas of technology are also involved, to the point where it is hard to find an area that does not have a direct impact on the food industry. Computer technology is also a central force, with computer networks and specialized software providing the support infrastructure to allow global movement of the myriad components involved.

Marketing

As consumers grow increasingly removed from food production, the role of product creation, advertising, publicity become the primary vehicles for information about food. With processed food as the dominant category, marketers have almost infinite possibilities in product creation. The smooth flow of international trade is critical to the functioning of the modern food industry. Government regulations have to be synchronized to some greater degree to allow this.

Labour and Education

Until the last 100 years, agriculture was labour intensive. Farming was a common occupation. Food production flowed from millions of farms. Farmers, largely trained from generation to generation, carried on the family business. That situation has changed dramatically. In North America, over 50% of the population were farm families only a few decades ago; now, that figure is around 1-2%, and some 80% of the population lives in cities. The food industry as a complex whole requires an incredibly wide range of skills. Several hundred occupation types exist within the food industry.

Research and Development

Research in agricultural and food processing technologies happens in great part in university research environments. Projects are often funded by companies from the food industry. There is therefore a direct relationship between the academic and commercial sectors, as far as scientific research.

Prominent Food Companies

Monsanto is a leading producer of pesticide, seeds, and other farming products. Both Archer Daniels Midland and Cargill process grain into animal feed and a diverse group of products. ADM also provides agricultural storage and transportation services, while Cargill operates a finance wing.

Bunge is a global soybean exporter and is also involved in food processing, grain trading, and fertilizer. Dole Food Company is the world's largest fruit company. Chiquita Brands International, another US based fruit company, is the leading distributor of bananas in the United States. Sunkist Growers, Incorporated is a U.S. based grower's cooperative. Tyson Foods is the world's largest processor and marketer of chicken and the largest beef exporter from the United States. Smithfield is the world's largest pork processor and hog producer.

Nestlé is the world's largest food and beverage company. The Altria Group owns 88.1% of Kraft Foods, the largest U.S. based food and beverage company. Unilever is an Anglo-Dutch company that owns many of the world's consumer product brands in foods and beverages.

FOOD MANAGEMENT

Food habits in India are traditional in nature and are varied across the country. Changing consumer mentalities, busier schedules, and a growing number of working women has collectively led to an increase in the demand for ready-to-eat traditional foods. These foods are based on a variety of raw materials such as cereals, milk, fruits and vegetables, and are prepared in large varieties in the country.

As a segment of the food industry, traditional foods are the largest, both in terms of tonnage and value. However, production is done at different scales, mostly in the unrecognized sector, barring a few large-scale industries. Most of the operations are manual at best batch type even in relatively large-scale units. This causes variation in quality and shelf life. Hence, the need of the hour is automation of the traditional food industry, irrespective of the scale.

FOOD SERVICE

Food service managers are responsible for the daily operations of restaurants and other establishments that prepare and serve meals and beverages to customers. Besides coordinating activities among various departments, such as kitchen, dining room, and banquet operations, food service managers ensure that customers are satisfied with their dining experience.

In addition, they oversee the inventory and ordering of food, equipment, and supplies and arrange for the routine maintenance and upkeep of the restaurant, its equipment, and facilities. Managers generally are responsible for all of the administrative and human-resource functions of running the business, including recruiting new employees and monitoring employee performance and training.

In most full-service restaurants and institutional food service facilities, the management team consists of a general manager, one or more assistant managers, and an executive chef. The executive chef is responsible for all food preparation activities, including running kitchen operations, planning menus, and maintaining quality standards for food service. In limited-service eating places, such as sandwich shops, coffee bars, or fast-food establishments, managers, not executive chefs, are responsible for supervising routine food preparation operations.

Assistant managers in full-service facilities generally oversee service in the dining rooms and banquet areas. In larger restaurants and fast-food or other food service facilities that serve meals daily and maintain longer hours, individual assistant managers may supervise different shifts of workers. In smaller restaurants, formal titles may be less important, and one person may undertake the work of one or more food service positions. For example, the executive chef also may be the general manager or even sometimes an owner.

One of the most important tasks of food service managers is assisting executive chefs as they select successful menu items. This task varies by establishment depending on the seasonality of menu items, the frequency with which restaurants change their menus, and the introduction of daily or weekly specials. Many restaurants rarely change their menus while others make frequent alterations. Managers or executive chefs select menu items, taking into account the likely number of customers and the past popularity of dishes. Other issues considered when planning a menu include whether there was any unserved food left over from prior meals that should not be wasted, the need for variety, and the seasonal availability of foods. Managers or executive chefs analyze the recipes of the dishes to determine food, labour, and overhead costs and to assign prices to various dishes. Menus must be developed far enough in advance that supplies can be ordered and received in time.

Managers or executive chefs estimate food needs, place orders with distributors, and schedule the delivery of fresh food and supplies. They plan for routine services or deliveries, such as linen services or the heavy cleaning of dining rooms or kitchen equipment, to occur during slow times or when the dining room is closed. Managers also arrange for equipment maintenance and repairs, and coordinate a variety of services such as waste removal and pest control. Managers or executive chefs receive deliveries and check the contents against order records. They inspect the quality of fresh meats, poultry, fish, fruits, vegetables, and baked goods to ensure that expectations are met. They meet with representatives from restaurant supply companies and place orders to replenish stocks of tableware, linens, paper products, cleaning supplies, cooking utensils, and furniture and fixtures.

Managers must be good communicators. They need to speak well, often in several languages, with a diverse clientele and staff. They must motivate employees to work as a team, to ensure that food and service meet appropriate standards. Managers also must ensure that written supply orders are clear and unambiguous.

Managers interview, hire, train, and, when necessary, fire employees. Retaining good employees is a major challenge facing food service managers. Managers recruit employees at career fairs, contact schools that offer academic programmes in hospitality or culinary arts, and arrange for newspaper advertising to attract additional applicants. Managers oversee the training of new employees and explain the establishment's policies and practices. They schedule work hours, making sure that enough workers are present to cover each shift. If employees are unable to work, managers may have to call in alternates to cover for them or fill in themselves when needed. Some managers may help with cooking, clearing tables, or other tasks when the restaurant becomes extremely busy.

Food service managers ensure that diners are served properly and in a timely manner. They investigate and resolve customers' complaints about food quality or service. They monitor orders in the kitchen to determine where backups may occur, and they work with the chef to remedy any delays in service. Managers direct the cleaning of the dining areas and the washing of tableware, kitchen utensils, and equipment to comply with company and government sanitation standards. Managers also monitor the actions of their employees and patrons on a continual basis to ensure the personal safety of everyone. They make sure that health and safety standards and local liquor regulations are obeyed.

In addition to their regular duties, food service managers perform a variety of administrative assignments, such as keeping employee work records, preparing the payroll, and completing paperwork to comply with licensing laws and reporting requirements of tax, wage and hour, unemployment compensation, and Social Security laws. Some of this work may be delegated to an assistant manager or bookkeeper, or it may be contracted out, but most general managers retain responsibility for the accuracy of business records. Managers also maintain records of supply and equipment purchases and ensure that accounts with suppliers are paid.

Technology influences the jobs of food service managers in many ways, enhancing efficiency and productivity. Many restaurants use computers to track orders, inventory, and the seating of patrons. Point-of-service (POS) systems allow servers to key in a customer's order, either at the table, using a hand-held device, or from a computer terminal in the dining room, and send the order to the kitchen instantaneously so preparation can begin. The same system totals and prints checks, functions as a cash register, connect to credit card authorizers, and tracks sales. To minimize food costs and spoilage, many managers use inventory-tracking software to compare the record of sales from the POS with a record of the current inventory. Some establishments enter an inventory of standard ingredients and suppliers into their POS system. When supplies of particular ingredients run low, they can be ordered directly from the supplier using preprogrammed information. Computers also allow restaurant and food service managers to keep track of employee schedules and paychecks more efficiently.

Food service managers use the Internet to track industry news, find recipes, conduct market research, purchase supplies or equipment, recruit employees, and train staff. Internet access also makes service to customers more efficient. Many restaurants maintain Web sites that include menus and online promotions, provide information about the restaurant's location, and offer patrons the option to make a reservation.

Managers tally the cash and charge receipts received and balance them against the record of sales. They are responsible for depositing the day's receipts at the bank or securing them in a safe place. Finally, managers are responsible for locking up the establishment, checking that ovens, grills, and lights are off, and switching on alarm systems.

The hospitality industry is notorious for their staffs turn over which costs untold millions of dollars. Experienced employees are difficult to find, and even if hired, still require additional training to understand the inner workings of the procedures of each department in the property. Managers often fail to understand that they must know each facet in every operation and then manage detail. After all, the success of each hospitality business depends on detail. In order to achieve any level of perfection, each manager must first learn, and then get subordinates to perform the task. There is always something new to learn if you want to implement a procedure. The business environment changes constantly as do the expectations of guests. What have been acceptable a year ago my not be so today. The challenge to learn new things daily and implement him or her in the operation is the responsibility of each manager.

Technology changed needs and expectations. While only a few years ago running an operation was a relatively simple task, today's managers must, in addition to all other tasks, be able to understand and manipulate electronic systems. The flow of information and intelligence accelerated due to such devices, and response time decreased accordingly. A guest expects a certain level of comfort and service based on the category of establishment. In many instances, imagers and all employees must anticipate needs and deliver them before the guests asks, This requires not only experience but also an innate sense of service and study of human behaviour. Good management goes beyond technically achieving objectives by co-ordinating human resources with materials to produce profits.

Leadership requires a thorough knowledge of the job, extreme commitment to duty, interpersonal skills, delegation of responsibilities, anticipating changes, and ability to deal with stress on individuals and its ill effects. Hospitality employees are particularly exposed to stress, as there is no formula or set workflow to serve a guest.

They are in constant, direct contact with guests whose needs; wants, moods and demands change from minute to minute. Successful operations have an informal mentoring system. Experienced managers take potential managerial "material" under their wings and guide them to techniques "reserved" for privileged managers. They spend time with their understudies and impart information on how to speak with important business partners, how to present themselves, how to behave in formal settings and the finer points of delivering an important proposal. They stress the importance of teamwork, the importance of structure, process, planning and human resources development.

Processes must be based on solid criteria in an attempt to be able to deliver services if an important (key) employee is absent, or leaves unexpectedly, or even must be relieved of his/her duties. Respected leaders know the importance of communication in daily management, planning and implementation of strategies.

Leaders have visions, and it is ultimately a vision that drives an organization. A leader knows that a title looks on paper, and that a true leader makes the world believe in his/her beliefs and visions by making a guest feel at ease.

MANAGING FOOD MATERIALS

Proper control of final products, and the waste streams associated with food preparation is an important source reduction technique. Improved ordering and inventory control significantly affect the three major sources of waste resulting from improper inventory control: excess, out-of-date, and obsolete raw goods. Below are options for reduction at the start.

- Order bulk supplies.
- Terminate useless packaging from the vendor.
- Refuse samples that will become waste.
- Work with suppliers to return shipping materials and packaging.
- Purchase reusable items.
- Purchase durable items such as air hand dryers that are designed to reduce waste.
- Purchase only the amount of raw goods needed for a set period of time. This practice will help eliminate out-of-date and excess goods and products.
- Develop a review and approval procedure for all raw goods and products purchased. The primary purchaser can regulate the quantity of materials purchased by other personnel to reduce excess and outof-date inventory.
- Clearly label all materials. Labels can indicate contents, storage and handling, and expiration dates.

Donations, Sales, and Composting of Food Material

Food preparation businesses seeking to reduce food waste should look for opportunities to work closely with potential reusers such as food donor programmes. After donating edible food to reusers, food businesses may work with facilities such as grease renderers, animal food manufacturers, local farmers, or composters who can collect food materials and use them in their operations. Composting is also an option for managing solid food waste.

Segregate Food Wastes for Beneficial Uses

To increase their recyclable potential, food materials should be clean and free of trash such as paper, glass, and plastic. Also, depending upon the requirements of recyclers, solid food wastes should be separated from liquid food wastes to enhance their recyclability.

Excess edible food should be kept separate from waste food and routed to a local food bank or food donor programme. North Carolina.s model .Good Samaritan Law. was enacted in 1989 and revised in 1991. This law protects any good faith donor from civil or criminal liability unless injury is caused by gross negligence, recklessness, or intentional misconduct of the donor. The local health department can provide handling and storage procedures applicable to your area. Currently, more than four million pounds of food materials are donated each year to North Carolina food rescue programmes alone.

Solid food waste should be segregated from waste oils and greases. Hog, cattle, and poultry producers are interested in collecting food waste to use as animal feed. Dairy and bread waste may be fed to hogs without further handling, but other food waste or mixed food waste must be cooked before being fed to hogs. Farmers who use other or mixed food materials must be licensed garbage feeders. Zylphia Smith of the U.S. Department of Agriculture, Animal Plant Health Inspection Services (APHIS) at (919) 856-4170 can provide information about state regulations and a list of licensed garbage feeders. Local cooperative extension agents also may assist with locating markets for waste food.

Waste Oils and Grease

Free grease is that used for or generated by cooking and has not been mixed with water. It is generated from pots, pans, grills, and deep fat fryers and comes from butter, lard, vegetable fats and oils, meats, nuts, and cereals. Free grease should be kept out of the drains and handled separately. Rendering facilities mays purchase free grease and meat wastes and provide storage and collection. The market price depends upon factors such as volume, quality, and hauling distances. The rendering services will process free grease by sampling it for pesticides and other chemicals and filtering and volatizing impurities before reselling it, where prices may range from one to three cents per pound. If the volume of the wastes generated from one restaurant or cafeteria is too small for the rendering facility, businesses should explore the feasibility of setting up a cooperative collection among similar businesses.

Trap Grease is that Collected in a Grease Trap

Because fats coat, congeal, and accumulate on pipes and pumps and sometimes obstruct sewer lines, some food service establishments may be required by their local government to maintain grease traps. Specific information about trap maintenance is presented below. Some rendering services and local septage haulers will service or pump out these traps for a fee, and some services may reduce the pumping fee if the restaurant is a free grease customer.

Dry Cleanup To Keep Wastes Out of the Drain

Food preparation facilities should develop dry cleanup procedures to the greatest possible extent. Some municipalities will charge (surcharge) for any discharge of BOD, COD, TSS, and O/G above a certain level. For a restaurant that uses 3,000 gallons of water per day, serves seven days a week, and has an average BOD of 1,250 milligrams per liter (mg/L), an annual surcharge could be as much as $1,173.1 Dry cleanup procedures will reduce the amount of food waste that enters the drains and, thus, help reduce the possible surcharges.

The "first pass" in equipment and utensil cleaning should be made with scrapers, squeegees, or absorbents to prevent the bulk of food materials from going down the drain. Studies have shown that for a fast food restaurant, 93 percent of the oil and grease discharged to the wastewater treatment plant is generated from ware washing. For a full service restaurant, 75 percent of the oil and grease discharged to the wastewater treatment plant is generated from the pot sink. Waste collected on this first pass. could be set aside for rendering or, possibly, composting.

Spills

Dry cleanup can be applied also to spills in the kitchen. Spills of dry ingredients should be swept up or vacuumed to prevent them from being washed down the drain.

Garbage Disposals

Businesses that use garbage disposals to dispose of food waste are simply transferring disposal from a landfill to a wastewater treatment plant. Disposal of food waste via the sewer system is more costly than landfill disposal and acts as a disincentive to reduce generation of food waste or to separate food for donations, rendering, animal feed, or composting.

Maintaining Grease Traps

Food preparation facilities that discharge to a municipal sewer should contact the local wastewater treatment plant (WWTP) for any requirements concerning the need for interceptors and grease trap management. The most important management procedure for grease traps is that a company representative be present during any cleaning, pumping, or skimming performed by a contractor. This safeguard permits management to respond appropriately to any questions about the services performed.

Pump out schedules should be properly established and strictly followed to prevent overflows, downstream blockage, excessive oil and grease, and BOD loading to wastewater. It is important that these pump outs are complete, i.e., the grease caps removed, the sides scraped or hosed down, and the trap refilled with water. The contractor should indicate whether the trap is refilled with clean water or water from the trap. P A food preparation facility should never "hot flush"(continuously run hot water) the grease trap as the heated, liquefied grease will be flushed down the sewer. While hot flushing may divert the need for pumping, the facility is liable for any costs associated with clogs caused by the flushing. Skimming services are available to skim grease traps on a regular basis. These facilities will reprocess the grease collected and notify owners when complete grease trap pump outs are necessary.

Bioaugmentation, the addition of selected microorganisms (primarily bacteria) to the trap for improved operation, should be evaluated for each case. The bioaugmentation process is basically a passive treatment system to facilitate grease digestion and control buildup of the grease cap. The effectiveness of bioaugmentation is determined by a variety of factors including retention time in the trap, temperature of the wastewater, strength of the wastewater, and contact surface area. Some information indicates that for completely effective bioaugmentation, a retention time of one to five days is needed; however, a typical grease trap is designed for only one day of hydraulic retention. Since these parameters vary with location, an evaluation of each case should be made. The local WWTP should be contacted before any additives are used.

Alternative Grease Trap Designs

Some grease trap systems are designed to periodically heat the trap to de-solidify grease so that it can be automatically skimmed and collected. The high-quality grease collected from these systems may have high reuse potential. These grease traps, which may also be smaller than standard traps, can be located under a specific device above ground (i.e., the pot sink).

Management Commitment

The most critical step to successful waste reduction is commitment by the owner(s)/managers of a facility to a waste management plan. A detailed waste reduction programme should be developed that outlines policies and procedures for dealing with waste and assigns individual responsibilities for all waste related activities. Employees will be aware of the degree of commitment by management and will rise or fall to the level that is expected or allowed. It is, therefore, important to have realistic goals that can be achieved, recognized, and rewarded.

Employee training is a significant component of a waste reduction programme, and all employees from managers to the clean-up crew should be included. The training

sessions, which should be repeated on a regular basis, should teach waste awareness, the impact of various food wastes on the wastewater stream, proper waste handling methods, and the importance of keeping non-food garbage out of food waste containers.

An Employee Suggestion/Awards Programme should be established to maintain employee motivation. Employees can be rewarded for proper waste handling practices. Current incentive programmes (.employee of the month.) can also incorporate employee waste handling practices as evaluation criteria.

An employee awareness programme should be highly visible, and managers and supervisors must strongly support these programmes.

Also, employees should be solicited for ideas/suggestions for conducting efficient dry cleanups, segregating food wastes, or recycling other solid waste products. Employees also may have ideas about methods to generate less food waste or more effectively manage inventory. The most effective waste reduction programmes make use of a team concept in which employees at all levels make contributions.

FOOD SCRAP MANAGEMENT

The intensification of agriculture and food production in recent years has led to an increase in the production of food co-products and wastes. Their disposal by incineration or landfill is often expensive as well as environmentally sensitive.

Methods to valorise unused co-products and improve the management of wastes that cannot be reused, as well as techniques to reduce the quantity of waste produced in the first place, are increasingly important to the food industry. With its distinguished editor and array of international contributors, Waste management and co-product recovery in food processing reviews the latest developments in this area and describes how they can be used to reduce waste.

Californians throw away more than 5 million tons of food scraps each year. That's 16 percent of all disposed materials going into landfills from businesses, residents, and institutions such as schools and prisons. Although green material collection programmes have been implemented in many cities and counties, management of food scraps provides additional opportunities to help meet the State's diversion goals as well as provide greater uses for this resource.

A suggested order for food scrap management is to (1) prevent food waste, (2) feed people, (3) convert to animal feed and/or rendering, and (4) compost.

Restaurants, fast food establishments, and cafeterias can do a lot to minimize or reduce potential cost increases by incorporating simple waste prevention and recycling programmes and procedures that will eliminate much of the waste that is thrown away.

With proper purchasing and handling, and careful preparation and storage, food service establishments can help reduce waste and save money! Your restaurant may already be using many of these ideas to reduce costs as well as waste. Try a few new suggestions, see how they work, and then continue to expand your waste reduction programme.

FOOD DIVERSION THROUGH ANIMAL FEED

Does your business or institution dispose of bakery or food preparation wastes, or post-consumer food scraps that might be used as animal feed? Diverting food scraps to animal feed can help food generators by:

- Decreasing disposal costs.
- Assisting local governments in meeting mandated waste reduction goals.
- Earning payment for food residuals.
- Enhancing food generators' public image.
- Supporting local farmers, dairies, or livestock producers.

The two main ways to divert food to animal feed are (1) direct feed to animals, and (2) converting residuals to a grain supplement, which is then fed to animals. Food scraps include anything from plate scrapings (postconsumer) to produce culls to food processing waste (preconsumer). Key factors in deciding whether this diversion option works for you are the quality of the food residuals, rate of generation, and existence of animal feed operations in your area appropriate for the type of food scraps generated.

Animal feed can be a viable option if a significant quantity of food residuals is generated on a regular basis and storage space is available to keep the material fresh until it can be transported.

Direct Feed to Animals

While care must be taken to prevent the spread of diseases such as swine fever, Exotic Newcastle disease, and Bovine Spongiform Encephalitis (BSE), also known as "Mad Cow Disease" (BSE update), farmers and ranchers can supplement their livestock's diet with the right type of food scraps, given a consistent supply. Food material generators and farmers or ranchers often have an informal arrangement. The generator must find a farmer willing to take the food scraps.

Pigs Are Swine

Some hog farmers participate in the "Garbage Feeding Programme" administered jointly by the U.S. Department of Agriculture (USDA) and the California Department of Food and Agriculture (CDFA). This programme requires a license and regular inspections. The collector must heat-treat all post consumer food scraps and food scraps that have been in any contact with meat scraps. At a minimum, the materials must be heated to 212 degrees Fahrenheit for 30 minutes prior to feeding it to swine. Some counties have further requirements. This heat treatment prevents potential transmission of diseases such as Trichonella, enteric coliform bacteria, swine fever, and foot and mouth disease. Food scrap generators should verify licensing prior to making arrangements with any pig farmer. Licensing is obtained through the CDFA for $20 per year and includes a booklet that describes how to set up a heating or steaming system.

Four Stomachs Are Better Than One

Cattle, sheep, and other ruminants are more restricted in what they can eat, but many dairy farmers or ranchers will accept certain types of food residuals as a feed supplement. If you have pre-consumer vegetable material, such as produce culls or a fruit or vegetable processing byproduct, it may be suitable for a local farm or ranch. Many types of food scraps can be fed directly to ruminants; however, some are not acceptable to cattle. To prevent the transmission of disease, ruminants should not be fed anything containing mammalian flesh. Also, certain vegetables such as onions or garlic are known to taint the flavor of milk from dairy cows. Contact a local dairy farmer, sheep ranch, or cattle rancher (or their animal nutritionist) to determine if your food scraps are appropriate for ruminants.

Poultry and Other Flying Objects

Chickens, turkeys, ducks, and geese love most fresh foods and have a broad diet. They can eat spaghetti with tomato sauce, steamed brown rice, grapes, fresh greens and lettuce, chopped cooked potatoes, corncobs, apple cores, whole grain bread, raw tomatoes, and their own eggs hard-boiled, including the ground shells. Kelp or blood meal are good sources of needed minerals. Any egg, meat, blood, or feather meal must be cooked to prevent the spread of disease. It is also important to note that chickens should be fed fresh, preconsumer foods, not plate scrapings or foods that have spoiled.

Exotic Animals

Exotic or less common animals at zoos and specialty farms may be potential consumers of unwanted food residuals. Some exotic animals have diets that allow them to eat foods unsuitable for traditional farm animals, such as citrus fruits. Check with local farms and zoos to see if the material you have is suited for these animals.

Feed Manufacturers

Ever wonder what animal feed is made of? While most feed is made from agricultural crops such as alfalfa, corn, wheat, soy, and rice, some also contains food residuals from large bakeries, food processing plants, rendering plants, and sometimes even candy factories. Animal feed manufacturers that use food residuals combine foods to make a "recipe" that is appropriate for specific animals. If the supplier has a surplus that is high in proteins and/or carbohydrates, there is a chance they may receive payment for the material. Bakery wastes in particular are of interest to many animal feed manufacturers, as well as other dry, high-protein and/or carbohydrate materials.

Prevent Spread of Diseases

Not all food residuals are suitable for animals. For example, no vessel or aircraft waste, whether it is foreign or domestic in origin, should ever be fed to livestock. Serious animal diseases are spread by this illegal practice. As mentioned above, ruminants should not be fed anything containing mammalian protein due to the risk of BSE, or "Mad Cow Disease." Also, all animal products should be cooked to prevent the spread of other diseases such as Salmonella, Trichonella, and Exotic Newcastle Disease.

Rendering

If you have excess grease or uncooked meat, bone or animal blood, contact a local renderer for collection. These companies collect and process these materials into feedstock for a variety of products, usually for a small fee. Improper disposal of grease can cause many environmental problems and is a leading cause of beach closures. Rendering companies are listed in the yellow pages under "rendering" or "grease collection."

Half of US Food Goes to Waste

The new study, from the University of Arizona (UA) in Tucson, indicates that a shocking forty to fifty per cent of all food ready for harvest never gets eaten. Timothy Jones, an anthropologist at the UA Bureau of Applied Research in Anthropology, has spent the last 10 years measuring food loss, including the last eight under a grant from the US department of agriculture (USDA). Jones started examining practices in farms and orchards, before going onto food production, retail, consumption and waste disposal.

What he found was that not only is edible food discarded that could feed people who need it, but the rate of loss, even partially corrected, could save US consumers and manufacturers tens of billions of dollars each year. Jones says these losses also can be framed in terms of environmental degradation and national security. Jones' research evolved from and builds on earlier work done at the University of Arizona. Archaeologists there began measuring garbage in the 1970s to see what was being thrown away and discovered that people were not fully aware of what they were using and discarding.

Those earlier studies evolved into more sophisticated research using contemporary archaeology and ethnography to understand not only the path food travels from farms and orchards to landfills, but also the culture and psychology behind the process. The fact that the US is a wasteful nation is not necessarily news, of course. The country has long has been chastised for its wilful consumption of the world's resources, and many aspects of the country's culture encapsulate what environmentalists disparagingly refer to as today's "throw-away society."

Similarly, researchers have known for years about the volumes of food Americans toss into the trash. But only recently, though, has that been quantified as a percentage of what is produced, and the UA statistics are the first tangible proof that Us food production is frighteningly wasteful. A certain amount of waste in the food stream cannot be helped of course. Little can be done, for instance, about weather and crop deterioration. The apple industry, for instance, loses on average about 12 per cent of its crop on the way to market.

Apples in the US are harvested over a two-month period and then stored and sold year-round. People in the apple business use aggressive methods to maintain their crop, with fresh apples hitting the supermarkets on a regular basis and marginal ones sent to be made into applesauce and other products. The goal of apple growers is to provide a nutritious product, all year long, at fairly constant prices. Jones says they've adopted a conservative business plan that forgoes the boom-and-bust cycles that other fruit and vegetable growers aim for and opts instead for a steady income stream.

But Jones argues that fresh fruit and vegetable growers, in contrast, often behave like riverboat gamblers. They will take a risk on the commodity markets if they think it will help them make a financial killing. A bad bet often means an entire crop is left in the field to be ploughed under. Jones' research also shows that by measuring how much food is actually being brought into households.

On average, households waste 14 per cent of their food purchases. Fifteen per cent of that includes products still within their expiration date but never opened. Jones estimates an average family of four currently tosses out $590 per year, just in meat, fruits, vegetables and grain products. Jones says that consumers better need to understand that many kinds of food can be refrigerated or frozen and eaten later. Nationwide, he says, household food waste alone adds up to $43 billion, making it a serious economic problem.

Cutting food waste would also go a long way toward reducing serious environmental problems. Jones estimates that reducing food waste by half could reduce adverse environmental impacts by 25 per cent through reduced landfill use, soil depletion and applications of fertilisers, pesticides and herbicides. Consumers and retailers are also of course responsible for minimising food waste, but it is manufacturers, who are being squeezed by high raw material prices and low retail costs, that stand to gain most by establishing greater operational efficiencies to cut out unnecessary waste. By demonstrating how wasteful food production in the US currently is, the UA study suggests not only where savings could be made, but also how far many companies are from making them.

THE FOOD PROCESSING INDUSTRY

MEAT PACKING INDUSTRY

The meat packing industry is an industry that handles the slaughtering, processing and distribution of animals such as cattle, pigs, sheep and other livestock. The industry is primarily focused on producing meat for human consumption, but it also yields a variety of by-products including hides, feathers, dried blood, and through the process of rendering, fat such as tallow and protein meals such as meat & bone meal. In the U.S. and some other countries the place where the meat packing is done is called a meat packing plant; in New Zealand, where most of the produce is exported, it is called a freezing works. An abattoir is a place where animals are slaughtered for food.

Because no two animals are the same, the meat packing industry has not been able to automate to the same extent that some other food processors have and remains very labour-intensive. If the meat is to be processed in as cost-effective a manner as possible, labour costs must be minimized by paying the lowest wages possible and maximizing productivity from the workforce. This combined with the nature of the work makes conditions intolerable to many people. In many plants, fewer than one out of ten recruits remains beyond the probationary period.

For this reason, many meat packing plants in the developed world are unionized while those that are not are often prime targets for labour organizers.

Relations between management and organized labour in meat packing plants can be strained at the best of times. Strikes and lockouts are fairly common occurrences in the meat packing industry. Because much of the work is relatively unskilled, it is possible to bring in replacement workers so long as such a workforce is available and the laws of the jurisdiction in question allow replacements to be hired. If management does attempt this route, the possibility for violence on the picket line can be great.

The United States meat packing industry held a prominent focus in the 1906 novel The Jungle by Upton Sinclair, which criticized the treatment of workers and the safety of the products themselves. Rendering is an industrial process that converts waste animal tissue into stable, value-added materials. The majority of tissue processed comes from slaughterhouses but also includes restaurant grease and butcher shop trimmings. This material can include the fatty tissue, bones, and offal, as well as entire carcasses of animals condemned at slaughterhouses, and those that have died on farms (deadstock), in transit, etc. The most common animal sources are beef, pork, sheep or poultry.

The rendering process simultaneously dries the material and separates the fat from the bone and protein. A rendering process yields a fat commodity (yellow grease, choice white grease, bleachable fancy tallow, etc.) and a protein meal (meat & bone meal, poultry byproduct meal, etc.). Rendering plants often also handle other materials, such as slaughterhouse blood, feathers and hair, but do so using processes otherwise distinct from true rendering.

Process Variations

The rendering process varies from plant to plant in a number of ways:

1. Whether the end products are to be used as human food is based on the type of raw material and the processing methods.
2. Whether the end products are to be used as animal or pet food

3. The material may be processed wet or dry. In wet processing, water in the form of liquid or steam is added to the material during the rendering process
4. The temperature range used, whether high or low.
5. Processing may be either in discrete batches or in a continuous process.
6. The processing plant may be operated by an independent company that collects the material on the open market, or by the packing plant that produced the material.

Rendering Processes for Edible Products

Edible rendering processes are basically meat processing operations and produce lard or edible tallow for use in food products. Edible rendering is generally carried out in a continuous process at low temperature (less than the boiling point of water).

The process usually consists of finely chopping the edible fat materials (generally fat trimmings from meat cuts), heating them with or without added steam, and then carrying out two or more stages of centrifugal separation. The first stage separates the liquid water and fat mixture from the solids. The second stage further separates the fat from the water. The solids may be used in food products, pet foods, etc, depending on the original materials. The separated fat may be used in food products, or if in surplus, it may be diverted to soap making operations. Most edible rendering is done by meat packing or processing companies.

Rendering Processes for Inedible Products

Materials that for aesthetic or sanitary reasons are not suitable for human food are the feedstocks for inedible rendering processes. Much of the inedible raw material is rendered using the "dry" method. This may be a batch or a continuous process in which the material is heated in a steam jacketed vessel to drive off the moisture and simultaneously release the fat from the fat cells. The material is first ground, then heated to release the fat and drive off the moisture, percolated to drain off the free fat, and then more fat is pressed out of the solids, which at this stage are called "cracklings" or "dry-rendered tankage". The cracklings are further ground to make meat and bone meal.

A variation on a dry process involves finely chopping the material, fluidizing it with hot fat, and then evapourating the mixture in one or more evapourator stages. Some inedible rendering is done using a wet process, which is generally a continuous process similar in some ways to that used for edible materials. The material is heated with added steam and then pressed to remove a water-fat mixture which is then separated into fat, water and fine solids by stages of centrifuging and/or evapouration. The solids from the press are dried and then ground into meat and bone meal. Most independent renderers process only inedible material.

Benefits of Rendering

After rendering, the materials are much more resistant to spoiling. The fat can be used in animal feed, in soap-making, in candles, as a raw material for biodiesel production, and as a feed-stock for the chemical industry. The bone and protein becomes dry particles known as meat and bone meal. For many years meat and bone meal were fed to cattle. This practice is now prohibited in developed countries because it is believed to be the main route for the spread of BSE (mad-cow disease). Meat and bone meal is still fed to non-ruminant animals in the United States.

Tallow, derived from beef waste, is an important raw material in the steel rolling industry providing the required lubrication as the sheet steel is compressed through the rollers. In the absence of the rendering industry, the cost of waste disposal of waste animal material would be very high and would place a significant economic and environmental burden on areas involved in industrial scale slaughtering.

Economic Impacts

Other major factors which impacted the industry in the 20th century were the popularization of chemical fertilizers, the development of synthetic detergents, the widespread adoption of "boxed beef" in the USA, and the change in consumer eating habits to reject animal fats. In the early 20th century the low cost of synthesis of artificial nitrogen fertilizers undermined the economic use of animal waste to enrich soils.

This resulted in the loss of a substantial market for meat by-product solids. But this lost market was replaced by the realisation that these products made good feed for animals. After World War II synthetic detergents came on the scene which eventually displaced soaps for both domestic and industrial washing uses. Thus, in the early 1950's over 50% of the inedible fat market disappeared. Diversion in these materials into animal feeds soon replaced the lost soap market and eventually became the single largest use for inedible fats.

The widespread use of "boxed beef" in which the beef was cut up into consumer portions at the packing plant rather than at the retail level in local butcher shops and markets meant that the fat and meat scrap raw materials for renderers stayed at the packing plants and were rendered there by packer renderers, rather than by the "independent" rendérering companies. The rejection of animal fats by diet-conscious consumers led to a surplus of edible fats and their resultant diversion into soapmaking and oleochemicals, displacing inedible fats and contributing to the market volatility of this commodity.

The rendering industry is one of the oldest recycling industries, and made possible the development of a large food industry. The industry takes what would otherwise be waste materials and makes useful products such as fuels, soaps, rubber, plastics, etc. At the same time, rendering solves what would otherwise be a major disposal problem. As an example, the USA recycles more than 21 million metric tons annually of highly perishable and noxious organic matter. In 2004, the U.S. industry produced over 8 million metric tons of products, of which 1.6 million metric tons were exported.

FOOD PRESERVATION SYSTEM

Since the earliest times humankind has searched for ways to make the food supply safer and to make food last longer. Without the use of some preservation technique, the natural microorganisms that are present everywhere in the environment will grow and multiply in foods. Preservation aims either to destroy or inhibit the growth of harmful microorganisms in food by making an environment unsuitable for them. The earliest recorded instances of food preservation date back to ancient Egypt and the drying of grains and subsequent storage in sealed silos.

The stored grain could be kept for several years to insure against famine in case the Nile River flooded. People in many parts of the world developed techniques for drying and smoking foods as far back as 6000 B.C.E. Microorganisms need water to carry out their metabolic processes. Many preservation techniques that are familiar to us, such as drying, smoking, and salting, seek to reduce available water in a product. Freezing foods and making foods more acidic through fermentation and pickling also inhibit microorganism growth. Salting was so important in Roman life that Roman soldiers received "salarium," or salt, as payment. This is the origin of today's term "salary."

Large-scale deployment of armed forces led to the need for more advanced methods of food preservation to keep food safe for troops in the field. Napoleon's realization that armies do indeed travel on their stomach caused him to offer a prize for an improved food preservation method. In response to this need, Nicolas Appert, a French candy maker, developed a process by which he placed food in bottles, sealed the bottles, and then heated them for hours in boiling water. When Appert published his method in 1810 he had no knowledge of bacteria. It took another 50 years and Louis Pasteur to elucidate the relationship between microorganisms and the spoilage of food. What Appert developed is essentially the process for canning food. Over 28 the years, food scientists have made many improvements in the canning process, but the basic idea of using high heat remains the same. As testimony to the durability of canned foods, a can of meat from Captain Parry's 1824 expedition to the Northwest Passage opened 114 years later in 1938 was still perfectly safe and edible.

Most American homes have a device that is extremely useful for keeping foods safe—the refrigerator. Although refrigeration was developed in the early 1800s, refrigerators were not readily available for home use until the 1930s. Most pathogenic bacteria do not grow at all, or grow very slowly, at refrigerated temperatures. However, spoilage bacteria, those that cause food to smell or taste bad, can grow in the refrigerator. While spoilage bacteria cause foods to become of unacceptable quality, they do not cause illness. Spoilage bacteria serve a good purpose in that they prevent people from eating food that may contain harmful bacteria.

Freezing, except in cold climates, did not fully develop until the 1950s. Freezing keeps food safe by slowing the movement of molecules, causing microbes to enter a dormant stage. Freezing preserves food for extended periods of time because it prevents the growth of microorganisms that cause both food spoilage and foodborne illness; so frozen food is theoretically safe forever. The quality of frozen food, however, diminishes quickly with time. For example, when air reaches the surface of food, it causes dry grayish-brown leathery spots to appear. A turkey kept in the freezer for 10 years would be perfectly safe, but may be dried to little more than skin and bones. One can only wonder about the quality of the meal served in 1799 by William Buckland, dean of Westminster, England, who reportedly served his unsuspecting dinner guests meat from a recently discovered frozen mammoth that was 100,000 years old.

A method of making food safer that is well-known and accepted today is pasteurization. Pasteurization is the process of heating foods to a temperature for a designated period of time to destroy disease-causing and/or food spoilage bacteria. The amount of time the product is heated depends on the temperature; higher temperatures require less time. It is different from sterilization in that some spoilage bacteria survive. Pasteurization takes its name from its inventor, Louis Pasteur. The most familiar pasteurized product in the United States is milk. Before milk was routinely pasteurized it spread tuberculosis, brucellosis, typhoid fever, diphtheria, and scarlet fever. Pasteurized milk made its debut in the United States in the 1880s, but took 30 years to gain full acceptance. Milk is not the only pasteurized food product available in grocery stores.

In the mid-1990s there were several high-publicity foodborne illness outbreaks traced back to unpasteurized juice. Now, 98 percent of all juices in the United States are pasteurized. Eggs are another product that has benefited from pasteurization. While estimates are that Salmonella enteritidis infects only one in 20,000 eggs, with a production rate of almost 60 billion eggs per year, that still leaves close to three million infected eggs. Egg products, which are eggs removed from their shells for use in processed foods and available in liquid, frozen, and dried forms, must be pasteurized by law. The latest product to undergo pasteurization is intact shell eggs. Shell eggs are pasteurized with a combination water bath and hot air treatment under relatively low temperatures but longer times so that the nature of the egg does not change.

A newer form of pasteurization is called ultrahigh temperature (UHT) pasteurization. The amount of bacteria killed with a heat method such as pasteurization depends on how high the temperature is, and how long the food is held at that temperature. For instance, heating to a lower temperature requires that the food be held at the low temperature for a longer time. But using very high heat means that the food can be kept at that heat for a shorter time. UHT pasteurization takes advantage of this principle by using a very high temperature for a very short time. This provides an almost sterile product with an increased shelf life, but without significant changes in colour, flavor, or texture of the food. Many countries use UHT for processing milk, which allows consumers to purchase cartons of milk that do not need refrigeration.

Preservation techniques that limit the availability of water, such as drying, salting, and smoking, and those that use heat, such as canning and pasteurization, dramatically alter the nature of the food itself. These processes degrade the colour, flavor, texture, and nutrients in food. Today's consumers want their food to appear fresh and natural, as close to just-picked or just-slaughtered as possible.

They don't want preservatives and other chemicals added to their foods, and at the same time they want convenience. But not many American consumers are willing to shop for fresh produce or meats every day. A number of new techniques are in use or in development that try to meet this demand for food with fresher, more natural qualities. There are several methods of applying electricity instead of heat to pasteurize food; these techniques are referred to as cold pasteurization. Irradiation, ohmic heating, and high-intensity pulsed electric fields are some of these technologies.

One of the earliest examples of applying electricity to foods is ohmic heating. In this process, a continuous electric current, which generates heat, is passed through the food. Experiments with ohmic heating began in the early 1900s. This method of processing is useful for viscous liquids and foods containing particles. High-intensity pulsed electric fields (PEF) is another emerging nonthermal technique. Unlike ohmic heating, PEF does not cause an increase in the temperature of food. PEF involves applying a short burst of high voltage to a food placed between two electrodes, which destroys bacterial cell membranes. This process has the potential to be used on juices, cream soups, milk, and egg products—all products in which heat produces undesirable changes.

Food irradiation is another technology to make food safe that, like canning, got its start in feeding the military. After World War II, the U.S. Army began experiments irradiating fresh foods for troops in the field. All irradiation is energy moving through space in invisible waves. The length of the wave determines the nature of the energy. As the wavelength gets shorter, the energy of the wave increases. Microwaves have a relatively long wavelength, so they have lower energy that is strong enough to move molecules and cause heat through friction, but not strong enough to structurally change atoms in the molecules. Ionizing radiation has a shorter wavelength and therefore higher energy—enough energy to change atoms by knocking electrons from them to form ions, but not enough energy to split atoms and cause exposed objects to become radioactive. Food irradiation exposes foods to very high-energy, short-length invisible waves. Depending on the dose, irradiation performs different functions.

Low doses delay ripening and sprouting in fresh fruits and vegetables, and control insects and parasites in foods. Medium doses extend the shelf life of foods and reduce both spoilage and pathogenic microorganisms by damaging the genetic material of bacteria so they can no longer survive or multiply. High doses disinfect certain food ingredients, such as spices, and sterilize meat, poultry, seafood, and prepared foods. NASA began irradiating foods for astronauts in 1972; a case of foodborne illness while in space could be deadly, since no medical care would be available. Similarly, some hospitals use irradiated foods to feed their more susceptible patients.

Irradiation is regulated in the United States as a food additive, therefore FDA approves the process. Each new food is approved separately with a specific dosage level. After FDA grants approval, guidelines are established. USDA writes the guidelines for irradiation of meat and poultry products. The latest approval for irradiation in the United States was granted in 2000 for eggs. A petition is pending for permission to irradiate ready-to-eat meat and poultry products. Foods that are irradiated must display the radura and the words "treated with radiation" or "treated by irradiation." Although 40 countries currently permit irradiation of food, its usage has been slow to catch on in the United States.

This is mainly due to high start-up costs and to fears about consumer acceptance of the process. When the technology was new, many thought irradiation meant the food would be radioactive. As consumers have become more educated, they have realized that is not the case. Opponents of irradiation argue that irradiating foods produces chemical changes in the food. Proponents of the technology answer that these same chemical changes occur when food is cooked. Recent outbreaks of E. coli O157:H7, Listeria, and other bacteria are creating a demand for irradiated products. Irradiated foods also retain their texture, colour, and taste better than do foods that are preserved by heat treatments.

Applying high pressure uniformly throughout a food product is another method of nonthermal food preservation. This inactivates microorganisms, spores, and undesirable enzymes, and increases the shelf life of foods. Japan is a leader in this technology. Although this method was initially studied at the end of the nineteenth century, consumer demand has caused renewed interest in commercializing the process. Jams made by high-pressure processing retain the taste and colour of fresh fruit, unlike conventionally cooked jams. High-pressure processing is currently used in yogurts, salad dressings, and citrus juices. It has the potential to be used for minimally processed meat and fish products, convenience foods with long shelf lives and fresh and natural colours, and frozen foods with improved quality. The major drawback to this method is that it is costly to implement. Future usage will depend on how much the consumer is willing to pay for more natural food.

Modified atmosphere packaging (MAP) is a process in which oxygen is removed from a food package and other gases, usually carbon dioxide and/ or nitrogen, are added. Vacuum-packaging, in which oxygen is removed but no other gases are added is also a type of MAP. The role of oxygen in food is that of a spoiler, one that causes degradation and spoilage of foods. Thus eliminating or reducing the amount of oxygen in a package prolongs the shelf life of the product. Examples of MAP products are fresh-cut produce, ready-to-eat salads, fresh pasta, lunch meats, and other meat products. These are the convenience food products that consumers want. However, from a food safety standpoint, there are some dangers with MAP products.

Because lack of oxygen suppresses most spoilage bacteria in MAP products, the odors that would normally warn consumers that a food is spoiled are not present. There are some pathogenic bacteria, notably C. botulinum, that do not need oxygen to survive. Without the competition for food and water from spoilage bacteria, these bacteria can thrive. Manufacturers combat this by adding other gases such as carbon dioxide, which lowers the pH; decreasing the available water in a food; adding salt; and keeping the temperature low. It is important for consumers to understand that these types of products must be kept at the proper temperatures to keep them safe.

Ultraviolet (UV) radiation is the major bacteria-destroying factor in sunlight. Scientists are using UV light to kill pathogenic microorganisms. The most prevalent use of this technology is to kill pathogens in water systems. It is environmentally friendly, safe, more cost-effective than chlorination, and doesn't affect the taste of water as chlorination does. One problem with this technique is that it doesn't penetrate substances very deeply, so action is limited to the surface. At high doses products develop off flavors and odors, but at low doses it can extend the shelf life of foods without damaging quality. It is used in dairy plants, in meat and vegetable processing plants, in the ice cream industry, and to sterilize packaging materials.

As consumers have become chemical- and preservative-phobic, food preservation using natural antimicrobials has evolved. This concept involves a more natural and milder alternative to making food safer. By their very nature of being milder, natural antimicrobials by themselves are not sufficient to control pathogens. However, when used in combination with other food preservation methods they can improve the safety of foods without the use of traditional chemical preservatives such as sorbate or benzoate, which consumers no longer consider natural and healthy. Nature contains many antimicrobial compounds.

Those used in food processing are derived from either plants or microorganisms. Spices and herbs have long been used to inhibit yeasts, bacteria, and molds. However, the spices and herbs themselves are less effective than the active ingredients such as essential oils, organic acids, and phenols found in them. Scientists are working to more actively exploit these active ingredients rather than using the whole spice or herb. As part of their life cycle, microorganisms produce compounds that affect the growth of other microorganisms around them. Many of these compounds inhibit microbial growth to increase the competitive edge of the producing organism. Lactic acid bacteria are the most important of these natural antimicrobials. Lactic acid bacteria have been used for centuries in fermentation, cheeses, and sausages. Many natural antimicrobials also have the advantage of being regulated as generally recognized as safe (GRAS) substances.

FREEZING AND FOOD SAFETY MANAGEMENT

Food safety is a matter that affects anyone who eats food. Whether or not a person consciously thinks about food safety before eating a meal, a host of other people have thought about the safety of that food, from farmers to scientists to company presidents to federal government officials and sanitarians. This chapter serves as a broad introduction to food safety and the concerns facing those who work with food. A history of food safety concentrates on scientific discoveries from the 1600s to modern times. The chapter ends with a look at food preservation techniques that humankind has practiced over the millennia to make food safer. These techniques range from the earliest methods of drying to newer high-tech methods such as food irradiation, and newer lower-tech methods such as using natural antimicrobials. Foods in the freezer are they safe? Every year, thousands of callers to the USDA Meat and Poultry Hotline aren't sure about the safety of items stored in their own home freezers. The confusion seems to be based on the fact that few people understand how freezing protects food. Here is some information on how to freeze food safely and how long to keep it.

What Can You Freeze?

You can freeze almost any food. Some exceptions are canned food or eggs in shells. However, once the food (such as a ham) is out of the can, you may freeze it. Being able to freeze food and being pleased with the quality after defrosting are two different things. Some foods simply don't freeze well. Examples are mayonnaise, cream sauce and lettuce. Raw meat and poultry maintain their quality longer than their cooked counterparts because moisture is lost during cooking.

Is Frozen Food Safe?

Food stored constantly at 0 °F will always be safe. Only the quality suffers with lengthy freezer storage. Freezing keeps food safe by slowing the movement of molecules, causing microbes to enter a dormant stage. Freezing preserves food for extended periods because it prevents the growth of microorganisms that cause both food spoilage and food borne illness.

Does Freezing Destroy Bacteria & Parasites?

Freezing to 0 °F inactivates any microbes bacteria, yeasts and molds present in food. Once thawed, however, these microbes can again become active, multiplying under the right conditions to levels that can lead to food borne illness. Since they will then grow at about the same rate as microorganisms on fresh food, you must handle thawed items as you would any perishable food. Trichina and other parasites can be destroyed by sub-zero freezing temperatures. However, very strict government-supervised conditions must be met. It is not recommended to rely on home freezing to destroy trichina. Thorough cooking will destroy all parasites.

Freshness and Quality

Freshness and quality at the time of freezing affect the condition of frozen foods. If frozen at peak quality, foods emerge tasting better than foods frozen near the end of their useful life. So freeze items you won't use quickly sooner rather than later. Store all foods at 0° F or lower to retain vitamin content, colour, flavor and texture.

Nutrient Retention

The freezing process itself does not destroy nutrients. In meat and poultry products, there is little change in nutrient value during freezer storage.

Enzymes

Enzyme activity can lead to the deterioration of food quality. Enzymes present in animals, vegetables and fruit promote chemical reactions, such as ripening. Freezing only slows the enzyme activity that takes place in foods. It does not halt these reactions which continue after harvesting. Enzyme activity does not harm frozen meats or fish and is neutralized by the acids in frozen fruits. But most vegetables that freeze well are low acid and require a brief, partial cooking to prevent deterioration. This is called "blanching." For successful freezing, blanch or partially cook vegetables in boiling water or in a microwave oven. Then rapidly chill the vegetables prior to freezing and storage. Consult a cookbook for timing.

Packaging

Proper packaging helps maintain quality and prevent "freezer burn." It is safe to freeze meat or poultry directly in its supermarket wrapping but this type of wrap is permeable to air. Unless you will be using the food in a month or two, overwrap these packages as you would any food for long-term storage using airtight heavy-duty foil, (freezer) plastic wrap or freezer paper, or place the package inside a (freezer) plastic bag. Use these materials or airtight freezer containers to repackage family packs into smaller amounts. It is not necessary to rinse meat and poultry before freezing. Freeze unopened vacuum packages as is. If you notice that a package has accidentally been torn or has opened while food is in the freezer, the food is still safe to use; merely overwrap or rewrap it.

Freezer Burn

Freezer burn does not make food unsafe, merely dry in spots. It appears as grayish-brown leathery spots and is caused by air reaching the surface of the food. Cut freezer-burned portions away either before or after cooking the food. Heavily freezer-burned foods may have to be discarded for quality reasons.

Colour Changes

Colour changes can occur in frozen foods. The bright red colour of meat as purchased usually turns dark or pale brown depending on its variety. This may be due to lack of oxygen, freezer burn or abnormally long storage. Freezing doesn't usually cause colour changes in poultry. However, the bones and the meat near them can become dark. Bone darkening results when pigment seeps through the porous bones of young poultry into the surrounding tissues when the poultry meat is frozen and thawed. The dulling of colour in frozen vegetables and cooked foods is usually the result of excessive drying due to improper packaging or over-lengthy storage.

Freeze Rapidly

Freeze food as fast as possible to maintain its quality. Rapid freezing prevents undesirable large ice crystals from forming throughout the product because the molecules don't have time to take their positions in the characteristic six-sided snowflake. Slow freezing creates large, disruptive ice crystals.

During thawing, they damage the cells and dissolve emulsions. This causes meat to "drip"—lose juiciness. Emulsions such as mayonnaise or cream will separate and appear curdled. Ideally, a food 2-inches thick should freeze completely in about 2 hours. If your home freezer has a "quick-freeze" shelf, use it. Never stack packages to be frozen. Instead, spread them out in one layer on various shelves, stacking them only after frozen solid.

Refrigerator – Freezers

If a refrigerator freezing compartment can't maintain zero degrees or if the door is opened frequently, use it for short-term food storage. Eat those foods as soon as possible for best quality. Use a free-standing freezer set at 0° F or below for long-term storage of frozen foods.

Keep a thermometer in your freezing compartment or freezer to check the temperature. This is important if you experience power-out or mechanical problems. Because freezing keeps food safe almost indefinitely, recommended storage times are for quality only.

Refer to the freezer storage chart at the end of this document, which lists optimum freezing times for best quality. If a food is not listed on the chart, you may determine its quality after defrosting. First check the odor. Some foods will develop a rancid or off odor when frozen too long and should be discarded. Some may not look picture perfect or be of high enough quality to serve alone but may be edible; use them to make soups or stews. Cook raw food and if you like the taste and texture, use it.

Safe Defrosting

Never defrost foods in a garage, basement, car, dishwasher or plastic garbage bag; out on the kitchen counter, outdoors or on the porch. These methods can leave your foods unsafe to eat. There are three safe ways to defrost food: in the refrigerator, in cold water, or in the microwave.

It's best to plan ahead for slow, safe thawing in the refrigerator. Small items may defrost overnight; most foods require a day or two. And large items like turkeys may take longer, approximately one day for each 5 pounds of weight. For faster defrosting, place food in a leak proof plastic bag and immerse it in cold water. (If the bag leaks, bacteria from the air or surrounding environment could be introduced into the food. Tissues can also absorb water like a sponge, resulting in a watery product.) Check the water frequently to be sure it stays cold. Change the water every 30 minutes. After thawing, cook immediately. When microwave-defrosting food, plan to cook it immediately after thawing because some areas of the food may become warm and begin to cook during microwaving.

Refreezing

Once food is thawed in the refrigerator, it is safe to refreeze it without cooking, although there may be a loss of quality due to the moisture lost through defrosting.

After cooking raw foods which were previously frozen, it is safe to freeze the cooked foods. If previously cooked foods are thawed in the refrigerator, you may refreeze the unused portion. If you purchase previously frozen meat, poultry or fish at a retail store, you can refreeze if it has been handled properly.

Cooking Frozen Foods

Raw or cooked meat, poultry or casseroles can be cooked or reheated from the frozen state. However, it will take approximately one and a half times the usual cooking time for food which has been thawed. Remember to discard any wrapping or absorbent paper from meat or poultry. When cooking whole poultry, remove the giblet pack from the cavity as soon as you can loosen it. Cook the giblets separately. Read the label on USDA-inspected frozen meat and poultry products. Some, such as pre-stuffed whole birds, must be cooked from the frozen state to ensure a safely cooked product.

A Brief History of Food Safety

Very little about food borne illness or food safety is found in historical records. Scientists did not begin to understand bacteria, and their relationship to disease, until the late nineteenth century. People did recognize that food spoils, but the reasons for that and the potential for becoming ill from food were not known. Perhaps the absence of food safety from historical chronicles is an indication that it was less of a concern than were other problems in the past. Even early food regulations were not aimed at making food safer, but rather at preventing economic fraud. So, a history of food safety really does not exist, but numerous discoveries, inventions, and regulations have led to the present knowledge and state of affairs in food safety.

Food preservation methods such as drying, smoking, freezing, marinating, salting, and pickling had their beginnings thousands of years ago. Whether these methods were employed solely to keep food for later use, to improve flavor, or for other reasons is not known. But they also had the effect of keeping food safer. Even cooking can be viewed as an ancient method of making food safer.

The Chinese Confucian Analects of 500 B.C.E. warned against consumption of sour rice, spoiled fish or flesh, food kept too long or insufficiently cooked food. The Chinese disliked eating uncooked food believing, "Anything boiled or cooked cannot be poisonous." Among the earliest of food safety manuals was one published in China in the year 2 (Needham 1962). It is possible that the practice of drinking tea originated because tea required using hot water, which would make it safer than using unheated contaminated water (Trager 1995). Doubtless other cultures in antiquity, while oblivious to the causes or prevention of foodborne disease, experienced it and prescribed methods to avoid it.

Early scientists grappled with the nature of disease and bacteria, which would set the stage for later discoveries. Much of the present knowledge about pathogens that cause food borne illness is built on a foundation of scientific discoveries spanning back over three centuries. Aristotle (384–322 B.C.E.) and his Greek philosopher/scientist predecessors believed in the spontaneous generation of organisms—that insects and animals arose spontaneously from soil, plants, or other species of animals. Francisco Redi, an Italian physician and poet, set out to disprove this theory in 1668. He believed that maggots did not arise spontaneously in meat, which challenged the common wisdom of the day. He prepared eight flasks with meat in them; four sealed and four left open to the air. No flies could land on the meat in the sealed flasks, thus no maggots grew. The clear conclusion was that maggots did not form by spontaneous generation, but that flies laid eggs that were too small to be seen.

This, however, was not enough to convince skeptics. Italian biologist Lazzaro Spallanzani in 1768 disproved the spontaneous generation theory. Even though Redi proved that insects did not arise from spontaneous generation, scientists still believed that microorganisms did. In his experiments, Spallanzani boiled solutions that would normally breed microorganisms for prolonged periods of time, which killed any microorganisms that might be in the solution, on the walls of the flask, or in the air inside the flask. Then he sealed the flasks to prevent any new spores or microorganisms from entering. No microorganisms grew no matter how long he left them standing. The fact that no new microorganisms appeared meant that there was no spontaneous generation.

The discovery of bacteria in the late nineteenth century, the increased understanding of bacteria's role in disease, and the realization that there is a connection between human diseases and animal diseases led to the ideas that cleanliness is important and that unsanitary conditions can contribute to disease. In 1847 Hungarian physician Ignaz Semmelweiss wondered why women who bore their children in hospitals died of fever during childbirth, while those who gave birth at home usually did not. Noting that doctors went straight from the operating room to labouring mothers, he concluded that the doctors themselves were carrying disease to the women from the dissecting room. In those days the doctors didn't wash their hands, but wiped them on their aprons, which were already coated with body fluids. Semmelweiss ran experiments in which he had the doctors wash their hands with soap and water, and then rinse them in a chlorinated lime solution before entering the maternity wards.

Death rates plummeted from 10 percent to 1.5 percent, only to climb again when the experiments were discontinued. Thereafter, he forced doctors to wash their hands before treating patients. Unfortunately, the validity of his work was not recognized at the time. His colleagues greeted his theory with ridicule, refusing to believe that their own hands were a vehicle for disease. Instead they attributed the deaths to a phenomenon arising from the "combustible" nature of the pregnant women. Historians attribute Semmelweiss's eventual despondency to the ridicule of his theories and attacks on his character. He was committed to an insane asylum, where he died of blood poisoning. Lack of personal hygiene remains one of the main causes of food borne illness 150 years later.

In a classic case of epidemiologic sleuthing, Dr. John Snow demonstrated in 1848 how cholera spread throughout London. He noticed that people who obtained their water from a particular well were more likely to become ill than those drawing their water from another well. He persuaded city officials to remove the pump handle from that particular well, which forced inhabitants to draw water from another well. The number of cholera cases dropped immediately. Louis Pasteur further elucidated the linkage among spoilage, disease, and microorganisms with his work on fermentation and pasteurization in the 1860s and 1870s. In 1872 German scientist Ferdinand Julius Cohn published a three-volume treatise on bacteria, and essentially founded the science of bacteriology. He was the first to attempt to classify bacteria into genera and species, and the first to describe bacterial spores. But this new field of bacteriology needed bacteria on which to conduct experiments and to study. It took Robert Koch in the 1880s to perfect the process of growing pure strains of bacteria in the labouratory.

At first he used flat glass slides to grow the bacteria. His assistant, Julius Richard Petri, suggested using shallow glass dishes with covers, now commonly called Petri dishes. Koch also established strict criteria for showing that a specific microbe causes a specific disease. These are now known as Koch's Postulates. Using these criteria scientists can identify bacteria that cause a number of diseases, including food borne diseases. In 1947 Joshua Lederberg and Edward Lawrie Tatum discovered that bacteria reproduce sexually, and opened up a whole new field of bacterial genetics.

Even though Anthony van Leeuwenhook, a Dutch biologist and microscopist, had improved the microscope to the degree that small microscopic organisms could be seen for the first time as far back as 1673, the discovery of food borne disease–causing microorganisms developed slowly. In 1835 James Paget and Richard Owen described the parasite Trichinella spiralis for the first time. German pathologists Friedrich Albert von Zenker and Rudolph Virchow were the first to note the clinical symptoms of trichinosis in 1860. However, the association between trichinosis and the parasite Trichinella spiralis was not realized until much later. In 1855 the non-pathogenic form of Escherichia coli was discovered. It later became a major research tool for biotechnology. Englishman William Taylor showed in 1857 that milk can transmit typhoid fever. In1885 USDA veterinarian Daniel Salmon described a microorganism that caused gastroenteritis with fever when ingested in contaminated food.

The bacteria were eventually named Salmonellae. August Gärtner, a German scientist, was the first to isolate Bacillus enteritidis from a case of food poisoning in 1888. The case was the result of a cow with diarrhea slaughtered for meat; 57 people who ate the meat become ill (Satin 1999). Emilie Pierre-Mare van Ermengem, a Belgian bacteriologist, was the first to isolate the bacterium that causes botulism, Clostridium botulinum, in 1895.

The case concerned an uncooked, salted ham served at a wake in Belgium. Twenty-three people became ill; three died. Van Ermengem isolated C. botulinum from both the ham and one of the victim's intestines. He demonstrated that the organism grows in an oxygen-free environment, and that it produces a toxin that causes the illness. In a perhaps overzealous use of the scientific method, M.A. Barber demonstrated that Staphylococcus aureus causes food poisoning.

He became ill after each of three visits to a farm in the Philippines in 1914. Suspecting cream from a cow with an udder infection, Barber took home two bottles of cream, let them sit out for five hours, drank some of the cream, and became ill two hours later with the same symptoms he experienced on the farm. He isolated a bacterium from the milk, placed it in a germ-free container of milk, waited a while, and then convinced two hapless volunteers to drink the milk with him. They all became ill with the same symptoms (Asimov 1972). In 1945 Clostridium perfringens was first recognized as a cause of foodborne illness. It wasn't until the years between 1975 and 1985 that some of today's major foodborne pathogens—Campylobacter jejuni, Yersinia enterocolitica, Escherichia coli O157:H7, and Vibrio cholerae—were first recognized.

FOOD PROSPECTIVE OF INDIA

India is one of the world's major food producers but accounts for less than 1.5 per cent of international food trade. This indicates vast scope for both investors and exporters. Food exports in 1998 stood at US $5.8 billion whereas the world total was US $438 billion.

The Indian food industry's sales turnover is Rs 140,000 crore (1 crore = 10 million) annually as at the start of year 2000. The industry requires about Rs 29,000 crore in investment over the next five years to 2005 to create necessary infrastructure, expand production facilities and state-of-the-art-technology to match the international quality and standards.

The office of the Agricultural Affairs of the USDA / Foreign Agricultural Services in New Delhi says that one of India's proudest accomplishments has been achieving a tenuous self-sufficiency in food production and that the country produces a wide variety of agricultural products at prices that are at or below world values in most cases. The Indian palate is accustomed to traditional foods, mostly wheat and rice-based, rather than potato and corn-based western palate. In marketing perspective, this is considered an important factor for foreign marketers.

The USDA report says initially consumer-ready food products may have to be tailored to include Indian spices and traditional ingredients. In addition to traditional tastes, there are other social factors which affect consumption in India. Hindus account for approximately 80 per cent of India's population, and while only 25 or 30 per cent are strict vegetarians, beef slaughter is prohibited in all but two states (Kerala and West Bengal) and consumption of other meats is limited. Incidentally, India is the only country where the US-based MacDonalds sells its burgers without any beef content and even offers purely vegetarian burgers. India's middle class segment will hold the key to success or failure of the processed food market in India. Of the country's total population of one billion, the middle class segments account for about 350-370 million. Though a majority of families in this segment have non-working housewives or can afford hired domestic help and thus prepare foods of their taste in their own kitchens, the profile of the middle class is changing steadily and hired domestic help is becoming costlier. This is conducive to an expansion in demand for ready-to-eat Indian-style foods.

India's food processing sector covers fruit and vegetables; meat and poultry; milk and milk products, alcoholic beverages, fisheries, plantation, grain processing and other consumer product groups like confectionery, chocolates and cocoa products, Soya-based products, mineral water, high protein foods etc. According to latest official statistics, India exported processed fruits and vegetables worth Rs 5240 million in 1997-98. The horticulture production is around 102 million tonnes. Foreign investment since 1991, when economic liberalisation started, stood at Rs 8,800 crore. Products that have growing demand, especially in the Middle East countries include pickles, chutneys, fruit pulps, canned fruits, and vegetables, concentrated pulps and juices, dehydrated vegetables and frozen fruits and vegetables.

Another potential processed food product is meat and poultry products. India ranks first in world cattle population, 50 per cent of buffalo population and one-sixth of total goat population of the world. Buffalo meat is surplus in India. There is vast scope to set up modern slaughter facilities and cold store chains in meat and poultry processing sector. India's current level of meat and meat-based exports is around Rs 8,000 million. In last six years foreign investment in this segment stood at Rs 5,000 million which is more than 50 per cent of the total investment made in this sector.

Compared with meat, poultry industry has registered significant growth. India ranks fifth in the world with annual egg production of 1.61 million tones. Both poultry and egg processing units have come in a very big way in the country. India is exporting egg powder, frozen egg yolk and albumin powder to Europe, Japan and other countries. Poultry exports are mostly to Maldives and Oman. Indian poultry meat products have good markets in Japan, Malaysia, Indonesia and Singapore. While meat products registered a growth of 10 per cent, eggs and broilers registered 16-20 per cent growth. There are about 15 pure line and grand parent franchise projects in India. There are 115 layer and 280 broiler hatcheries producing 1.3 million layer parents and 280 million broiler parents. They in turn supply 95 million hybrid layer and 275 million broilers, day-old chick. Presently there are only five egg powder plants in India which is considered insufficient in view of growing export demand for different kind of powder - whole egg, yolk and albumen. The scope of foreign investment and state-of-the-art technology in this field is therefore tremendous.

Milk and milk products is rated as one of the most promising sectors which deserves foreign investment in a big way. When the world milk production registered a negative growth of 2 per cent , India performed much better with 4 per cent growth. The total milk production is around 72 million tonnes and the demand for milk is estimated at around 80 million tonnes. By 2005, the value of Indian dairy produce is expected to be Rs 1,000,000 million. In last six years foreign investment in this sector stood at Rs 3600 million which is about one-forth of total investment made in this sector. Manufacture of casein and lactose, largely being imported presently, has good scope. Exports of milk products have been decanalised.

Grains could emerge as a major export earner for India in coming years. India's food grains production is now at around 225-230 million tones. These include rice, jawar, bajra, maize, wheat, gram and pulses. Indian basmati rice enjoys command in the international market. Besides growing Middle east market for basmati rive, many other countries are showing interest for this food grain. In 1998-99 export of basmati and non-basmati rice stood at Rs62000 million. There is a total rice milling capacity of 186 million tones in the country. Among plantation, tea emerged as major foreign exchange earner. India is the largest producer and exporter of black tea. However, the most worrying factor for Indian tea industry is that from early next year with the implementation of tea imports into the country, India tea may face a stiff competition within the country as well, specially threat of Sri Lanka's presence in the Indian market is looming large.

The current year's tea export prospect is not that very good in terms of forex earnings because international prices has fallen significantly this year . India exports between 150-170 million kilogram's of tea per annum. Of course, the scope of foreign investment in this sector is good and the multinational tea companies would either be trying for marketing joint ventures with the Indian producers or acquire stakes in Indian tea companies. There is strong possibilities of third country exports through such joint venture as quality wise still Indian teas are ruling the international market. Alcoholic beverages is another are where India witnessed substantial foreign investment. Foreign investment in this sector stood at Rs 7000 million which about 70 percent of the total investment made so far. The IMFL (Indian Made Foreign Liquor) primarily comprises wine, vodka, gin, whisky, rum and brandy. Draught beer is a comparatively recent introduction in the Indian market. The Indian beer market is estimated at Rs7000 million a year. One of the major advantages for any investor eyeing the Indian liquor market is that India offers enough raw materials like molasses, barely, maize, potatoes, grapes, yeast and hops for the industry.

Yet another catchy investment sector is fisheries. There is growing canned and processed fishes from India. The marine fish include prawns, shrimps, tuna, cuttlefish, squids, octopus, red snappers, ribbon fish, mackerel, lobsters, cat fish etc. In last six years there was substantial investment in fisheries to the tune of Rs 30,000 million of which foreign investments were of the order of Rs 7000 million. The potential could be gauged by the fact that against fish production potential in the Exclusive Economic Zone of 3.9 million tones, actual catch is to the tune of 2.87 million tones. Harvesting from inland sources is around 2.7 million tones.

The biggest bottleneck in expanding the food processing sector, in terms of both investment and exports, is lack of adequate infrastructure. Without a strong and dependable cold chain vital sector like food processing industry which is based mostly on perishable products cannot survive and grow. Even at current level of production, farm produce valued at Rs 70,000 million is being wasted every year only because there is no adequate storage, transportation, cold chain facilities and other infrastructure supports. Cold chain facilities are miserably inadequate to meet the increasing production of various perishable products like milk, fruits, vegetables, poultry, fisheries etc. Prevention of Food Adulteration laws is not only stringent one but time consuming also. It is considered as an archaic and no industry friendly food law. It substantial varies from Codex standard. Harmonization of multiple food laws is an urgent necessity.

Many of India's food-processing companies are known to be keen to import intermediate food products. As India's food-processing industry grows and becomes more sophisticated, there is no doubt that the market for intermediate food products and ingredients will grow. It is important that you, or your agents in India, ensure that intermediate food products are considered by customs officials as industrial intermediates and not as consumer products to minimise customs duty. Though law looks at intermediate food products as industrial intermediates, there have been reports that uninformed customs officials have treated them as consumer products.

Selection of Food

The concept of safe and wholesome food encompasses many diverse elements. From a nutritional aspect, it is food that contains the nutrients humans need and that helps prevent long-term chronic disease, promoting health into old age. From a food safety aspect, it is food that is free not only from toxins, pesticides, and chemical and physical contaminants, but also from microbiological pathogens such as bacteria and viruses that can cause illness.

While America's food supply is among the safest in the world, there are still numerous threats to the safety of the food supply. Some of these threats have been around since ancient times, while others are newer, the result of changing lifestyles, production practices, and even evolution of microorganisms themselves. Ensuring the safety of food is a shared responsibility among producers, industry, government, and consumers.

A major focus of this chapter is microbial food borne illness, a widespread, but often unrecognized, sickness that affects most people at one time or another. It is caused by eating food that is contaminated with pathogens such as bacteria, viruses, or parasites. At least four factors are necessary for food borne illness to occur: (1) a pathogen; (2) a food vehicle; (3) conditions that allow the pathogen to survive, reproduce, or produce a toxin; and (4) a susceptible person who ingests enough of the pathogen or its toxin to cause illness. The symptoms often are similar to those associated with the flu-nausea, vomiting, diarrhea, abdominal pain, fever, and headache.

Most people have experienced food borne illness, even though they might not recognize it as such, instead blaming it on the "stomach flu" or "24-hour bug." Symptoms usually disappear within a few days, but in some cases there can be more long-lasting effects such as joint inflammation or kidney failure. In the most severe cases people die from food borne illness. Every year more than 5,000 Americans die from eating contaminated food.

It is difficult to trace a bout of food borne illness back to a particular food because illness can occur anywhere from an hour to several days, or even weeks, after eating the contaminated food. Epidemiologists faced with tracing a food borne illness outbreak may have to interview dozens of people, asking them to recall everything they ate for the past week. It is difficult for people to remember everything they ate yesterday, much less one week ago. Further complicating the picture is that one person may eat the contaminated food and not become ill, while someone else in a higher-risk group does. In 81 percent of food borne illnesses the cause remains unknown.

Additives

The use of food additives dates back to ancient times. Examples of these early additives are salt to preserve meats and fish, herbs and spices for seasoning foods, sugar to preserve fruits, and vinegar to preserve vegetables. Today manufacturers use more than 3,000 food additives. A commonly used definitition of a food additive is any substance added to a food either directly or indirectly through production, processing, storing, or packaging. Food additives serve a number of functions:

Preservatives to keep food fresh and to prevent spoilage. This is important, as in our modern lifestyle food is rarely eaten at the time or place it is produced. Calcium propionate inhibits molds and is often added to bread products for this purpose.

Nutrients to improve or maintain the nutritional quality of foods. Most salt contains iodine to prevent goiter, a condition resulting from iodine deficiency. Processing aids to maintain product texture such as retaining moisture, preventing lumping, or adding stability. Powdered foods such as cocoa contain silicon dioxide to prevent clumping when water is added.

Flavours to enhance or change the taste or aroma of a food. These include spices, herbs, flavor enhancers, natural and synthetic flavors, and sweeteners. Colours to give foods an appealing look. Many of the colours we associate with foods are from added colourings, such as caramel to make cola drinks brown and annatto to make margarine yellow.

Food additives are derived from naturally occurring and synthetic materials. Scientists can now synthesize in the labouratory many additives that used to be derived from natural substances, creating a larger and cheaper supply. Americans consume from 140 to 150 pounds of additives a year, mostly due to additives such as sugar, corn sweeteners, salt, pepper, vegetable colours, yeast, and baking soda. Food additives allow us to enjoy safe, wholesome, tasty foods year-round without the inconvenience of growing our own foods or shopping daily. Convenience foods are made possible by the use of food additives.

FDA approves all food additives before they can be added to foods. USDA authorizes additives used in meat and poultry products. Before manufacturers may use an additive, they must prove that the additive does what it was intended to do and that it will not be harmful to humans at the expected level of consumption. Two groups of additives are not subject to FDA's strict approval process—those that are prior sanctioned and those that are generally recognized as safe (GRAS). Prior sanctioned substances were already approved by FDA before the 1958 Food Additives Amendment to the Food, Drug and Cosmetic Act.

GRAS substances, including salt, sugar, spices, and vitamins, have been used extensively in the past with no known harmful effects, and therefore experts believe them to be safe. FDA may also label an additive as GRAS based on scientific evidence that it is safe. FDA and USDA continue to monitor prior sanctioned and GRAS substances to ensure that they really are safe as new evidence emerges. In addition, FDA operates the Adverse Reaction Monitoring System (ARMS) to investigate all complaints related to specific foods, food and colour additives, or vitamin and mineral supplements.

While the overwhelming majority of additives are safe for all people, small segments of the population are sensitive to some. Sulfites are an example of this; they cause hives, nausea, shortness of breath, or shock in some people. For this reason, in 1986 FDA banned the use of sulfites on fresh fruits and vegetables, such as in salad bars where they were used to keep lettuce and other produce looking fresh. Product labels must list sulfites if they are added. In the 1970s it was thought by some individuals that additives may contribute to childhood hyperactivity, but studies conducted since then have found no link.

Index